WOMEN ON THE POLISH LABOR MARKET

WOMEN ON THE POLISH LABOR MARKET

MIKE INGHAM,
HILARY INGHAM
and
HENRYK DOMAŃSKI

CEU PRESS

Central European University Press

Published by

Central European University Press

Nádor utca 15
H-1051 Budapest
Hungary

400 West 59th Street
New York, NY 10019
USA

An imprint of the
Central European University Share Company

Distributed in the United Kingdom and Western Europe by
Plymbridge Distributors Ltd., Estover Road, Plymouth PL6 7PZ
United Kingdom

ISBN: 978-963-9241-13-8

Library of Congress Cataloging-in-Publication Data
A CIP catalog record for this book is available upon request

CONTENTS

CONTRIBUTORS

Henryk Domański, Professor of Sociology in the Institute of Philosophy and Sociology, Polish Academy of Sciences, Warsaw, Poland

Aleksandra Dukaczewska-Nałęcz, Assistant Professor in the Institute of Philosophy and Sociology, Polish Academy of Sciences, Warsaw, Poland

Anna Firkowska-Mankiewicz, Associate Professor in the Institute of Philosophy and Sociology, Polish Academy of Sciences, Warsaw, Poland

Krzysztof Gorlach, Associate Professor in the Institute of Sociology, Jagellonian University, Kraków, Poland

Hilary Ingham, Senior Lecturer, Department of Economics, Lancaster University, UK

Mike Ingham, Associate Director, European Studies Research Institute, University of Salford, UK

Anna Karwińska, Associate Professor in the Academy of Economics, Kraków, Poland

Irena Kotowska, Professor of Demography, Institute of Statistics and Demography, Warsaw School of Economics, Warsaw, Poland

Ewa Malinowska, Assistant Professor in the Institute of Sociology in Łódź University, Łódź, Poland

Irena Reszke, Professor of Sociology in the Institute of Philosophy and Sociology, Polish Academy of Sciences, Warsaw, Poland

Anna Titkow, Associate Professor in the Institute of Philosophy and Sociology, Polish Academy of Sciences, Warsaw, Poland

Grzegorz Węcławowicz, Professor of Social Geography, Institute of Geography and Spatial Organization of the Polish Academy of Sciences, Warsaw, Poland

LIST OF FIGURES

LIST OF TABLES

LIST OF MAPS

PREFACE

For the second time in the lives of many of its citizens, Poland is currently undergoing a transformation unknown in kind or magnitude in the western world. On this occasion, however, change was embraced freely in the widespread anticipation that the circumstances of the population could and would improve. More than a decade later, it is clear that for many the expected benefits have been long delayed and much energy is still consumed in the identification of winners and losers from the forces unleashed in 1989. Equally clearly, many of the consequences, good and bad, of the move to a free market democracy are transmitted through the labor market, although we still know insufficient about what these are and who they affect. Such ignorance has a multiplicity of causes, amongst which must be noted the inadequacy of much available data, although the sheer diversity of the implications of reform also plays its part. Recognition of this latter fact spawned the idea for the current volume, which brings together a multi-disciplinary collection of twelve original papers, each addressing some important aspect of the impact of systemic transformation on the position and role of Polish women in relation to the world of work. That women should not suffer disproportionate disadvantage in this critical arena is vital to the efficiency and equity of the economic and social configuration to which the transition eventually leads the country. Ensuring that the outcome has these desirable properties is above all an issue for policy makers, but it must be assumed that they will not act in ways that will assist in bringing this about without there being a wider awareness of the scope and complexity of the issues involved. It is hoped that this volume will assist in this process.

The book is addressed primarily to all with an interest in labor market and social change in the economies in transition, although its mix of theoretical and applied perspectives should appeal to those whose usual geographic focus lies elsewhere. It is intended as both a research and policy resource and as an input to the teaching of a wide range of social science and humanities courses, including those that concentrate on gender and women's issues, labor markets, sociology and post-socialist transformation. While focusing on one country, the volume contains important spatial insights in view of the evident fact that the current and future labor market status of women in Poland has a distinct regional dimension. The many shared experiences of the countries in the old Soviet realm of influence also lends a wider generality to many of the issues examined by the contributors. Furthermore, while women occupy center-stage in each of the chapters, the work is also, and inevitably, about men. Indeed, it is the gendered dimension of reform that provides so much of the substance in the contributions that follow and the differences of emphasis between them. With but one exception, the papers are written, in whole or in part, by Polish academics, a quality that introduces a domestic insight that is absent too frequently in English language writings on labor market change in Central and Eastern Europe.

We wish to acknowledge support from the Department for International Development (ESCOR Grant R6601) for the project entitled 'The Gender Dynamics of the Polish Labour Market in Transition' from which this volume emerged. The process of editing the volume has been a long one and it would probably have remained incomplete without the cheerful support of E.D. and G.R.

CHAPTER 1

WOMEN ON THE LABOR MARKET: POLAND'S SECOND GREAT TRANSFORMATION

The core of much of the literature devoted to the analysis of the transformation of Polish society from state socialism to capitalism has been premised on the belief that the process, at least in the short run, would expose women to the danger of losing valuable economic and social welfare rights. Many of the early predictions were, however, formed in an empirical vacuum; communist to capitalist transitions are novel phenomena and lively academic and political debate was often pursued in the absence of factual information. As a decade of reform has now furnished data and observation, it is timely to examine the facts and to subject the early hypotheses to test. It is with this end in mind that the contributions contained within this volume have been assembled, each of which constitutes a reconsideration of some of the many unresolved questions concerning the roles of the sexes in the labor market, the division of labor and the women's movement. The findings reveal a complex situation.

Gender has been viewed as the prism through which the shifts in the socio-political configuration of the former communist countries of Central and Eastern Europe (CEE) can be evaluated (Einhorn, 1993, p. 2) and, while focused upon Poland, the contributions presented here have relevance for the whole of the region. Gender issues lie at the hub of the potentially explosive processes of social and political transformation now underway, and major currents of debate on the role of gender revolve around the question of whether the newly emerging democratic societies have transformed women into active agents who enjoy full democratic citizenship rights in the new market conditions. Did the collapse of communism affect the structural underpinnings of gender inequality and, if so, in which direction? How have gender relations on the labor market changed as the transformation has unfolded? Economic and political freedom could have found resonance in a greater equality of the sexes, but some recent empirical studies reveal evidence of a reinforcement of the oppression of women and growing rigidities in the stratification systems of post-communist countries. As such, they merely serve to underline the fact that it remains impossible to ignore the legacy of the past and the following section is devoted to an outline of the historical contexts within which women's status on the labor market of Poland is evolving.

HISTORICAL CONTEXT: GENDER RELATIONS UNDER SOCIALISM

Contrary to the impression conveyed in popular discourse, Poland is now in the process of its second great transformation and the events of the preceding decade represent the second occasion on which the labor market position of women has assumed particular prominence. On the first occasion, the country's transition to communism, the concern was essentially pragmatic. A war-torn economy had to be rebuilt quickly, but without the assistance of the millions of prime-age males who had lost their lives during the course of the preceding hostilities. The rhetoric, and perhaps even the initial intent, was subtler, involving a commitment on the part of the communist government to women's emancipation. Constitutions, Labor and Family Codes established women's right to work and to acquire education, and to social provisions guaranteeing that they could fulfil their role as a worker while being simultaneously a mother. In fact, it is possible to view the development trajectory of state socialist society as one which created the conditions under which inequalities of gender might be have been eliminated.

In proclaiming equality with men in all spheres of life, the constitutions of the newly formed socialist societies of CEE granted women legal majority and personal autonomy, both of which they were largely denied in the pre-war period, when Poland, at least, retained many semifeudal characteristics. Seemingly, state socialist legislation was more path-breaking than that enacted in the capitalist west: for example, women were granted the right to equal pay by Article 67 of the first Constitution of the Polish People's Republic of 1952. The same entitlement was only secured in the Federal Republic of Germany in 1955 (Einhorn, 1993, p. 23), while it was not until 1963 that equivalent legislation was passed in the United States (Fuchs, 1988, p. 1). Yet, radical as the approach taken by the communist authorities may seem, there were yawning gaps between rhetoric and reality.

Even laws enacted to promote positive discrimination and to advance women's emancipation operated to disadvantage their position on the labor market, barring them from promotion tracks and serving to create distinct patterns of occupational segregation. In Poland, according to a Labor Code, it was 'prohibited to employ women in jobs which are particularly arduous and detrimental to health': a general restriction followed by a list of 90 particular occupations to which it was to apply (Rozporządzenie, 1979). Perhaps the most conspicuous evidence of the gendered stratification of the workforce was the persistent gap between the incomes of women and men, with national surveys indicating that the divide remained within the range 65–75 per cent over the whole communist period (Domański, 1992; Łobodzińska, 1983).

Whatever the failings, paid employment in the period of socialism is often considered to have been life-enhancing for women. Female full-time labor force participation was much higher than was usual in the west and women accounted for almost 45 per cent of all Polish workers in 1989. However, the reasons for the high rate of female participation were essentially negative in character. First, the inefficiencies of socialist production brought about constant labor shortages that required the economic activation of women; second, as in all CEE countries, at least two wages per family were necessary in order to fulfil basic household needs. Notwithstanding the real benefits of economic activity—itself a necessary condition for socio-economic achievement, personal independence and autonomy—there were also profound costs associated with women's involvement in work. In particular, they had to endure an onerous double burden, which had adverse effects on both their social situation and their self-esteem (Plakwicz, 1992).

Nevertheless, the social policy of the time was framed so as to alleviate the exigencies of combining household responsibilities with the participation of women in the labor force, and the state attempted accordingly to socialize some parts of domestic labor and childcare. In many cases, benefits dispensed in the form of affordable housing, subsidized transport, food and children's clothing, public facilities, and extended maternity and childcare leave were taken utterly for granted. Viewed from the perspective of 'emancipation', some authors saw these provisions as resulting in a shift from the economic dependence of women on individual men to their dependence on the state; that is, from private to public patriarchy. Be this as it may, similar critiques could also be applied, at the time, to the social democratic welfare model espoused by the Scandinavian countries, given their similarly large female labor market participation rates and generous welfare benefit systems.

A largely unintended by-product of the educational policies pursued by the state, which were designed primarily to expand technical and vocational provision, was to ensure that females were generally better educated than males, at least in terms of years of schooling, and women outnumbered men at post-secondary educational institutions (Białecki and Heyns, 1993). The fact that boys tended to enter the vocational schools, which state policy emphasized but which required fewer years of attendance, generated an intellectual gender imbalance in education that favored women. This educational superiority did not, however, benefit females by granting them access to the channels of recruitment to higher positions in the occupational ladder and their investments were not converted into commensurate social or economic rewards. On the whole, women occupied middle-level and lower positions in the service sector—in administration and the vast clerical workforce—thereby preserving a distinctive pattern of segregation.

Beginning in the late 1940s, the state embarked upon a program of rapid industrialization, nationalization and the collectivization of private farms. Although the latter was to prove conspicuously unsuccessful, the overall impact of these policies was virtually to force the transfer of manpower from agriculture to heavy industry and to secure the promotion of large numbers of workers and peasants to positions within governmental and industrial bureaucracies. These mass transitions shortened temporarily the social distances between the intelligentsia, the working class and peasants (Erikson and Goldthorpe, 1992, p. 101). However, they did not restructure the basic shape of the social hierarchy and analyses undertaken for later periods of time reported declining mobility rates; that is, the openness of the social structure displayed in the 1950s was effectively reversed (Andorka and Zagórski, 1980). All the same, the educational achievements of individuals appeared to determine their occupational career more than in the United States, and the inter-generation transmission of social status came to be weaker (Tuma, et al., 1979). Nevertheless, the reduction in the strength of ascriptive factors and the rise in the importance of achievements as a determinant of personal success, supposedly the strength of the communist system, failed to operate to the benefit of women.

There was a marked distinction between the east and the west in the mechanism underpinning the distribution of incomes. Administrative control by the state resulted in the determination of remuneration according to industrial divisions in the Polish economy: enterprises within these then competed for the available state subsidies and each thereby attempted to maximize its control of resources. In consequence, realized wages and benefits were a result of the exercise of bargaining power in a world of scarcity. Industrial branch of employment was the single most important factor predicting wages, overshadowing education, occupational position, age, working years and other social and demographic variables. Only sex competed in importance as a determinant of an individual's income (Domański, 1990), but the Polish case did not depart from the experience of the western world in this respect.

A further distinctive feature of the communist regime was its success in bringing about significant change in the hierarchy of occupational prestige. In particular, as compared to their position in the west, it succeeded in upgrading the status of skilled manual workers, which was unusual given the stability in the occupational prestige ladder observed in other contemporary societies (Treiman, 1977; Sawiński and Domański, 1991). This increase in the occupational prestige of skilled manual workers was paralleled by their attainment of relatively high wages, buttressed of course by the greater bargaining power of heavy industry (but particularly coal mining), which was both the stronghold of the skilled workforce and traditionally favored by the policies of the communist state. As such, the pre-existing logic of social stratification proved insufficiently entrenched to be immune to the counter pressures applied by the communist creed and the planned allocation of resources within the economy. It was more insulated, however, from relations of gender: sex inequalities appeared to be deeply ingrained, structurally based and not susceptible to disruptions in the social system. Even the chaos and political turmoil of the 1980s had little impact on the relative positions of men and women: the gender gap in incomes, sex segregation across occupations and discriminatory labor market regulations persisted.

THE TURNING POINT?

In many respects, the market transition in Poland was more radical than in other eastern European countries: at the least, it was more rapid at the outset of the transformation. Monetary reform, trade liberalization and the removal of price supports were initiated with unprecedented speed, launching what some have described approvingly as a period of 'shock therapy' and others with disapprobation as an era of 'turkey capitalism' (Wechsler, 1989). The centralized legal and political structures exercising control of the command economy were dismantled, an Act of Parliament in 1990 abolished the system of segmented industrial ministries directing economic policy and replaced them with a single Ministry of Industry and Trade and various privatization schemes were introduced although, in the case of the large state enterprises, the plans have stalled repeatedly. New Polish businesses were established by expansions in the private sector, but the political leverage of state-owned enterprises has persisted as a factor in bargaining, even though the allocation of state funds, investment credits and other subsidies are based on calculations that now have little, if any, political content. At the same time, privatization has brought about major structural changes in the configuration of the labor market, with the private sector accounting for over 70 per cent of total employment in 1998. Even when private agriculture is excluded, a sector which remained almost intact under the communist system in Poland, this figure only falls to 60 per cent (GUS, 1999, p. 12).

The collapse of extensive political control over economic life has fostered a proliferation of new and different distributive mechanisms. Under the guidance of market forces, the earnings returns to education and occupational position increased substantially between the 1980s and the 1990s (Domański, 1994); a finding that is indicative of the growing role of meritocratic principles of distribution. The rules underpinning the operation of the post-communist labor market seem to be approaching those of the capitalist economy. The closer relationship between human capital investments and financial rewards, along with the growth of unemployment (which peaked in Poland in 1994 at just under 17 per cent of the total labor force), has operated to the benefit of the intelligentsia and to the detriment of the working class. Market forces have created a growing gap between the earnings of white and blue-collar workers, with skilled workers suffering the heaviest losses (Domański, 1994).

Proprietors can also be counted amongst the losers from transformation, with the 1990s witnessing a systematic decline in property-based incomes. While small private entrepreneurs received the highest incomes throughout the communist period, they have faced obstacles typically encountered by the 'old middle classes' in capitalist countries in the 1990s and have been overtaken by professional and managerial workers (*ibid.*). This suggests that, in Poland, the high school diploma and the possession of professional assets have begun to count more than the sheer ownership of the means of production, to put it in neo-Marxist terms. The fate of proprietors reflects the inevitable logic of the mechanisms of the capitalist economy; the private sector no longer constitutes a privileged economic enclave, drawing profits from its monopolistic position. At the same time, the *nomenklatura* system, which made Communist Party credentials a requirement for important jobs in both the economy and politics, has been abolished.

THE PROBLEMS CONFRONTING WOMEN

How have the changes outlined above affected women and how have they responded to the new challenges? The readings to follow provide some of the important clues and illuminate the range of experience encountered by Polish women and the extent to which this has been typical of other, both post-communist and capitalist, societies. Here the aim is merely to provide an overview of some of the major issues to have confronted women in the first decade after communism. In particular, consideration is given to their labor force participation, access to higher occupational positions, self-employment opportunities, earnings levels and unemployment. Some initial attention is also paid to the fundamental question of the impact of systemic change on the citizenship role of women and the degree to which they have grasped the opportunity afforded by democratic freedom to enhance their positions on the labor market and in society at large.

PARTICIPATION IN THE LABOR FORCE

Problems of definition and measurement arise when women's work is subjected to standard economic analysis and these serve to demonstrate certain shortcomings of the neo-classical model. A considerable amount of production takes place in the household and, without an examination of the social relations of domestic work, it is not possible to understand fully the nature of women's participation in the labor force. Moreover, the use of many standard indicators leads to the under-reporting of women's economic participation, both because of their involvement in the informal sector and as unpaid family workers. With this caveat in mind, a consideration of women's formal employment must be an important first step in the assessment of the place of men and women in the transforming economy.

The results of opinion polls conducted in Poland indicate that women do derive a sense of identity, worth and esteem from their working lives, in addition to the relative economic independence that their jobs bring to them. The national survey carried out in 1993 by the Center of Social Opinion Research (CSOR) found that only 3.2 per cent of adult women regarded the role of housewife as the most prestigious 'job', compared to 48.2 per cent who felt that the performance of occupational roles on the labor market was more esteemed. When an identical question was asked of another representative, random sample three years later, in 1996, it appeared that the social prestige of the working female had increased dramatically, with 70.2 per cent of respondents according highest prestige to regular jobs and only 2.3 per cent to domestic duties. This rapid growth of favorable attitudes towards employment came about chiefly from a decline in the proportion of those who were undecided and who asserted originally that it did not matter whether one performs an occupational role or stays at home. The 1996 CSOR survey also found that more women (35.5 per cent) felt that a woman's extra-household economic activity 'provided the family with more advantages than disadvantages', compared to 19.9 per cent who claimed to the contrary and 26.1 per cent who perceived a balance of benefits and costs.

Paid work was the norm for women in east European countries for 45 years. What remains to be seen in the coming years is whether, under economic restructuring, their employment opportunities will remain higher than has been the case in the west. So far, some of the omens suggest that it might. For example, the International Social Sciences Survey (ISSP) for 1994 found that women working full-time in Poland accounted for 53 per cent of the female population aged above 18, with even higher figures being recorded in Bulgaria, Hungary and Russia. In Great Britain, Germany and Sweden, on the other hand, the comparable figures were only 35, 37 and 38 per cent, respectively. Official statistics further indicate that, in Poland, the share of the active labor force (employed plus unemployed) accounted for by females has risen during the current decade, amounting to 45.2, 46.2 and 47.2 per cent in 1990, 1995 and 1998, respectively (GUS, 1999a, p. 129).

SEGREGATION BY SEX

The Labor Force Survey (LFS) of February 1998 found there to be 6.8 million working women in Poland (GUS, 1998, p. XXI), but this statistic obscures as much information as it reveals. Many jobs are considered to be either 'men's jobs' or 'women's jobs' and this fact is often regarded as the key to the inferior position of women on the labor market. The truth is that a large proportion of 'women's jobs' are bad jobs; poorly paid, boring and dead-end. Under state socialism, women's employment was marked by a paradox: while they succeeded in entering several traditionally male-dominated occupations, professions and branches of economy, there was marked and continuing occupational segregation of a kind not dissimilar to that obtaining in the capitalist world. Despite proverbial socialist stereotypes of the female tractor driver, most women worked in the over-staffed clerical and low-level administrative areas of the economy.

Sex segregation attracts renewed interest in the face of the rapid and radical transformation of the occupational structure of the Polish economy resulting from market liberalization. What nowadays may keep women out of the good jobs? Some traditional constraints that pushed them out of certain male-dominated occupations remain in force, while it seems also that some new ones have been added. The former include regulations of the Labor Code, such as those banning women from night shifts or over-time work, as well as hiring practices that reflect the view that women are unreliable because of the high absenteeism associated with maternity leave and child-care. Well known socio-cultural factors also contribute to this vicious circle; for example, Polish women previously displayed far less willingness than men to accept promotion and were reluctant to accept responsible positions at work (Siemieńska, 1990). Findings of low occupational aspirations on the part of women are, however, by no means unique to Poland (Komarowsky, 1987; McDowell and Priangle, 1994).

The process of marketization has been accompanied by the closure of old, under-invested industries, by the removal of subsidies for child-care facilities and a dearth of retraining programs geared to the needs of women. The introduction of new technology has created jobs that require specialist training (for example, computing courses), for which women are less likely to volunteer because of their family responsibilities. Another bizarre illustration of the new impediments to the advancement of women is the proliferation of blatantly gender-specific advertisements for jobs, but particularly those for better positions. The requirement, often stated by employment agencies, that a person seeking a job be 'available' at any time also disadvantages women with young children. The banking and financial services industries now offer a lot of new opportunities and it will become important to monitor whether the very good occupational career prospects there lead to the displacement of women by men, following mechanisms referred to by American students as 'resegregation' (Reskin and Roos, 1990).

Work by Domański (1992) and Dukaczewska (1997) indicated that, at least in its incipient phase, the systemic upheaval did not undermine existing patterns of occupational segregation. With later evidence revealing no signs of improvement, the situation accords well with the early thesis that it would be women who carry the main load of systemic transition. Furthermore, the expansion of self-employment and the privatization of the economy so favored by policy makers has not eased segregation, but achieved the reverse. Both the LFS and the PGSS indicate that women account for less than forty per cent of all business owners. At the same time, while growing, opportunities for part-time work and various non-standard job forms continue to lag well behind the levels experienced in Great Britain and Australia (Domański, 1998).

UNEMPLOYMENT

The struggle to survive the introduction of market forces accompanied by the pressures of the privatization process, created an inexorable logic for enterprises to shed labor. It has been argued frequently that, in this process, women will be the first to go. While the threat of job loss almost always comes to the fore in analyses of the position of women on the contemporary labor market, the issue was gender-neutral for many decades in Eastern Europe. People living there were unfamiliar with unemployment, which essentially was an abstract notion viewed as a problem encountered only in capitalist society. Since the beginning of the 1990s, however, it has added a new dimension to the discussion of gender inequality in the region. The most visible aspect of the new unemployment is its differential impact by gender, but such a cursory consideration obscures the multi-dimensional nature of the phenomenon. As such, the true social significance of unemployment is often left unexplored and its economic implications are frequently distorted. In many ways, what matters most is job matching and, on the Polish labor market, there are seemingly fewer job offers for women than for men

(Kotowska and Podogrodzka, 1994). This fact underpins the longer durations of unemployment that women are observed to experience.

The possibility is that women may withdraw from the labor force voluntarily, or delay their re-entry, because of a lack of available jobs. For example, in both Sweden and the US during the 1970s, the probability of unemployed women leaving the labor force—and thus disappearing from the unemployment statistics—was about twice as high as that of men (Björklund, 1984, p. 29). This point is especially important because official counts of the unemployed include only those workers actively seeking work and exclude discouraged workers. In Canada, for example, it has been observed that the discouraged worker effect is stronger for women than for men, with the former being more likely to cease to look for work because they believe none is available (Agarwal, 1985). Moreover, in some countries (for example, the United Kingdom), married women do not register as unemployed because the coverage of unemployment and related benefits can be restricted according to marital status. To the extent that such programmatic details operate in eastern European countries and that they increase the tendency for unemployed women, but not men, to be excluded from the unemployment statistics, this will perpetuate the view that female unemployment is somehow a less serious problem than actually is.

INEQUALITY OF EARNINGS

The gender gap in earnings is perhaps the most widely used indicator of sex inequality on the labor market. As such, two constants merit special attention: first, the prevalence of the phenomenon is independent of economic, political and cultural context; second, the gap appears to be relatively immune to the passage of both time and legislation. Studies that have examined the pay differential in several countries have found that, on average, women earn 20–40 per cent less than men (Madden, 1988; Baron and Newman, 1989; Lane, 1995). Despite some signs of a slight narrowing in the earnings gap in the OECD countries (OECD, 1985), its presence remains an enduring sociological regularity. Bearing these previous findings in mind, it may seem puzzling that, in post-communist Poland, the gender gap in earnings actually fell over the period 1992–1995, in spite of the rising levels of overall wage inequality as marketization of the economy gained momentum. After a decade in which the ratio of women's to men's pay stood in the range 67–69 per cent, the female–male mean monthly earnings ratio was observed to have fallen to 55.9 per cent in 1992, but to have increased to 74.2 per cent in 1995 (Domański, 1998).

Western authors probe the underlying causes of the residual gap in gender incomes using a multiplicity of individual and aggregated data sets and statistical techniques. Even then, however, it becomes difficult to discuss the gender gap without reference to the concept of discrimination, which is commonly identified in economic and sociological literature as the underpayment resulting from the adverse treatment of women by employers. It is that difference in earnings that remains after controlling for male–female difference in skills and many other 'measurable' factors affecting the absolute pay gap. In Poland, this net gap also appears to have been reduced over the years 1992–1995. After taking account of factors such as years of schooling, experience in work, occupational and industrial segregation, age and place of residence, the residual declined from 16.5 per cent in 1992 to ten per cent in 1995 (*ibid.*, 1998). While Blau and Kahn (1997) ascribed a falling gap in the USA in the 1980s to either an upgrading of women's unmeasured labor market skills or to a decline in labor market discrimination against them, neither of these possibilities seems credible in the case of Poland. However, many observers would be unwilling to accept that there has been a pro-female shift in skills or an increased marketability of education, and neither would many concede that statistical discrimination against women has diminished in recent years.

MOBILIZATION AND ARTICULATION OF COLLECTIVE INTERESTS

Not unlike activists in western countries, women in eastern Europe assert that the 'Polish democracy is a masculine democracy' (Heinen, 1992, p. 135), which suggests that women are in some way not allowed to participate in decision-making on the public stage. It may well be wrong, however, to impose norms derived from the western European experience of feminist activism in the 1970s and 1980s on a situation that is politically and culturally different. As women stand to lose the welfare and employment rights they enjoyed under state socialism, the non-emergence of a mass women's movement may seem paradoxical, but the slow pace of development of women's citizenship needs to be viewed from a more neutral perspective for at least two reasons. First, women were unable to gain experience of defending, and fighting for, their rights under the old autocratic regime; they must now learn how to self-organize like other social categories in post-communist countries.

Second, one cannot overlook looming 'organic' forms of civic society in Poland, such as the 'abortion' campaign that followed the restrictive anti-abortion bill and the debates on sex education in schools, which accelerated the growth of new women's organizations. In fact, there is an incipient growth of grassroots activity and organizations defending the interests of various groups. These represent a vast spectrum of ideological and political orientations, from extreme right to the radical left, and they exist as groups working within national political structures, or as organizations dedicated to working at the local level devoted to the establishment of women's centers, feminist libraries and sports clubs.

THE STRUCTURE OF THE BOOK

Systemic change is the clear objective in Poland, yet few will deny the significance of the past in the determination of current events. Titkow therefore provides the necessary anchor in her consideration of the historical, rather elevated, role of women in Polish society, even though that society was patriarchal and viewed the world in terms of family, class and national unity. The communist epoch, through its mass professional activation of women, could have enhanced their, always heroic, social standing further although, in the event, it served merely to sustain and in many ways to reinforce the traditional model. Liberalization of the Polish economy and its society presents the ideal opportunity to rewrite the basic gender contract and to undermine the received stereotype.

In the space of just ten years, empirical analysts of the Polish labor market have experienced an enormous increase in the raw material of their trade, data. Furthermore, the windfall has not been one-dimensional; the increase in the quantity of information generated by official governmental sources has been accompanied by a commensurate improvement in its quality. While there have been teething problems as new surveys have been introduced and reporting conventions have been modified, sometimes radically, to conform to those of the world from which the country was isolated formerly, there now exists a wealth of statistical material with which to evaluate the impact of labor market change on men and women. Ingham and Ingham exploit a variety of these sources in order to provide an overview of the evolving relationship of men and women to the world of work. Covering market participation, employment, hours of work, earnings and unemployment they portray a situation that is not as simple as might once have been imagined and one which provides food for thought to those who claimed that the costs of transformation, at least as those are conveyed through the labor market, would be borne mainly by women.

Demographic processes represent the fundamental determinant of the supply of labor to the economy and Kotowska's contribution highlights the significant changes in fertility and nuptiality that have taken place in the past twenty years and which will impose additional pressures on the labor market in the coming decade. The labor force is set to increase until 2010, while the omens suggest that the pace of the positive economic developments of the mid-1990s will not be maintained with equal velocity into the future. Falling labor demand and rising labor supply imply more unemployment and Kotowska reminds us of the disproportionate share of unemployment that has been borne by women. The processes she identifies are not uni-directional, with labor market phenomena generally regarded as important influences on fertility, nuptiality and migration. That the latter is a weak force in Poland serves to intensify the marked disparities in economic well-being to be observed across the regions of the country and to increase the difficulties to be overcome before the transformation process can be considered to be complete.

While both of the two preceding contributions highlight employment changes in the first decade that appear to have been more favorable to women than to men, Domański's comparative study of occupational mobility is the first of several papers in this volume to stress the need to look behind raw statistical aggregates in order to examine the kinds of work that are available to the sexes. Increased flexibility has occasioned greater cross-strata mobility on labor markets throughout Eastern Europe and it has done so for men and women alike. However, in all of the nations studied by Domański, women remain entrenched in relatively disadvantaged employments and, in the case of Poland, their propensity to enter supervisory positions actually declined in the first years of the new capitalism. Nevertheless, that country lies at one extreme of a range of outcomes unearthed by his research and there may be lessons to be learned for all transforming economies from the more positive developments uncovered in the Czech Republic.

The concept of success, implicit in many of the contributions to this volume, is rendered explicit in the study discussed by Firkowska-Mankiewicz. Utilizing a carefully constructed longitudinal panel of men and women and controlling for social background and level of intelligence, both of which can invalidate comparisons of the relationships between personal aspirations and realized outcomes, her results violate many popular stereotypes. At least amongst the intellectually gifted, Polish women have more positive images of their social position and success in life than do men, even though their parents usually held lower expectations for their future careers than did the direct ancestors of equivalent boys. Indeed, the more optimistic view of the transformation held by women actually leads them to expect that their occupational status will exceed that of men in the coming years. Nonetheless, the persistence of traditional family structures represents an unwelcome constant in Polish life and serves to emphasize the fact that not all stereotypes can yet be discarded.

If women in conventional employment remain trapped under the glass ceiling, the formation of their own businesses may present a possible escape and an alternative route to the apex of the occupational hierarchy. The problem is that such a course of action might itself challenge traditional mores and thereby be the trigger for the erection of a new set of obstacles. In fact, Reszke's examination of the opinions of the urban population of Poland reveals that, on the whole, both men and women hold largely positive views of female entrepreneurs. However, just as in the case of paid employment, domestic obligations are seen to represent a barrier to the pursuit of a successful entrepreneurial career. Also, the reasons why women are seen potentially to be successful as business owners differ markedly from those that underpin the supposed ability of men to rise to the challenge of entrepreneurship. Stereotypes may once again therefore constitute an ongoing threat to the advancement of women, although the image of the successful entrepreneur held by the population may, in many ways, be equally unhelpful in the near future.

During the communist era, there existed two major women's organizations, although one was effectively an organ of the state, with ideological functions and subjected to political pressure, leaving only the Circle of Rural Housewives (CRH) as a largely independent, albeit functionally limited, undertaking. Malinowska's survey indicates that, by 1995, sixty-eight independent, although very heterogeneous, women's groupings could be identified, each typically formed with the aim of promoting the interests of women of a given, endangered economic status. With the exception of the CRH, however, which retains its rural outlook, most of the groups operate from urban locations, as might be expected from the intelligentsia and professional backgrounds of their activists. A major positive initiative of many of these groups is their attempt to combat long-term female unemployment, numerically mainly an urban problem. The women's movement in Poland is, however, weakened by its fragmentation and the failure of its constituent bodies to co-operate. As such, it cannot yet be said to exhibit western-style characteristics.

Dukaczewska-Nałęcz develops the theme of women's participation in public life one stage further and links it to their access to positions of power. In looking at the situation in both politics and the world of business, she brings to the fore the question of where the true locus of power actually resides in democratic market economies. The comprehensive survey findings in the paper indicate clearly that the representative tokenism existing under communist rule has been replaced by a situation in which, notwithstanding their educational attainments, women now enjoy merely minority status in parliament, the civil service and on the management boards of the most powerful companies in the new economy. The divide that separates the male sphere (the public) from the female sphere (the private) has apparently yet to be bridged.

It would be disingenuous to attempt to convey the impression that Poland constitutes a spatially homogeneous society in economic, political or social terms and three contributions to this volume are dedicated to the illumination of regional difference. In the first of these, Ingham and Węcławowicz draw attention to the fact that the earnings gap between men and women observable at the national level displays wide variation across the voivodships of the country. Nevertheless, and in spite of the major changes in the distribution of earnings nationally, nowhere do the earnings of women achieve parity with those of men. Nonetheless, on the basis of the model constructed within the paper, it is economic and structural factors, rather than purely local forces, that would seem to be responsible for the majority of the variation in women's relative earnings across space, although the specter of the past looms large in the process.

The retention of a significant private agricultural sector rendered Poland unique amongst the states to fall under the influence of the Soviet Union following the Second World War, although the price to be paid was that of a rural community dominated by an essentially time-warped peasant-farming sector. While many women did leave the farms during the rapid industrialization program followed by the communists for the great number who remained there existed a fuzzy distinction between market and non-market work. Gorlach's contribution develops these themes and shows how the rural communities have suffered increased hardships in the 1990s. The return of men released from alternative, industrial employment to positions of hidden unemployment on the farms has had severe impacts on the women who previously managed the enterprises. Because the prevailing cultural mores dictate that they continue to perform all of the domestic chores, their entrepreneurial inventiveness and willingness to migrate in search of additional income are subjected to damaging constraints.

The concluding work in the volume, by Ingham and Karwińska, examines the impact of reform on women's labor market position in the city of Kraków. As the historical center of academia, but also the home of the Huta Sendzimira steelworks, this is an area of stark contrasts, but it is one in which women have fared relatively well. Using official statistics and sample survey data, the authors find that women have enjoyed a better employment record than men in the current decade, have a more diversified employment base and are held in a positive light by employers in the region. The caveats are that women have been more prone to unemployment and hold far more negative views of the transformation process than men. In the future, the rationalization of the steel industry will have its immediate impact on the unemployment rate of males, although it will simultaneously impose a severe shock on the whole of the local economy. The threat to women is clear; less so is the likely success of the city's development strategy.

REFERENCES

Agarwal, N. (1985) "Economic Costs of Discrimination in Canada," in: *Research Studies of Commission on Equality in Employment*, Ottawa: Commission of Equality and Employment.

Andorka, R. and K. Zagórski (1980) *Socio-occupational Mobility in Hungary and Poland*, Budapest–Warszawa: IFiS Publishers.

Baron, J.N. and A.E. Newman (1989) "Pay the Man: Effects of Demographic Composition on Prescribed Wage Rates in the California Civil Service," in: R.T. Michael, H.I. Hartmann and B. O'Farrel (eds), *Pay Equity: Empirical Inquiries*, Washington D.C.: National Academy Press.

Białecki, I. and B. Heyns (1993) "Educational Attainment, the Status of Women, and The Private School Movement in Poland," in: V. Moghadam (ed.), *Democratic Reform and the Position of Women in Transitional Economies*, Oxford: Clarendon Series.

Björklund, A. (1984) "Evaluations of labour market policy in Sweden," *International Journal of Manpower*, vol. 15, no. 5, pp. 16–31.

Blau, F.D. and L.M. Kahn (1997) "Swimming Upstream: Trends in the Gender Wage Differential in the 1980s," *Journal of Labor Economics*, vol. 15, no.1, pp. 1–42.

Domański, H. (1990) "Dynamics of the Labour Market Segmentation in Poland," *Social Forces*, vol. 69, no. 2, pp. 423–438.

Domański, H. (1992) *Zadowolony niewolnik. Studium o nierównościach społecznych między mężczyznami i kobietami w Polsce* (The grateful slave. The study of inequalities between men and women in Poland), Warszawa: IFiS PAN.

Domański, H. (1994) "The Recomposition of Social Stratification in Poland," *Polish Sociological Review*, vol. 108, no. 4, pp. 335–358.

Domański, H. (1998) *Zadowolony niewolnik idzie do pracy. Analiza porownawcza wobec pracy kobiet z 23 krajow* (The grateful slave goes to market. A comparative analysis of attitudes towards the occupational activity of women for 23 countries), Warszawa: IFiS PAN.

Dukaczewska, A. (1997) Aktywność kobiet w sferze prywatnej jako substytut dominacji mężczyzn w sferze publicznej (Women's activity in the private sphere as a substitute for men's domination in the public sphere), Ph.D. Dissertation, Warszawa: IFiS PAN.

Einhorn, B. (1993) *Cinderella Goes to Market. Citizienship, Gender and Women's Movements in East Central Europe*, London: Verso.

Erikson, R. and J.H. Goldthorpe (1992) *Constant Flux*, Oxford: Clarendon Press.

Fuchs, V.R. (1988) *Women's Quest for Economic Equality*, Cambridge: Harvard University Press.

GUS (1993) *Aktywność zawodowa i bezrobocie w Polsce* (Occupational activity and unemployment in Poland), Warszawa: Główny Urząd Statystyczny.

GUS (1998) *Aktywność Ekonomiczna Ludnosci Polski May 1998* (Economic activity in Poland May 1998), Warszawa: Główny Urząd Statystyczny.

GUS (1999) *Pracujacy w Gospodarce Narodewej w 1998 R* (Employment in national economy in 1998 revised), Warszawa: Główny Urząd Statystyczny.

GUS (1999) *Rocznik Statystyczny 1999* (Statistical yearbook 1999), Warszawa: Główny Urząd Statystyczny.

Heinen, J. (1992) "Linking Women East and West: French–Polish Cooperation," *Women's Studies International Forum*, vol. 15, no. 1, pp. 134–135.

Komarowsky, M. (1987) *Blue-Collar Marriage*, New York: Yale University Press.

Kotowska, I. and M. Podogrodzka (1994) "Women's Discrimination in the Labour Market and its Possible Demographic Effects," Paper prepared for the meeting *Women in Business, Society and Family*, Warszawa: Central School of Statistics and Economics, 5–6 May.

Lane, C. (1995) "Gender and the labor market in Europe: Britain, Germany, and France Compared," *International Journal of Sociology*, vol. 41, no. 2, pp. 8–38.

Łobodzińska, B. (1983) "Urban and Rural Working Women in Poland Today: Between Social Change and Social Conflict," in H. Lopata and J. Pleck (eds), *Research in the Interweave of Social Roles: Families and Jobs*, vol. 3, Greenwich: JAI Press Inc.

Madden, J.F. (1988) "The Persistence of Pay Differentials. The Economics of Sex Discrimination," in: L. Larwood, A.H. Stromberg and B.A. Gutek (eds), *Women and Work: An Annual Review*, vol. 1., London: Sage.

McDowell, I. and R. Priangle (1994) "Defining Work," in: I. McDowell and R. Priangle (eds), *Defining Women. Social Institutions and Gender Divisions,* Cambridge: Polity Press.

OECD (Organization for Economic Co-operation and Development) (1985) *The Integration of Women in the Economy*, Paris: OECD.

Plakwicz, J. (1992) "Between Church and State: Polish Women's Experience," in C. Corrin (ed.), *Superwomen and the Double Burden: Women's Experience of Change in Central and Eastern Europe and the Former Soviet Union*, London: Scarlett Press.

Reskin, B.F. and P. Roos (1990) *Job Queues, Gender Queues: Explaining Women's Inroads Into Male Occupations*, Philadelphia; Temple University Press.

Rozporządzenie Rady Ministrów z dn. 19 stycznia 1979 r. w sprawie prac wzbronionych kobietom. Dziennik ustaw z dn. 27 lutego 1979 r., No. 4 (Regulation of the council of ministries from January 19th on jobs prohibited for women), Zmiana w Dzienniku Ustaw z 1984 r. No. 44.

Sawiński, Z. and H. Domański (1991) "Stability of Prestige Hierarchies in the Face of Social Changes—Poland, 1958–1987," *International Sociology*, vol. 6, no. 2, pp. 227–241.

Siemieńska, R. (1990) "Women, Work and Gender Equality in Poland: Reality and Its Social Perception," in: S.I. Wolchik and A.G. Meyer (eds), *Women, State and Party in Eastern Europe*, Durham: Duke University Press.

Treiman, D.J. (1977) *Occupational Prestige in Comparative Perspective*, New York: Academic Press.

Tuma, N.B., M.T. Hannan and L.P. Groeneveld (1979) "Dynamic Analysis of Event Histories," *American Journal of Sociology*, vol. 84, no. 4, pp. 820–854.

Wechsler, L. (1989) "A Grand Experiment," *The New Yorker*, 13 November, pp. 59–104.

CHAPTER 2

ON THE APPRECIATED ROLE OF WOMEN[1]

The election of June 1989 symbolized the change of political and economic systems in Poland and marked the beginning of a remarkable transformation in the norms, role models, needs and customs of social behavior. However, change is not so transparent in all spheres shaping the relationships between men and women, which condition the principles of production and reproduction and delineate the respective social positions of the sexes; that is, in the terms of the gender contract. In fact, the only claim that can be made regarding this contract is that the process by which it is formed started anew at the beginning of transition.

Verification of certain stereotypes, or social myths, is an integral part of the evolution of the gender contract. Among those stereotypes one will undoubtedly encounter impressions, deeply rooted in the Polish culture and shared by both men and women alike, of the special role played by Polish women. The democratic character of Poland's new political system, as well as its market economy mechanisms, is gradually revealing what 'the appreciated role of women' actually means. Political, legislative and economic decisions are now taken openly and, as a result, they give rise to public debates. The form and content of these debates—the way they are held and concluded—provide an opportunity to observe the enlivenment of the stereotype under which Polish women have been given a social status of particular importance. More generally, there is a reiteration of the requirement to subordinate the needs and interests of women to those of family, nation and country.

It is of important to enquire whether the historical scheme that stresses the 'special importance of women' will re-emerge in its old shape or whether it will be modified to a certain extent, if only by women themselves. Equally significant is the question of whether the contemporary perspective leads to a negative evaluation of the whole of the historical heritage conditioning the present position and status of Polish women. Needless to say, this chapter will not provide any definitive answers to these questions. Instead, given that other chapters in this volume refer to hard indices of women's social position, the present contribution represents what might be regarded as a sociological tale on the appreciated role of Polish women, with due consideration paid to the question of whether or not life will continue to liberate them against their own will.

THE AMBIGUOUS HERITAGE OF THE PAST

The Polish nobility ethos seems to have a relatively clear conscience as far as women are concerned. Fifteenth century court records kept in archives in the city of Kraków contain lists of women who managed vast landed properties or who represented their husbands in court. There is also evidence that women of lower classes enjoyed similar rights and had abilities similar to those of men (Koestler, 1992). Later, during the partition of Poland, women were allowed to participate actively in all aspects of the drive to regain independence and thereby, in the eyes of the nobility, freedom. That is, the entry of women into public life was facilitated by the 'in the name of freedom for the nation' principle. On the whole, however, women did not constitute a significant social group and their individual positions depended heavily on class affiliation and the financial situation of their families. Nonetheless, in the noble class, women were equal to men and, in the seventeenth century, the nobility code of honor told men to pay due respect to their wives (Lorence-Kot, 1985). With the nobility constituting ten per cent of the whole population, the precepts of this code were important.[2] In consequence, the Polish nobility ethos granted women a relatively high social position by giving them the right to individual and independent attitudes. However, the mild patriarchalism it contained forged a perception in which the world was viewed in terms of family, class and national unity and this was later to foster circumstances under which women became entangled in their heroic role of Polish Mother.

Poland's loss of independence was an ambiguous influence on the situation of women, at least in terms of the common understanding of their social position and interests. After partition, bringing up children became a political matter, since the family was then the only guarantee that the identity of the nation could be preserved. Family, an area for which women were solely responsible, became the place in which patriots were supposed to be shaped. As such, women gained in importance, because cultural, national and political significance was added to society's traditional perception of their position, and this happened without the previous gender division of social roles being questioned. This development had both positive and negative consequences:

> The Catholic Church and the society formed a new pattern of woman characterized by moral and emotional elements. The religious tradition required females to be ready for various sacrifices offering them in return a new significance contained in the symbol of Polish Mother. Although it strengthened national resistance, this idealization of woman created very strong bonds between family and nation, and the bondage was such that any attempt undertaken by women to free themselves from traditional family dependence was perceived as betraying the nation and apostasy. Liberation of women interpreted in this way was considered a social taboo. This is proved by the fact that the notion of women's liberation was used to show disapproval [as it still is—A.T.] and gained meanings commonly associated with the behavior of women like George Sand. (Pietrow-Ennker, 1992, p. 22).

The period of lost independence and statehood created an image of the Polish woman as a heroic figure, capable of undertaking a variety of duties and burdens. She was expected to be strong and faithful to her tasks. Her role in educating children was emphasized constantly; and she was responsible for preserving the national tradition, the language and culture, and the Christian faith: a very rich role-set. Moreover, women were used to fulfilling the roles traditionally ascribed to men, typified as those of managing a husband's property or business when he was imprisoned or dead.

It was during this difficult period of the lost state that the social genotype of woman as capable of enduring even the most severe hardships of social reality was created. Following the loss of independence, women were required to surrender their aspirations to the needs of the group and were supposed to do so in the name of nation and family, and assumed not to expect any gratification, other than the symbolic one, for their sacrifice. In spite, but at the same time because, of this, women acquired a remarkably prestigious position in both the family and society (Titkow, 1992, 1993).

Polish women, particularly in the first years of partition, had hardly any choice but to accept the foregoing attitudes and behaviors: they were placed on a pedestal that subordinated them to social norms and expectations. However, the pressure exerted on women by this idealization also had its benefits. It prompted, and later sustained, the need to include women in the formal schooling system. Before the partitions, even the most enlightened members of Polish society were of the opinion that women were to be educated only as good mothers and housewives. The drive to prevent denationalization changed this belief and the need for well-educated mothers was acknowledged (Winiarz, 1992).

The reality of partition influenced the collective activities of women in two ways. On the one hand, the loss of independence included women in public life, mainly by transforming their charitable activities into pro-national ones. On the other hand, the national cause united women of different social classes, thus preventing the formation of a strong and unambiguous women's liberation movement. The pressure and priority of fighting for the national identity and regaining independence left hardly any room for activities other than the performance of the roles of wife, mother, daughter and patriot. Women directed their protest against the oppressive political system and not against the patriarchal structures dominant in social life. This facilitated the inclusion of the Polish women's movement into the national pro-independence activities and undoubtedly permitted the existence of a women's liberation movement, albeit one that was weakened from its very inception.

Polish historians emphasize how the crisis of the noble—agricultural economy after the 1864 enfranchisement of peasants and the industrialization of the Silesia region initiated the process of women's emergence from the family into public life (Żarnowska and Szwarc, 1992).[3] It was then that the general formula for women's participation on the labor market was shaped in a way that discriminated against them. They were not at all prepared for their new life situation, and society was not ready to accept their greater independence. The upgrading of women's education, which was initiated after the partition, proved insufficient; women of the upper classes suffered from their impractical upbringing and the superficiality of their schooling (Rzepniewska, 1990). On the other hand, women from the lower classes had no education and no economic means to support themselves. Thus, both groups of women were not prepared to compete against men on the labor market. At the same time, many women were forced to take a job if they wanted to provide for their families and for themselves, and the absence of choice prevented them from negotiating better working conditions.

Each of the social classes had its own norms determining the degree of approval afforded to working-women. Next to the relatively small group of well-educated people, middle-class townspeople, particularly those not too well off, accepted women's professional activities. In the latter class, so closely connected with the development of trade and craftsmanship, the participation of women in family businesses was natural, and even expected (Kowalska-Glikman, 1990). The lower classes, on the other hand, where women were forced to work if they wanted to survive, were unwilling to approve of women working in industry.[4] Working-class families were characterized by the woman submitting herself totally to the man of the house, even if she was the only provider. This situation was often realized only with a great deal of deception, not infrequently to the detriment of the woman.

Many historians of both the nineteenth century and the post-World War I period emphasize the extent of social approval for women's participation in the fight for national independence. However, other research testifies to the contrary; for example, one study suggests social disapproval of the legendary Emilia Plater, the woman who fought in the army disguised as a man (Śliwowska, 1994). Another scholar points to the 'paralyzing effect of stereotype' in the case of women actively engaged in the pro-independence military campaign of Józef Piłsudski, the leader of Polish pro-independence movement (Nałęcz, 1994). Piłsudski's army did have female conscripts, but they were made to wear men's uniforms, their squads were commanded by men and they were registered under masculine names, even on their personal identity cards. Piłsudski was afraid to expose himself to ridicule by openly admitting that he had women among his soldiers, although he did admit how much the success of his pro-independence movement owed to women.

It seems that this involved more than just the belief that women should support soldiers but not themselves become one. The social disapproval of women soldiers reflected a great ambivalence in the attitudes of both sexes towards the transgression of traditional female roles. Paraphrasing the 'women as a reserve labor army' thesis, it might be said that Polish women constituted a reserve army of society, or better still, a reserve army of the nation. Eighty years later, the functioning of women within the structures of Solidarity, the famous social movement that remained illegal until 1989, was based on the same principles (Penn, 1994).

Thus, the stereotype ascribing women to their traditional roles is still alive today and reducing their participation in public life solely to emergency situations, such as threats to national independence or sovereignty. However, the force of the stereotype may have been reduced under the circumstances that appeared after 1945, when both the level of women's education and their participation in the labor market rose dramatically. Also, when confronted with the reality of the new democratic system constructed in Poland after 1989, the stereotype seems to have weakened further.

It should be emphasized that some protection of the equality of Polish women's political and educational rights was enacted in the years 1918–1920, in the aftermath of the country regaining independence. Nevertheless, formal equal civil rights for the sexes did not encourage women to take an active part in the public life of the newly independent state and, in this sense, the legal innovation was not of great importance to women's liberation movements. However, post-World War I Poland was an arena in which the most active and self-confident women could realize their ambitions; in particular, they could enter Parliament, in which women MPs and senators 'held the rule over others'. Thus, while there were not many women in the legislature—1.9 per cent of members of the lower chamber of Parliament and 3.8 per cent of the upper chamber throughout all the terms of office in the inter-war period—they nevertheless were much better educated than their male parliamentary colleagues. For example, half the females in the Sejm (the Lower House of Parliament) held university diplomas, while one-quarter of the men in Parliament had no education at all, or had graduated only from elementary school.

Women's parliamentary activities during that time achieved the passage of the prohibition law, the law granting women equal rights with men under the civil code, the law on social services, and the law on the principles of employment of under-age women. As a result of these enactments, Poland found itself among those countries with the most advanced legal regulations on social security (Śliwa, 1996). In a similar vein, professionally active women included not only those who 'had to' work, but also those who 'wanted to'. The former group probably consisted of women employed in industry while the latter group included, for example, female doctors of medicine, who amounted for 15.7 per cent of the total number of practitioners (Siemieńska, 1990).[5]

The years 1945–1989 marked the next important period in shaping the specificity of the social prestige of Polish women. This epoch witnessed a massive, and largely forced, professional activation of women. The process was based primarily on ideology, enforced by the rapid growth of the industrial labor market and the economic pressures this created. Low wages for almost all workers made women's earnings a necessary part of family budgets, with the associated pressure to take a job being exerted on women of all social classes. It was egalitarian.

Such professional activation could have extended the social position of women and enriched it with new elements: they could have become success-oriented; they could have started to believe in themselves, and developed partnership relationships with both their families and with society at large. Instead, the process sustained and enforced the traditional pattern, entailing protective—supporting virtues and sacrifice (Titkow, 1993). This meant losing the chance to change the contents of social and cultural identification. Consequently, an opportunity was lost to transform the identity of women from that defined by a traditional role-set into one defined by personal choice.

The professional activation of women resulted in an extension of their social role by imparting a duty upon them to earn money rather than by opening-up new opportunities of self-realization. It was accepted as another element of the pattern of daily life, uncompensated by the introduction of change in the traditional role division, most particularly within the family. Furthermore, little change is evident in the current era, with research indicating that women devote five times more of their time to household drudgeries than do men (Kalkhoff, 1995). In 70 per cent of all Polish families, women do all the housework; professionally active women can count on the help of their husbands only slightly more than can women who do not work (CBOS, 1993a). Adding professional work to the role-set of women was not necessarily helpful as activation merely added one more element to their social genotype, without destroying that which existed previously. Neither the previous system of meanings nor the cognitive terminology were disturbed, let alone changed. Moreover, and following the deeply rooted cultural pattern, women expected no gratification for the additional burden of earning money that was placed upon them.

In the case of Poland, it is probably correct to hypothesize that women did not feel a dramatic role conflict because of their professional activation. Even if, at the very beginning, their traditional roles and those resulting from their newly taken professional activities were equally important for themselves, most soon made a choice that diminished the importance of the latter. A similar hypothesis argues that professional roles only supplemented an already existing pattern in which heroism and sacrifice were the most conspicuous elements. If this hypothesis is true, we should expect that the opportunity to meet the requirements sanctioned by historical tradition added to women's self-esteem. If so, this opportunity constituted not only an important reward, a buffer softening mental and physical discomforts, but also a factor legitimizing their authority in the family. The difficult life situation created a specific kind of matriarchy, a formation characteristic of the countries of Eastern Europe in both communist and post-communist times. In this matriarchy, a woman is loaded with bags of shopping, often extremely tired and lacking sleep but, at the same time, she has a legitimate feeling of being an irreplaceable manager of family life, single-handedly fulfilling duties which would be a burden for a number of people. This managerial success, supported by the restrictive, commanding style so popular in Polish culture, legitimizes the feeling of domination. And domination can be very rewarding.

Perhaps gratification, which is a traditional way of improving one's self-evaluation, has always been much more important for the majority of Polish women than the satisfactions related to pursuing either a professional career or participating in public life. It certainly seems to have been more important than the related needs of self-realization, recognition, respect, financial reward and a high position in the social hierarchy. As such, we can assume that gratification can compensate for the physical strains women suffer in consequence of having to combine family and professional roles (Titkow, 1993). Research indicates that professional activation has not created a subculture of professional women: both professionally active women and those who are not working outside the home are equally satisfied with their lives. Both groups declare identical sets of preferred general values, as well as the same sets of desired qualities in a child. Furthermore, both groups perceive the institution of marriage in the same way, which is not surprising in view of their declared preferences (Titkow, 1984a).

The period after 1945 may be seen as one of lost opportunity for women since it has not added any new elements to the binding cultural image of woman. Nevertheless, it should be remembered that women's massive professional activation was accompanied by an unprecedented increase in the level of their education. This increase, however, has not prevented discrimination against women, as manifested in their salaries, professional paths and lesser participation in public life. By making their life choices, women themselves reinforce this discrimination. They participate in the process of constructing 'the Bastille of discrimination' (Titkow, 1984b), as is evident from their declared beliefs. Although they claim to be better managers than men—and men declare the same opinion—they prefer to have male bosses (CBOS, 1993a).

Does this approval of discrimination result from the fact that women are not conscious of their political, economic and social group interests? Such an attitude would be understandable and justified in a country where, for hundreds of years, the notion of interest was associated with either the well being of one's own family or with that of the country. Or perhaps such approval should be seen as resulting from gratification related to a managerial matriarchy. These two interpretations are not mutually exclusive. Moreover, gratification related to managerial matriarchy may have prevented the creation of a women's group-interest consciousness. It might be hypothesized that women have gained a sense of their own value from operating under the extremely difficult daily life conditions associated with real socialism: "living the life within the circle of one's own daily life and the immediate future of the family." (Nowak, 1979, p. 124). Indeed, it could be argued that, within the sphere of female responsibilities, such feelings merely served to elevate the status of the family; a possibility enhanced by the plebeian component of the Polish Mother syndrome.

The period after 1945 was the period of lost opportunity for women in another sense as well. A managerial matriarchy was created as a result of the necessity to solve the daily problems of a difficult economic reality and it may have given women the feeling of domination within their families. Nevertheless, it also laid the foundations for the opinion that there are much more important matters than the problems of women themselves; an opinion in a recent survey expressed by 70 per cent of women (OBOP, 1995).

The above considerations outline the nature of the process that transformed Polish women into a highly homogeneous group, defined by the roles of mother and wife, in which all share the same dreams, goals and patterns of life.[6] This process can also be seen as a kind of training aimed at convincing women that no joint action could possibly change anything in their lives and, as a result of which, the notion of 'women's rights' became perceived with hostility. With their rhetoric, the Communists tried particularly hard to convince society that 'privileges', such as social benefits, should be identified with the rights of women: the myth of the existence of equality between sexes was being created. In consequence, one should not be surprised that the movements for women's rights started in Poland after 1989 have been perceived either as instruments in a fight for additional privileges or as tools with which to discriminate against men.[7] This also explains why the so-called 'Ruch Komitetów,' a union of committees supporting the idea of a national referendum on abortion, emphasized the necessity to defend democracy and preserve the ideological neutrality of the state, rather than women's reproductive rights per se.

Polish society is dominated by one traditional way of thinking about the social functioning of men and women. According to it, the burdens of family life should be borne by women and their professional careers must be subordinated to family needs. However, certain exceptions to this rule are beginning to appear; in particular, a diversification of opinions regarding women's position in the social structure. Even if the exceptions are not yet pervasive enough to change the general character of the gender contract, they permit speculation that changes in that contract are possible. Perhaps the starting point for change is data, ironic and intriguing as this may seem in the light of what has been said so far. According to survey evidence, 80 per cent of Polish women and 60 per cent of Polish men, declare that women are in a worse situation than men, both professionally and socially. Obviously, such findings do not necessarily mean that 80 per cent of Polish women also think that there is no equality between the sexes and that women's status and prospects are worse than those of men: this opinion is voiced by only four per cent of adult women in Poland. Furthermore, only three per cent of Polish women use derivatives of the word 'discrimination' in describing their own position (CBOS, 1993b).

Attempts to explain this false self-consciousness should point to double standards as one of the main mechanisms creating and regulating the phenomenon of social differences between men and women. Double standards can be found in morality, in the ways that law and social policy function and in the labor market. Double standards dominate sexual and marital life. They also underlie the principles of the role division between the sexes, thus influencing both family life and the lives of individual women. Double standards start to function at an early age due to the different ways in which boys and girls are reared (see Titkow and Domański, 1995).

THE AMBIGUOUS CONSEQUENCES OF DEMOCRACY AND BACKLASH

The role of historical heritage is ambiguous if analyzed from the standpoint of the social appreciation of women. On the one hand, women have achieved remarkable prestige through sacrificing their own interests to those of society and, because of this, they have high self-esteem. On the other hand, women have gathered a common pool of experience through the generations as a result of participating both in private and public spheres. This accumulation is particularly important in the current period of social and economic transformation in that it may change the way women understand their own interests and how they define the indices of their social position and prestige.

Evidence on the situation of Polish women after 1989 indicates that, despite all the changes in the political system, the place of women in society has consistently been the subject of public discussions which have resulted in various decisions that have been taken by everyone but women themselves. Even if this can be explained, it is much more difficult to accept. Freedom came as a surprise and necessitated clarification of a vision of the new socio-economic deal to be constructed as part of it. It also created the need to evaluate justly the period after 1945, with those in some political circles pointing to the necessity to condemn the era totally. Under such circumstances, public attention and political activities have naturally focused on those spheres of social life that yield easily to arguments referring to culture, tradition and religious persuasion. Nevertheless, those arguments are abused in all discussions of the social position of women.

The notion of backlash seems to describe accurately the situation of Polish women after 1989, even if in Poland it did not start as a reaction against 'the achievements of feminism', as was the case in the United States. Rather, backlash here refers to the reaction of men to the position occupied by women in society. It should be remembered that this reaction is taking place in a situation colored by various threats, uncertainties and changes typical of radical socio-political transformation, on the one hand, and the various accompanying opportunities brought by democracy, on the other. Both the requirements and the opportunities impose stringent demands, particularly for those in government. Polish men, having for so long dominated the arena of public and political life, are having serious problems meeting the requirements of democracy and a market economy, and this clearly causes fear. It is quite probable—

following Faludi (1991)—that men personify this fear as a female figure, with whom the easiest way to fight is by control and the imposition of convenient solutions. Thus it may be assumed that backlash is to a large degree motivated by the fact that men realize the profits they reap from the traditional division of sex roles. This claim seems to be supported by research results: while men generally accept women working professionally and an equal division of responsibilities between the sexes, they are rather reluctant, particularly if they are urban residents, to see their own wives working on the external labor market (Firlit, 1995).

Reproductive rights became one of the main theaters of social war after 1989. This aspect of life highlights potentials which, with the help of political and legal decisions taken in the name of the highest moral and religious values, allow men to gain political gratification by reinstigating the program of reducing the world of women to that of *Kirche, Küche, Kinder*. The anti-abortion law drafted in 1992 and revised in 1993, which allows abortion, but only partly, gives rise for concern. Equally alarming are the style and content of the discussions held on abortion before and after the passing of the 1993 act, as well as the ways in which the law has been interpreted (e.g. in the fields of sexual education and availability of contraceptives). All of these activities may be seen as attempts to prevent a situation in which the social roles played by women—mother, wife, 'guardian of family life' and professionally and publicly active person—are encoded in social patterns as equally valued (Matuchniak-Krasuska, 1995; Titkow, 1995). So far, all of the attempts by women members of parliament to pass a law on the equal status of men and women have been unsuccessful (Fuszara, 1998).

Such thinking also makes it easier to have women carry the burden of systemic transformation. That this strategy has been adopted is evident in many fields of social life. For example, there are not enough projects for the professional re-training of women, which intensifies the nature of women's unemployment. Furthermore, the number of nursery schools is being reduced, while regulations protecting the working environment of pregnant women and women bringing up children are subject to mass violation. It has also been argued that women are the first to be dismissed during layoffs and the number of women employed in new companies is decreasing (Fuszara and Tarnowska, 1995; Lisowska, 1994).

Unemployment appears to be an inevitable consequence of introducing the market economy. However, it seems to operate according to sex, in that men and women do not have equal opportunities in the labor market. Since 1990, unemployment amongst women has been growing faster than it has amongst men: in June 1990, women constituted 48 per cent of the unemployed (GUS, 1991), this figure had risen to 53 per cent by July 1994 when the national unemployment rate peaked (GUS, 1995). By December 1998, despite the fact that the aggregate unemployment rate was declining, the percentage of the unemployed who were female had risen further to 58 per cent (GUS, 1999).

So far, the unemployment rate of women has always been higher than the unemployment rate of men. For example, in September 1993 the rates stood at 17.3 per cent and 13.5 per cent, respectively (Kotowska and Podogrodzka, 1994). Women have to look for a job much longer than men: in 1993 more men than women got a job within six months, and more women than men remained unemployed for longer than one year (Reszke, 1995). Forty-six women out of each hundred of those registered in unemployment offices remain unemployed for longer than one year. The situation of women on the labor market is more difficult than the situation of men mainly because they have to wait for a job much longer than men: their unemployment is greater and is of a chronic character (Beskid, 1996). This situation persists even though they are usually better educated than men (Kowalska, 1996). In short, the attack on the social position occupied by Polish women is concentrated in two main spheres: their participation in the labor market and their reproductive rights

Certain politicians view women's professional careers as being part of the heritage of the communist regime and as a burden of which women would gladly divest themselves. However, women seem to be of a different opinion. Over the period 1992 to 1995, professionally active women were repeatedly asked whether they would continue to work if they did not have to (Cichomski and Morawski, 1995). In 1995, 75.2 per cent of women answered they would, while in 1992 and 1994 the numbers were 70.2 per cent and 72.2 per cent, respectively. Thus it seems obvious that the restrictions of the market economy actually make a job more attractive than was the case before 1989. It may be expected that, in spite of the unemployment barrier, women will, to a greater extent than before, decide on the forms of their participation in the labor market. The latter claim is supported by research conducted in Poland in 1995 which showed that women accounted for one-third of all business owners, about the average ratio for OECD countries in 1986 (Lisowska, 1997). Likewise, they have now started to win positions on boards of stock-quoted companies and boards of trustees in big companies (Dukaczewska-Nałęcz, *this volume*).

This optimism can be justified on the grounds that women have specific psychological resources that can help them in these activities. Numerous studies point to the fact that women, more so than men, are characterized by a generalized locus of external control ('what will happen does not depend on me'), and this feeling may intensify as result of the hardships and challenges of the transition period. At the same time, the results of research conducted in 1984, 1989 and 1995 show that women move less frequently than men on the continuum from a generalized locus of internal control ('what will happen is a consequence of my behavior') to a generalized locus of external control (Titkow, 1997). It is therefore possible that the multitude of roles and duties that women typically perform lessen the impact of external factors. This argument is supported by their stronger bondage with the private sphere of life and by their historical 'training' in how to meet even the most demanding challenges.

Restrictive legislation, low levels of sexual education and infrequent use of contraceptives are not likely to change demographic trends significantly. For the past decades Polish society has realized its procreation plans with hardly any modern contraception with, in 1991, contraceptive pills being taken by only 6.3 per cent of women and IUD coils being used by 7.1 per cent (Titkow, 1999). Negligence in sexual education and a restricted supply of contraceptives forced the use of abortion as the method of birth control during the period of real socialism, a fact that has fuelled an inexhaustible supply of arguments for the supporters of fetal life protection ideology.

'Real life' evidence of reproduction and fertility indices as well as the number of marriages, testify to the fact that the anti-abortion law, with all its accompanying propaganda and subsequent government regulations, has not created 'pro-family' and 'pro-conception' attitudes in society. Such a lack of reaction to this anti-abortion backlash leaves a price to be paid by women. The list of consequences is a long one, to mention only fear of unwanted pregnancy and 'abortion tourism', with their related mental, financial and sometimes medical consequences. However, the real cost for Polish women for the realization of restricted procreation plans (which are not only theirs) in a situation of limited reproduction rights and scarcity of successful birth control methods is not clear and cannot be estimated.

Never before have the tendencies to stop the gender equality process been so clearly presented and so rigorously realized. It is possible that the arguments put forward on this occasion, particularly those quoting the stereotype of 'Polish Catholic Mother,' will make women think about themselves as subjects and not objects much more than was the case after their initial professional activation. As we enter the twenty-first century, use of the 'Polish Catholic Mother' arguments may accelerate the emergence of women's group consciousness.

Polish women are used to discrepancies between their status and what should be its underlying determinants, such as those between the level of their education and the position they attain in social structures, public life and the centers of power. However, they have also got used to the various compensations they were granted because of this. One of these was the high social prestige that resulted from the co-operation of history, tradition and managerial matriarchy. In the past, Polish women were abused, although not in a way that would openly threaten their self-esteem and dignity. Even if they found themselves in a 'no choice situation' (it was hardly possible to reject the call for sacrifices in the name of the country's independence), they never lost a sense of their importance nor of their high position in social structures. During the present-day systemic transformations, in which they are both actors and observers, the subtle balance between the various factors defining women's position has been disturbed. It is only in the post-communist era that a clear pattern of discrimination against women has appeared (Titkow, 1995). Perhaps the creators of the backlash have good reasons to assume that, even if Polish women have not gained equal rights so far, they may achieve them under democracy.

Social space does have areas which women can use to articulate their interests and their needs, where they can voice the need to change their situation and to level the nature of the relationships between themselves and men, as is clearly testified by the research conducted by Malinowska (*this volume*). Obviously, this territory can be used as a result of opportunities created by the newly constructed democratic deal. Women will not try to undertake any activities leading to such a profound change of their personality that they would lose their present privileged position of the dominating 'mother-manager'. Equally difficult to imagine is a scenario in which women would continue with the heroic attitude and realize the social genotype of woman as one who has to meet even the hardest challenges of social reality. After all, the elements of individualism that have appeared in Polish social life affect not only men. Thus, we can postulate a middle course of changes, namely a long-range process broadening women's identity by the introduction of new elements. One of the mechanisms of this could be a stage during which more and more women will start to realize that they have needs that can be articulated in various ways. On this platform women will understand that they can gain an alternative identity that will not be reduced subsequently to the functional role of preserving the male-defined status quo.

Even a still fragile democracy is enough to reveal, at least in part, previously hidden social taboos. The issue of violence against women appeared in public life and the media after 1990. Before that date, the media were silent about it and the phenomenon did not even exist officially. Now, not only has the reality been exposed, it has also become the subject of numerous articles, conferences and research. According to CBOS, 18 per cent of women suffered from family violence in 1993 (CBOS, 1993b). Organizations are being created, both governmental and non-governmental, to support women who have suffered in this way, such as the Centrum Praw Kobiet and Niebieska Linia. However, the present Government Minister for Family Affairs has actually been questioning the rationale behind the latter.

WHAT ABOUT THE FUTURE?

Will democracy allow the re-implementation of the schema in which Polish women gain social value and appreciation through submission to the requirement of sacrificing their own interests and needs to the interests of family, nation and state? Will women continue to function as a homogeneous mass (without a sense of common interest) that is distinguished for this very sacrifice? Will Poland continue the social contract under which women are appreciated for as long as they remain useful without threatening patriarchal structures? Has the way in which the newly democratic state has treated the issue of reproduction undermined women's confidence in the ways society trusts and evaluates them?

Experience of the past decade suggests the hypothesis that systematic attempts to preserve the basic principles of the Polish gender contract in a situation of political independence, democracy and a market economy will prove unsuccessful, even if the principles have operated for centuries in our history. Polish women value highly a professional career for its own sake, give birth to as many children as they want to, sit on boards of stock-market quoted companies and big financial institutions, and have gathered the courage to speak about the violence they suffer in families. They have created their own women's organizations and undertaken numerous initiatives whose very variety offers a perfect way to undermine the importance of the stereotype under which Polish women are perceived as a monolithic social category with non-diversified needs and orientations.

Democracy has revealed the truth about the appreciation given to women and this will certainly accelerate the changes in the position they take in their discussions with society and its structures. Women are likely to become the subject rather than the object of social relationships; at the very least, the thesis about women being liberated by life against their own will, voiced several decades ago by Ludwik Krzywicki (1960), one of the founding fathers of Polish sociology, may become obsolete. And then the nature and the scope of 'women's liberation' will depend more than ever before on, and result from, their own consciously chosen activities.

NOTES

1 This chapter was translated by Paweł Cichawa.

2 In a comparative context, only in Spain were the nobility similarly numerous (Tazbir, 1978).

3 Of course, albeit under different circumstances, the same process was occurring simultaneously in other countries as well.

4 One-quarter of all the working women were the sole providers for their families (Żarnowska, 1990).

5 In 1938, women constituted 23.5 per cent of those employed in industry, although their salaries averaged only 55 per cent those of men.

6 After 1945 this process was facilitated by the only two 'politically correct' women's organisations, Liga Kobiet and Koła Gospodyń Wiejskich.

7 For a detailed description of the growth of the women's movement post-1989, see Malinowska (*this volume*).

REFERENCES

Beskid, L. (1996) "Bezrobocie kobiet" (Women's unemployment), in J. Sikorska (ed.), *Kobiety i ich mężowie. Studium porównawcze*, Warszawa: Wydawnictwo IFiS PAN.

Cichomski, B. and P. Morawski (1995) *Polish General Social Survey*, Warszawa: Uniwersytet Warszawski.

(CBOS) Centrum Badania Opinii Społecznej (1993a) "Kobiety w pracy zawodowej i życiu publicznym" (Women, work and public life), Warszawa: Research report, February.

(CBOS) Centrum Badania Opinii Społecznej (1993b) "Kobiety o swoim życiu osobistym" (Women and their personal life), Warszawa: Research report, October.

Dukaczewska-Nałęcz, A. (2001) "The Participation and Power of Women in Public Life", *this volume.*

Faludi, S. (1991) *Backlash. The Undeclared War Against American Women,* New York: Anchor Books.

Firlit, G. (1995) "Tradycja a partnerstwo. Zmieniająca się rola ojca w rodzinie wschodnioeuropejskiej" (Tradition and partnership. Change the father's role in east European families) *Rodzina, jej funkcje przystosowawcze i ochronne,* Warszawa: PAN, Centrum Upowszechniania Nauki.

Fuszara, M., (1998) *Niedokończona demokracja: problemy reprezentacji politycznej kobiet w Polsce* (Unfinished democracy: problems of Polish women's political representation), Warszawa: IPSiR, Warsaw University.

Fuszara, M., and M. Tarnowska (1995) "Kobiety—kategoria 'szczególnie chronionych' pracowników" (Women—a 'differently situated' category), in: Titkow and Domański (eds).

GUS (1991) *Bezrobocie w Polsce I–IV Kwartał 1991* (Unemployment in Poland I–IV quarter 1991), Warszawa: Główny Urząd Statystyczny.

GUS (1995) *Bezrobocie Rejestrowane w Polsce I Kwartał 1995* (Registered unemployment in Poland I quarter 1995), Warszawa: Główny Urząd Statystyczny.

GUS (1999) *Bezrobocie Rejestrowane w Polsce I–IV Kwartał 1998* (Registered unemployment in Poland I–IV quarter 1998), Warszawa: Główny Urząd Statystyczny.

Kalkhoff, B. (1995) "Prowadzenie domu" (Houskeeping), Warszawa: Research Report.

Koestler, N. (1992) "Kobiety polskie między społeczeństwem tradycyjnym a nowoczesnym" (The place of Polish women in traditional and modern societies), in: Żarnowska and Szwarc (eds).

Kotowska, I.E., and M. Podogrodzka (1994) "Dyskryminacja kobiet na rynku pracy" (Labour market and discrimination of women), *Kobieta i Biznes,* no. 2–3, pp. 29–35.

Kowalska, A. (1996) "Aktywność ekonomiczna kobiet i ich pozycja na rynku pracy" (Women's productive activity and the labour market), Warszawa: Główny Urząd Statystyczny, Department Pracy.

Kowalska-Glikman, S. (1990) "Kobiety w procesie przemian społecznych" (Social change and women), in: Żarnowska and Szwarc (eds).

Krzywicki, L. (1960) "Sprawa Kobiece" (Women's Issues), in: *Dzieła,* vol. V, Warszawa: PWN.

Lisowska, E. (1994) Współczesna kobieta w rodzinie i pracy zawodowej—czy konflikt ról?. (Women, family life, work—or role conflict?). *Kobieta i Biznes,* nos. 2–3, pp. 48–51.

Lisowska, E. (1997) "Women Entrepreneurs in Poland, Lithuania and Ukraine—a Comparative Analysis", *Women and Business,* nos.1–2, pp. 14–19.

Lorence-Kot, B. (1985) *Adults and Children in Eighteenth Century Poland,* Michigan: Ann Arbor.

Malinowska, E. (2001) "Women's Organizations in Poland," *this volume.*

Matuchniak-Krasuska, A. (1995) "Czym była dyskusja o aborcji" (The abortion debate: what really happened), in: Titkow and Domański (eds).

Nałęcz, T. (1994) "Kobiety w walce o niepodległość w czasie I wojny światowej" (Women and the struggle for independence during World War I), in: Żarnowska and Szwarc (eds).

Nowak, S. (1979) "Przekonania i odczucia współczesnych" (Feelings and beliefs of contemporary Poles), in: *Polaków portret własny*, Praca zbiorowa: Kraków: Wydawnictwo Literackie.

OBOP (Ośrodek Badania Opinii Publicznej) (1995) Warszawa: Research Newsletter, August.

Penn, S. (1994) "Tajemnica pa ństwowa. Kobiety w Solidarności" (State secret. Women in Solidarity), Pełnym Głosem, no. 2, pp. 3–16.

Pietrow-Ennker, B. (1992) "Tradycje szlacheckie a dążenie emancypacyjne kobiet w społeczeństwie polskim w dobie rozbiorów" (Nobleman's tradition and women's aspirations towards emancipation. The time of the partitions of Poland), in: Żarnowska and Szwarc (eds).

Reszke, I. (1995) "Stereotypy bezrobotnych i opinie o bezrobociu w Polsce" (Stereotypes of the unemployed and beliefs about unemployment in Poland), Warszawa: Friedrich Ebert Stiftung.

Rzeczypospolita (1997) 28th September, 1997.

Rzepniewska, D. (1990) "Kobieta w rodzinie ziemiańskiej w XIX w. Królestwo Polskie" (Women in landed aristocracy families. The congress kingdom of Poland in XIX century), in: Ż.arnowska and Szwarc (eds).

Siemieńska, R. (1990) "Płeć, zawód, polityka. Kobiety w życiu publicznym w Polsce" (Gender, profession, politics. Women in public life in Poland), Warszawa: Uniwerstytet Warszawski, Instytut Socjologii.

Śliwa, M. (1996) "Kobiety w parlamencie II Rzeczypospolitej" (Women in the Parliament of the II Polish republic) in: A. Ż.arnowska and A. Szwarc (eds), *Kobieta i świat polityki w niepodległej Polsce 1918–1939* (Women and the world of politics in independent Poland 1918–1939), Warszawa: Wydawnictwo Sejmowe.

Śliwowska, W. (1994) "Kobiety w konspiracjach patriotycznych lat czterdziestych XIX" (Women in the patriotic conspiracy of the nineteenth century) in: Żarnowska and Szwarc (eds).

Tazbir, J. (1978) *Polska szlachecka* (Noble Poland), Warszawa: Książka i Wiedza.

Tikow, A. (1984a) *Child and Values*, Warszawa: IFiS PAN.

Titkow, A. (1984b) "Let's Pull Down Bastilles Before They are Built," in: R. Morgan (ed.), *Sisterhood is Global. The International Women's Movement Anthology*, New York: Anchor Press Doubleday.

Titkow, A. (1992) "Słowo wstępne" (Introduction), in: S. Walczewska (ed.), *Głos mają kobiety*, (Women speak), Kraków: Convinium.

Titkow, A. (1993) *Stres i życie społeczne. Polskie doświadczenia* (Stress and social life. Polish experiences) Warszawa: Państwowy Instytut Wydawniczy.

Titkow, A. (1995) "Kobiety pod presją? Proces kształtowania się tożsamości" (Women under pressure? The gender identity process), in: Titkow and Domański (eds).

Titkow, A. (1997) "Poczucie kontroli nad zdarzeniami" (Locus of control), in: H. Domański and A. Rychard (eds), *Elementy Nowego Ładu*, (Elements of a new deal), Warszawa: IFiS PAN.

Titkow, A. (1999) "Poland", in: H.P. David (ed.), *From Abortion to Contraception*, Westport: Greenwood Publishing Group Inc.

Titkow, A. and H. Domański (eds) (1995) *Co to znaczy być kobietą w Polsce?* (What does it mean to be a woman in Poland?), Warszawa: IFiS PAN.

Winiarz, A. (1992) "Kształcenie i wychowanie dziewcząt w Księstwie Warszawskim i Królestwie Polskim (1807–1905)" (Girls' education and upbringing in the congress kingdom of Poland (1807–1905)), in: Żarnowska and Szwarc (eds).

Żarnowska, A. (1990) 'Kobieta w rodzinie robotniczej. Królestwo Polskie u schyłku XIX i na początku XX w.' (Woman in a worker's family. The congress kingdom of Poland in the nineteenth and early twentieth centuries), in: Żarnowska and Szwarc (eds).

Żarnowska, A. and A. Szwarc (eds) (1990) *Kobieta i społeczeństwo na ziemiach polskich w XIX w* (Women and society in nineteenth century Poland), Warszawa: Instytut Historyczny Universytetu Warszawskiego.

Żarnowska, A. and A. Szwarc (eds) (1992) *Kobieta i edukacja na ziemiach polskick w XIX i XX w* (Women and education in Poland in the nineteenth and twentieth centuries), Warszawa: Instytut Historyczny Universytetu Warszawskiego.

Żarnowska, A. and A. Szwarc (eds) (1994) *Kobieta i świat polityki. Polska na tle porównawczym w XIX i początkach XX w* (Women and the world of politics. Poland in the nineteenth and early twentieth centuries), Warszawa: Instytut Historyczny Universytetu Warszawskiego.

CHAPTER 3

GENDER AND LABOR MARKET CHANGE: WHAT DO THE OFFICIAL STATISTICS SHOW?

Adoption of the Soviet tool of extensive economic growth by the communist authorities of Poland was always going to be problematic, given that the country suffered the largest percentage population losses of any independent state during the course of the Second World War (Kolankiewicz and Lewis, 1986, p. 11). The difficulties were exacerbated by the abandonment of the attempt to collectivize the agricultural sector in 1956. In the longer term, labor supply growth was ensured through a birth rate that was consistently amongst the highest in Europe (Kotowska, *this volume*), with the statistics suggesting that this was attained neither at a cost of reductions in labor force participation nor by the spread of part-time working. A large part of the explanation for this outcome lies in the existence of a plethora of benefits and facilities made available to working mothers by the state. For a variety of reasons that extended beyond the time when the limitations of the extensive growth strategy were finally accepted, the communist labor market displayed a remarkable ability to absorb workers and, notwithstanding the existence of so-called 'job-seekers', open unemployment was effectively zero. Nevertheless, all of the evidence indicates that women were more lowly paid than men and, furthermore, that the differences could not be accounted for simply by differences in the human capital endowments of the sexes or by their occupational and industrial locations (Domański, 1992).

As the current transformation process commenced, many observers feared that reform would be detrimental to women's position in relation to the world of work. While this is a concern that presumably should be addressed in comparison to the impact of change upon the standing of men, this exercise in benchmarking has frequently been underplayed in the literature. In any event, many of the issues raised in the early debates have yet to be resolved satisfactorily and, as a backcloth to the more narrowly focused contributions that follow in this volume, it is useful to examine the broad insights which can be offered by the official statistics. In pursuit of this objective, the chapter contains five substantive sections covering, in turn, participation, employment, hours of work, earnings and unemployment. The picture uncovered is mixed and points clearly to the need for the exercise of care when interpreting selected pieces of evidence as indicative of the presence of gender-bias in the process of transformation.

PARTICIPATION

Labor force participation rates in the former communist countries were widely acknowledged, perhaps too uncritically, to be high. On an ideological level this was seen to be the outcome of a system under which it was considered to be the duty of citizens to engage in productive labor. From a more instrumental perspective, it could be regarded as the inevitable corollary of the rapid, forced industrialization that occurred after the communists took power. Rates of participation for selected CEE countries and for the EU in 1989 are highlighted in Table 3.1. Those in Poland were fairly low for an Eastern bloc country, although that for females appears as particularly so. However, note should made of the higher cut-off age for women in the Polish data, although the Population Census of 1988 indicates that the omission of women over the age of 55 would raise the participation rate only marginally. By way of comparison, the labor market participation rate of women in Denmark in 1989 for those aged 15–64 had reached almost 60 per cent, although it was only 31.4 per cent in Spain (Eurostat, 1991).

The liberalization of the labor market at the start of the transformation should, in theory at least, have unleashed a variety of pressures on the participation patterns observed in the communist era, not all of which would necessarily be expected to reduce the size of the workforce. A consideration of the relevant behavioral factors follows although, prior to this, one potentially important administrative change needs to be noted: the overthrow of the old regime meant a shift to a more rational—and probably more honest—system of record keeping. Past participation rates were undoubtedly inflated to some extent by the inclusion of workers, but particularly women, on extended absences from employment. All else equal, the elimination of this statistical artifact should have served to reduce the count of the economically active.

Table 3.1 Labour Force Participation Rates, 1989[1]

	Male (%)	Female (%)
Bulgaria	82.5	92.9
Czechoslovakia	93.6	83.4
Hungary	85.1	78.5
POLAND	85.3	68.1
Romania	87.5	80.7
EC 12	67.9	41.7
Denmark (highest female rate)	74.0	59.9
Spain (lowest female rate)	64.1	31.4

[1] *Working ages*: Bulgaria (m) 16–60, (f) 16–55; Czechoslovakia (m) 15–60, (f) 15–55; Hungary (m) 15–56, (f) 15–55; Poland (m) 15–60, (f) 15–60; Romania (m) 16–59, (f) 16–55; Denmark and Spain (m and f) 15–64.

Source: CEE Participation Rates from EC (1992, p. 35). EC Participation Rates from Eurostat (1991, p. 44–5).

First and foremost, reform meant that choice could more freely be exercised; in short, tastes were liberated, although there is no way of knowing directly what the impact of this might have been. Indeed, it is important to recognize that liberalization did not imply that the past became an irrelevance: *Homo sovieticus* has received a good deal of attention in the literature (Kolarska-Bobińska, 1994) and the species was accustomed to being in the labor market. Furthermore, retention of certain free welfare benefits by the unemployed was made conditional on their registration with the employment service and thereby, at least on one method of compiling the statistics, continuing to participate.

Two of the possible impacts of transition on labor supply have probably received the most attention. The first is the disincentive to female participation generated by the removal or reduction of subsidies on numerous family benefits such as kindergartens, sanatoria and holidays for children. The second is the deterrent effect associated with the emergence of open discrimination against women that some believed free markets would elicit. There can be little argument with the first of these concerns, irrespective of whether the impact on those affected is assumed to be a money or a time cost (Killingsworth, 1983, pp. 23–28), although the second is more contentious. The problem in the latter case is the assumption that free markets will generate more discrimination than ones in which the imperative to utilize labor efficiently is not so strong. However, these two popular concerns alone fail to capture all of the possible influences on participation invoked by transformation.

Following Mincer (1966) and his predecessors, it is possible to identify both discouraged and added-worker effects associated with a downturn in economic activity, such as that which occurred during the early reform period. Neither of these is necessarily sex-specific, although the latter, under which unemployment for one household worker should encourage participation by other family members, is most frequently applied to married women. Pissarides (1976) further shows the importance of unemployment compensation, the recruitment standards of firms, the costs of search and attitudes towards risk to the participation decision: all factors which underwent rapid change with the collapse of socialism. At the empirical level, Kabaj (1996, pp. 7–8) demonstrates clearly that the introduction of early retirement schemes to ease the short-run impacts of the transition recession certainly achieved their goal of reducing market activity, but most particularly amongst males. Finally, the opening of Polish commodity markets enhanced the prospect of labor-saving changes in household production techniques. Confronted by such a multiplicity of forces, each with different expected effects, it would be foolhardy to assume any uni-directional impact of reform on the labor market participation of either sex.

Table 3.2 presents two alternative measures of the changes in participation that have taken place in the recent past: one based on the summation of firm survey employment statistics and registered unemployment data, the other drawn from the Labour Force Survey (LFS). In both cases, a baseline is provided by the results obtained from the 1988 Census of Population. Fortunately, the series convey roughly the same message, although the larger discrepancy between the two sets of data in the case of females will be shown to have particular significance later in the chapter. Ignoring unusual year-on-year changes, both series indicate that the labor force participation of women has fallen by less than that of men, with the registration-based data actually indicating an absolute increase for the former. Furthermore, these conclusions hold whichever early year is taken as the base. The concordance between data from two independent sources certainly inspires confidence in the rejection of early fears that women would in some way be forced out of the market in disproportionately large numbers by the process of liberalization.

Table 3.2 Labour Force Participation, 1988–1998 ('000s)

	Registration (December)		LFS (May)	
	Male	Female	Male	Female
1988 (Census)	10070.0	8382.2	10070.0	8382.2
1990	9579.5	8031.3		
1991	9684.3	8243.6		
1992	9591.4	8274.4	9467	7971
1993	9519.8	8487.3	9247	7944
1994	9541.9	8578.0	9182	7857
1995	9427.9	8525.4	9195	7851
1996	9435.8	8765.6	9179	7844
1997	9428.7	8692.2	9275	7785
1998	9079.5	8673.0	9292	7825

Source: 1988 Census data from GUS (1997, p. 6). Employment data (1990–96) from GUS (1997a, p. 128), 1997 from GUS (1998, p. 1), 1998 from (GUS, 1999, p. 1). Registered Unemployment data (1990–98) from GUS (1999a, p. 2). LFS data from GUS (1999b).

Any attempt to draw definitive conclusions regarding the causes of the observed behavior of labor market participation would require considerably more information than the preceding discussion has brought to bear upon the issue. The conduct of such an in-depth analysis goes some way beyond the ambition of the present chapter, which is to provide a context within which to locate later contributions to this volume. Nevertheless, the simple finding that female participation has withstood the shocks of the early transformation period introduces the possibility that their employment experiences during the last decade may not have been as adverse as some feared initially.

EMPLOYMENT

Considerable emphasis has been placed on the segregation of employment by sex that characterized the labor markets of the communist countries. This section reviews some of the major characteristics of the past Polish situation and extends the analysis into the first decade of post-socialist experience. It should be noted immediately, however, that the majority of the official statistics produced by the communist authorities, but especially those broken down by sex, covered only those workers employed in the so-called productive sector who worked in state-owned enterprises. This introduces an important caveat when attempting to interpret historical data, given the size of the private agricultural sector in Poland.[1]

The hardening of budget constraints in the Polish economy implied a reduction in the employment levels of at least some surviving enterprises (Pissarides, 1993). Under the previous system, firms had no incentive to economize upon their labor usage and there were a variety of reasons (including state subsidies, plan fulfillment, insurance against high absenteeism and turnover etc.) to hoard workers (see, for example, Góra, 1993). As well as attempting to force enterprises to be more self-sufficient, the Balcerowicz 'big bang' package imposed a severe recession on an already chaotic economy, seemingly thereby adding to the pressures on employment levels. In the event, neither the overall impact of these shocks nor their distribution across the sexes was altogether in line with initial predictions.

Between 1989 and 1991, GDP fell by some 18 per cent although, as shown in Table 3.3, employment fell by only just over eleven per cent.[2] Estimates of labor hoarding in Poland under planning vary wildly, running as high as 74 per cent and as low as zero, although the true figure was most probably in the order of 25 per cent *(ibid.)*. In any event, it is clear that the process of adjustment had not been fully completed by the end of 1991; indeed, while GDP began to increase from 1992, employment continued to fall. At its nadir, in 1993, the number of jobs in the economy stood at just over 15 million, some 2.2 million less than at the end of 1989. However, whether 1988, 1989 or 1990 is chosen as the base, both the absolute and the proportionate reductions in male employment to 1993 exceeded those experienced by females. Put slightly differently; the initial employment shake out did not have a more serious impact on women than on men, the reverse was true.

Between 1993 and 1997, the Polish economy generated almost 1.2 million new jobs, although this was not perhaps as many as might have been expected from a country that, since 1994, has posted some of the highest GDP growth figures in the world (WERI, 1998). The figures become easier to rationalize when it is noted that only in 1996 did the country's real level of GDP exceed its 1989 level. Nevertheless, of the new jobs created, 51.7 per cent were taken by women: the early upturn in employment did not favor males. Fears that women would come to constitute a "reserve labor army" (Titkow, 1994, p. 325) or that "[I]t is women who are fired first and given jobs last" (Malinowska, 1995, p. 40) appear, on this evidence at least, to have been unfounded.[3] What is more, even though total employment turned down again in 1998, the impact was borne entirely by men.

Table 3.3 Employment and GDP, 1985–1997

	GDP	Employment ('000s)		
	(1989 = 100)	Total	Male	Female
1985	90.2			
1988	–	18452.2 (a)	10070.0 (a)	8382.2 (a)
1989	100.0	17760.0 (b)	9855 (b)	7905 (b)
1990	88.4	16484.7	9027.1	7457.6
1991	82.2	15772.3	8662.8	7109.5
1992	84.4	15356.5	8420.9	6935.6
1993	87.5	15117.5	8137.5	6980.0
1994	92.1	15281.9	8198.9	7083.0
1995	98.6	15324.5	8247.7	7076.8
1996	104.6	15841.9	8451.9	7390.0
1997	111.8	16294.5	8705.5	7589.0
1998	117.1	15921.1	8319.4	7601.7

Source: GDP data are rebased from figures in *Poland: Quarterly Statistics*, GUS, Warsaw, various issues. The employment data for 1988 are from GUS (1997, p. 6); for 1989 from EC (1992, p. 18); for 1990–96 from GUS (1997a, p. 128), and for 1998 from GUS (1999, p. 1).

Further insight into the evolving employment structure requires the data to be disaggregated in various ways, but this frequently demands that the results be interpreted with caution. The most important watershed for the purposes of analyzing employment movements in the Polish economy occurred in 1994, when the industrial classification was changed from the old, Marxist-inspired KGN (Klasyfikacji Gospodarki Narodowej) to the European-based EKD (Europejskiej Klasyfikacji Dzialalnośći). This is particularly troublesome insofar as the statistics were not reported on both bases in the year that the change was enacted. Furthermore, employment under the new arrangement was only disaggregated to sections of the EKD until 1996, when reporting by industrial division was introduced.

The KGN was concerned only with the measurement of activity in the socialized, material branches of the economy. In most of the communist bloc, this yielded a tolerable approximation to employment although it did not, of course, capture activity in the black economy. The Polish case was somewhat different insofar as the bulk of agriculture always remained in private ownership. Also, a certain expansion of other non-state enterprise was sanctioned in the 1980s. From a statistical point of view this is clearly unsatisfactory, but the excluded agricultural employment (approximately four million jobs) is known to have accounted for roughly equal proportions of economically active men and women. The official employment series continued to cover only the socialized sector until 1993, although certain estimates of overall employment have been made available for the years from 1989 onwards, as already witnessed above.[4] However, finer disaggregations of the data by sex were not made available until the quarterly LFS estimates were introduced in May 1992.

EMPLOYMENT BY SECTOR AND OWNERSHIP

Looking at the Polish economy in terms of just three broad sectors—agriculture (including forestry and fishing), industry (including mining, the utilities and construction) and services—reveals a good deal about the degree of post-communist economic development. Most striking of all is the continued importance of employment in agriculture, the extent of which far exceeds that prevailing in any of the EU partners that Poland might acquire in the near future.[5] After initially falling quite rapidly in absolute terms, but somewhat more slowly in relation to employment as a whole (Table 3.4), the workforce in this sector actually grew again, although it has been relatively stable since 1996. In fact, much of the early reduction was due to the liquidation of the state farms and what remains is composed overwhelmingly of a patchwork of small, highly inefficient family enterprises (Ingham et al., 1998).[6] The failure to address agricultural reform, with over 27 per cent of all workers still engaged on farms, is one of the most important factors conditioning interpretation of labor market change in the past decade.

It has been argued elsewhere (Ingham et al., 1998a) that the recent growth of employment in small-scale agriculture was fueled by the release of males in possession of farming land from industrial enterprises undertaking rationalization on an 'equitable' basis. However, the apparent increase, albeit small, in the female intensity of the sector suggests that this is only part of a more complex story.[7] Nevertheless, it remains true that Polish agriculture is comprised predominantly of workers who are both relatively old and poorly educated (EC, 1998). When reform eventually comes to this mainly peasant sector, with its large body of 'family workers', two-thirds of whom are female, it will have severe implications for both sexes.[8]

Turning briefly to the other macro sectors identified in Table 3.4, it is first of all clear that women are under-represented in industry although, in comparison to the situation in the EU in 1989, their presence was matched only in Portugal and was considerably in excess of that found elsewhere (Eurostat, 1991). Given the diversity of economic structures within the west, with both Austria and Portugal having industrial sectors of similar size to that of Poland (GUS, 1997, p. 201), it is by no means obvious how Polish industry will evolve in the future. Nevertheless, competitiveness remains a huge problem, most particularly perhaps to Poland's coal and steel sectors, great swathes of which remain largely unreformed and state owned (EIU, 1999).[9]

Table 3.4 Employment by Major Sectors, 1989–1997

	Agriculture (% women)	Industry (% women)	Services (% women)
1989	4969.8	6201.0	6218.6
1990	4629.4	5495.1	6020.9
1991	4357.6	5079.7	6005.3
1992	4027.8	4792.4	6190.7
1993	3938.3	4522.1	6300.8
	(48.8)	(30.0)	(57.3)
1994	4054.4	4570.0	6299.6
	(48.9)	(30.8)	(57.4)
1995	4045.9	4556.2	6365.8
	(46.8)	(31.1)	(58.0)
1996	4371.5	4626.0	6489.9
	(49.2)	(30.6)	(57.7)
1997	4377.8	4708.8	6854.1
	(49.2)	(30.2)	(57.4)
1998	4343.7	4588.6	6988.8
	(49.5)	(30.3)	(58.1)

Source: The data for 1989–91 are from GUS (1997, p. 217); for 1992–96, GUS (1997a, p. 129); for 1997, GUS (1998, pp. 1–4); for 1998, GUS (1999, pp. 1–4). The gender breakdown is taken from *Pracujacy w Gospodarce Narodowej* (Employment in the national economy), GUS, Warsaw, various issues.

The communist economies had under-developed service sectors and liberalization was seen as a major potential impetus towards the market-led correction of the imbalance. In fact—and in spite of the unraveling of many state enterprise conglomerates, the small privatization program and a fundamental revision of the industrial classification—the number of service sector workers in Poland grew by less than three-quarters of a million between 1989 and 1997. Consequently, the relative size of the sector still lags far behind the levels typically observed in western economies. As Zienkowski (1997, p. 25) argues: "those types of services that are responsible for large share to GDP in highly developed countries are rather poorly developed in Poland (financial services, telecommunications, different types of consulting services, research and development, tourism and recreation, etc.)." [*sic.*]. In line with experience in the first world, the expected growth of service activity was predicted to bring with it a marked increase in opportunities for female workers. As with the size of the sector as a whole, this does not as yet appear to have happened; women's share of service sector employment has not risen to any appreciable extent, although they are nevertheless over-represented within it. As such, women have not benefited to the extent that was assumed initially and the current reforms in the female-intensive education and health services may herald deterioration in their position before any genuine improvement is observed.

It has been intimated already that, in addition to industry, the distribution of employment across ownership sectors of the economy could be of some relevance for the future. From Table 3.5 it can be seen that, while diminishing in overall importance, the public sector has become notably more feminized during the course of the last decade, at the same time as an ever growing gap between its importance to the overall employment of men and women has emerged. It is therefore apparent that the early shrinkage of the sector was felt most acutely by males, although those displaced did not necessarily flow into the unemployment pool: in particular, privatization could, at least in part, be seen as a statistical sleight of hand. At the same time, mention has already been made of the early retirement schemes that were targeted more clearly at jobs held typically by males in state-owned enterprises. As just noted, however, the next wave of public sector reforms might be expected to impinge most heavily on females.

The growth in self-employment, in part fueled by the early success of the small privatization program, is amongst the Polish economic 'miracles' cited most frequently in the literature (e.g. Sachs, 1992, p. 6). However, it is possible to dispute the economic significance of some of the small-scale activity observed (Ingham et al., 1998a): it is certainly known that the survival rate of small enterprises in Poland is low (Jackson et al., 1997). Taking the UK as a comparator, where 12.1 per cent of workers were classed as self-employed in 1998 (ONS, 1999: p. S18), the situation in Poland, where between one-fifth and one-quarter have had this independent status in the 1990s, is certainly striking.[10] Yet, notwithstanding the interest shown in self-employment as a vehicle for improving the labor market status of women (Reszke, *this volume*), they are rather less likely than men to work for themselves. The small firm sector is of importance if it constitutes an engine of growth and, more particularly, if it is a significant provider of employment. The Polish record on this latter score does not appear to be impressive: while growing slowly, at least up to 1996, only one-fifth of self-employed males and 15 per cent of self-employed females had any employees in 1998. Nevertheless, the rate of growth of the propensity of female entrepreneurs to employ others has exceeded that observed for males by some margin.

Table 3.5 Public Sector Employment, 1989–1997

	Women as a % of Total Employment (1)	Public Sector as a % of Total Employment (2)	% in Public Sector (3)[1]		% of Public Sector (3)	
			Male	Female	Male	Female
1989	44.5	53.4				
1990	45.2	51.1				
1991	45.1	45.7	79.7	77.5	53.5	46.5
1992	45.2	44.0	74.8	76.2	52.2	47.8
1993	46.2	41.1	69.0	73.1	50.9	49.1
1993	46.2	41.1	39.3	43.1	50.9	49.1
1994	46.3	39.4	37.1	42.0	49.9	50.1
1995	46.2	37.6	34.6	40.9	49.0	51.0
1996	46.6	34.9	31.9	38.4	48.1	51.9
1997	47.1	31.8	28.3	35.8	47.0	53.0
1998	47.7	29.3	25.5	33.5	45.4	54.6

[1] The old, restricted basis of data collection was replaced by a fully inclusive series from 1993 onwards.

Source: (1) 1989 data are from EC (1992); for 1990–96 from GUS (1997a: 128) and for 1997 from GUS (1998, p.1). (2) 1989–96 data are from GUS (1997, p. 23 & p. 217); 1997 from GUS (1998, p. 5), 1998 from (GUS (1999, p. 1). (3) Public Sector data are from *Pracujacy w Gospodarce Narodewej* (Employment in national economy), GUS, Warsaw, various issues.

Although the transformation was well underway by the time that the first LFS was conducted (May 1992), it must be noted that self-employment has not increased since. Nevertheless, even those holding great faith in the belief that there was a rich vein of entrepreneurial talent waiting to be unleashed by the power of the market in CEE could not fail to be impressed by the seemingly spontaneous explosion in self-employment in Poland. However, once agriculture is excluded from the calculations, the LFS indicates a much lower incidence of own-account working and, at 10–12 per cent, the corrected figures resemble those typically observed in Western Europe.[11]

Omitting agriculture actually increases the male-intensity of self-employment, although there has been a tendency for this to fall slightly. At the same time, once employed on their own account outside agriculture, women are about as likely as men to employ others. Even so, self-employment in Poland, and its concentration in the agricultural sector, looks less like a miracle of transition than a legacy of the communist past.

To conclude this section, note can be made of one more historical continuity: gender-based employment segregation. Considerable weight is usually attached to the degree of segregation under communism (e.g. Einhorn, 1993; Fong and Paull, 1993) and Ingham and Ingham (2001), using a variety of statistical indicators, not only confirm the usual impression but also show that it increased through time. Furthermore, they find that degree of industrial segregation continued to grow during the early years of transition. While the change of industrial classification, and the short-run restrictions on data availability that were associated with it, make definitive pronouncements impossible, it would appear that little changed in subsequent years (*ibid.*).

HOURS OF WORK

Accounts of communist labor markets generally contain very little direct evidence on hours of work. This may be because the extent of labor hoarding rendered such information of dubious value, but it is more likely to be a reflection of the paucity of data on working time that existed previously. Whatever the reason, the issue is worthy of attention, even if the discussion must be relatively brief. It is made all the more interesting by the contrasts between descriptions of hard labor in dangerous and dirty conditions (Bromke and Strong, 1973, p. 213), the double (or even triple) burden faced by women (Einhorn, 1993, p. 117), the huge labor hoarding (Góra, 1993) and the well known workers' maxim that 'they pretend to pay us and we pretend to work'.

In practice, the socialist economies operated with some notion of a standard working week, with the observed consequence being that workers took 'leisure on the job'; that is, they shirked. Local, but assuredly implicit, bargains between management and workers eased the tensions somewhat further by condoning periods of unofficial absence, during which workers could either queue or engage in other shortage-relieving activities. Reasoning along similar lines undoubtedly goes some way towards a rationalization of how the social system continued to function with high market participation rates for both sexes and in the apparent absence of part-time working.[12] Some such explanation is surely required, given the failure of actual levels of social and welfare aid to achieve the comprehensive levels assumed in theory (Ciechocińska, 1993).[13]

The longest available series of data on hours of work is that which the authorities reported to the International Labor Organization (ILO) for manufacturing.[14] Predictably, the data are not disaggregated by gender and, furthermore, the information is provided in terms of hours per month rather than hours per week. Nevertheless, the statistics suggest that working hours in communist Poland fell gradually, in line with the trend throughout much of western Europe, although possibly for somewhat different reasons (Ingham and Ingham, 2001a). The reduction in labor hoarding, the emergence of the profit motive, the growth of consumer-oriented service sector activities, the erosion of state provided welfare programs and the widening of data coverage might all be expected to have led to a more varied pattern of working hours in the current decade. From May 1992 onwards, the LFS became a new source of information on working time in the Polish economy and, at the national level at least, is in many ways the richest available. As reported in Table 3.6, both men and women worked considerably longer hours than those suggested by the old ILO series, even at the height of the transition-induced recession. On average, men do work longer than women, although the difference is sufficiently small that, in view of evidence that women continue to perform the majority of household chores (Leven, 1994), the 'double-burden' argument advanced by authors such as Einhorn (1993) is provided with considerable empirical weight.

Table 3.6 Annual Average Hours of Work: 1992–1998

	1992	1993	1994	1995	1996	1997	1998
Male	45.7	44.5	45.0	44.6	45.0	44.8	44.3
Female	40.7	39.3	39.4	39.3	39.6	39.5	39.0

Source: GUS (1999b, pp. 92–93).

Of course, the economy-wide figures conceal variations in hours of work across sub-groups and disaggregation forms one of the building blocks for reasoned interpretation of the gender earnings differential considered below and is essential for the study of productivity trends. It also represents a necessary point of departure in debates about whether transformation has witnessed the growth of a new flexibility in the Polish labor market. Space constraints preclude a detailed discussion of the evidence, although the main findings contained within Ingham and Ingham (2001a) can be outlined briefly.

Given the gradual attempts to de-bureaucratize the public sector; along with the continued existence of largely uneconomic state-owned enterprises and frequently voiced fears that private sector enterprises would somehow exploit their workers, the public–private sector split of working hours may seem somewhat surprising. Notwithstanding an evident, albeit slow, downward trend of hours of work in the public sector, there is currently little difference in the length of the working week by ownership form, particularly in the case of males.[15] There are, however, some rather large differences in working time between employed and self-employed workers, with the latter claiming to work for noticeably longer. Also, the hours differential between the sexes is much larger for those who work on their own account. As might be expected, paid employees work considerably longer than do unpaid workers, although the latter claim on average to work for more than 30 hours per week, with virtually no difference between the sexes evident.

The observations regarding unpaid helpers lead directly to reference to the persistence of low rates of part-time working in the Polish labor market throughout the current decade. In particular, the LFS indicates that only about seven per cent of workers are employed for less than 30 hours per week, the usual definition of part-time working (GUS, 1999b, p. 91). This is certainly low by western standards and might be compared with the 1998 UK figure of 24.8 per cent (ONS, 1999, p. S18). Nevertheless, women are approximately twice as likely as men to be employed part-time but, rather surprisingly, there is some evidence that the trend for both sexes might be downward. Such information alone is insufficient to enable one to adjudicate in the debate between those who argue that differentiation in hours of work would be one way in which the liberalization of the labor market will marginalize women and others who assert that the market economy will be beneficial insofar as it provides women with greater choice. It might be noted, however, that the data indicate that considerably fewer women than men claim to be working less than a standard week involuntarily.

In line with previous suggestions that part-time working was present, in fact, in the communist labor market, although somewhat contrary to the expectation that transformation would lead to the growth of secondary labor market, consumer service activity, the proportion of employees working for less than thirty hours is considerably larger in the public sector than it is in the private sector of the economy. Once again though, the evidence does nothing to alter the overall conclusion that women are twice as likely as men to be employed for less than a full week. The same is true when the working hours of the employed and the self-employed are compared, although an interesting trend emerges then. Thus, while early LFS returns indicated that employees were, as might be expected, more likely than the self-employed to be part-time, the position was reversed in 1996, in the case of males, and in 1997, in the case of females. It would appear, as noted above, that the retreat to agriculture was an important influence on this outcome. At the risk of being seen to assume an equivalence, the absence of any upward trend in paid part-time employment between 1992 and 1998 might be taken as further evidence of the ongoing failure of a western-style service sector to emerge in Poland.

EARNINGS

Employment and hours of work differences notwithstanding, "to a number of economists the issue of inequality between the sexes may be reduced to what is its most visible symptom—the difference in earnings between men and women." (Joseph, 1983, p. 204). However, the assumptions under which all workers will earn the same are rather extreme (e.g. Fallon and Verry, 1988, p. 135) and it is unrealistic to treat such global equality as a benchmark. Rather, differences between the sexes will be considered in the light of a number of the factors other than gender that are normally assumed to influence earnings.

Discussion of earnings, or indeed income, under socialism is complicated by the divergence between nominal and real magnitudes that resulted from the importance of non-pecuniary payments (Gorecki, 1994, p. 33).[16] Nevertheless, there are no grounds for supposing that the distribution of non-wage benefits was 'equalizing', with the privileges enjoyed by the nomenklatura being a constant source of disquiet (Bromke and Strong, 1973, pp. 231–4; Wiatr, 1987, p. 27). At the same time, the question arises of how the distribution of family welfare benefits between the sexes should be treated: as Fuszara (1993, p. 47) argues, most of these were in fact women's benefits. Although no attempt at quantification of such payments is made in this chapter, the general issue will be returned to below.

A central feature of the measured wage structure in communist economies was its narrow dispersion relative to that observed in market economies (Kramer, 1995, p. 78). As a result, the tangible returns to human capital accumulation were negligible, with unskilled manual workers often receiving higher wages than those with university education (Gorecki, 1994, p. 33).[17] Nevertheless, it has been argued that wages were determined in ways that were not entirely dissimilar to those in the west; the key difference being in the manner that the output of workers was valued (Rutkowski, 1994).[18]

In 1952, Article 67 of the Polish Constitution guaranteed equal pay for women and stated that all citizens were to be treated as equals regardless of their sex. The equal rights of men and women in all activities were confirmed in Article 78 of the same document and Poland was a signatory to the United Nations Convention on the Elimination of all Forms of Discrimination, which was ratified in 1980 (Leven, 1994, p. 28). The mere existence of these formal safeguards seemingly encouraged the authorities to assume that gendered pay differentials were not an issue and, as a result, little official data was published on the earnings of the sexes in communist times.

Evidence has already been presented which indicates that there was marked segregation in the employment of the sexes by industry under the planned economy and there are numerous references to a similar maldistribution across occupations (e.g. Mach and Słomczyński, 1995, p. 142). Overall, the highest benefits were afforded to those workers in primary sector employment and to those in the most senior positions, in whichever sector of the economy they were employed.[19] As Rutkowski (1994, p. 140) notes, and as was confirmed by the evidence presented above, primary sector jobs tended to be male and, furthermore, senior positions were, on the whole, denied to women (Fuszara, 1994, p. 41). The existence of a large black economy probably made male–female earnings differentials higher still.

The foregoing impressions were confirmed by such surveys, both official and otherwise, as were undertaken during the era. That is, they uniformly reported that women received lower pay than men in all industries and occupations (see, Domański, 1992; Kuratowska, 1991, p. 56; Leven, 1994, pp. 29–30; Łobodzińska, 1983, p. 17). For example, Leven (*op. cit.*, p. 29–30) reports that the average earnings of women white-collar workers were 68 per cent of those of similar men in 1987, while the equivalent figure for blue-collar workers was 73 per cent. Table 3.7, reproduced from Łobodzińska (*op. cit.*, p. 17), indicates that this picture from the late socialist period was merely a reflection of the situation in earlier times. Women were disproportionately to be found in the lower echelons of the salary distribution and their estimated median incomes fluctuated between two-thirds and three-quarters of those for men.

Table 3.7 Salaries in the Nationalized Economy by Sex (%)

Salaries in złoty	1960		1965		1973	
	Men	Women	Men	Women	Men	Women
Total	100.0	100.0	100.0	100.0	100.0	100.0
Less than 800	4.2	15.2	1.1	7.1	–	–
801–900	2.4	6.8	1.0	4.8	–	–
901–1000[1]	2.9	7.6	1.4	5.4	0.4	1.4
1101–1200[2]	8.5	7.6	4.4	12.3	0.3	2.3
1201–1500	16.4	24.5	10.1	22.6	1.7	8.2
1501–2000	27.3	20.7	23.2	30.0	6.8	24.1
2001–2500	18.5	5.4	22.1	11.6	19.9	29.4
2501–3000	9.8	1.5	15.5	3.9	19.5	19.1
3001–5000	9.0	0.7	18.5	2.3	44.3	14.4
5001 and over	1.0	0.0	2.6	0.0	12.1	1.1
Median[3]	1786	1357	2200	1471	3064	2239

[1] In 1973, 1100 złoty and less.
[2] In 1973, 1001–1200 złoty.
[3] Medians imputed from the distribution presented in the source.

Interpretation of any of the foregoing information on earnings as evidence of gender discrimination is rendered problematic by the usual absence of suitable multivariate disaggregations of the data, including the absence of control for hours worked. Indeed, the latter holds even for those studies that have attempted to examine earnings differentials conditioned upon relevant individual characteristics (e.g. Domański, 1992). The previous section produced important evidence to suggest that working time differed by sex, while Fong and Paull (1993, p. 235) report a Hungarian survey which found that "mothers worked on the average 50 per cent of the standard working hours as a result of their legal concessions and leave taken for children's illnesses".[20] With the average female–male wage differential being similar in Hungary to Poland (73.4% and 76.7%, respectively; *ibid.*, p. 227), it is certainly not possible to conclude decisively that there was pay discrimination.[21]

Turning to the transition era, a variety of different data sets on earnings have become available, all of which indicate that women continue to earn less than men, irrespective of how the data are disaggregated or the year in question. As an indication of the situation as the labor market has taken on a progressively more liberal character, Table 3.8 shows that women continued to earn less than men, almost irrespective of industry or ownership in 1998.[22] However, it is surely important to note that their disadvantage is somewhat smaller in the private sector than it is in public enterprises. The pitfall is that the absolute earnings of both sexes tend to be lower in private enterprises than they are in the state sector (GUS, 1997, 1998b). This may be a surprising finding in view of arguments that foresee private employers exchanging current for future gains with their employees, but it is nonetheless a very significant one.

Bearing in mind the caveats, a somewhat stronger picture of gender-based earnings differentials by sector emerges when the data are disaggregated by occupation. Utilizing a survey undertaken in March 1996 of enterprises employing five or more workers (GUS, 1997b), Table 3.9 indicates that women generally fare considerably better in the non-state sector, with only female machine operators and fitters enjoying a more favorable earnings differential in public enterprises. This is not to say that there is any evidence of earnings equality in the private sector: overall, women in private enterprises earn only 82 per cent as much as men, and more than men in only eight of the 83 three-digit occupations underlying the aggregate data in the Table.[23] Furthermore, the evidence has nothing to say about earnings differentials in the smallest enterprises in the economy.

While the estimation of multivariate earnings functions lies beyond the scope of this chapter, comment can be made on certain other features of the data from the 1996 survey. First, male and female university graduates earn considerably more than other workers of the same sex, irrespective of the sector in which they are employed, while women fare relatively worse at all levels of education, other than general secondary, if they work in the state sector. Second, women of all ages, except for those between 60 and 65, achieve earnings somewhat closer to those of men in private undertakings than they do in the public sector. That females under 35 years of age fare particularly well in the private sector might be seen as surprising: it is just such women who, employers might feel, are the 'high risk' maternity and family crisis absentees. Third, when disaggregated by seniority, the data reveal that the female–male earnings ratio is always higher in the private than in the public sector.

Perhaps the most unexpected outcome from this disaggregation is that women with the longest labor market histories, in either sector of the economy, fail to achieve earnings that are noticeably closer to parity with those of men than do others.

Table 3.8 Female–Male Average Earnings (%), September 1997

	Public Sector	Private Sector
Total	74.5	81.5
A. Agriculture	88.9	103.0
B. Fishing	133.9	103.7
C. Mining	70.7	76.7
D. Manufacturing	65.9	88.4
E. Utilities	79.2	76.7
D. Construction	86.0	86.2
G. Trade	90.5	99.9
H. Catering	79.4	78.4
I. Transport	85.7	80.3
J. Finance	95.0	97.4
K. Real Estate	74.4	63.7
L. Public Admin.	85.8	83.2
M. Education	90.2	94.1
N. Health	82.8	80.8
O. Other Community	76.5	78.3
P. Budgetary Units	91.7	80.8

Source: GUS (1998a, p. 88–92).

Table 3.9 Female–Male Average Earnings by Occupation and Sector (%), October 1998

	Public Sector	Private Sector
Total	77.3	82.3
Parliamentarians, higher officials and managers	74.0	78.8
Specialists	73.9	82.0
Technicians and other middle grade personnel	70.7	82.4
Office workers	91.9	94.7
Service workers and sales assistants	68.6	81.6
Agricultural, garden, forestry and fishery workers	88.6	97.5
Industrial workers and craftsmen	66.3	71.3
Machine operatives and fitters	87.3	86.0
Laborers	80.4	87.6

Source: GUS (1999c, p. 58–63).

Finally, reference can be made to the gender earnings differentials by sector and establishment size, which, as reported in Ingham and Ingham (2001a), present a rather confused picture. First, and in some contrast to earlier findings, private organizations do not monopolize the highest female earnings ratios. Second, it is certainly not the case that women are most disadvantaged in the smallest private sector firms, thereby suggesting that fears that such employers would be most likely to flout laws on wage payments may be a little too simplistic. Third, while it might be expected that large organizations would more often have gender-blind salary scales, this supposition receives only partial support in the private sector and female relative earnings appear remarkably low in very large public enterprises.

The data presented in this section indicate that there is no iron law of gender pay differentials and that the issue is worthy of much more in-depth study than it has been possible to undertake here. One reading of the simple evidence might conclude that transition has failed to eradicate the inherited gender earnings gap, although this would ignore the tendency observed in the private sector for women to earn, relative to men, more than they do in the public sector. Whatever the interpretation, earnings accrue only to those in work and, as described in the following section, a vast number of both men and women have been jobless during the course of the past decade.

UNEMPLOYMENT

Opinions differ on whether the pace of change in many labor market magnitudes during the present decade has been rapid or slow, appropriate or destabilizing. In the case of unemployment, however, there is less scope for disagreement. The impact of the change of regime was immediate, large and has been prolonged. As such, it is not difficult to see why the behavior of unemployment has captured public attention and why the distribution of joblessness has so frequently been used as a barometer to assess the distribution of the costs of transformation throughout the working population.

The historical backcloth can be brief. Notwithstanding the existence of a small body of so-called job seekers, unemployment was officially and effectively zero prior to 1990. The labor market was in a state of constant excess demand, with reference to vacancy to job-seeker ratios of 1.5, 6.3 and 86.8 in the years 1955, 1975 and 1988 (Chilosi, 1991,

p. 73), respectively, being sufficient to illustrate the point. To the extent that all conceivable outputs could have been produced with less labor than enterprises actually retained, there was labor hoarding (Góra, 1993).[24] However, confronted with problems of low morale and no means of overcoming this by means of suitably tailored reward structures, it is likely that technical efficiency was impossible, even within the confines of a relatively backward technology.

In the current era, the behavior of unemployment can be analyzed using one of two major sources of data: registration statistics and the quarterly LFS. To the extent that these series convey conflicting information, it is tempting to engage in a discussion of which is 'right'. This temptation is to be avoided: the data do not measure exactly the same thing and it is only by chance that they will agree. The registration data record the number of people who declare themselves as jobless at a local labor office and who satisfy a number of administratively determined criteria. The LFS data, on the other hand, are based on household surveys in which those who declare that they have not worked in the survey period but who want a job and would be willing and able to perform one are counted as unemployed. The pictures conveyed by these alternative sources will be analyzed in turn.

REGISTRATION DATA

Issued monthly from January 1990, at first in limited form and then in progressively more detail, the registered unemployment figures rose inexorably over the early post-socialist years. Over half a million people were without work by June 1990, over one million by the end of that year, over two and a half million by the end of 1992 and, ultimately, the jobless total peaked at just a fraction under three million in July 1994. In September 1990, the number of females without work exceeded the equivalent number of males for the first time and has continued to do so at each subsequent observation point. With women constituting less than half of the labor force, this simple fact appeared to confirm the fears of those who believed that the burden of transformation would fall disproportionately upon their shoulders.

Having stagnated at over 2.8 million from July 1993 to February 1995, the level of unemployment remained in excess of 2.5 million until June 1996, when it commenced a somewhat erratic descent to its low of 1.67 million (9.5%) in August 1998. Since that date, the figure has risen again and, as Kotowska (*this volume*) argues, the signs are that no further falls are likely in the foreseeable future. Both sexes shared in the decline of unemployment from its peak, although women to a lesser extent than men. Furthermore, from the middle of 1996, the trend decline in male unemployment was markedly stronger than that evident in the figures for females, of whom more than one million remain jobless. This is confirmed by the behavior of the female-to-male unemployment ratio depicted in Figure 3.1.

While the apparently disadvantageous situation with which women have been confronted may be a cause for concern, it is important that the simple unemployment stock figures are placed in a wider context, if they are to be understood properly. Some unemployment was inevitable, although just how much has been the cause of a debate that has yet to be resolved (Blanchard, 1997). Under the optimistic scenario, as the public sector withered, so the private sector would expand to absorb those workers displaced by restructuring.[25] This naturally suggests that the length of time people remain without work might be equally as important as the number unemployed. That is, a reasoned evaluation of labor market change and the distribution of its costs must take into account unemployment durations.

Data on registered unemployment durations began to be published, on a quarterly basis, from July 1992, with the series being reproduced in Figure 3.2.[26] From just short of one million at the first enumeration, the numbers registered as without work for over 12 months rose to a peak of 1.33 million in September 1994; that is, at approximately the same point in time as the total stock of jobless was at its height. Although not reported until March 1994, very long-term unemployment—over two years—also appeared to peak in September 1994, at almost 600,000 people. Figure 3.2 portrays the over-representation of women amongst the ranks of the long-term unemployed, which is even more marked than it is amongst the jobless pool overall. They now account for over seven-in-ten of those registered as without work for over one year and almost 80 per cent of those who have been unemployed for more than two years. Such differences are extraordinary by western standards: amongst the EU twelve in 1989 women accounted for 53.3 per cent of those without work for over one year and 52.1 per cent of those unemployed for more than two years (Eurostat, 1991, p. 182).[27] For some reason, women have considerable difficulty exiting the unemployment register and this directs attention to the flows underlying the basic stock statistics.

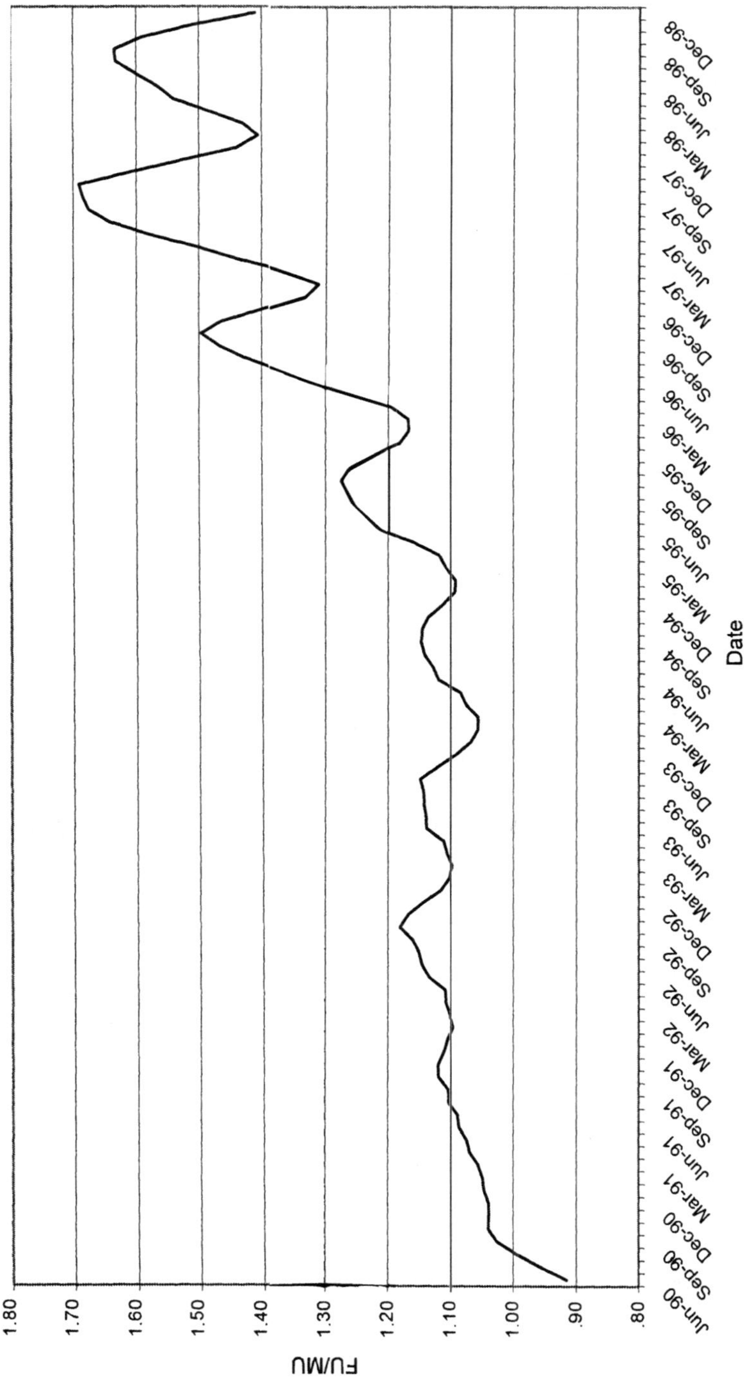

Figure 3.1 Female–Male Unemployment Ratio—Registration Data: June 1990–December 1998
[*Source: Bezrobocie Rejestrowane w Polsce* (Registered Unemployment in Poland), GUS, Warsaw, various issues].

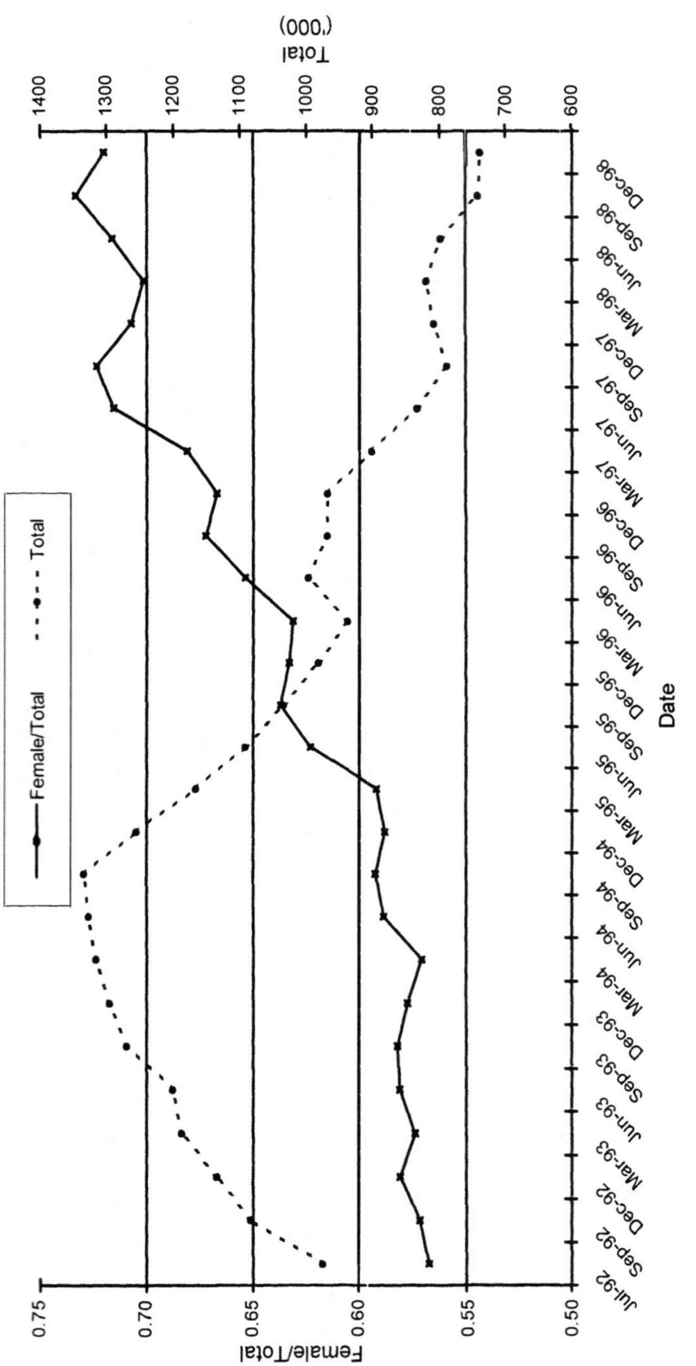

Figure 3.2 **Total and Female–Male Long-term Unemployment Ratio—Registration Data: June 1990–December 1998**
(*Source:* As for Figure 3.1).

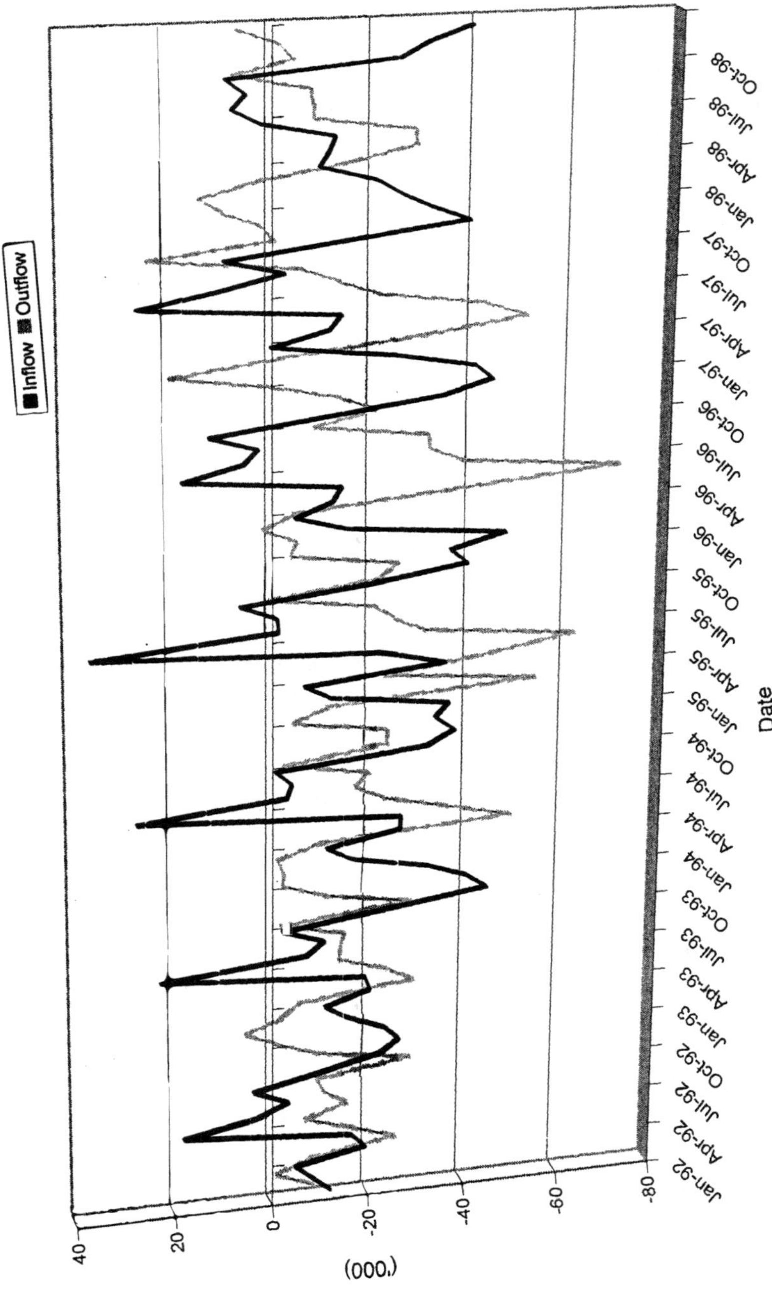

Figure 3.3 Differences between Female and Male Unemployment Inflows and Outflows: January 1992–December 1998 (*Source:* As for Figure 3.1).

Figure 3.3 shows that, in general, the monthly inflow of women to unemployment has been less than that of men and, over the whole period January 1992 to December 1998, the average number of entrants were 92,230 males and 79,190 females. This, along with the earlier discussion of employment trends in the first decade of reform, is hardly consistent with early predictions that women would bear the brunt of the job losses associated with transformation. However, Figure 3.3 also plots the difference in unemployment outflows, with the exit of women from the registration pool exceeding that of men in only ten of the 84 months for which data has been reported. Visual impressions are reinforced by the summary statistics, which reveal that the average monthly outflow of women was only 79,460 compared to a figure of 95,340 for men. Yet even this picture is not as straightforward as it may appear: on average, only about half of all outflows from unemployment (52% for men, 48% for women) are into jobs. This obviously raises the question of where the remaining deregistrants have been going.

It is now widely accepted that the initial unemployment benefit regulations in Poland were too lax (Blanchard, 1997; Góra et al., 1996; Kotowska, *this volume*). In particular, one can point to universal coverage, open-endedness and the absence of disqualification criteria as particularly distortionary. Over time, the system has been tightened considerably and this contributed much to the sharp reductions in the stock of unemployment in 1996 and 1997. However, there is some suspicion, as noted in Kotowska (*ibid.*), that the largest impact of these changes may have been on the male registration count. Unfortunately, information on destinations other than into work was not made available until 1994 (retrospectively in 1998) and, even now, the data is not disaggregated by sex. In 1994, the outflow to jobs accounted for 51 per cent of all exits from the unemployment pool, while deregistrations on account of inability to confirm the willingness to undertake a job accounted for a further 34 per cent. In 1995, these figures were 49.1 per cent and 36.8 per cent, respectively; in 1996, 52.3 per cent and 37.1 per cent; in 1997, 48.7 per cent and 31.7 per cent; and, in 1998, 48.2 per cent and 34.4 per cent. From 1996 onwards (again retrospectively), further information on the destinations of leavers became available, with entry into training being by far the largest element of the residual, accounting for about seven per cent of those leaving the pool.

LFS DATA

Contrary to the situation in most countries, unemployment according to the registration statistics exceeded that reported by the LFS from the second quarter of 1992 to the end of 1997. Furthermore, the differences were in general non-trivial, averaging almost eleven per cent over the run of the LFS to November 1998 and having been as high as twenty-five per cent. That the figures would now appear to have assumed their expected relationship is merely indicative of the shakeout of the register as eligibility criteria have been tightened. As shown in Figure 3.4, however, the earlier figures were driven largely by the female counts, with the register sometimes containing thirty per cent more jobless women than the LFS reported. To the extent that the differential movements in the two series have been driven by changes in the administrative regulations governing registration, these have clearly influenced men relatively more than women, as was suggested above.

None of the foregoing can be taken as evidence that women have not faced a disproportionate share of the unemployment burden, all that has been shown is that the registration data would appear to exaggerate the handicap. As shown in Figure 3.5, the unemployment rate of women uncovered by the LFS has always been in excess of that for men, with the situation deteriorating sharply in 1996 and 1997, although there is at least some evidence from 1998 that this latter shift might have been temporary. Furthermore, the series plotted in Figure 3.5 display marked seasonal variations, due to the greater volatility of male than female employment and unemployment over the course of a year. In particular, males find relatively more work to do in the summer months than do females. As the relevant series are more seasonal in rural than urban areas (GUS, 1999b), it must be surmised that the pattern is driven by the annual agricultural cycle. Although further consideration is beyond the remit of this particular chapter, one might question for how much longer males will enjoy this particular 'advantage'.

Finally, as with the registration data, it is females who have shouldered the majority of the burden of long-term unemployment (in excess of one year) uncovered by the LFS, although the figures have exhibited a downward trend since the beginning of 1994 for both sexes. Nevertheless, in line with the registration figures, the female share of the burden has tended to increase in recent years. Thus, whichever data source is consulted, the conclusion is that once women become unemployed, they face a higher risk than men of remaining so for a long period of time. In

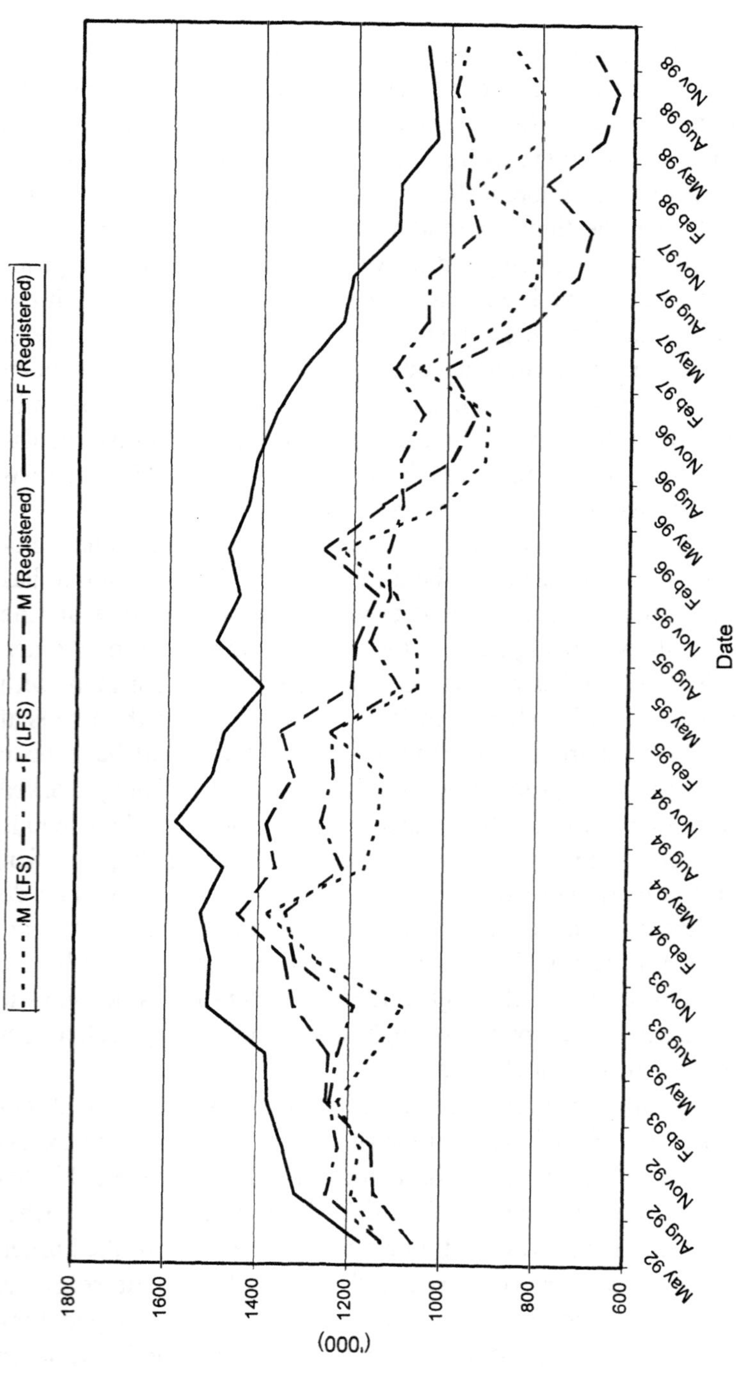

Figure 3.4 Registered vs. LFS Unemployment Counts [*Source:* Registration data are as for Figure 3.1, LFS data are from GUS (1999b)].

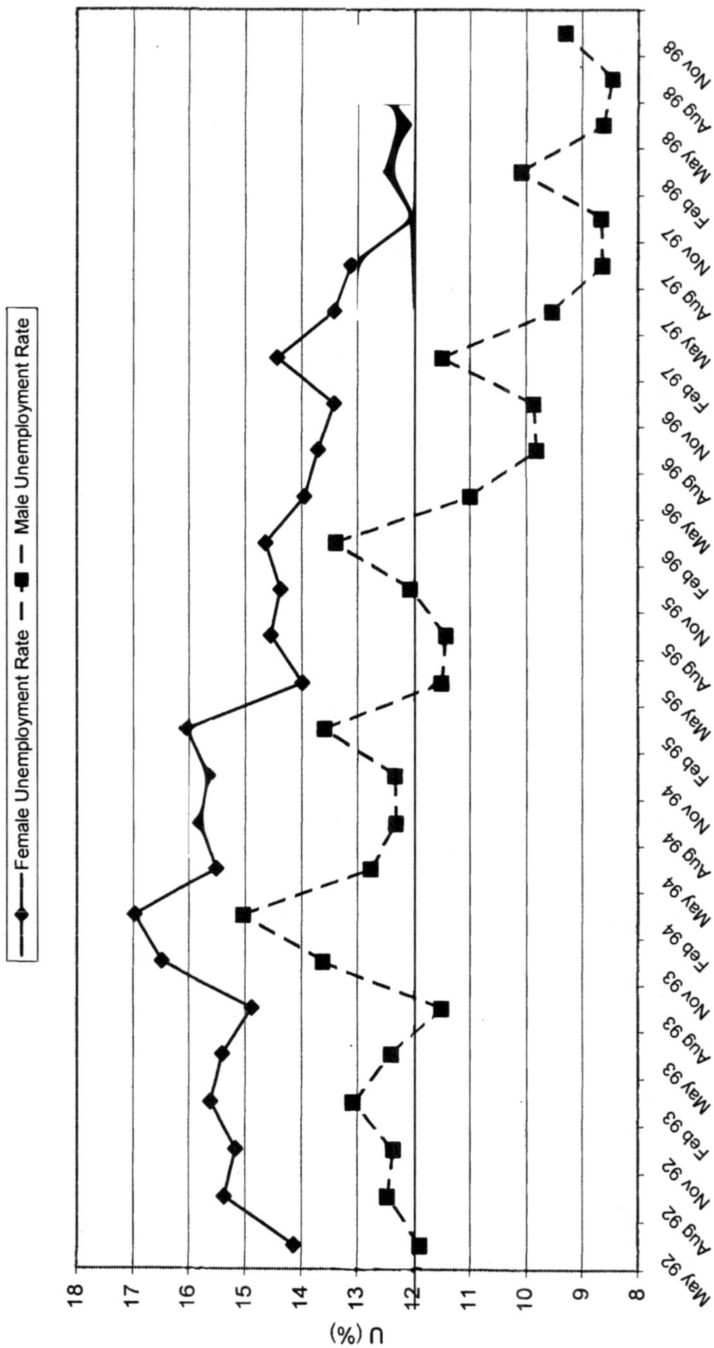

Figure 3.5 **Unemployment Rates—LFS Data** (*Source:* GUS (1999b)).

view of the contrary evidence on employment presented above, efforts to understand clearly why this discrepancy exists deserve a high priority in future research looking at the impacts of transformation on the labor market status of the sexes.

CONCLUSION

Although the discussion has of necessity been brief, this chapter has brought a considerable weight of evidence to bear on the question of whether women have suffered more than men from the effects of the shocks experienced by the Polish labor market in the course of the last decade. In purely quantitative terms, the answer in the case of both employment and labor force participation must surely be that they have not. Other chapters in this volume consider the more qualitative dimensions of these phenomena, while here attention is merely directed to the still incomplete character of labor market reform and realignment. The jobs of many more women than men will surely be threatened by the impending changes to the education and health services, although the sexes will share the burden of agricultural restructuring equally. It is likely, however, that women will have much to gain once the emergence of a modern service sector finally begins in earnest.

Conclusions regarding the earnings differential between men and women must be more circumspect. There can be no doubt that women continue to earn less than men, but is this the result of discrimination? Any adequate answer must be based on the findings of the overdue multivariate analyses of earnings and, as has been stressed in this paper, these must include controls for hours of work. It is quite clear that while women earn less, they also work less, at least in the formal labor market. A similarly guarded conclusion must also be applied to the evidence on unemployment. Women have faced considerably more joblessness than men, but this is certainly not because they have been at greater risk of losing their jobs. Nevertheless, once unemployed, women have greater difficulty than men re-entering work. Understanding more fully why this should be so is an important item on the agenda of research needing to be undertaken.

NOTES

1 For a detailed discussion of the difficulties encountered when comparing labor market data from the former central planned economies with those from free markets, see Nesporová (1993).

2 In both cases, the statements refer to recorded figures and these make no attempt to control for unofficial economic activity. For an introduction to the importance of the black economy to output and employment in the Polish economy, see the papers contained in RECESS (1996). However, even the most extreme speculations about the importance of such activity do not alter the qualitative impression conveyed in the text.

3 The LFS suggests that, on the basis of annual averages, employment fell from 1992 up to and including 1994, but that women lost almost 450,000 fewer jobs than men. Between 1994 and 1998 it reports that male employment grew by 462,800 compared to only 234,500 for women. On the other hand, while total employment did not fall in 1998 according to the LFS, the growth of female employment was fifty per cent higher than that of men during the year. Between 1992 and 1998 male employment grew by 1.6% and that of women by 0.7% (GUS, 1999b). While painting a slightly different picture to the establishment survey data presented in the text, the evidence from the LFS is hardly sufficient to substantiate claims regarding the existence of widespread discrimination.

4 Certain detailed Census of Population information was also made available, as with the 1988 employment data presented earlier.

5 That is, assuming Romania is not accepted into membership in the short-term.

6 The increases in agricultural employment described in the text are in fact somewhat understated owing to the continuous declines that have occurred in the workforces of the fishery and forestry industries over the period covered. However, as these comprise rather less than five per cent of the aggregate discussed, the damage is minimal.

7 Official data on employment on an inclusive basis (i.e. incorporating both public and private sector activity) was not disaggregated by sex before 1993.

8 This is not to deny that the pressures placed on agriculture by reform elsewhere in the Polish economy have had profound effects on gender relations within the sector (Gorlach, *in this volume*).

9 Some progress was made with the rationalization and potential privatization of the Huta Katowice steel plant in 2000, although the sale to Corus eventually collapsed. However, no such positive developments have occurred at Huta Sendzimira because of the failure to attract the interest of foreign investors. Further discussion of these issues can be found in Ingham and Karwińska *(in this volume)*. Little change has taken place, or is in prospect, within the coal industry (Ratajczyk, 2000).

10 Amongst the economies in transition for which any reliable data is available, self-employment levels in Poland are second only to those reported in Romania and considerably larger than those seen elsewhere (Ingham and Ingham, 2001). In 1989, the twelve country average EU rate of self-employment was 15.8 per cent (Eurostat, 1991, p. 94). The Polish data on self-employment discussed in this section are calculated from GUS (1999b).

11 Even then, however, interpretation is clouded by the existence of a limited, but growing, private enterprise sector during the 1980s, mostly composed of small firms (Schaffer, 1992).

12 This is not to suggest that it is women who should undertake the domestic chores implied in this statement, merely that it was a fact of socialist existence.

13 The initial impression of universal full-time working is further reinforced by the failure to record hours of work outside manufacturing, where certain occupations, particularly feminized ones such as teaching, were known to have much lower working hours than the 'norm' (Krajewska, 1995).

14 Note that the reported hours are explicitly recorded as hours worked as opposed to hours paid for.

15 This comparison says nothing about weeks worked per year, overtime payments or any of the other factors that could introduce differences in employment conditions across sectors. This reservation applies equally to the discussion of other disaggregations of the hours of work data that follows.

16 The reliance on fringe benefits was exacerbated by the existence of incomes policies throughout most of the communist period.

17 However, membership of the intelligentsia was not a reward to be discounted in the closed communist world.

18 Gorecki (1994) indicates that the Gini coefficient for per capita household income in 1987 was similar to that typically registered in market economies. However, the discussion in the text is about individual earnings from work.

19 Primary in this context relates to those sectors which the authorities, not the market, adjudged to be the most valuable.

20 It must be borne in mind, however, that the state and not the enterprise was the ultimate paymaster. Nevertheless, to the extent that the absences were unrelated to the pace of activity within the employing enterprise, they may have been costly to an employer faced with harsh target plans and irregular and unpredictable raw material supplies.

21 This is not to argue that "the objective is to add more and more variables ... so that the residual, which is equated with the irrational element discrimination, is minimized." (Rubery, 1997, p. 339). Rather, the discussion is meant to point to the need for some care in making valid earnings comparisons between the sexes, either before or after the systemic watershed.

22 While the data for the fishing industry certainly appear odd, it employed only 1231 women in 1997; that is, 9.8 per cent of its total workforce (GUS, 1998, p. 1).

23 This last figure might be compared to the total of seven three-digit occupations where this was true in the public sector.

24 Although Taylor (1970) uses the terminology to refer to the cyclical sensitivity of the labor force, it is hard to resist the temptation to equate labor hoarding with hidden unemployment given that there was zero overt unemployment.

25 When enterprises are privatized, at least some workers will be able to change sectors without passing the transition through unemployment.

26 To be precise, the first figures were published in July 1992, the second in September 1992 and they were then issued quarterly.

27 Note, however, that the EU data refer to LFS findings.

REFERENCES

Blanchard, O. (1997) *The Economics of Post-Communist Transition*, Oxford: Clarendon Press.

Bromke, A. and J. Strong (eds.) (1973) *Gierek's Poland*, New York: Praeger Publishers.

Chilosi, A. (1991) "The Impact on Employment of Institutional Transformation in Eastern Europe and the Tasks of Social Policy, with Particular Reference to the Polish Case," *Moct—Most*, vol. 1, no. 3, pp. 71–92.

Ciechocińska, M. (1993) "Gender Aspects of Dismantling the Command Economy in Eastern Europe: The Case of Poland", in: Moghadam (ed.).

Domański, H. (1992) *Zadowolony niewolnik? Studium o nierównóśchiach między mezczyznami i kobietami w Polsce* (Grateful slave? A study of inequality among men and women in Poland), Warsaw: IFiS PAN.

EC (European Commission) (1992) *Employment Observatory Central and Eastern Europe*, 3, December, Brussels.

EC (European Commission) (1998) *Agricultural Situation and Prospects in the Central and Eastern European Countries: Poland*, Directorate General for Agriculture (DG VI) Working Document, June.

Einhorn, B. (1993) *Cinderella Goes to Market*, London: Verso.

EIU (Economist Intelligence Unit) (1999) *Poland: Country Report* 1st quarter 1999, London: EIU.

Eurostat (1991) *Labour Force Survey Results 1989*, Luxembourg: Statistical Office of the European Commission.

Fallon, P. and D. Verry (1988) *The Economics of Labour Markets*, Oxford: Philip Allan.

Fong, M. and G. Paull (1993) "Women's Economic Status in the Restructuring of Eastern Europe," in: Moghadam (ed.).

Fuszara, M. (1993) "Women's Legal Rights in Poland and the Process of Transformation," *Beyond Law*, vol. 3, no. 8, pp. 35–47.

Góra, M. (1993) "Labour Hoarding and its Estimates in Central and Eastern European Economies in Transition," in: OECD *Employment and Unemployment in Economies in Transition: Conceptual and Measurement Issues*, Paris: OECD.

Góra, M., H. Lehmann, M. Socha and U. Sztanderska (1996) "Labour Market Policies in Poland," in: OECD *Lessons From Labour Market Policies in the Transition Countries*, Paris: OECD.

Gorecki, B. (1994) "Evidence of a New Shape of Income Distribution in Poland," *Eastern European Economics*, vol. 32, no. 3, pp. 32–51.

Gorlach, K. (2001) "Agricultural Change and the Labor Market Status of Women," *this volume.*

GUS (1997) *Rocznik Statystyczny Pracy 1997* (Yearbook of labour 1997), Warszawa: Główny Urząd Statystyczny.

GUS (1997a) *Rocznik Statystyczny 1997* (Statistical yearbook 1997), Warszawa: Główny Urząd Statystyczny.

GUS (1997b) *Wynagrodzenia zatrudnionych w gospodarce narodowej wed ug zavwodów za Marzec 1996* (Earnings of the employees in the national economy by occupations as of March 1996). Warszawa: Główny Urząd Statystyczny.

GUS (1998) *Pracujacy w Gospodarce Narodewej w 1997 R* (Employment in national economy in 1997), Warszawa: Główny Urząd Statystyczny.

GUS (1998a) *Earnings Distribution in National Economy: September 1997*, Warszawa: Główny Urząd Statystyczny.

GUS (1999) *Pracujacy w Gospodarce Narodewej w 1998 R* (Employment in national economy in 1998), Warszawa: Główny Urząd Statystyczny.

GUS (1999a) *bezrobocie rejestrowane w Polsce: I–IV Kwartal 1998* (Registered unemployment in Poland: I–IV quarter 1998), Warszawa: Główny Urząd Statystyczny.

GUS (1999b) *Aktywność Ekonomiczna Ludności Polski w Latach 1992–1998* (Polish labour force survey: 1992–1998), Warszawa: Główny Urząd Statystyczny.

GUS (1999c) *Wynagrodzenia Według Zawodów w Październiku 1998R* (Earnings by occupations in October 1998), Warszawa: Główny Urząd Statystyczny.

Ingham, H. and A. Karwińska (2001) "Women on the Kraków Labor Market," *this volume.*

Ingham, H., M. Ingham and G. Węcławowicz (1998) "Agricultural Reform in Post-Transition Poland", *Tijdschrift voor Economische en Sociale Geografie*, vol. 89, no. 2, pp. 150–160.

Ingham, M and H. Ingham (2001) "Gender and Labour Market Restructuring in Central and Eastern Europe: A Cross-Country Comparison," in: A. Smith, A. Rainnie and A. Swain (eds), *Work, Employment and Transition: Restructuring Livelihoods in 'Post-Communist' Eastern Europe.*

Ingham, M. and H. Ingham (2001a) *The Gender Dynamics of the Polish Labour Market in Transition*, Basingstoke: Macmillan, forthcoming.

Ingham, M., H. Ingham, A. Karwińska and G. Węcławowicz (1998a) "Women in the Polish Labour Market: Is Transition a Threat?," in: M. Bull and M. Ingham (eds.), *Reform of the Socialist System in Central and Eastern Europe*, Basingstoke: Macmillan.

Jackson, J., J. Klich, K. Poznanska and J. Chmiel (1997) "Economic Change in Poland: 1990–1994," *Research Bulletin* of the Research Centre for Economic and Statistical Studies of the Central Statistical Office and the Polish Academy of Sciences, vol. 6, no. 1, pp. 7–20.

Joseph, G. (1983) *Women at Work*, Oxford: Philip Allan.

Kabaj, M. (1996) "Programs and Strategies for Counteracting Unemployment and the Promotion of Productive Employment in Poland," ILO–CEET Report No. 15, Hungary: International Labor Office.

Killingsworth, M. (1983) *Labor Supply*, Cambridge: Cambridge University Press.

Kolankiewicz, G. and P. Lewis (1986) *Poland: Politics, Economics and Society*, London: Pinter.

Kolarska-Bobińska, L. (1994) *Aspirations, Values and Interests: Poland 1989–94*, Warsaw: IFiS Publishers.

Kotowska, I.E. (2001) "Demographic and Labor Market Developments in the 1990s," *this volume.*

Krajewska, A. (1995) "Education in Poland," *Eastern European Economics*, vol. 33, no. 4, pp. 38—54.

Kramer, M. (1995) "Polish Workers and the Post-Communist Transition, 1989–1993," *Communist and Post Communist Studies*, vol. 28, no. 1, pp. 71–114.

Kuratowska, Z. (1991) "Present Situation of Women," in: *Impact of Economic and Political Reform on the Status of Women in Eastern Europe*, Proceedings of a UN seminar, UN Centre for Social Development and Humanitarian Affairs, Vienna, 8–12 April 1991.

Leven, B. (1994) "The Status of Women and Poland's Transition to a Market Economy", in: N. Aslanbeigui, S. Pressman and G. Summerfield (eds), *Women in the Age of Economic Transformation*, London: Routledge.

Łobodzińska, B. (1983) "Urban and Rural Working Women in Poland Today: Between Social Change and Social Conflict," in H. Lopata and J. Pleck (eds.), *Research in the Interweave of Social Roles: Families and Jobs*, vol. 3, Greenwich: JAI Press Inc.

Mach, B. and K. Słomczyński (1995) "Occupational Structure and Mobility in the Transition from Communism to Post-Communist Capitalism," in: E. Wnuk-Lipinski (ed.), *After Communism: A Multidisciplinary Approach to Radical Social Change*, Warsaw: ISP PAN.

Malinowska, E. (1995) "Socio-Political Changes in Poland and the Problem of Sex Discrimination," *Women's Studies International Forum*, vol. 18, no. 1, pp. 35–43.

Mincer, J. (1966) "Labor Force Participation and Unemployment: A Review of Recent Evidence," in: R. Gordon and M. Gordon (eds), *Prosperity and Unemployment*, New York: Wiley.

Moghadam, V. (ed.) (1993) *Democratic Reform and the Position of Women in Transitional Economies*, Oxford: Clarendon Press.

Nesporová, A. (1993) "Measuring Employment in Central and Eastern Europe," in OECD.

OECD (Organization for Economic Co-operation and Development) (1993) *Employment and Unemployment in Economies in Transition; Conceptual and Measurement Issues*, Paris: OECD.

ONS (Office for National Statistics) (1999) *Labour Market Trends*, vol. 107, no. 6, London: The Stationery Office.

Pissarides, C. (1976) *Labour Market Adjustment*, Cambridge: Cambridge University Press.

Pissarides, C. (1993) "Labour Hoarding in Industrial Countries: Concept and Measurement," in OECD.

Ratajczyk, A. (2000) "Privatization: Past Successes, Future Plans," *Warsaw Voice*, no. 2, 9th January.

RECESS (1996) *Research Bulletin*, vol. 5, no. 1, Warsaw: Research Centre for Economic and Statistical Studies of the Central Statistical Office and the Polish Academy of Sciences.

Reszke, I. (2001) "Stereotypes: Opinions of Women Entrepreneurs in Poland," *this volume.*

Rubery, J. (1997) "Wages and the Labour Market," *British Journal of Industrial Relations*, vol. 35, no. 3, pp. 337–366.

Rutkowski, J. (1994) "Wage Determination in Late Socialism: The Case of Poland," *Economics of Planning*, vol. 27, no. 3, pp. 135–164.

Sachs, J. (1992) "The Economic transformation of Eastern Europe: The Case of Poland," *The American Economist*, vol. 36, no. 2, pp. 3–11.

Schaffer, M. (1992) "The Economy of Poland", *Centre for Economic Performance*, Discussion Paper no. 67, LSE.

Taylor, J. (1970) "Hidden Unemployment, Hoarded Labour and the Phillips Curve," *Southern Economic Journal*, vol. 37, no. 1, pp. 1–16.

Titkow, A. (1994) "Status Evolution of Polish Women—The Paradox and the Chances", in: M. Alestalo, E. Allardt, A. Rychard and W. Wesolowski (eds), *The Transformation of Europe: Social Conditions and Consequences*, Warsaw: IFiS Publishers.

Wiatr, J. (1987) "The Party System, Involvement in Politics, and Political Leadership," in: L. Graham (ed.) *The Polish Dilemma: Views from Within*, Boulder, Colorado: Westview Press.

Witkowski, J. (1995) "Labour Market in Poland in 1994: New Trends, Old Problems," Warszawa: GUS.

WERI (World Economy Research Institute) (1998) *Poland: International Economic Report 1997/98*, Warszawa: Warsaw School of Economics.

Zienkowski, L. (1997) "Why Do Regional Gross Products Differ?," *Research Bulletin*, Research Centre for Economic and Statistical Studies, Central Statistical Office, Warsaw, vol. 6, no. 4, pp. 7–32.

CHAPTER 4

DEMOGRAPHIC AND LABOR MARKET DEVELOPMENTS IN THE 1990S

Recent changes in fertility and nuptiality in the countries undergoing transformation to a market economy are similar to those that took place earlier in Western Europe and which became known as the second demographic transition (see e.g. van de Kaa 1987, 994; Lesthaeghe, 1991). This terminology was adopted initially to describe the radical shifts in fertility and nuptiality behaviors that had been observed in developed countries since the middle of the nineteen-sixties. The changes can be characterized as having two component elements. First, a decline in fertility to a point below replacement level, accompanied by changes in its pattern, as manifested by the postponement of birth, a growing proportion of children born out of wedlock (to both cohabiting couples and single mothers), and a growing proportion of childless couples. Second, the increasingly widespread use of contraceptive practices by all social groups in order to limit family size according to preference. These trends were accompanied by an increasing social acceptance of couples having children out of wedlock, while their manifestations included a decline in the propensity to marry, postponement of marriage, an increase in cohabitation and LAT (Living–Apart–Together) relations, a rise in divorce rates and a growing number of single parents.

The conceptual framework underpinning analysis of the second demographic transition focuses on changes in fertility and nuptiality as these relate to changes in family formation and dissolution patterns. Fertility and nuptiality are decisive for the emergence of a course of reproduction far removed from that expected under classical theory for the last stage of demographic development, and much less attention is paid under the new approach to the behavior of mortality and migration than was the case previously. In accord with the modern paradigm, the emphasis in Section 2 of the present chapter, which provides a brief description of demographic developments in Poland in the 1990s, is directed towards changes in fertility and nuptiality.

The demographic evolutions currently underway are taking place in the context of a society in the throes of a fundamental systemic transformation, in which change is being witnessed in all spheres of economic, political and social life. As a fundamental determinant of the supply of workers, demographic developments inevitably impact upon the labor market. However, the economic reforms introduced under Balcerowicz's program of liberalization, restructuring and stabilization also imposed a fundamental reconstruction of labor market control mechanisms aimed at the more effective management of the workforce, a rise in labor productivity and an improvement in the quality of work. Nonetheless, the process of conversion from a job-rights to a job-search economy has been strongly influenced by the economic and social relations existing under the previous system, including the structure of employment, the pattern of labor hoarding and inherited attitudes towards work. To these pressures need also to be added those arising from current economic phenomena, such as recession, the course of privatization and the development of the fiscal framework. In encapsulating these developments, the discussion in Section 3 of the chapter focuses upon changes in the labor force participation behavior of different population groups, the decline in the demand for labor, changes in the employment structure (by ownership, broad economic sectors and employment status) and the emergence and trend of unemployment. Remarks on future changes in the Polish labor market conclude the chapter, with the expectation being that demographic pressure, together with a slowdown of economic growth, restructuring of the coal and steel sectors, and reforms introduced in 1999 will contribute to bring past positive developments to a halt.

DEMOGRAPHIC DEVELOPMENTS IN POLAND

Although the Polish population rose from 38.04 million in 1989 to 38.65 million in 1999, this represented a remarkable decrease in its dynamic in comparison with earlier years. The reduction in the rate of natural increase was due mainly to a rapid drop in fertility and not, as shown in Table 4.1, to an increase in emigration. The downward trend in fertility and nuptiality, already observable in the 1980s, accelerated in the 1990s, but the latest decline has been accompanied by changes in procreative and marriage patterns (a postponement of marriage and births, a rise in cohabitation and LAT relations, increasing extra-marital births and divorces). However, reproduction in Poland differs by urban/rural regions and its changes over the period considered in this chapter were not uniform across these areas, even though the share of the urban population remained stable at about 62 per cent of the total. Also, and contrary to the expectations of some authors, improvements in mortality have been observed since 1992.

Table 4.1 Population Dynamics in Poland: 1980–1998

Year	Rate of Natural Increase (%)	Rate of Net Migration (%)
1980	0.97	–0.06
1989	0.48	–0.06
1993	0.26	–0.04
1996	0.11	–0.03
1997	0.09	–0.03
1998	0.05	–0.03

Source: Demographic Yearbook, GUS, various issues.

Also characteristic of the demographic developments in the period of transformation are the changes in external and internal migration. While spatial mobility within the country declined remarkably, official statistics and sample surveys both indicate that international migration intensified. The shifts in internal flows are relatively well-documented and can be discussed with some confidence, although comments on international migration patterns need to be more circumspect, owing to the problematic nature of the data.

CHANGES IN THE AGE STRUCTURE

The main changes in the age composition of Poland's population can be characterized as a steady decline in the share of the youngest cohort (aged 0–17 years), combined with a rising share of those of working-age (18–59 for women and 18–64 for males) and of older persons (65 and over). As a result of the decline in fertility, the percentage of the first group in the population decreased from 29.8 per cent in 1989 to 25.6 per cent in 1998, while that of older persons increased from 10 per cent in 1989 to 11.9 per cent in 1998 (Table 4.2). The increase in the percentage of persons of retirement age (i.e. men 65 years and more, women 60 years and more) was even more visible—from 12.6 per cent to 14.4 per cent. Nevertheless, at the end of the 1980s, cohorts of the second-wave of the post-war baby boom started to enter the labor market. During the years 1989–1998 the working-age population increased by 1.34 million (by 686,000 in the years 1990–1995)—that is, by 6.1 per cent—and its share in the total population rose from 57.6 per cent to 60 per cent. Anticipating later discussion, the total further increase predicted for the years 1996–2000 is 1,018,000; a figure which leaves no room to doubt the potential importance of this factor in influencing the future labor market situation.

Table 4.2 Age Composition of the Polish Population: 1989–1998

Age	1989 (%)	1990 (%)	1991 (%)	1992 (%)	1993 (%)	1994 (%)	1995 (%)	1996 (%)	1997 (%)	1998 (%)
0–17	29.8	29.7	29.4	29.1	28.7	28.2	27.6	27.0	26.3	25.6
18–59/64	57.6	57.5	57.6	57.7	58.0	58.3	58.6	59.0	59.5	60.0
60/65 +	12.6	12.8	13.0	13.2	13.3	13.5	13.8	14.0	14.2	14.4
0–14	25.3	24.9	24.6	24.1	23.7	23.1	22.5	21.9	21.1	20.3
15–64	64.7	64.9	65.1	65.4	65.7	66.0	66.3	66.6	66.9	67.8
65 +	10.0	10.2	10.3	10.5	10.7	10.9	11.2	11.5	11.7	11.9

Source: Demographic Yearbook, GUS, various issues.

The largest observed increases in population in recent years occurred in those groups aged 45–54 (by 38.9%) and 18–24 (by 25.8%). As a result, the population in the so-called 'immobile age' (45–59 for females and 45–64 for males) rose more strongly than did the total population of working-age: the absolute increase in the former being some 1,190,500, or 16.7 per cent. In consequence, this group accounted for 33.0 per cent of the total population of working-age in 1998, which is to be compared with a figure of 29.9 per cent in 1989.

FERTILITY AND NUPTIALITY

As shown in Table 4.3, Poland had a relatively high total fertility rate (TFR) of 2.28 in 1980 a figure that might be compared with those observed in Sweden (1.68), the UK (1.89), Belgium (1.69) and France (1.95). The decline of the Polish TFR over the course of the subsequent decade led to a situation in which reproduction below replacement was observed for the total population in 1989.[1] Over the period 1989–1998 the decline accelerated, with the TFR for the urban and rural populations alike falling by 31 per cent. The reduction in fertility was accompanied by shifts in the age distribution of mothers, a feature that can be synthesized by data on changes in the mean age of childbearing. This measure highlights the contribution of age-specific factors to the overall decrease in fertility. Prior to 1992, changes in the fertility of women of different ages contributed roughly equally to the observed, gradual overall decrease, thereby allowing the mean age at birth to remain relatively stable. In the years that followed, however, a particularly strong fertility decline occurred amongst women aged 20–24; a reduction followed in intensity by that exhibited among those aged 25–29. The result was that the mean age at birth began to rise. As indicated by Figure 4.1, the fertility of women aged 20–24 declined by 40 per cent over the period 1989–1997, while that for the age group 25–29 fell by 20 per cent. The upshot was that these groups came to share equal status as most fertile cohorts amongst Polish women (100 births per 1000 women), whereas those aged 20–24 had been dominant previously. In fact, the shifts in fertility patterns are most visible in urban regions, where those aged 25–29 actually became more productive than those aged 20–24, as shown in Figures 4.2 and 4.3.

Table 4.3 **Selected Polish Fertility Indicators: 1980–1988**

Year	Fertility Rate			Extra-marital Births (Per 100 Births)			Mean Age at First Birth	
	Total	Urban	Rural	Total	Urban	Rural	Urban	Rural
1980	2.276	1.928	2.908	4.7	5.2	4.2	26.5	23.4
1989	2.078	1.817	2.506	5.8	7.3	4.1	26.3	23.6
1993	1.847	1.558	2.273	8.2	10.5	5.6	26.6	23.4
1996	1.580	1.371	1.924	10.2	12.8	7.8	26.9	23.6
1997	1.508	1.305	1.843	11.0	13.7	7.8	26.9	23.7
1998	1.430	1.251	1.730	11.6	14.3	8.3	26.6	23.8

Source: *Demographic Yearbook*, GUS, various issues; "Basic Information on Poland's Demographic Development," Central Statistical Office, 1999.

At the same time, and in parallel to the fertility decline, Table 4.3 shows the visible increase in extra-marital births, although the trend was especially marked in urban areas. While the spread of out-of-wedlock births is related to changes in marital behaviors, the changes in nuptiality are even more pronounced than those in fertility, with the reduction

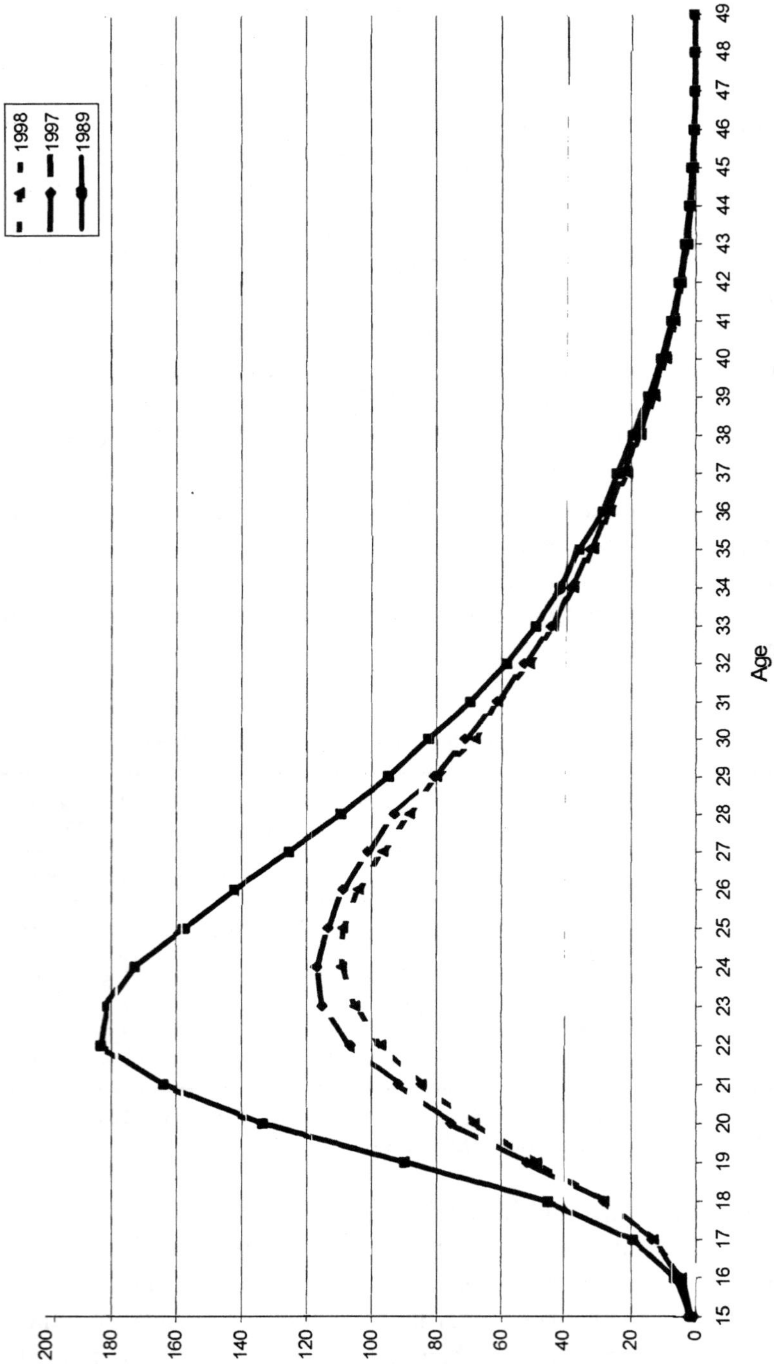

Figure 4.1 Age-specific Fertility Rates: 1989, 1997 and 1998—Poland

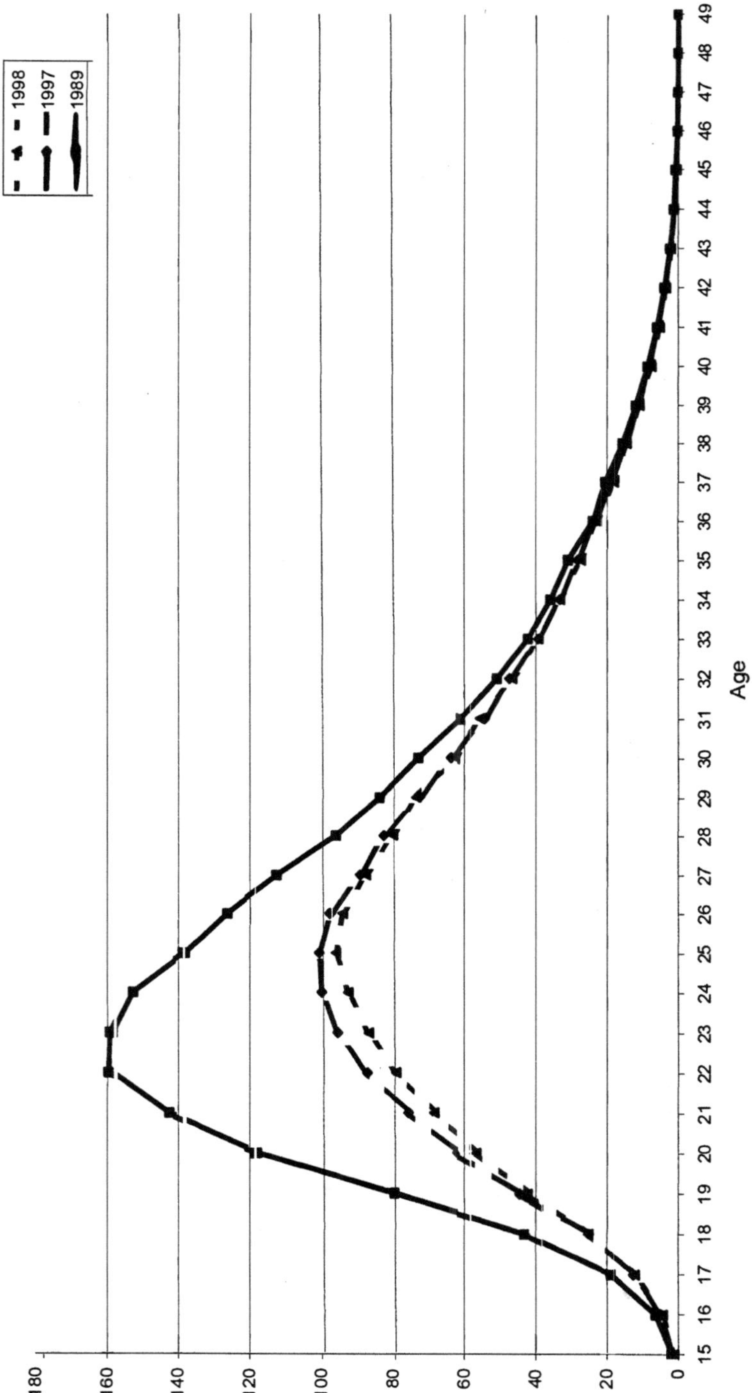

Figure 4.2 **Age-specific Fertility Rates: 1989, 1997 and 1998—Urban**

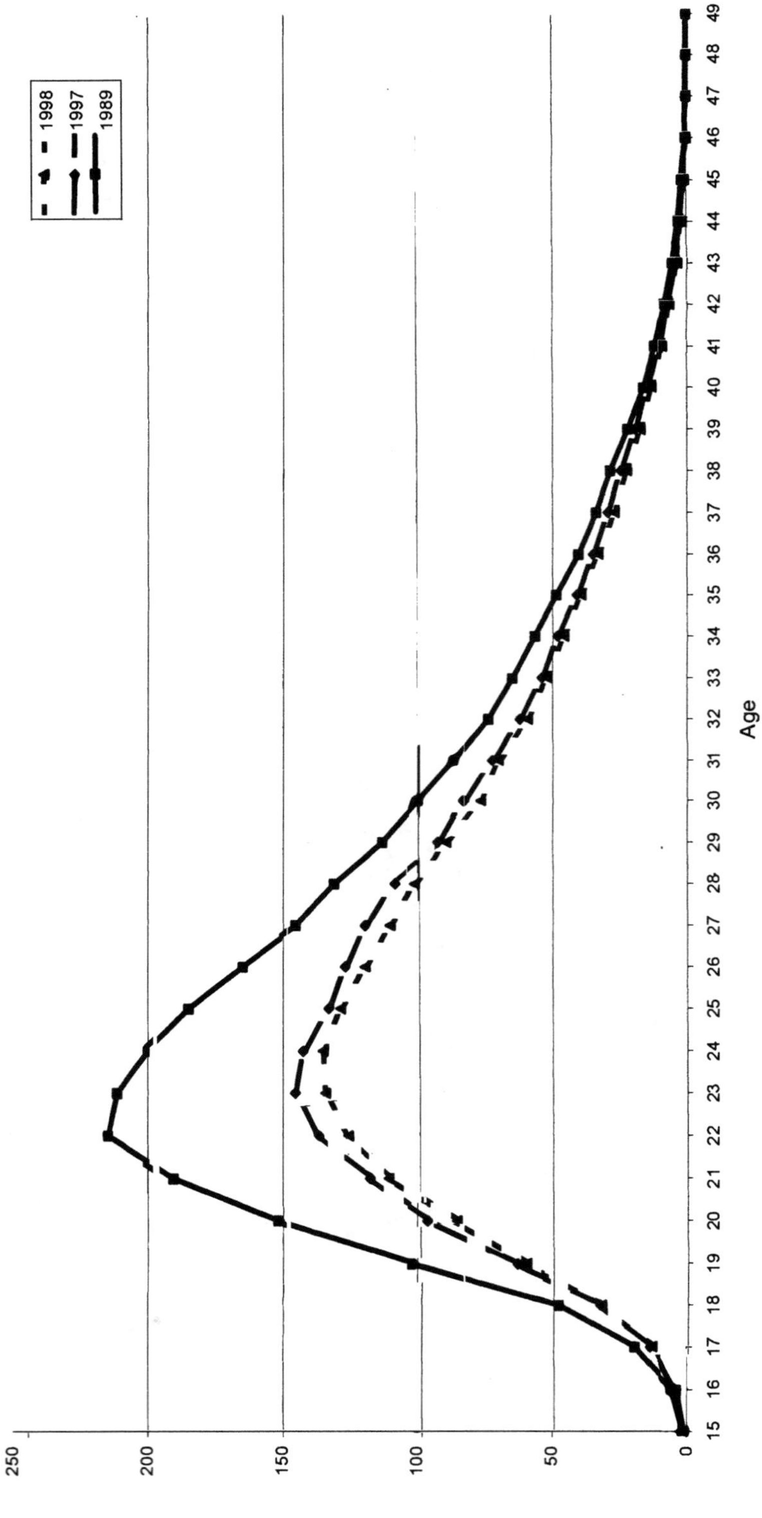

Figure 4.3 **Age-specific Fertility Rates: 1989, 1997 and 1998—Rural**

in nuptiality having begun one year earlier than the onset of the decline in fertility (Macura, 1995). As shown in Table 4.4, nuptiality changes are manifested mainly by a decline in the propensity to marry and, in 1996, crude marriage rates were considerably lower than in 1989 (by 43 per cent for the urban population and by 31 per cent for rural residents). In 1980, Polish marriage rates had been higher still and were generally in excess of the rates observed in developed countries. The impact of the decline in marriage rates in rural areas was diminished by changes in their age and sex structures, both of which resulted from the diminution of migration flows to urban areas. As its strongly Catholic orientation would suggest, Poland's divorce rate has been low in comparison to the figures witnessed in most of the western world. Indeed, in the years 1989–1993, the figure declined even further and, as detailed in Table 4.4, still remains at its original, pre-1990 level. Also, 1998 seems to have been a turning point for nuptiality changes: crude marriage rates exhibited a slight increase, a shift confirmed by the figures for 1999 which indicated that the total marriage rate had risen to a level of 5.7 marriages per 1,000 population.

Table 4.4 Selected Polish Nuptiality Indicators: 1980–1998

Year	Crude Marriage Rate (Per 1000 of Population)			Crude Divorce Rate (Per 1000 of Population)		
	Total	Urban	Rural	Total	Urban	Rural
1980	8.6	9.0	8.1	1.1	1.6	0.4
1989	6.7	6.8	6.7	1.2	1.8	0.5
1993	5.4	5.1	5.9	0.7	1.0	0.3
1996	5.3	5.1	5.6	1.0	1.4	0.4
1997	5.3	5.1	5.6	1.1	1.5	0.5
1998	5.4	5.3	5.7	1.1	1.6	0.5

Source: *Demographic Yearbook*, GUS, various issues.

The decline in overall nuptiality has come about mostly from a decline in first marriages, a fact that is reflected in the changes that have occurred in the age pattern of marriage, as illustrated by the data in Table 4.5. Following a slight decline in 1990, both the median ages of first and of all marriages remained stable until 1992, but began to increase from 1993 onwards. Figures 4.4 and 4.5 indicate that these increases were due to a stronger decline in the marriage propensity of those aged 20–24 than of those aged 25–29. The slight increase in the marriage rate of persons aged 25–29 in 1997, as compared to 1996, might be taken as a sign that some of the marriages postponed in the earliest years of transformation had eventually to occur.

Table 4.5 Median Age of Marriage in Poland: 1980–1998

Year	Median Age of Women at First Marriage	Median Age of Women at Marriage	Median Age of Males at Marriage
1980	22.0	22.8	24.4
1989	21.9	22.4	24.9
1993	21.8	22.2	24.7
1996	22.3	22.6	24.9
1997	22.5	22.9	25.1
1998	22.9	23.1	25.2

Source: GUS (1998b, 1999d); *Demographic Yearbook*, GUS, various issues.

Unfortunately, there are no official data on cohabitation and LAT relations. However, some evidence is available from opinion polls and this points to the emergence of both more frequent pre-marital cohabitation and of LAT relations, especially among young persons. Cohabitation will, in general, postpone a decision to enter into wedlock, hence the evidence leads to an expectation of a declining number of marriages in the future, in spite of the growing number of persons of marriageable age.

Nevertheless, all of these changes exhibit marked differences across the urban and rural areas of the country and detailed scrutiny of the regional disparities reveals a more uniform pattern of change in the former than in the latter. Using a taxonomy for voivodships—the main administrative units in Poland—developed in an OECD paper by Scarpetta and Huber (1995) as the basis for analysis, it is further possible to conclude that more pronounced changes (in terms of the overall and age-specific fertility decline) occurred in more developed regions.[2] The same conclusion also emerges for the marriage rates of women aged 20–24 and 25–29. On the other hand, the propensity of males aged 20–24 to marry has declined, irrespective of the type of region in which they are domiciled and notwithstanding the fact that the urban/rural divide re-emerges for changes in the marriage rates of males in the age groups 25–29 and 30–34 (Kotowska et al., 1998).

In summary, the patterns of change described above indicate that the postponement of marriage and childbearing is manifested, firstly, by shifts in intensity rates and then, at a later date, by changes in the char-

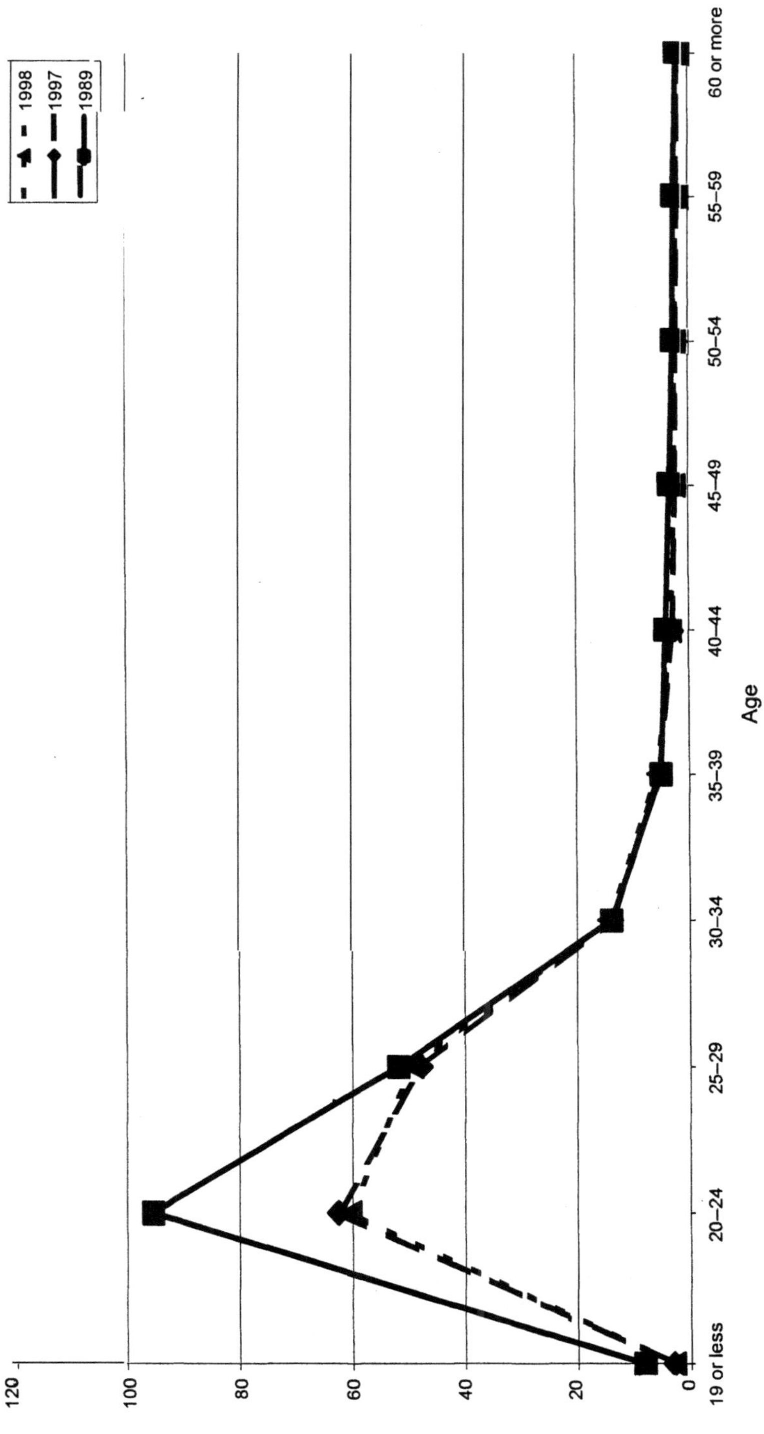

Figure 4.4 **Age-specific Marriage Rates: 1989, 1997 and 1998—Males**

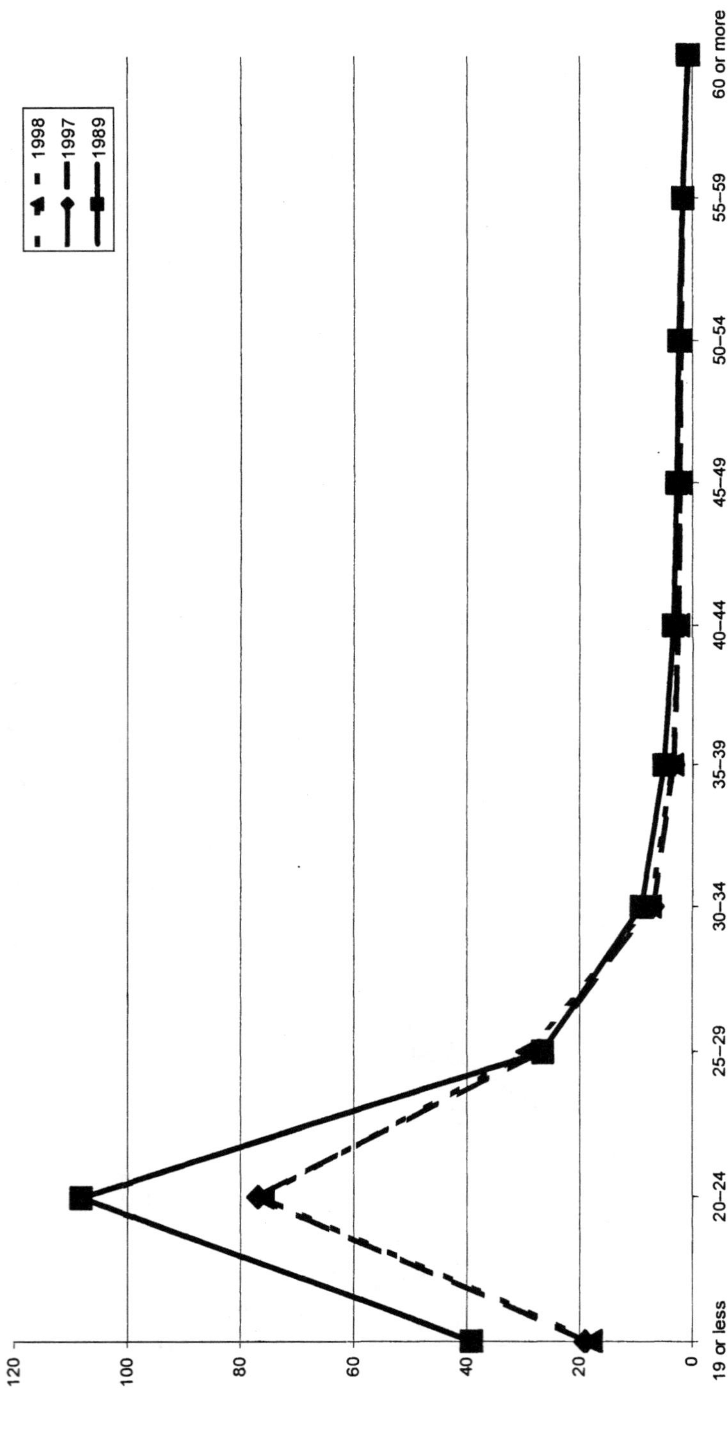

Figure 4.5 **Age-specific Marriage Rates: 1989, 1997 and 1998—Females**

acteristics of the relevant distributions. In explaining current developments and in the construction of hypotheses regarding future shifts, it is clear that the different behavioral aspects of the various demographic behaviors (e.g., fertility versus nuptiality, migration versus mortality) cannot be ignored. For instance, there is only a limited degree of freedom in the choice of timing of the birth of a child, especially the first one, due to the restricted distribution of advanced family planning practices. At the same time, changes in norms and attitudes, as reflected in the growing social approval of extra-marital sexual experiences are likely to be influential. The latter is reflected in a decline in the age at first intercourse and in the rise of extra-marital births. Because of limited sexual education and family planning, the tendency for there to be an increase in the age at first birth for married couples could be counteracted by these developments. Nevertheless, one might expect there to be improvements in sexual education, along with the more widespread use of family planning methods, both of which should stimulate delays in—or cancellations of—births, including the first. But marriage is the more 'decisive' behavioral variable, as can be observed from the stronger decline in marriage rates than in the indicators of fertility.

MORTALITY

At the beginning of the 1990s, Poles experienced a worsening of their chances of survival, as manifested by the deterioration of life expectancy at birth, a statistic that was already low by western standards. After the 'black' year of 1991, some improvement in the mortality rates of both sexes occurred (see also Tabeau, 1996) and, between 1991 and 1998, the life expectancy of males grew by 3.0 years, while that of women increased by 2.3 years. However, as shown in Table 4.6, progress in human survival has been more pronounced for the urban population, where the indicators rose by 3.3 and 2.6 years for males and females, respectively, while males in rural areas gained only 2.4 years and women 1.9 years of additional expected life.

Despite these visible improvements, life expectancy, particularly for males, is still much lower than in developed European countries, mostly due to the excess mortality of men aged 40–60 in Poland. While this excess mortality has fallen slightly, the death rates of Polish males aged 45–55 remain comparable with those observed at the beginning of the 1950s (GUS, 1998b, p. 19). Nonetheless, the decline in infant mortality, which fell by 51 per cent in the years 1990–1998, made a remarkable contribution to the recent improvement in survival chances, although the rate remains relatively high by European standards.

Table 4.6 Selected Polish Mortality Indicators: 1980–1998

Year	Life Expectancy at Birth			Life Expectancy at Birth			Infant Mortality Rate (Per 1,000 Live Births)
	Males			Females			
	Total	Urban	Rural	Total	Urban	Rural	
1980	66.01	65.81	66.13	74.44	74.22	74.75	21.3
1990	66.24	66.16	66.30	75.24	74.88	75.79	19.3
1991	65.88	65.76	66.04	75.06	74.63	75.73	18.2
1992	67.17	67.10	67.23	75.81	75.49	76.32	16.1
1996	68.12	68.35	67.75	76.57	76.39	76.89	12.2
1997	68.45	68.69	68.04	76.99	76.88	77.28	10.2
1998	68.87	69.13	68.44	77.34	77.18	77.65	9.5

Source: GUS (1998a, 1999d).

INTERNAL MIGRATION

Past demographic developments in Poland were strongly influenced by internal migration, and especially by flows from rural to urban areas. In the 1980s, this migration declined both in absolute and relative terms. The yearly number of migrants per 1,000 of population dropped from 26 in 1971–1980 to 21 in 1981–1985 and to 16 in 1989. The fall intensified in the 1990s: net migration in 1998 was the lowest recorded in the post-war period, with the net migration into urban areas being only 8,600 and there were only ten migrants per 1,000 of population. The slowdown of inflows from rural areas, which were always highly selective by sex and age, improved the sex–age composition of the rural population slightly and reduced the trend decline in marriage and fertility rates in those regions. Another quite new phenomenon was the slight decline observed in the populations of big cities, accompanied by a rise in the population residing in small towns situated close to them. In general, the reduction in spatial mobility can be explained by the difficult situation in many regional labor markets, housing shortages and the high cost of houses, as well as by the overall uncertainty introduced by the period of reform.

INTERNATIONAL MIGRATION

The political and economic situation in both Poland and other CEE countries has led to a clear increase in international population flows. Net migration since 1980 has been negative (that is, emigration has exceeded immigration), although it has exhibited a downward trend. Many factors underlie the summary statistics, although it is difficult to quantify most of them precisely due to the scarcity of reliable data. The national registration system does not deliver complete data on migration categories (labor and trade migrants, refugees, ethnic migrants, etc.). But, even if that data source is improved, it will not ensure that data covering all aspects of international migration will become available because a marked proportion of migrants go abroad irregularly and stay in their destination countries illegally. In consequence, researchers have relied increasingly upon data collected from sample surveys to supplement official sources. As such, the following discussion utilizes both in order to indicate directions of changes in migration and generally does not purport to statistical exactitude.

The liberal legal regulations governing international migration that came into effect at the end of 1989 created new opportunities for people to move between Poland and other countries, and the emigration flows that occurred in 1989 and 1990 could be considered as an immediate response to that change in legislative climate. Nevertheless, unemployment and economic deprivation were undoubtedly acting as push factors underlying the emigration decision. However, immigration policies in western countries also changed, with the emergence of an enhanced emphasis on the protection of their own labor markets. As a result, the expected high labor inflows from Poland and other transition countries to the developed world did not materialize at the beginning of the 1990s (see e.g. Kotowska and Witkowski, 1996). Nonetheless, moves for jobs contribute more and more to the total volume of flows out of Poland, while re-settlement migration has declined remarkably (see e.g. Jaźwińska and Okólski, 1996).

New national regulations that exhibit a preference for the import of seasonal workers, combined with a more rigid system of stable work contracts for residents, have resulted in a shift from long-term migration to short-term moves for temporary jobs. Although part of the rise in short-term movement is in accordance with the fulfillment of official job contracts, a marked share of these moves is still related to illegal jobs (see e.g. Okólski, 1996). Around 90 per cent of job migration now involves developed countries while, in the past, the majority of such moves were to and from the former socialist countries. Migrants in both directions have become older, less educated and their jobs tend to be low skilled and situated at the bottom of the hierarchy of blue-collar occupations. The 'brain-drain' that characterized flows from Poland in the 1980s has stopped.

Differences in living conditions underlie inflows to Poland from other Central and Eastern regions of Europe, and these inflows persist in spite of hardened immigration policies and levels of unemployment that remain uncomfortably high. Inflows to Poland grew considerably following the downfall of the communist authorities, with refugees, transitory migrants and trade migrants constituting a large share of these movements (see e.g. Kozłowski, 1994; Stola 1997). The growth in the number of shadow economy employees, both national and foreign, has ensured that the problems associated with unregistered employment have increased in importance during the course of the current decade.

LABOR MARKET DEVELOPMENTS

The transition to a market economy started in 1990 with the introduction of Balcerowicz's 'shock therapy' program. The liberalization of prices, a drastic reduction in state subsidies, controls over wage growth, a tight monetary policy, liberal trade regulations, privatization and restructuring of the labor market were the hallmarks of this radical strategy. Predictably, its efforts to control inflation were accompanied by steep declines in output and real wages and a rapid rise in unemployment. During the first two years of the program, the cumulative decline in GDP reached some 20 per cent and unemployment rose to over 2.1 million by December 1991. Economic recovery commenced with the onset of GDP growth in 1992, which was followed, at later dates, by other signs that the worst of the transition crisis might be over: a declining rate of inflation, a decrease in the budget deficit, growing real wages (from 1995), as well as an increase in employment and a decline in unemployment (from 1994). The rapidly developing private sector was one of the main sources of this recovery. Fundamentally, however, restructuring the labor market required the establishment of a new institutional framework and this was sensitive to current economic developments, the position of trade unions and the demographic pressures discussed above. Nevertheless the process was also heavily influenced by the economic and social relations established under communism (the structure of employment, labor hoarding, attitudes to work, social protection at work, etc.).

It can be expected that the trends in reproductive patterns described earlier will continue. Those entering the working-age population are now confronted with more opportunities regarding their choice of professional career and life style, and with more possibilities to influence their economic and social position, as well as their life course in general. An individual's position has become more dependent upon their personal skills and their ability to act in the circumstances imposed by the transition process. However, as a result of increased competition on the labor market and changes in the employment status of workers (from employed towards self-employed and employer and from the state to the private sector), much more effort is required to gain any desired status. In conjunction with richer consumption opportunities, the enhanced importance of economic considerations to the choices that individuals make is evident. A professional career orientation and a growing awareness of the relevance of skills and education as determinants of labor market status could motivate young people either to delay starting a family or even to resign from family formation altogether.

The evident weakening of the position of women on the labor market under the transition process contributes an additional force for change in procreative and marital attitudes and behaviors. The economic and ideological reasoning underpinning women's participation in paid work that characterized the centrally planned economy has been replaced by purely economic arguments. The efficiency and cost criteria applied in the economy, together with the significant decline in demand for labor, have led to visible preferences for males in employment. However, services remain under-developed, rigid working-time schedules still predominate and unfortunate changes in the social infrastructure (education, child-care facilities, health care) have had negative affects on women's opportunities to combine paid work and family duties: the domestic situation has become a more important factor in determining their economic activity. At the same time, employers' hiring procedures use the age and family situation (marital status, number and age of children) of women as a proxy for their production-related attributes.

Re-entering the labor market following a period of child-care leave is confronted by serious obstacles, while threats of job loss during such leave have resulted in a marked drop in the percentage of mothers taking advantage of their legal rights in this area (see e.g. Kotowska and Witkowski, 1996). Adjustment to the new labor market requirements is conditioned by, among other things, labor force mobility. However, institutional, economic and social changes—external to females—have served to reduce radically their flexibility on the labor market. Additionally, the rising costs of child-rearing as a result of changes in family assistance (limited access to child-care facilities and the costs of such care; the costs of the educational system and of health care being shifted to households, a relative decline in family allowances, etc.), without any family-oriented changes in tax policy, can also be cited as factors influencing attitudes towards children. The impact of forces prompting reductions in fertility and nuptiality could be intensified by concomitant shifts in values and norms towards more individual independence, autonomy and self-realization, combined with a stronger orientation towards the attainment of a successful professional career.

Table 4.7 Changes in the Polish Working-age Population: 1990–1998[1]

Year	Population as on January 1	Persons Reaching Working Age	Persons Reaching Post-working Age	Balance[2]	Real Decrease[3]	Net Increase	Population as on December 31
	('000)	('000)	('000)	('000)	('000)	('000)	('000)
1990	21889.6	562.6	364.7	+197.9	−125.7	+72.2	21961.8
1991	21961.8	572.5	345.4	+227.1	−133.4	+93.7	22055.5
1992	22055.5	598.2	347.1	+251.1	−125.3	+125.8	22181.3
1993	22181.3	621.1	348.2	+272.9	−121.7	+151.2	22332.5
1994	22332.5	640.3	347.8	+292.5	−123.6	+168.9	22501.4
1995	22501.4	631.2	361.2	+270.0	−124.0	+146.0	22647.4
1996	22647.4	643.5	355.2	+288.3	−115.7	+172.6	22820.0
1997	22820.0	654.3	344.5	+309.8	−115.8	+194.0	23014.0
1998	23014.0	662.8	335.2	+327.6	−115.3	+212.3	23226.3

[1] Females ages 18–59 years and males aged 18–64.
[2] The difference between persons reaching working-age and post-working age.
[3] Due to mortality and out-migration.

Nevertheless, as noted above, economic reform in Poland started at just the time when a greater number of young people were entering the labor market. The strength of the demographic pressure this exerted on the labor market over the period 1989–1998 is illustrated by the data reported in Table 4.7: year by year, with just one exception, a larger cohort entered the world of work. It is expected that during the decade 1990–2000, the working-age population will increase by 1.7 million (Table 4.8). Thus the country has to deal with the shocks of transition at the same time as it is facing an extremely large increase in potential labor supply. However, the reality is that this growth is translating into a higher dependency ratio as early retirements and delayed school leaving counter the effects of the demographic bulge; and this burden may persist as the impact of the falling TFR becomes dominant, unless economic growth is either very high, very labor intensive, or both.

Table 4.8 Selected Labour Market Indicators by Gender and Region: 1990–2000

Indicators	1990	1995	2000[1]	95–90[2]	00–95[3]
Population ('000)	38183	38609	38649	426	40
Males	18606	18786	18777	180	–9
Females	19577	19823	19872	246	49
Urban	23614	23877	23897	263	20
Rural	14569	14732	14752	193	20
Working-age population ('000)	21962	22647	23665	685	1018
Males	11364	11702	12201	338	499
Females	10598	10945	11464	347	519
Urban	14068	14555	15203	487	648
Rural	7894	8092	8462	198	370
Working-age in % of population	57.5	58.6	61.2	–	–
Males	57.5	62.3	65.0	–	–
Females	54.3	55.2	57.7	–	–
Urban	59.6	60.9	63.6	–	–
Rural	54.2	54.9	57.4	–	–
Labor force participation rate[4]					
Males	74.3	66.4	67.0	–	–
Females	57.0	53.0	51.6	–	–

[1] CSO 1999 population forecast.
[2] Population increments in respective periods.
[3] As note 2.
[4] The labor force relates to the population aged 15 and over; 1990 data are drawn from the 1988 Population Census, 1995 data are drawn from the 1995 Microcensus, 2000 data are own estimates based on labor force projections.
Source: GUS (1995, 1996, 2000) and Microcensus 1995.

ECONOMIC ACTIVITY

Declining labor force participation rates have been a common feature of the economies undergoing transition to free market configurations. In Poland, as highlighted in Table 4.8, the overall participation rate, defined as the percentage of the population aged 15 years and over active in the labor force, dropped from 57 per cent in 1988 to 53 per cent in 1995 for females, and from 74 per cent to 66 per cent for males.[3] Employment rates, defined as the percentage of the population aged 15 years and over in employment, calculated on data from the 1995 Microcensus, revealed an even stronger decline: to 46 per cent for females and 59 per cent for males.

The reduction in the economic activity of men was even sharper than that of women and the fall exhibited by the former was more uniform by age. The significant decrease in the economic activity of both young women and young men can be linked to higher post-compulsory school enrollment rates resulting from the troubles experienced by new entrants to the labor market: by far the highest rates of unemployment are observed for those aged between 15 and 24 years. The significantly lower labor force participation rate of women aged between 20 and 34 years witnessed in recent years results partly from interruptions to their professional careers to raise children and partly from difficulties in returning to work. The decline in the economic activity of persons in the 'immobile age' can, to some extent, be attributed to new labor market regulations, which allow enhanced opportunities for, or impose pressures to accept, early retirement. In general, it can be concluded that the reduction in labor force participation has been driven mainly by the exit from the market of either unskilled persons (with education no higher than primary or with general secondary education), from the withdrawal of persons with low skills (vocational education), and from the prolongation of educational careers by young people.

CHANGES IN EMPLOYMENT AND ITS STRUCTURE

The reduction in the demand for labor, a major characteristic of the early years of transformation, was reflected in a sharp decline in employment: in the year 1990, by approximately 1.3 million workers and, in 1991, by around 713,000. Over the whole period of 1990–95, the total reduction amounted to about one million persons. The first signs of increasing labor demand emerged in 1994, although the employment increase observed since then has been strongest in agriculture, where the real need is to shed, rather than attract, workers. Non-agricultural activities contributed only 51 per cent of the employment increment observed in recent years (Table 4.9). Given the already bloated size of the agricultural workforce, the increased employment in that sector actually amounted to an increase in labor hoarding; a finding confirmed by the Agricultural Census of 1996, from which it has been estimated that there are approximately 890,000 workers (of whom 54 per cent are of working age) who are effectively idle on Poland's farms (Kowalska, 1999).

Table 4.9 Selected Polish Employment Indicators: 1989–1998[1]

Variables	1989	1990	1991	1992	1993	1994	1995	1996	1997	1998
Employment ('000)	17746	16485	15772	15357	15118	15282	15486	15842	16229	16174
Non-agricultural employment ('000)	13879	12276	12153	11802	11562	11565	11569	11768	12155	12044
Employment by Sector (%):										
Agriculture	29.3	30.1	29.5	26.8	26.7	27.2	27.0	28.2	27.5	27.4
Industry	35.5	33.3	32.0	31.9	30.6	30.6	30.4	27.7	29.5	28.8
Services	35.4	36.6	38.5	41.3	42.2	42.2	42.6	44.1	43.0	43.8
Employment by Ownership (%):										
Public	54.3	51.0	45.7	44.0	41.1	39.4	37.6	34.9	31.8	29.3
Private	45.7	49.0	54.3	56.0	58.9	60.6	62.4	65.1	68.2	70.7

[1] The employment data relate to December 31st and exclude employment in the Ministry of Internal Affairs, the Ministry of Defence and the State Security Agency.

Source: GUS (1992, 1995, 1997, 1998c); own calculations; Kotowska and Kowalska (2000).

Outside agriculture, employment change differed considerably across industries. In the years 1990–1993, the strongest declines were observed in manufacturing, construction and transport and, in total, these branches of the economy were responsible for 75 per cent of the overall fall in non-agricultural employment. Over the same time period, relatively large reductions were also observed in education, health care, culture and arts, sports and recreation, while employment in agriculture declined more slowly. Services such as wholesale and retail trade, state administration and justice, finance and insurance experienced growing employment from the beginning of the reforms. For the period 1994–1996, employment increased in all branches of activity, except mining (Kowalska, 1999). The result is that the main shifts in employment by broad economic sector can be characterized, as shown in Table 4.9, by a decline in the share of industrial employment, a rise in the share of services and an increase in the percentage of jobs accounted for by agriculture. The latter plays the role of a buffer for shedded labor that cannot be absorbed by other sectors.

Changes in employment structure during the period of transformation have differed by gender, although no change has been observed in either agriculture or industry, where males continue to account for approximately 54 and 68 per cent of the workforces, respectively. This can be explained by parallel declines in male-dominated branches of the economy (heavy industry) and in those branches which employ predominately women (light industry). The upward trend in female participation in services has stopped—mainly due to the decrease in female employment in retailing and state administration—and it accounted for 21.7 per cent of total female employment in 1995. The most feminized areas of activity are health care (82.7%) and education (75.6%), which together account for one-fifth of total female employment (Kotowska, 1996).

Marked change has also been evident in the employment structure by ownership sector and status. In Poland's centrally planned economy, the private sector was mainly composed of agricultural undertakings but, in 1998, 71 per cent of all in work were to be found outside the public sphere. Changes in employment by status are manifested by the considerable increases that have been observed in the numbers of those self-employed and, included amongst these, those acting as employers of others. In 1995, 15 per cent of men and 8 per cent of women were self-employed in urban areas while, in rural areas, self-employment accounts for about forty per cent of all employment (Kotowska, 1996).

Employment in the shadow economy is important in Poland. While this phenomenon also existed under the previous system, it then constituted work that was supplementary to official employment. Estimates of the labor force involved in some form of informal employment vary considerably (from several hundred thousand to several million people). According to the Yearbook of Labor 1997 (p. 21), between 805,000 and 850,000 persons held unregistered jobs during the years 1994–1996. More and more, unregistered work is becoming the main job (Kotowska and Witkowski, 1996). Recent evaluations based on the sample survey made in August 1998 under the regular wave of the Labor Force Survey (LFS) indicated that about 1.4 million persons were in informal employment. Those employed informally are also likely to register as unemployed, despite engaging in remunerated work (OECD, 1995). On the other hand, hidden unemployment is also a problem faced by the country, as intimated above: in particular, there are a significant number of agricultural workers who are recorded as being employed by the LFS but who are not in receipt of wages.

UNEMPLOYMENT

The most important change to affect the labor market in the past decade has been the emergence of open unemployment. Indeed, large-scale joblessness in Poland appeared during the first two years of the transition process, with unemployment rising from 55,700 in January 1990 to 2,156,000 in December 1991, as shown in Table 4.10. Over the next two years the rise was considerably slower, although by no means insignificant. Since 1994, the number of unemployed persons has been trended downwards and, in December 1997, the unemployment rate stood at 10.3 per cent.[4] However, the Table also shows that the downward trend has stopped and registered unemployment rose by over 500,000 during 1999, which returned the unemployment rate to its 1996 level of 13.0 per cent.

Several factors underlie the emergence of unemployment on such a large and unanticipated scale. First, there was a general decline in the demand for labor; second, there were inflows from out of the labor market. These factors are considered elsewhere (Ingham and Ingham, *this volume*) and will not be discussed further. Third, as described earlier, there was an increase in the population of working-age. Last, some of the unemployment was generated by the operation of labor market institutions, an issue that is worthy of elaboration.

Table 4.10 Selected Unemployment Indicators

Indicators	1990	1991	1992	1993	1994	1995	1996	1997	1998	1999
Unemployment ('000)[1]	1126	2156	2509	2890	2839	2629	2360	1826	1831	2350
Unemployment ('000)[2]	–	–	2394	2595	2375	2233	1961	1737	1827	–
Females as % of total unemp.[3]	50.9	52.6	53.6	52.2	52.7	55.1	58.4	60.4	58.5	55.6
School-leavers as % of total unemp.[4]	14.6	10.3	7.4	7.1	7.4	8.3	3.6	4.7	6.0	6.4
Unemployment rate[5]	6.5	12.2	14.3	16.4	16.0	14.9	13.2	10.3	10.4	13.0
Unemployment rate[6]	–	–	13.7	14.9	13.9	13.1	11.6	10.2	10.6	–
Inflows ('000)[7]	1595	1720	1560	1970	2094	2371	2225	2051	2128	2563
Outflows ('000s)	469	690	1207	1589	2145	2581	2494	2584	2123	2044

1 Registration data, 31st December.
2 LFS, November.
3 As note 1.
4 As note 1.
5 As note 1.
6 As note 2.
7 Registration data, flows for 1990 and 1991 estimated by Witowski (1994).
Source: *Registered Unemployment*, GUS, various issues; *Economic Activity in Poland*, GUS, various issues.

Especially during 1990 and 1991, observed changes in unemployment could not be attributed wholly to the process of labor market adjustment. For instance, a large inflow into unemployment of persons who were previously economically inactive contributed strongly to the dramatic rise of unemployment (Góra, 1996; Góra et al., 1995). At first, the relevant regulations included incentives to register as unemployed that are normally absent in developed economies. For example, the eligibility criteria did not refer to previous labor market status, unemployment benefits were open-ended in duration and few procedures were in place to record those who had actually left the unemployment register (which was just one symptom of the poor monitoring procedures in place at the time). Despite the gradual tightening of the eligibility criteria for unemployment benefits and improvements in the management of the system, some groups who initially registered as unemployed remain as members of the long-term unemployed, notwithstanding their unavailability for work. Evidence for the existence of this phenomenon can be obtained by comparisons between unemployment rates from the unemployment register and from the LFS. It has been shown that the differences result mostly from different numbers of long-term unemployed in the two sets of statistics (Góra et al., 1995). The share of long-term unemployment in the total registration count as of December 1996 was about 42 per cent, while the LFS for November 1996 returned a figure of 40 per cent.

The probability of being unemployed varies by gender, age, place of residence and educational attainment. Young persons under 35 years of age, persons with low-level skills (the majority of whom have no more than a basic vocational education), persons living in urban areas and women are the groups most exposed to the threat of unemployment. Despite the high incidence of unemployment among young people, their chances of leaving the jobless pool have improved, especially in the case of males, and the share of unemployed persons under 35 years of age has declined gradually, from 64 per cent in December 1992 to 58 per cent in December 1999. The rising value attached to educational attainment in the new marketized economy can be illustrated by the fact that 67 per cent of the unemployed had no more than basic vocational education in December 1991, while eight years later that proportion had increased to 71 per cent.

For women, there is a higher risk of becoming unemployed and remaining so than is the case for men. The prevalence of women amongst the unemployed has been a consistent feature of the data since the middle of 1990. In December 1999, women constituted 55.6 per cent of the total unemployed, in spite of the fact that since 1992, when flows started to be registered, male inflows were greater than those for women.[5] The explanation of this apparent contradiction is that women exhibit considerably lower outflows from the pool than do men. Estimates of the probabilities of falling into and out of unemployment, based on panel data from the LFS, have confirmed this pattern (Góra, et al. 1995a). The risk of long-term unemployment also varies by sex: in December 1999, the percentage of each sex who were long-term unemployed was 28 per cent for men and 47 per cent for women. Inflows to employment are similarly gender-related and reveal that women experience more difficulty entering the labor market and returning to work (Kotowska, 1996). The much lower mobility of unemployed women is due both to individual characteristics and to employers' attitudes. Unfavorable changes in the social infrastructure (e.g. in the organization of pre-school and primary education, in declining access to child-care facilities, etc.) limit women's ability to combine paid work and family duties.

Spatial differentials in labor market developments are a distinctive feature of the transformation process in Poland and the evidence suggests that the differences will not be transient (Kwiatkowski et al., 1992; Góra and Lehmann, 1995; GUS, 1995a; Kwiatkowski et al., 1995; Kotowska and Podogrodzka, 1995; OECD, 1995). There are several reasons for the marked disparities, some of which can be related to the economic development of regions and to the role of specific industries in local economies and the associated degree of industrial specialization, in particular. These factors, stemming from spatial industrial history, have been compounded by the progress of the economic reforms undertaken to date. The contraction in aggregate demand and consequent fall in employment were experienced unevenly across regions, while advances in privatization, levels of labor mobility and wage differences have all varied across space.

The distribution of unemployment in Poland has its origins in the early transition years of 1990 and 1991. Despite the steady increase in total unemployment until the end of 1993, there was little change in the ranking of voivodships by unemployment over time (Kotowska and Podogrodzka, 1995), as shown in Table 4.11.[6] Moreover, there are indications that the unfavorable situation in some regions and the favorable one in others, as characterized both by unemployment rates and by the associated inflow and outflow rates, has stabilized. This lends support to the view that market mechanisms alone are not able to reduce existing regional imbalances and that some form of state intervention is needed, particularly in regions of high and stagnant unemployment (OECD, 1995).

Table 4.11 Voivodships with the Highest and Lowest Unemployment Rates (UNR): 1991–1998[1,2]

Year	The Highest Rate	The Lowest Rate
December 1991	UNR ≥ 17.0	UNR ≤ 8.2
	Suwalskie (B)	Wrocławskie (F)
	Olsztyńskie (G)	Katowickie (D)
	Koszalińskie (G)	Krakowskie (F)
	Słupskie (G)	Poznańskie (F)
	Wałbrzyskie (D)	Warszawskie (F)
	Ciechanowskie (B)	
December 1994	UNR ≥ 27.0	UNR ≤ 13.0
	Suwalskie (B)*	Bielskie (C)
	Olsztyńskie (G)*	Katowickie (D)*
	Koszalińskie (G)*	Krakowskie (F)*
	Słupskie (G)*	Poznańskie (F)*
	Wałbrzyskie (D)*	Warszawskie (F)*
December 1996	UNR ≥ 23.6	UNR ≤ 9.7
	Suwalskie (B)*	Wrocławskie (F)*
	Olsztyńskie (G)*	Katowickie (D)*
	Koszalińskie (G)*	Krakowskie (F)*
	Słupskie (G)*	Poznańskie (F)*
	Elbląskie (G)	Warszawskie (F)*
December 1998	UNR ≥ 18.0	UNR ≤ 7.3
	Słupskie (G)*	Katowickie (D)*
	Suwalskie (B)*	Gdańskie (F)
	Elbląskie (G)*	Krakowskie (F)*
	Koszalińskie (G)*	Poznańskie (F)*
	Wałbrzyskie (D)	Warszawskie (F)*

[1] The letters in the brackets are the regional groupings proposed by Scarpetta and Huber (1995).

[2] A '*' indicates that a voivodship was in the same group in the preceeding time period.

Source: Updated from Kotowska and Podogrodzka (1995).

The highest levels of unemployment are found mostly in voivodships in the industrialized regions and in those with a relatively underdeveloped industrial infrastructure, while the lowest levels are observed in agricultural regions and those with a varied industrial complexion (Góra and Lehmann, 1995; Kotowska and Podogrodzka, 1995). Labor markets with the highest unemployment rates are, in general, more threatened by long-term unemployment, although less developed agricultural regions also experienced this combination of adverse circumstances. In an attempt to diminish these inequalities, a great number of labor market related initiatives have been undertaken at both the regional level and below for different specific purposes. However, despite some attempts to encourage activity in 'crisis regions' (supported at the national level through tax breaks and preferential loans for investment, for example), the disparities remain. A recent suggestion aimed at trying to offset this differentiation (subsequently acted upon) was that 'economic zones', with significant privileges for investment, as well as for launching specific developments, should be established.[7]

The official unemployment regulations have been subject to considerable adjustment and re-adjustment over the years 1990–99. These changes have related to qualifying conditions; waiting periods; reasons for disqualification; eligibility criteria for benefit, its duration and rate. In short, all have been oriented towards reducing the disincentives to work. Yet despite the fact that the system has become increasingly strict in terms of registration, ongoing registration, entitlement to unemployment benefit, access to training, etc., problems still exist because of interactions between these regulations and those of the wider social security system. For instance, the relatively rapid increase in registered unemployment observed since December 1998 may be related partly to changes in the health care system introduced in January 1999, as a result of which health insurance tax is now paid from the Labor Fund for those on the unemployment register.

CONCLUDING REMARKS

There are now signs that the positive labor market developments of recent years, reflected in the decline in unemployment, have come to an end. The future trajectory of this key indicator will depend mainly upon demographic trends, the rate of economic growth, the progress in restructuring the coal and steel sectors, the pace of agricultural reform and upon reforms in the social security system, education and health care. Each of these are likely to be associated with further adverse shocks to the labor market.

The supply of labor will continue to increase in the coming years, with Poland's labor force expected to rise until 2010. Its rate of growth is one of the highest in Europe, accounting for about 25 per cent of the total increase projected for the continent as a whole. At the same time, a further slowdown in the country's economic growth (in 1997 GDP rose by 6.8 per cent while in 1998 and 1999 the figures were 4.8 and 4.1 per cent, respectively) can be expected, both for internal reasons (a drop in economic activity, a worsening of the economic situation of firms, a reduction in the growth of consumption and insufficient competitiveness of the economy) and on account of external factors (a reduction in the economic growth of European countries). Both the LFS data for November 1998 and the registration data for February 1999 show a decline in the demand for labor and the associated employment decrease is reflected in a drop of both employment rates and labor force participation rates (GUS 1999a, GUS 1999b, GUS 2000a). Group layoffs increased in 1999 and further declines in employment can be expected to follow from the reforms in the education and health care sectors, with individuals previously working in these areas now beginning to register as unemployed. The rise in unemployment is confirmed by more recent data; at the end of March 2000, the rate of registered unemployment was 13.9 per cent and the unemployment stock stood at 2,533,600 (GUS 2000a). The continued restructuring of the mining and steel sectors, together with the increasingly urgent need for agricultural reform, suggest that a reversal in the current upward trend of unemployment is unlikely in the near future.

Recent and impending reforms of the social security and health care systems will undoubtedly affect behavior on the labor market. It can be expected that changes in the pension system will create new incentives to work. According to the new regulations, contributions to pension funds are obligatory for persons under 30 years, while persons aged between 30 and 50 years can decide on either shared contributions to the Social Insurance Institution (ZUS) and to pension funds or on contributions paid entirely to ZUS. Older persons have to rely totally on ZUS pensions, collected according to new rules. A clear and strict link between formal employment and pensions, non-existent under the old system, has been created. This could motivate workers to prefer formal jobs and some flows from informal employment to registered work might be expected. On the other hand, contributions to the health care system can be covered from the salaries of those in work and from the Labor Fund for those without a job. This creates some incentive for people to register at the labor office, even if they are not interested in taking a job. As noted above, this reaction to the new regulations has already been observed.

Adjustments to the conditions prevailing in the labor market under the transformation process have resulted in the need to distinguish a phenomenon labeled as 'transitional unemployment' (Boeri, 1994). Its important features include remarkable spatial differentials across regional labor markets, combined with a low level of mobility of the labor force. Very low unemployment turnover rates, due to marked regional and occupational mismatch, recruitment policies resulting in job-to-job flows and the hiring of new entrants indicate that long-term unemployment and the pushing of workers out of the labor force are serious threats. In fact, even in a situation of rising flexibility, the flows into and out of unemployment observed recently reinforce the concern that long-term unemployment and recurrent spells of joblessness are becoming more and more important. At the same time, it must be recognized that outflows from unemployment are not synonymous with moves to a job. The percentage of the unemployed taking up work is not high, accounting for only about 50 per cent of the total outflow from the pool. Moreover, many persons return to the register, with re-entrants constituting 43 per cent of those newly registered in 1994, a figure which increased to 70 per cent in 1997 and to 71 per cent in the last quarter of 1999.

Regional inequalities remain stable despite attempts to improve capabilities to cope with the problems arising from the transformation process, such as the creation of 'economic zones'. It seems that in order to reduce regional differences in the labor market, more complex policies aimed at influencing labor force mobility are required. As such, the development of transport and communication networks, together with improvements in the housing situation, have to be considered, along with improvements to regional infrastructures and educational provision. The housing shortage is estimated currently at 1.5 million flats although, if EU standards are taken into account, the figure increases to approximately two million (GCSS, 1998). Change in rural areas is especially necessary, particularly from the perspective of Poland's potential integration into the EU. The necessary restructuring of the agricultural sector will release large segments of the rural labor force but, because of the difficult housing situation, outflows to urban regions cannot be regarded as a realistic way of relieving the associated pressures on the labor market. Therefore, productive reallocation of the rural labor force will depend upon the development of a non-agricultural sector in the countryside. At the same time, the low level of human capital embedded in the rural population, including its younger generations, will be an obstacle to the movement of workers to urban areas and to the kind of new industry that can be operated successfully within the rural regions themselves.

In general, education is a crucial determinant of the ability to adjust to the new labor market conditions prevailing in Poland. The gap between the types of skills now demanded and those which many in the population can supply is still large, as well as differentiated spatially. Yet the rising costs of education, in conjunction with the uneven development of education centers in different regions, create inequalities of access for different segments of population. Reforms to the educational system alongside proper financial regulations are needed if these inequalities are to be diminished.

NOTES

1 In urban areas this phenomenon had been observed once before, in 1963.

2 The 49 voivodships were classified into the following types by Scarpetta and Huber (1995):
1—developed agricultural regions (3 voivodships)
2—less developed agricultural regions (17 voivodships)
3—more developed heavily industrialized regions (6 voivodships)
4—less developed heavily industrialized regions (6 voivodships)
5—developed diversified regions (7 voivodships)
6—underdeveloped regions (10 voivodships).

3 In Poland's centrally planned economy the labor force participation rate referred to the so-called 'economically active population'—a category that corresponds to employment in current statistics. Therefore, for purposes of comparison, labor force participation rates based on the Population Census of 1988 and the Microcensus of 1995 as well as employment rates should be calculated.

4 There is an opinion that the outflows in 1996 could, to some extent, have been accounted for by the more restrictive de-registration procedures introduced in the first half of the year. However, CSO data show that outflows to jobs increased by 36,800 while inflows to registration declined by 146,000, compared to 1995. Changes in the regulations in 1997 might have diminished the incentives for registration: in 1997 outflows to jobs declined by 45,600 while inflows to registration declined by 174,000, compared to 1996 (based on Registered Unemployment in Poland, I–IV Quarter 1997, Warsaw, 1998, see also Table 4.8).

5 Data from the LFS also confirm the predominance of females amongst the unemployed.

6 Voivodships represent the regional ties of administration in Poland. Their number was reduced from 49 to 16 by the local government reform that came into being at the beginning of 1999.

7 Up to 1998, twelve 'economic zones' had been established.

REFERENCES

Boeri, T. (1994) "Transitional' unemployment," *The Economics of Transition*, vol. 2, no. 2, pp. 1–25.

GCSS (1998) (Government Center for Strategic Studies) *Sfera społeczna w Polsce. Przesłnki rozwoju* (Social sphere in Poland. Development premises), Warszawa: GCSS.

Góra, M. (1996) "The Labour Market in Poland: 1990–1995. Empirical and Methodological Studies," *Monografie i Opracowania*. no. 421, Warsaw School of Economics: Warszawa.

Góra, M. and H. Lehmann (1995) "How Divergent is Regional Labour Market Adjustment in Poland?", in: OECD (ed.).

Góra, M., M.W. Socha and U. Sztanderska (1995) "Zachowania bezrobotnych na rynku pracy. System rejestracji bezrobotnych i zasiłek dla bezrobotnych. Wpły w na zachowania na rynku pracy" (Behaviors of the unemployed in the labour market. unemployment registration and benefits), Zeszyty Centrum im. Adama Smitha, no. 5, September.

Góra, M., M.W. Socha and U. Sztanderska (1995a) "Analiza polskiego rynku pracy w latach 1990–1994: kierunki zmian i rola polityk rynku pracy" (An analysis of the Polish labor market in 1990–1994. The direction of changes and the role of labor market policies), Warsawa: Central Statistical Office Ministry of Labor and Social Policy.

GUS (1992) *Zatrudnienie w Gospodarce Narodowej 1991* (Employment in national economy in 1991), Warszawa: Główny Urząd Statystyczny.

GUS (1995) *Rocznik Statystyczny Pracy 1995* (Yearbook of labor), Warszawa: Główny Urząd Statystyczny.

GUS (1995a) *Regionalne zróżnicowanie rynku pracy w Polsce w latach 1989–1993* (Regional differentials of the labor market in Poland in the years 1989–1993), Warszawa: Główny Urząd Statystyczny.

GUS (1996) *Demographic Yearbook*, Warszawa: Główny Urząd Statystyczny.

GUS (1997) *Rocznik Statystyczny Pracy 1997* (Yearbook of labor), Warszawa: Główny Urząd Statystyczny.

GUS (1998) *Basic Information on Poland's Demographic Development*, Warszawa: Główny Urząd Statystyczny.

GUS (1998a) *Rocznik Demograficzny* (Demographic yearbook 1998), Warszawa: Główny Urząd Statystyczny.

GUS (1998b) *Podstawowe informacje o rozwoju demograficznym Polski. Zmiany demograficzne w okresie transformacji społeczno-ekonomicznej w latach 1989–1997* (Basic information on Poland's demographic development. Demographic changes under the socio-economic transformation in 1989–1997), Warszawa: Główny Urząd Statystyczny.

GUS (1998c) *Zatrudnienie w Gospodarce Narodowej 1997* (Employment in national economy in 1997), Warszawa: Główny Urząd Statystyczny.

GUS (1999) *Main Trends in Economy in 1998, Poland in Statistics*, Warszawa: Główny Urząd Statystyczny.

GUS (1999a) *Labour Market Monitoring*, February, Warszawa: Główny Urząd Statystyczny.

GUS (1999b) *Labour Market Monitoring*, April. Warszawa: Główny Urząd Statystyczny.

GUS (1999c) *Basic Information on Poland's Demographic Development.* Warszawa: Główny Urząd Statystyczny.

GUS (1999d) *Rocznik Demograficzny 1999* (Demographic yearbook 1999). Warszawa: Główny Urząd Statystyczny.

GUS (2000) *Prognoza lunności Plski według województw na lata 1999–2030* (Population forecasts for Poland by voivodship for the years 1999–2030). Warszawa: Główny Urząd Statystyczny.

GUS (2000a) *Biuletyn Statystyczny* (Statistical bulletin), no. 4, May. Warszawa: Główny Urząd Statystyczny.

Ingham, H. and M. Ingham (2001) "Gender and Labor Market Change: What Do the Official Statistics Show?", *this volume.*

Jaźwińska, E. and M. Okólski (eds) (1996) "Causes and Consequences of Migration from Central and Eastern Europe. Podlasie and Śląsk Opolski: Basic Trends in 1975–1994," Warszawa: Fridrich Ebert Stiftung.

Kotowska, I.E. (1996) "Women in the Polish Labour Market—Are They Benefiting from Economic Recovery?", paper prepared for the Eighth Annual Conference of EALE, Crete, September 1996.

Kotowska, I.E. and A. Kowalska (2000) "Labour Market," in: *Poland: International Economic Report 1999/2000*, Warsaw: Warsaw School of Economics.

Kotowska, I.E. and M. Podogrodzka (1995) "Spatial differences of Labour Market Developments in Poland", paper prepared for the Seventh Annual Conference of EALE, Lyon, September 1995.

Kotowska, I.E. and J. Witkowski (1996) "Labour Market Developments and Demographic Processes in Countries making the Transition to a Market Economy," *Studia Demograficzne*, nos.1–2/123–124, pp. 55–81.

Kotowska, I.E., R. Serek R., and P. Toński (1998) "Regionalne zróżnicowanie płodności i małżeńskości w Polsce, 1989–1997" (Regional differences in fertility and nuptiality in Poland, 1989–1997), mimeo, Institute of Statistics and Demography, Warsaw School of Economics, Warszawa.

Kowalska, A. (1999) "Zmiany na rynku pracy w okresie transformacji" (Changes in the labor market under the transition), in: I.E.Kotowska (ed.), *Demographic Changes in Poland in the 1990s from the Perspective of the Second Demographic Transition*, Warsaw: Warsaw School of Economics.

Kozłowski T.K. (1994) "Poland: Between Transit, Asylum Seeking and Immigration," paper prepared for the seminar: "Hearing on the Situation of Refugees and Asylum Seekers in Central and Eastern Europe," May 16, Warsaw.

Kwiatkowski, E., H. Lehmann and M.E. Schaffer (1992) "Bezrobocie i wolne miejsca pracy a struktura zatrudnienia w Polsce" (Unemployment, vacancies and pre-reform employment structure in Poland, an regional analysis), *Ekonomista* no. 2, pp. 229–246.

Kwiatkowski, E., T. Janusz and V. Steiner (1995) "Unemployment in light industry regions," in: OECD (ed.).

Lesthaeghe, R. (1991) "The Second Demographic Transition in Western Countries: An Interpretation," *IPD Working Papers*, 1991–2, Brussels.

Macura, M. (1995) "Fertility and Nuptiality Changes in Central and Eastern Europe: 1982–1993," *Studia Demograficzne*, no. 4/122, pp. 9–34.

OECD (ed.) (1995) *The Regional Dimension of Unemployment in Transition Countries*, A Challenge for Labour Market and Social Policies, OECD: Paris.

Okólski, M. (1996) "Czynniki zmian mobilności siły roboczej" (Factors of labour force mobility) in: M. Okólski and U.Sztanderska (eds), *Studia nad reformowaną gospodarką. Aspekty instytucjonalne* (Studies on economy undergoing reforms. Institutional aspect), Warszawa: Wydawnictwo Naukowe PWN.

Scarpetta, S. and P. Huber (1995) "Regional economic structures and unemployment in Central and Eastern Europe: an attempt to identify common patterns," in: OECD (ed.).

Stola, D. (1997) "Rodzaje i mechanizmy migracji zarobkowych do Polski" (Types and rules of job migration), Working Papers of Institute for Social Studies, Warszawa: Warsaw University, Migration Studies, No. 8.

Tabeau E. (1996) "Mortality in Poland in 1989–1993: A Response to Economic Reforms?", *Studia Demograficzne*, nos. 1–2/123–124, pp. 13–37.

Van de Kaa, D.J. (1987) "Europe's Second Demographic Transition," *Population Bulletin*, vol. 42, no.1, Population Reference Bureau: Washington D.C.

Van de Kaa D. J. (1994) "The Second Demographic Transition Revisited: Theories and Expectations, 1993," in: G.C.N. Beets, R.L. Cliquet, G. Dooge and J. de Jong Gierveld (eds), *Population and Family in the Low Countries 1993. Late Fertility and Other Current Issues*, Amsterdam: NIDI—CBGS Publications, Swets & Zeitlinger B.V.

Witkowski, J. (1994) "Podstawowe cechy bezrobocia w Polsce w okresie transformacji" (Unemployment in Poland in the period of transition), Warszawa: GUS.

CHAPTER 5

SOCIAL MOBILITY IN SIX EAST EUROPEAN NATIONS

It is clearly important to understand the effects of systemic transition in Eastern Europe on the relative occupational attainments of females and this chapter seeks to assess the dynamics of the mobility rates of women and men during the 1990s in the region. The ultimate concern is to establish whether the passage from communism has transformed the processes by which women are allocated to different positions on the labor market. Patterns of social mobility follow their own logic, which need not necessarily respond to institutional transformations, even if these are systemic in nature. If reform has impacted upon mobility, it might reasonably be expected that the evidence would have emerged early in the process, when there was a marked change in socio-occupational structures. The rapid expansion of the private sector after 1989 is of particular importance, as this should have engendered a mass inflow to the class of owners and thereby served to increase overall mobility. In 1994, owners accounted for 10.4 per cent of all actively employed persons in Poland, compared to only 4.3 per cent in 1988 and the present analysis will pay particular attention to this phenomenon, which is an important element of the formation of new social strata in the post-communist period.

The view is widely held that the prime objective of comparative macro-sociology must be to demonstrate differences in aspects of the social structure across nations and then to account for these differences by analyses in which the societies under study serve as the basic units of observation. However, studies have found little systematic cross-national variation in any of the measures of mobility that are commonly employed (Goldthorpe, 1987). Put slightly differently, any variation in mobility that does exist has not been found to be attributable to differences in, for example, the level of economic development or to the existence of democracy versus totalitarianism in the political system (see Grusky and Hauser, 1984; Erikson and Goldthorpe, 1992). The evidence for such relationships found in, for example, Tyree et al. (1979) has been challenged by recent national mobility enquiries that have introduced higher standards of data comparability (Erikson and Goldthorpe, 1992). Further, time-series analyses have emphasized the absence of uni-directional trends in mobility (Featherman and Hauser, 1978; Ganzeboom and de Graaf, 1984; Yamaguchi, 1987; Payne 1993). Nevertheless, it remains to be established whether these results are applicable to post-communist societies. In particular, all of these past findings track social movements in stable societies that were not in the process of systemic changes, while the East European countries have a distinctly different set of experiences. The pertinent question in the latter setting is whether mobility rates altered markedly in the early stages of the creation of a new social order and, if they did, whether the trend is towards greater openness, typified by an increased flow into the expanding 'old middle-class' of proprietorship.

The basic question of concern here is whether occupational mobility barriers came down for women as much as they did for men. Increasingly flexible labor markets are offering up the kinds of employment that promise either to enrich or to threaten the status of women in society. Under the old regime, a high level of female labor force participation was ensured by a dominant creed that emphasized the right to work, coupled with the ideology of equal opportunity, regardless of social origin and sex. At the same time, generous maternity provision and child-care facilities, in combination with economic necessity, encouraged females to work. The onset of systemic transformation brought a marked shift in these parameters, with the retreat from the state, coupled with budget-driven reductions in child-care facilities, increasing the weight of the 'double-burden' of bearing both domestic and market responsibilities. Furthermore, in Poland, the Catholic model of the family places women in the home and there have been renewed calls for women to withdraw from the market and return to their traditional role. On the other hand, falling real wages in the early years of transition rendered the two-income family no less necessary than in the past. The task is therefore to investigate the extent to which women have borne a disproportionate share of the costs of transition through a reduction in their labor market opportunities.

While institutional forces have been set in motion that seem capable of unleashing massive movements in the division of labor, this is not without precedent in the recent history of Poland and the other countries which found themselves in the communist camp in the years following World War II. Then the communist leaders initiated major reconstructions of the social order no less radical than those taking place in the 1990s. What appeared crucial at the time was rapid industrialization, driven centrally by the state, nationalization of manufacturing, transport and the majority of private firms in other industries and, starting from late 1940s, collectivization of private farms. These measures virtually forced the transfer of manpower from agriculture to heavy industry, while large numbers of workers and peasants were promoted to positions in governmental and industrial bureaucracies.

It is useful to recall the implications of these earlier structural changes for the composition of specific classes in Poland. As of the early 1970s, men of farm and of working-class origins formed 30 and 26 per cent, respectively, of the non-manual workforce (Zagórski, 1978, p. 132). Indeed, Erikson and Goldthorpe (1992, p. 101) found that the two most rigid barriers to mobility—namely those separating the intelligentsia from manual workers and farmers—were either almost nonexistent in Poland or were much weaker than in any of the eight other nations included in their study. Yet both barriers were apparent in Hungary, which underwent a similar trajectory of socialist transformation in the early post-war era. Nevertheless, even though it would appear that policies directed towards shaping new hierarchies and patterns of mobility were able to work in Poland and resulted in the temporary weakening of social rigidities, strict limitations were placed on individual entrepreneurship and, while private firms continued to exist, they did so only in vestigial forms.

Sight must not be lost of the duality between the 'phenotypical' perspective, with its focus on actually observed mobility rates, and the 'genotypical' perspective, which looks to the pattern of relative mobility chances (also referred to as 'social fluidity') underlying these rates (see Featherman et al., 1975). If mobility is considered at the former level, changes can easily be anticipated—precisely because observed rates are greatly influenced by the division of labor and, in turn, by effects deriving from a range of economic, technological and demographic circumstances that are known to vary through time. As far as mobility net of all such effects is concerned, the thesis of basic invariance in fluidity patterns through time also received empirical support in communist societies. Numerous studies of long-term trends carried out in Poland, Czechoslovakia, former East Germany, Russia and Hungary in the

1980s indicated that mobility regimes had not altered in a substantive way over recent decades and, furthermore, conformed to the patterns detected in the West (see Haller and Mach, 1984; Andorka, 1990; Boguszak, 1990; Marshall et al., 1995; Marshall, 1996). But, such findings do not remove the need to examine the consequences of the 'second transformation'. Did it give rise to any change in the dynamics of social mobility? Did mobility barriers fall more for men than for women? And is it true that the inflow into proprietorship impacted heavily on these transitions for both sexes?

WHAT MIGHT CHANGE?

Social mobility tables reflect both the relative chances of movement and the constraints imposed upon these by occupational origins and opportunities. Sociologists have recognized for some time this duality and have attempted to distinguish total movements between socio-occupational categories—which include both structural constraints and opportunities—from relative rates, also referred to as 'circulation', 'exchange', or 'pure' mobility. The latter encapsulate mobility rates net of changing distributions of origin and destination categories. Analyses of these two aspects of mobility address somewhat different theoretical and substantive issues. While total (absolute) rates can be used to map configurations of basic social distances, as determined both by factors influencing movement and those reflecting the 'inheritance' of positions, relative rates refer to the openness of specific social strata and of the social structure globally.

Previous mobility studies covering long periods of time reported changes in total movements over decades (Glass, 1954; Svalastoga, 1958; Featherman and Hauser, 1978). It was convincingly shown that these changes, insofar as they took place, were 'phenotypical' in kind; that is, they were mediated by a wide variety of economic, technological, demographic and political influences that were largely exogenous to the dynamics of social stratification *per se*. Above all, they derived chiefly from transformations of origin and destination categories. The driving force behind the occupational transformations in western countries after World War II was the prevailing economic boom. Its counterpart in Eastern Europe was the mass mobility associated with extensive industrialization, although this was quickly followed, perhaps as early as the 1960s (Andorka and Zagórski, 1980), by a decline in total mobility flows. However, the transformations in the economic and political systems underway in the 1990s might be expected to have occasioned a new growth in mobility. Given that the intention is to establish the effects of these institutional changes, the period immediately preceding the fall of communism represents a good referential base. As such, this study will compare and contrast mobility rates over the period 1983–1988 with those observed over the years 1988–1993.

It is only to be expected that mobility would increase in the 1990s as a result of structural change associated with systemic transformation, a process that has witnessed the emergence of both new jobs and new skills. Development of the capitalist market in post-communist societies has produced an expansion of the financial sector, banking, marketing and a wide area of personal services. Occupational roles have emerged that had no counterpart in the communist economy. For example, the growth of private security firms that, in Poland, employed some 200,000 persons in 1996 represents a quite new sector of activity that, in terms of numerical size, was the third largest broad occupational category, after teachers and miners. There was also a rapid expansion in the ownership of private businesses. However, there is little sign that the occupational structure is becoming less stratified by sex: the only high-status occupations that were previously the preserve of males and into which women have made significant inroads have been professions such as school teaching and some medical jobs.

In studies of social mobility, changes in the occupational distribution are referred to as the 'demand' side of the process governing the flow of persons through the life cycle during which newly created positions tend to 'attract' mobile persons. The 'supply' side consists of the relative advantages afforded to individuals by their different class origins; advantages which may be characterized in terms of their economic, cultural and social resources. In the interplay of supply and demand in the 1990s, the expansion of business may be attributed a decisive role. Representatives of the intelligentsia, the working class and farmers all witnessed the tangible effects of the growing opportunities to succeed that emerged in business, while middle-class women are entering occupations such as accountancy. After 1989, entrepreneurial orientations and possessive individualism found an outlet that was blocked both by administrative obstacles and systemic design under communism.

New patterns of mobility might also result from the changing educational system and the new forms of training for jobs that have emerged, with the rules of the capitalist market tending to convert the general knowledge received in schools into practical skills. From the beginning of the 1990s, in Hungary, Poland and the Czech Republic, new vocational courses based on western models have been developed. Some of these have provided individuals with widened opportunities and encouraged them to embark upon different occupational career paths. But, as the newly emerging educational structures have been the subject of a certain amount of experimentation and modification, institutions that might release permanently higher mobility flows cannot yet be identified. Nevertheless, educational reform is a new element in a changing context that should reshape the opportunities contained within the occupational system. At the same time, there has been an increase in the range of bargaining strategies adopted by trade unions in their negotiations with employers over wages and the licensing of recruitment to firms (see Esping-Andersen et al., 1993). In Eastern Europe, new labor market mechanisms have begun to be consolidated and their effects on mobility have slowly been coming into play. However, it is a common observation that women are less willing than men to participate in industrial action and, even when in trade unions, women are less likely than men to hold positions of responsibility, thereby denying them a toe-hold in the upper echelons of the power structure.

Of course, it is important to compare not only different occupational groups but also to examine the situation within each of them separately. The latter exercise reveals that women (both professional and working class) fare badly in comparison with men in terms of their grades within occupations. Even where a woman and a man are doing what is classified as the same job, the man is often in a higher position, typically because he has been employed longer and so qualifies for a length-of-service award or because he holds a position of seniority. It seems therefore that the key to understanding the dynamics of sex inequality in the labor market lies not simply in 'horizontal' segregation but must also take into account 'vertical' segregation, where men perform work that is of more authority.

What students of sex inequality refer to as the 'glass-ceiling' became a popular characterization of the simple fact that women are excluded from positions of power and influence at work. While discrimination against females in their access to supervisory positions in some western countries has been subjected to close scrutiny (see Wolf and Fliegstein, 1979; Freeman, 1990; Jacobs, 1995), empirical studies of this kind have been completely absent in the post-communist societies. The novelty of the present analysis resides in its attempt to go beyond the traditional concerns of occupational mobility studies and to cast light on women's under-representation in supervisory positions. This is achieved by asking whether, at a time when labor markets in Eastern Europe have been changing rapidly, the disproportionate representation of men in the upper reaches of job ladders persists.

In the light of the foregoing discussion, this chapter will, in subsequent sections, address four specific issues. The first examines the impact of systemic change upon mobility rates under the expectation that these were higher between 1988 and 1993 than in the immediate period preceding the collapse of the communist system. It is predicted, on the basis of experience elsewhere with market systems, that the mobility rates of women remain lower than those of men. The second issue introduces the distinction between total and relative rates of mobility; the former refers to all movements across the occupational matrix, the second to transitions net of changes in the distribution of occupational categories (i.e. in the distribution of 'origins' and 'destinations'). While there are reasons to expect that the removal of planning prompted occupational mobility, it is possible that this resulted mainly from changes in the social structure consequent upon economic reform. In particular, the vast privatization and restructuring program in the region inevitably unleashed mobility flows while the social changes post-1989 were prompted by new macro-structural arrangements that were exogenous with respect to the logic of social stratification. In brief, the growth in absolute rates of transitions might have resulted from the changing occupational distributions implied by the increasing size of some socio-occupational segments and the decrease in the proportions accounted for by others. If this is the case, relative occupational mobility will have remained basically unchanged for both women and men.

This does not necessarily imply that the access of the sexes to supervisory positions has been unchanged. In particular, it might be expected that with growing competition on the labor market the position of women would deteriorate. That is, men benefit most from the installation of capitalist structures, both in terms of their higher rates of gross inflow to supervisory positions and in terms of their relative net chances of recruitment into these posts. This represents the third specific issue to be addressed below. Finally, in the transformation of communist societies into market-oriented democracies, the inflow to private business might be expected to exceed the inflows to other occupational strata for both women and men. This possibility will be considered against the background of the theoretical debates in the sociological literature regarding the formation of classes and strata.

DATA AND VARIABLES

The data to be analyzed come from national surveys carried out in six countries as a part of the international *Social Stratification in Eastern Europe after 1989* project. Using a questionnaire common to all countries, nationally representative samples of the population were surveyed in Bulgaria (N=4907), Czech Republic (N=5621), Hungary (N=4285), Russia (N=4732), Slovakia (N=4876), (in 1993) and, Poland (N=3520) (in 1994). More detailed information about the project and methodology can be found in Treiman (1994). In seeking to isolate the effect of systemic transformation on rates of mobility, comparisons were made between tables of transitions across occupational categories for the periods 1983–88 and 1988–1993, respectively. Any substantial differences in mobility rates between these two periods are regarded as indicative of changes in social stratification. It is a matter of further debate as to whether, and to what extent, these potential changes were affected by transformations in the political and economic systems, rather than deriving simply from the 'endogenous' logic of social structuration.

There is no obvious or non-controversial method for establishing which set of categories should provide the basis for empirical work of this kind. With respect to the analysis of occupational mobility per se, the class schema proposed by Erikson, Goldthorpe, and Portorarero (EGP) in various publications (see Erikson and Goldthorpe, 1992), utilized by many students of social stratification in recent years, has been adopted. The EGP scheme possesses a theoretical rationale, derived particularly from Marx and Weber, which endows it with a measure of internal consistency. Its aim is to differentiate positions within labor markets and production units according to the nature of the employment relations implied by them and, by such means, to highlight the salient features of mobility amongst the populations of modern industrial societies.

In its most expansive form, EGP consists of eleven class categories. However, the number of observations within some categories of the original schema provided by the current data set is too small to support statistical analysis, particularly in the case of proprietors with employees, proprietors working on their own and farmers. Bearing this in mind, the variant of EGP adopted in this study utilizes six class categories: (1) higher-grade professionals, administrators, officials, managers of large industrial establishments and large-scale proprietors (referred to, interchangeably, as the intelligentsia); (2) other non-manuals (i.e. lower-grade professionals, administrators, officials, higher-grade technicians, managers of small industrial establishments and routine non-manual employees in administration, commerce, sales and service); (3) small-scale non-agricultural owners with and without employees; (4) skilled workers; (5) unskilled workers, and (6) farmers and agricultural workers. Nonetheless, useful as such descriptions are for the purpose of identifying the terrain of occupational mobility, they fail to isolate movements in 'vertical segregation' by sex. In order to detect patterns of flows in the job authority ladder, women and men were categorized into: (i) higher supervisors (i.e. those having at least 10 subordinates); (ii) lower supervisors with 1–9 subordinates, and (iii) the rank-and-file or supervisees. The analysis of mobility between subordinates and supervisors had to be restricted to five countries, as the extent of unreported data for Slovakia rendered reliable estimations impossible.

TOTAL MOBILITY RATES IN THE 1980S AND 1990S

Two sets of figures were compared in order to address the question of whether mobility rates increased as a consequence of systemic change: the percentage of movers over the years 1983–1988 and over 1988–1993 (1994 for Poland), as reported separately for women and for men in Table 5.1. The percentages provided in that Table were calculated on the basis of 6 x 6 matrices of transitions between occupational categories over the course of the two time periods.[1] The rates of mobility are the percentages of women and men in the national samples found in the cells off the main diagonal of the arrays; in other words, the percentage of women and men whose 'present' or 'destination' category (in 1988 or 1993) was different from their category of 'origin'—the latter being indexed by the respondent's category in 1983 or in 1988.

It can be seen that total mobility increased in all six countries. Amongst men, mover rates were also higher in the later period than in the earlier one, and the same is true for women, except for the slight decline—from 12.2 per cent to 11.6 per cent—observed in Russia. In the five other countries, women's mobility increased, but at a slower pace than that of men. The earlier suggestion that the transformation would unleash large movements in the occupational structure is therefore confirmed. However, it is simultaneously of interest that, in marked contrast to later years, males exhibited lower mobility than women in the 1980s.

Table 5.1 Total Mobility Rates (between EGP Categories) 1983–1988 and 1988–1993: (%)

	Men		Women	
	1983–1988	1988–1993	1983–1988	1988–1993
Bulgaria	12.2	17.2	13.1	14.6
Czech Republic	8.1	23.6	12.1	22.3
Hungary	13.4	19.5	16.1	16.3
Poland	9.7	20.0	11.5	14.6
Russia	11.2	15.1	12.2	11.6
Slovakia	8.8	19.7	8.4	12.9

INTER-COUNTRY COMPARISONS

It is natural to inquire which country exhibited the most intense mobility dynamic. In the case of women, movement was greatest in the Czech Republic, where over one-fifth of respondents changed occupation between 1988 and 1993, a figure which is almost double that observed in Russia, a country with distinctive patterns of gendered social stratification. Differences in male mobility between countries were less marked although, as in the case of females, transition rates grew most strongly, and were at their highest, in the Czech Republic. Mobility was once again both lowest and trended least steeply in Russia. Overall, it would appear that the Czech Republic, Poland and Slovakia have experienced the highest total mobility rates, while these have been somewhat lower in Bulgaria and Russia.

PROMOTION

For purposes of highlighting the unequal opportunities on the labor market by sex, gender-based differences in promotion to supervisory positions might be of greater importance than total mobility rates. Therefore, Tables 5.2 and 5.3 present the distributions of women and men by their levels of supervisory authority, as revealed by the data for the years 1988 and 1993. The figures expose marked differences at the end of that period, with men being 3.5 times more likely than women to be supervisors of the highest level in Poland. Overall, the data reveal that men are approximately three times more likely than women to be supervisors of ten or more employees. Women in Russia, where the multiple in 1993 was 2.7, fared best on this score.

Table 5.2 Supervisors by Number of Supervisees: 1988 (%)

Number of People Supervised	Bulgaria		Czech Republic		Hungary		Poland		Russia	
	Women	Men	Women	Men	Women	Men	Women	Men	Women	Men
0	93.1	87.4	85.3	75.3	89.6	81.0	86.6	76.5	83.3	74.5
1–9	4.9	6.0	11.8	13.3	6.5	8.5	9.6	14.1	11.2	12.1
10 or more	2.0	6.5	2.9	11.4	3.8	10.5	3.8	9.4	5.4	13.4
Total	100.0	100.0	100.0	100.0	100.0	100.0	100.0	100.0	100.0	100.0

Table 5.3 Supervisors by Number of Supervisees: 1993 (%)

Number of People Supervised	Bulgaria		Czech Republic		Hungary		Poland		Russia	
	Women	Men	Women	Men	Women	Men	Women	Men	Women	Men
0	91.2	85.8	85.2	75.2	90.2	80.8	87.3	77.4	83.6	74.1
1–9	6.5	7.7	11.7	15.2	6.6	10.9	10.4	14.2	11.3	12.1
10 or more	2.3	6.5	3.0	9.6	3.2	8.3	2.4	8.4	5.1	13.8
Total	100.0	100.0	100.0	100.0	100.0	100.0	100.0	100.0	100.0	100.0

Notwithstanding the increase in mobility occasioned by the new liberalism, the evidence indicates that there remains considerable vertical segregation between the sexes. However, there was a widespread decline in the proportions of both sexes who were higher supervisors in the first years of economic upheaval, although the fall of over 36 per cent in the number of Polish higher supervisors was particularly large. On the other hand, while insufficient to overturn the overall impression of decline, there was no reduction in the proportions of higher cadres of either sex with over 10 subordinates in Bulgaria, such females in the Czech Republic or such males in Russia. The proximate reason for the decline in the numerical importance of top-level positions lies in the increased efficiency of economies exposed to the exigencies of the capitalist market. The result has been the rationalization of unwieldy bureaucracies and the consequent elimination of redundant supervisory tiers in order to reduce the operating costs of firms. More efficient or not, transformation has largely failed to reduce the gender-based vertical segregation in employment inherited from the communist period, although western experience provides little evidence to suggest that any other result could have been expected (see Siltanen, 1994).

In terms of the dynamics of gender divisions on the labor market, it may be concluded that, in the infancy of capitalism in Eastern Europe, the position of women generally did not improve, although developments in Czech society may be one exception. However, suggestive as the evidence may appear, descriptive statistics such as those presented here do not actually allow authoritative statements to be made regarding the chances of different groups to rise to the higher echelons of job authority. Table 5.4 therefore reports the percentages of women and men who moved during the periods 1983–1988 and 1988–1993 within the tripartite division of higher and lower supervisors and subordinates. The patterns revealed by the data suggest that the dynamics of mobility along the hierarchy of supervision paralleled the dynamics of occupational mobility between EGP strata revealed earlier. This leads to the conclusion that mobility between the basic segments of social stratification increased during the first stages of the transformation. This might have resulted from a mutual reinforcement between restructurations (Giddens, 1973) in the social space and from changing economic and political structures, although this remains a conjecture. Nevertheless, mobility barriers fell less for women than they did for men. Thus, while the rates of transition of women between subordinate and supervisory positions were greatest in Poland in the 1990s, they faced a dramatic decline in mobility in the Czech Republic from ten per cent in 1988 to 5.4 per cent in 1993.

Table 5.4 Total Mobility Rates in Hierarchy of Job Authority: 1983–1988 and 1988–1993 (%)[1]

	Men		Women	
	1983–1988	1988–1993	1983–1988	1988–1993
Bulgaria	3.8	9.9	1.8	3.5
Czech Republic	6.5	13.6	10.0	5.4
Hungary	6.2	10.8	4.9	6.7
Poland	8.3	12.0	4.7	7.4
Russia	11.2	6.9	6.9	6.6
Slovakia	n.a.	n.a.	n.a.	n.a.

[1] n.a.—data not available.

OPENNESS

Although the evidence presented above is suggestive, it remains necessary to establish whether the labor market opened up less for women than it did for men as a result of the rejection of communism. It has been demonstrated that there was a systematic cross-country pattern of increase in absolute mobility rates, as determined via both the EGP class schema and divisions into subordinates and supervisors, from which it might be inferred that shifts in the occupational structure prompted by the restructuring of the economic system were the underlying cause. But the importance of the changing structural context for trends in absolute mobility rates remains open to question. Put differently, have the differences in objective opportunity structures been the sole source of variation in the mobility chances of men and women, or have differences in underlying patterns of social fluidity (the association between the jobs held by women and men during their careers net of structural effects) also contributed? An answer to this question must confront the issue of how mobility trends would appear if they could, in some way, be assessed independently of this structural context. In studies of social mobility, these net rates, which control for changing occupational distributions, are regarded as more direct estimates of the openness of the social structure. Therefore attention will now focus on a detailed examination of the set of relative mobility chances—the 'mobility regime', as Hauser

(Featherman and Hauser, 1978) termed it. In this field, sociologists have used different approaches, although all of them rest on a distinction between 'structural' (also known as 'demand' or 'forced') mobility and 'exchange' ('circular,' 'pure' or 'relative') mobility. The former is defined as that part of total observed mobility that is attributable directly to changes in the structure of objective mobility opportunities and the latter as that part which is unassociated with such changes: a conceptual distinction that is adopted below.

Several writers have proposed approaches to the problem of controlling for structural change that draw upon the application of log-linear models to the analysis of multivariate contingency tables (Goodman, 1972; Hout, 1982; Ishii-Kuntz, 1994). Here, emphasis is placed on the popular constant fluidity model (CFM; Erikson and Goldthorpe, 1992) to compare mobility over the periods 1983–1988 and 1988–1993. As the name of the technique implies, the effects of origins and destinations vary in time while the association between them is constant; that is, it is assumed that there are variations in absolute mobility between 1983–1988 and 1988–1993, but constant relative mobility. Stated differently, changes in structural mobility are taken to account for all changes in total observed mobility.

If mobility regimes changed at the beginning of the 1990s it would be unprecedented, given that relative mobility rates were basically constant through time. But the basic question is whether the dynamics of the fluidity patterns of women differed from those of men. To this end, Table 5.5 contains results obtained from fitting four separate log-linear models to the fluidity rates of men and women, for each of the nations covered by this study, for the periods 1983–1988 and 1988–1993. The calculated G^2 statistics are given in the first row of each country's cell, with the diagnostic rG^2 statistics ($0 < rG^2 < 100$) being provided in the second row. The rG^2 is the 'coefficient of multiple determination' applied to log-linear modeling by Goodman (1972) and it indicates how much of the total association between class of origin and class of destination is accounted for by a model.

The first model tests the hypothesis of conditional independence of class origins and destinations. Usually this model is employed as a baseline, with reference to the rG^2 statistics providing an assessment of how much of the total association between class of origin and class of destination are explained by other models. The statistics of fit for the conditional independence model are shown in the first columns of Tables 5.5 and 5.6. The second columns report statistics for the model that assumes that the occupational distributions of origin and destination states were different for women and men, and that these changed between 1983–1988 and 1988–1993, while still maintaining that these categories were independent.

Table 5.5 Origin by Destination Category (EGP Categories) by Sex and Time: 1983–1988 and 1988–1993[1]

	Model				
	O D T	OTS DTS	OTS DTS OD	OTS DTS ODT	BIC for OTS DTS ODT
Bulgaria					–359
G^2	122986	10829	106	71	
rG^2	–	11.9	99.1	99.4	
p	0.00	0.00	0.01	0.01	
Czech Republic					–358
G^2	14381	11765	131	81	
rG^2	–	1.9	99.4	99.1	
p	0.00	0.00	0.00	0.01	
Hungary					–341
G^2	9995	8592	172	81	
rG^2	–	13.1	98.3	99.2	
p	0.00	0.00	0.00	0.01	
Poland					–336
G^2	9667	8247	131	77	
rG^2	–	14.7	98.6	99.2	
p	0.00	0.00	0.00	0.01	
Russia					–395
G^2	13119	11549	77	40	
rG^2	–	12.0	99.4	99.7	
p	0.00	0.00	0.00	0.01	
Slovakia					–353
G^2	14130	11933	154	82	
rG^2	–	15.5	98.9	99.4	
p	0.00	0.00	0.00	0.01	
df (all countries)	131	100	75	50	

[1] O—category of origin in 1983–88 and 1988–93 tables; D—category of destination in 1983–88 and 1988–93 tables; S—sex; T—time (1=1983–88, 2=1988–93).

The third column of Table 5.5 reports the results of fitting the CFM to the occupational mobility matrices of women and men for 1983–1988 and 1988–1993. The rG^2 returned for the CFM is never less than 98.3 (significant at the .05 level for all societies except Russia), signifying that relative occupational mobility remained practically unchanged in the period of transition from communism for both sexes. Nevertheless, the deviations for the five countries indicate that some marginal change did take place in fluidity patterns in the 1990s.[2] However, these were not the same for women and men—again with the exception of the Russian case—as demonstrated by the application of the final model, which allows for changes in fluidity across time, although which still assumes they are uniform for women and for men. There is, in other words, some indication that the higher total mobility rates for women and men between 1988 and 1993 do not reflect differences in the underlying change in relative rates, as shown in Table 5.1. These findings suggest that the higher rates of absolute occupational mobility in the 1990s derived not only from the discrepant opportunity structures facing women and men, but also from net exchange between occupational categories.

Table 5.6 Origin by Destination Category (Categories of Job Authority) by Sex and Time: 1983–1988 and 1988–1993[1]

	Model				
	O D T	OTS DTS	OTS DTS OD	OTS DTS ODT	BIC for OTS DTS ODT
Bulgaria					11
G^2	2807	2443	112	58	
rG^2	–	13.0	96.0	97.9	
p	0.00	0.00	0.00	>0.05	
Czech Republic					4
G^2	4296	3943	131	81	
rG^2	–	8.2	98.0	98.3	
p	0.00	0.00	0.00	>0.05	
Hungary					–61
G^2	2755	2758	29	6	
rG^2	–	7.2	98.9	99.8	
p	0.00	0.00	0.00	0.01	
Poland					–59
G^2	2684	2505	32	7	
rG^2	–	6.7	98.8	99.7	
p	0.00	0.00	0.00	0.01	
Russia					–57
G^2	4783	4501	24	13	
rG^2	–	5.9	99.5	99.7	
p	0.00	0.00	0.00	0.01	
df (all countries)	29	16	12	8	

[1] As for Table 5.5.

When the CFM is fitted to arrays of mobility tables between the three categories of subordinate, lower and upper supervisor, as in Table 5.6, the results with respect to the relative dynamics of mobility rates are broadly similar. However, the fact that the CFM postulating identical rates for 1983–1988 and 1988–1993 does not fit indicates that the same pattern of fluidity did not underlie the total movements of women and men over the whole period 1983–1993. Nonetheless, in Hungary, Poland, and Russia, a preponderant common element for both sexes is clearly indicated when controls are applied for changes in fluidity over time. In these three countries, the relative chances of women entering supervisory positions were the same as those for men. However, this result does not emerge in either the Bulgarian or Czech cases, where a large measure of dissimilarity prevailed in men's and women's fluidity patterns, as the final model, which allows for changes in fluidity over time, demonstrates clearly. These findings reinforce conclusions reached by previous investigators on the basis of quite independent analyses for other countries: the relative chances of entering occupational positions are basically similar for women and men (Roos, 1985; Dunton and Featherman, 1985). The early period of transition from communism did not undermine this regularity.

Table 5.7 **Odds-Ratios for Higher Supervisors vs. Lower Supervisors and Subordinates**

Year	Bulgaria	Czech Republic	Hungary	Poland	Russia
1983	2.7	4.7	3.4	3.3	74.5
1988	3.4	4.4	2.9	2.6	12.1
1993	3.0	3.4	2.8	3.9	13.4

On the other hand, past generalizations regarding mobility patterns between tiers of the hierarchy of job authority are questioned to some extent by these findings. In particular, Table 5.7 reports ratios giving the relative odds of men and women being higher supervisors, rather than subordinates and lower supervisors, for the years 1983, 1988 and 1993. These ratios may be interpreted as showing the outcome of a series of 'competitions' between the sexes to achieve higher supervisory positions as the transition from communism proceeds. The more the ratio exceeds one, the more men win, and the closer is its value to unity, the more equal is the competition by sex. Used in analyses of mobility trends, these odds provide a more insightful picture of the gender-based relative chances of recruitment to the highest positions.

What the data reveal clearly is that men had greater access to positions on the top of the job authority ladder throughout the whole period from 1983 to 1993, although this generalization masks two trends that appeared during the course of the decade. The first was evident in the sub-period 1983 to 1988, when the set of odds tended to decrease in all countries, except Bulgaria, indicating that the relative position of women improved during the period of systemic decay. During the 1990s, on the other hand, there were different tendencies in the separate countries. Only in the Czech Republic (and to a much lower extent in Bulgaria) had competition between the sexes become more equal by 1993. In Hungary, men retained their privileged position, while in Poland and Russia, but most particularly the former, women had much lower chances of becoming higher supervisors in 1993 than they did in 1988.

The major advantage of thinking of the relative chances of females in terms of odds ratios is that the analysis reveals the specific kinds of interactions underlying the common fluidity patterns of the sexes in Poland, Hungary and Russia, while also indicating what might explain the significant change that was detected in the dynamic of sex inequality in the Czech Republic and Bulgaria. In particular, improvement observed in the latter two cases had its origins in the significant gains made by women in securing promotion to higher supervisory grades in the 1990s, as shown in Table 5.7. In the three former countries, the offsetting tendencies occurring during the whole 1983—1993 period did not generate any overall meaningful aggregate patterns of change. In Appendix Table A5.1 (see p. 143), values of the odds showing the competition by sex for vacancies in the lower rung of the job authority ladder are reported. These still indicate men's advantageous position, although this is not as substantial as in their access to positions at the highest levels of authority and, as the odds remained practically unchanged through time, they did not contribute anything new to an understanding of the dynamic of sex inequality.

One further question is suggested by the analysis. Differences between the fluidity patterns of men and women in relation to supervisory positions were discovered within the Czech Republic and Bulgaria while, in the case of occupational mobility, a large measure of similarity by sex prevailed across nations. Might it therefore be expected that there would be cross-time stability in the fluidity patterns of the sexes considered separately? This leads to an examination of the dynamic openness within the two distinct segments of the labor market, utilizing both the CFM and the diagonals model. The constrained diagonals model employed here specifies a single parameter for all diagonal cells of the mobility table, thereby testing the proposition that immobility exceeds that which would be expected on the basis of perfect mobility by the same proportion in all occupational categories (see Goodman, 1972, pp. 661–671; Hout, 1982, p. 28). The diagonals model refers to a state in which change is occurring only in occupational distributions, but not in either structural mobility or in exchange mobility: in other words, self-recruitment in the six occupational strata accounts for all associations in the mobility tables for both 1983–1988 and 1988–1993 in each country. The goodness of fit of this model casts light on the openness of stratification systems, since comparisons of transitions taking place over very short periods of time are being made. It may seem unlikely that radical changes in the opportunities for movement would emerge over a ten-year period and it might therefore be hypothesized that it is self-recruitment rather than circulation that has shaped the occupational careers of women during this time.

The results of applying these models are set out in Table 5.8 for men and in Table 5.9 for women. In these tables, the six countries are modeled separately and, in each case, both the diagonals model and the CFM are fitted to a three-way table that comprises the six EGP categories of origin, six destination categories and two transitions (those between 1983–1988 and 1988–1993). The results are in accord with the findings of previous studies; mobility doors in East-European countries basically remained as open (or as closed) in the 1990s as they were in the preceding decade. The second model, which tests the hypothesis that occupational distributions changed in the two consecutive decades, produces values of G^2 that are significant in each of the six countries. However, no more than four per cent of the total association is ever explained, as shown in the second rows of the Tables. Even so, there is a significant improvement in the goodness of fit, providing direct support for the thesis that occupational distributions had undergone major transformations by the end of the 1980s, although those for men were more significant than those for women. Occupational distributions for 1983, 1988, and 1993 are reported in Appendix Tables A5.2 and A5.3 (see pp. 144–145) and these make apparent the direction in which occupational structures in East European countries have been moving.

Table 5.8 Origin by Destination Category (EGP Categories): Women, 1983–1988 and 1988–1993[1]

	Model				
	O D T	OT DT	OT DT DIAG	OTS DTS ODT	BIC for OT DT OD
Bulgaria					–162
G2	5661	5610	193	35	
rG2	–	0.9	96.0	99.4	
p	0.00	0.00	0.00	>0.05	
Czech Repub-					–165
lic	5643	5533	243	36	
G2	–	1.9	95.7	99.4	
rG2	0.00	0.00	0.00	>0.05	
p					
Hungary					–143
G2	4169	4114	367	47	
rG2	–	1.3	91.2	98.9	
p	0.00	0.00	0.00	>0.05	
Poland					–159
G2	4098	4071	191	32	
rG2	–	0.7	95.3	99.2	
p	0.00	0.00	0.00	>0.05	
Russia					–186
G2	6689	6679	159	19	
rG2	–	0.3	97.6	99.7	
p	0.00	0.00	0.00	>0.05	
Slovakia					–167
G2	6051	6013	182	30	
rG2	–	0.6	97.0	99.5	
p	0.00	0.00	0.00	>0.05	
df (all countries)	60	50	49	25	

[1] O—category of origin in 1983–88 and 1988–93 tables; D—category of destination in 1983–88 and 1988–93 tables; T—time (1=1983–88, 2=1988–93); DIAG (1=off-diagonal cells, 2=diagonal cells).

The diagonals model also performs fairly well: although it does not fit the observed data in each country at the conventional 5 per cent level, statistical significance is not the only guide to substantive sociological significance. Holding immobility constant between 1983–1993 accounts for no less than 90 per cent of all of the associations investigated, which implies complete independence. It must therefore have been the case that self-recruitment prevailed over mobility in both time periods. Nevertheless, the reduction in G^2 proved unsatisfactory, which indicates that there was circulation between the six categories, notwithstanding the strong tendency for individuals to remain within their category of origin.

Table 5.9 **Origin by Destination Category (EGP Categories): Men, 1983–1988 and 1988–1993**[1]

	Model				
	O D T	OT DT	OT DT DIAG	OTS DTS ODT	BIC for OT DT OD
Bulgaria					–162
G^2	5288	5219	161	36	
rG^2	–	1.3	97.0	99.3	
p	0.00	0.00	0.00	>0.5	
Czech Republic					–159
G^2	6498	6233	197	45	
rG^2	–	4.1	96.7	99.3	
p	0.00	0.00	0.00	>0.5	
Hungary					–162
G^2	4543	4778	139	34	
rG^2	–	1.4	96.9	99.3	
p	0.00	0.00	0.00	>0.05	
Poland					–140
G^2	4231	4176	202	52	
rG^2	–	1.3	95.2	98.7	
p	0.00	0.00	0.00	>0.05	
Russia					–176
G^2	4903	4871	141	21	
rG^2	–	0.6	97.1	99.6	
p	0.00	0.00	0.00	>0.05	
Slovakia					–151
G^2	6060	5920	181	52	
rG^2	–	2.3	97.0	99.1	
p	0.00	0.00	0.00	>0.05	
df (all countries)	60	50	49	25	

[1] As for Table 5.8.

In the light of these findings, it is appropriate to consider whether the constant fluidity model, which assumes that circulation did take place, improves the fit. The results of fitting the CFM are presented in the fourth columns of Tables 5.8 and 5.9 and it is apparent that circulation between the six occupational strata remained basically constant over the decade 1983–1993. In other words, the CFM reproduces the observed data almost entirely and accounts for 99–100 per cent of the association between class of origin and class of destination in each country. Statistically significant deviations are present only in the Czech Republic, Slovakia and Poland, in the case of men, and in Hungary for women. The caveat must therefore be that, in these countries, some significant portion of the discrepancies between observed and expected values pertain to circulation, a suggestion that could only be explored by more detailed analysis that is beyond the scope of this contribution. Nonetheless, even in these four countries, circulation rates appear to be captured largely by the core model that assumes constant fluidity through time. Stability predominates insofar as the concern is with the openness of the social structure. It seemed reasonable to suppose that the collapse of communism and the re-birth of capitalism in Eastern Europe would imprint on the occupational structure by relaxing rigidities and closures in social space, but no support for this presumption could be found in the current data. Even the transformations of the political and economic systems, with their concomitant institutional changes, did not suffice to make class barriers more fluid by the middle of the 1990s. Nevertheless, it must be recognized that there might exist a delayed potential for growth in circulatory rates of mobility.

The absence of change in the openness of occupational structures was accompanied by a slight increase in total movement after 1988, with the sources of this increase to be found in changing occupational distributions. Indeed, it has already been shown that there was a particularly rapid growth in the class of proprietors in all six societies during the 1990s. The shift towards greater total mobility lends support to the prediction with which the chapter began: rising flows in the 1990s resulted from macro-structural changes, enforced chiefly by economic transformations that created new positions in the division of labor. Mobility regimes themselves remained stable.

Finally, consideration should be paid to the question of whether the fluidity patterns are a sociological constant, not only between occupational categories but also between subordinates and supervisors, in the post-communist societies of the 1990s. Following the same logic as in the comparison of EGP matrices for 1983–1988 and 1988–1993, the CFM was tested for the five national 3 x 3 matrices of transitions for these same time periods, with the results being presented in Tables 5.10 and 5.11.

The constant fluidity model reproduces patterns of women's transitions in the ladder of job authority that are satisfactory for Bulgaria, Hungary and Russia. In the Czech Republic and Poland, however, the model does not fit; not unexpectedly given the rapid improvement of women's relative odds on the Czech labor market and the deterioration of their position in Poland revealed earlier. In the case of men, the CFM does not reproduce the data; although it returns G^2s of no less than 97.9 (in the Czech Republic), it implies $p<0.05$ and there is therefore good reason to examine in more detail the fluidity between subordinates and supervisors. In order to examine by what means men experienced more mobility than women, inflow rates to the occupational categories and supervisory levels will now be considered.

Table 5.10 Origin by Destination by Time (Hierarchy of Job Authority): Women, 1983–1988 and 1988–1993[1]

	Model				
	O D T	OT DT	OT DT DIAG	OTS DTS ODT	BIC for OT DT OD
Bulgaria					–25
G^2	1115	1110	10	7	
rG^2	–	0.4	99.1	99.4	
p	0.00	0.00	0.00	0.01	
Czech Republic					5
G^2	1378	1377	45	27	
rG^2	–	0.0	96.7	98.8	
p	0.00	0.00	0.00	>0.05	
Hungary					–24
G^2	852	846	13	6	
rG^2	–	0.7	98.5	99.3	
p	0.00	0.00	0.00	0.01	
Poland					–20
G^2	949	946	11	10	
rG^2	–	0.3	98.8	98.9	
p	0.00	0.00	0.00	>0.05	
Russia					–30
G^2	2238	2237	8	3	
rG^2	–	0.0	99.6	99.9	
p	0.00	0.00	0.00	0.01	
df (all countries)	60	50	49	25	

[1] As for Table 5.7.

Table 5.11 Origin by Destination by Time (Hierarchy of Job Authority): Men, 1983–1988 and 1988–1993[1]

	Model				
	O D T	OT DT	OT DT DIAG	OTS DTS ODT	BIC for OT DT OD
Bulgaria					–11
G^2	1499	1495	21	15	
rG^2	–	0.3	98.6	99.0	
p	0.00	0.00	0.00	>0.05	
Czech Republic					23
G^2	2571	2566	69	55	
rG^2	–	0.2	97.3	97.9	
p	0.00	0.00	0.00	>0.05	
Hungary					–9
G^2	1722	1711	32	22	
rG^2	–	0.6	98.1	98.7	
p	0.00	0.00	0.00	>0.05	
Poland					–15
G^2	1561	1559	26	16	
rG^2	–	0.1	98.3	99.0	
p	0.00	0.00	0.00	>0.05	
Russia					–12
G^2	2265	2263	26	20	
Rg^2	–	0.1	98.6	99.2	
p	0.00	0.00	0.00	>0.05	
df (all countries)	12	8	7	4	

[1] As for Table 5.7.

INFLOWS TO BUSINESS AND SUPERVISORY POSITIONS

Tables 5.12 and 5.13 display the proportions of women and men across the six nations who, in 1988 and 1993, found themselves in an occupational category other than that in which they were located five years previously. In particular, they give the inflow rates to the intelligentsia, lower non-manual positions, ownership, skilled work, unskilled work and agricultural categories in 1988 and 1993. The rates presented in Table 5.12 are percentage distributions of the sexes for 1988, conditioned on their occupational category in 1983, while those given in Table 5.13 refer to percentage distributions for 1993, conditioned on 1988 origins.

Table 5.12 Inflow Rates: Women (%)

Socio-occupational Categories	Bulgaria		Czech Republic		Hungary		Poland		Russia		Slovakia	
	1983–1988	1988–1993	1983–1988	1988–1993	1983–1988	1988–1993	1983–1988	1988–1993	1983–1988	1988–1993	1983–1988	1988–1993
Higher & Lower Professionals, Managerial Cadres	9.9	15.6	9.0	23.3	14.9	23.4	15.0	14.3	7.0	13.7	5.7	17.8
Lower Non-Manual Workers	58.6	10.0	44.9	7.2	49.2	9.8	39.3	6.2	64.5	9.5	44.4	6.2
Owners	56.0	33.3	61.5	86.9	44.2	54.7	31.2	74.0	65.2	35.3	41.7	78.0
Skilled Workers	21.4	23.0	12.5	23.5	17.5	11.1	14.0	13.6	14.5	13.5	8.6	7.9
Unskilled Workers	8.7	14.7	9.7	19.5	13.0	14.2	9.0	11.4	15.9	9.5	8.9	9.5
Farmers & Farm Laborers	14.1	15.6	11.8	13.4	8.2	5.4	7.3	9.0	9.0	12.4	7.1	11.2

Table 5.13 Inflow Rates: Men (%)

Socio-occupational Categories	Bulgaria		Czech Republic		Hungary		Poland		Russia		Slovakia	
	1983–1988	1988–1993	1983–1988	1988–1993	1983–1988	1988–1993	1983–1988	1988–1993	1983–1988	1988–1993	1983–1988	1988–1993
Higher & Lower Professionals, Managerial Cadres	9.1	17.1	8.2	16.1	16.7	16.5	7.2	13.1	8.1	15.7	8.1	20.0
Lower Non-Manual Workers	79.3	.3	80.6	19.9	79.4	12.6	77.1	1.3	86.4	11.0	17.0	21.4
Owners	65.0	55.7	55.0	90.2	40.8	40.6	50.8	59.1	35.8	67.6	70.0	89.5
Skilled Workers	10.8	11.1	8.0	11.0	7.9	11.0	11.5	8.6	10.0	11.3	6.4	8.0
Unskilled Workers	8.7	14.7	8.9	13.6	12.2	12.3	14.7	11.4	11.4	15.1	8.5	15.5
Farmers & Farm Laborers	14.1	15.6	11.7	19.1	16.6	26.4	19.7	10.0	8.5	12.3	4.3	20.5

In the 1990s, owners displayed the highest proportion of newcomers in comparison with those in the other categories. Over the whole period 1983–1993, the class of lower non-manuals—clerical workers, teachers in elementary schools, nurses, technicians, shops assistants, receptionists, etc.—was also a significant external recruiter of labor. This latter category had the highest inflow rates in 1983–1988, although this distinction fell to proprietorship in the following five years. The increase in inflow rates to ownership was more apparent among men than among women. In Poland, for example, the inflow rate to the lower non-manual worker category stood at 77 per cent in 1988 and in Russia it was as high as 86.4 per cent. The high inflow rates to the lower non-manual category witnessed in the 1980s—Slovakia being an extreme outlier—had decreased greatly by 1993, except again in Slovakia where the rate actually increased. Simultaneously, the rate of inflow into ownership was generally either maintained or increased, with Bulgaria being the only exception by experiencing a reduction of ten per cent. In consequence, the class of owners remained, at the beginning of the 1990s, the most transient group. They received the highest influx in the Czech Republic and Slovakia, where only ten per cent of owners in 1993 were in the same positions as in 1988. Three-quarters and more of the intelligentsia, lower non-manuals and manual workers and farm categories were 'self-recruited' in 1993. The dynamics of the female labor market were somewhat different in that, as of the early and late 1980s, the owner and lower non-manual categories shared the highest recruitment rates. But the inflow rate to lower non-manual occupations decreased dramatically in the subsequent period, leaving proprietors as the single most transient category among the six strata, particularly in the Czech, Polish and Slovakian labor markets.

The volume of mobility is central to the issue of class formation. As such, questions pertaining to the homogeneity of different strata in terms of their recruitment patterns is simply another way of examining the degree of their 'demographic identity' (Goldthorpe, 1987): that is, the degree to which they have formed collectives of individuals and families identifiable by the continuity of their association with sets of strata positions over time. From this standpoint, there are certain contrasts in the patterns of self-recruitment of owners across nations. In the Czech Republic and Slovakia, owners seem the least homogeneous category in terms of job experience in business. Nine out of ten male proprietors in 1993 recruited themselves from a different 1988 category of origin. In Bulgaria, Hungary and Poland, on the other hand, this proportion did

Table 5.14 Inflow Rates to Supervisory Positions: Women (%)

Number of Subordinates	Bulgaria		Czech Republic		Hungary		Poland		Russia	
	1983–1988	1988–1993	1983–1988	1988–1993	1983–1988	1988–1993	1983–1988	1988–1993	1983–1988	1988–1993
0	0.7	0.9	1.6	4.8	1.1	3.7	3.5	6.8	3.3	2.9
1–9	16.9	18.4	23.2	35.6	32.4	30.3	20.2	30.9	20.7	21.6
10+	12.9	31.2	34.1	41.3	28.7	29.4	34.6	31.4	34.6	31.4
Total	100	100	100	100	100	100	100	100	100	100

Table 5.15 Inflow Rates to Supervisory Positions: Men (%)

Number of Subordinates	Bulgaria		Czech Republic		Hungary		Poland		Russia	
	1983–1988	1988–1993	1983–1988	1988–1993	1983–1988	1988–1993	1983–1988	1988–1993	1983–1988	1988–1993
0	1.0	1.0	2.1	6.5	5.4	2.6	3.5	6.8	3.0	4.9
1–9	25.0	34.4	16.9	40.2	31.6	22.2	20.2	30.9	21.2	27.6
10+	20.2	27.0	21.4	24.8	16.7	18.7	20.8	25.3	14.4	27.1
Total	100	100	100	100	100	100	100	100	100	100

not exceed one-half. Given such heterogeneity of origin, it is not possible to predict the direction in which the possible formation of owners into a socio-cultural entity might proceed. Mobility into business as a result of systemic transformation led to the disintegration of this category as a class. So far as the consequences of social mobility for class formation in the post-communist countries are concerned, the heterogeneity of owners seems to be the most striking by-product of the systemic changes that have taken place.

Finally, Tables 5.14 and 5.15 explore the entry of women and men into supervisory positions through time. The first column of each of these tables presents the percentages of the sexes in each nation who moved into the categories of: (i) subordinates, (ii) lower supervisors, and (iii) higher supervisors between 1983 and 1988. In the second columns, inflow rates for 1993 are reported. Comparison of these columns provides clear confirmation that mobility was everywhere higher in the 1990s than in the 1980s. Two regularities emerge: first, the rates of upward mobility of both men and women universally exceeded rates of demotion to subordinate positions; second, women experienced more mobility to higher supervisory positions than men—with Bulgaria, in the earlier period, representing the only exception. Nevertheless, sight should not be lost of the existence of the extensive crowding of women into lower supervisory and subordinate roles.

CONCLUSION

The aim of this study was to examine the mobility rates of women and men in a critical period of the systemic transformation. There is a large literature that suggests that females have borne a disproportionate share of the burden of the transition from communism to capitalism in Eastern Europe. The current analysis scrutinized the validity of these claims through an exploration of the barriers to mobility on the labor market, both before and after the collapse of the communist regime, in Bulgaria, the Czech Republic, Hungary, Poland, Russia and Slovakia.

The overall picture of flexibility on the labor market that emerged is not entirely encouraging for women, even though total mobility rates appeared higher in the 1990s than in the preceding decade for both sexes. This much was to be expected: in all six national economies, the indications are that the mechanisms of labor allocation under compulsion have begun to be modified by the rules of the capitalist market and the democratization of public life, thus removing formal access barriers to prominent positions in politics and private business. Social mobility in Eastern Europe responded to institutional transformation in just the way predicted by Sorokin (1958).

However, the labor market opened up more for men than for women. First, women have been shown to be concentrated in relatively disadvantaged non-manual or manual categories in all nations and they less often hold supervisory positions than do men in all countries. In other words, nothing changed in the pattern of either horizontal or vertical segregation by sex throughout the first years of transition. Second, while total rates of mobility rose, men enjoyed more intense movements in the 1990s and were more likely than women to cross the boundaries between occupational strata, as well as those between the categories of subordinates and supervisors.

In the light of previous research, it was of interest to test whether women's overall rates of fluidity were relatively more or less than those of men. The results indicate that they are higher in the Czech Republic and, to much lower extent, in Bulgaria, with women gaining greater access to higher supervisory levels in the 1990s, thereby suggesting a reduction in gender-based inequality in recruitment. In contrast, inequality persisted at the same level as in the 1980s in Hungary, while in Russia, and more particularly in Poland, women exhibited a lower propensity to enter supervisory positions in the first years of capitalism.

What is the most general interpretation that may be given to these empirical findings? Once conjectures regarding the impact of transition on the mobility chances of women were confronted with the evidence, cross-national uniformities failed to emerge. Subject to the caveat that the transition clearly still has many years to run, the results indicate that, by the middle of the 1990s, potent forces were in operation that were detrimental to the situation of women. According to the data analyzed in this chapter, the transition from communism generally did not remove the occupational barriers facing women to any significant degree. In Poland, albeit only temporarily perhaps, women found themselves in worse positions than before the political breakthrough and the introduction of market structures. It appears that social upheaval in this country has been the most detrimental to women. In Czech society, however, they were better off. These were the two extreme cases.

NOTES

1 Appendix Tables A5.2 and A5.3 report the distributions of the EGP categories.

2 The statistics of fit for the CFM are shown in the last line for each country of Tables 5.5 and 5.6 and Tables 5.7 and 5.8. In the last column of these tables, BIC (Bayesian Information Criterion) statistics, which are not sensitive to the number of cases employed in the analysis, are reported, although only for the full model. BIC is especially recommended for selection between models if the number of cases in an analysis is very large, that is when N makes it almost impossible to achieve a satisfactory fit according to standard criteria (i.e. the statistical significance of G^2). The decision rule is that the best model is that with the smallest BIC (see Raferty, 1986).

REFERENCES

Andorka, R. (1990) "Half a Century of Trends in Social Mobility in Hungary." in: J.L. Peschar (ed.), *Social Reproduction in Eastern and Western Europe*, Nijmegen: Institute for Applied Social Sciences.

Andorka, R. and K. Zagórski. (1980) *Socio-occupational Mobility in Hungary and Poland*, Budapest–Warszawa: IFiS Publishers.

Boguszak, M. (1990) "Transition to Socialism and Intergenerational Class Mobility. The Model of Core Social Fluidity Applied to Czechoslovakia," in: M. Haller (ed.), *Class Structure in Europe*, NewYork, Armonk: Sharpe.

Breen, R. and C.T. Whelan (1985) "Vertical Mobility and Class Inheritance in the British Isles," *British Journal of Sociology*, vol. 36, no. 2, pp. 175–92.

Domański, H. and Z. Sawiński (1992) "Dynamics of Occupational Mobility in Poland, 1972–1987," in: P. Clancy et al. (eds), *Ireland and Poland. Comparative Perspectives*, Dublin: University College.

Dunton, N. and D.L. Featherman (1985) "Social Mobility Through Marriage and Careers," in: J.T. Spence (ed.), *Achievement and Achievement Motives*, San Francisco: W.H. Freeman.

Erikson, R. and J.H. Goldthorpe (1992) *Constant Flux*, Oxford: Clarendon Press.

Esping-Andersen, G, Z. Assimakopulu and K. von Kersergen (1993) "Trends in contemporary class structuration: a six nation comparison," in G. Esping-Andersen (ed.), *Changing Classes. Stratification and Mobility in Post-Industrial Societies*, London: Sage.

Featherman, D. and R.M. Hauser (1978) *Opportunity and Change*, New York: Academic Press.

Featherman, D., F.L. Jones and R.M. Hauser (1975) "Assumptions of Social Mobility Research in the US: The Case of Occupational Status", *Social Science Research,* vol. 4, December, pp. 329–360.

Freeman, S.J.M. (1990) *Managing Lives. Corporate Women and Social Change*, Amherst: University of Massachusetts Press.

Ganzeboom, H. and P. de Graaf (1984) "Intergenerational Mobility in the Netherlands in 1983 and 1977: A Loglinear Analysis," in: B.F. Bakker et al. (eds), *Social Stratification and Mobility in the Netherlands*, Amsterdam: SISWO.

Giddens, A. (1973) *The Class Structure of the Advanced Societies*, London: Hutchinson.
Glass, D. (1954) *Social Mobility in Britain*, London: Routledge.
Goldthorpe, J.H. (1987) *Class Structure and Mobility in Modern Britain*, Oxford: Oxford University Press.
Goodman, L. (1972) "A General Model for the Analysis of Surveys," *American Journal of Sociology*, vol. 77, no. 6, pp. 1035–1086.
Grusky, D. and R.M. Hauser (1984) "Comparative Social Mobility Revisited: Models of Convergence and Divergence in 16 Countries," *American Sociological Review*, vol. 49, no. 1, pp. 19–38.
Haller, M. and B.W. Mach (1984) "Structural Changes and Mobility In a Capitalist and Socialist Society: A Comparison of Men and Women in Poland," in: M. Niessen, J. Peschar, and C. Kourilsky (eds), *International Comparative Research: Social Structure and Public Institutions in Eastern and Western Europe*, Oxford: Pergamon Press.
Hout, M. (1982) *Mobility Tables*, London: Sage.
Ishii-Kuntz, M. (1994) *Ordinal Log-linear Models*, London: Sage.
Jacobs, A.A. (1995) "Women's Entry into Management. Trends in Earnings, Authority, and Values among Salaried Managers," in: J.A. Jacobs (ed.), *Gender Inequality at Work*, Thousands Oaks: Sage.
Marshall, G. (1996) "Was Communism Good for Social Justice? A Comparative Analysis of Two Germanies," *British Journal of Sociology*, vol. 47, no. 3, pp. 397–426.
Marshall, G., S. Sidorenko and S. Roberts (1995) "Intergenerational Social Mobility in Communist Russia," *Work, Employment and Society*, vol. 9, no. 1, pp. 1–27.
Payne, G. (1993) "Competing views on Contemporary Social Mobility and Social Divisions," in: R. Burrows and C. Marsh (eds), *Consumption and Class*, London: Macmillan.
Raferty, A.E. (1986) "Chosing Models for Cross-Classifications," *American Sociological Review*, vol. 51, no. 1, pp. 145–146.
Roos, P. (1985) *Gender and Work: A Comparative Analysis of Industrial Societies*, Albany: State University of New York Press.
Sorokin, P. (1958) *Social and Cultural Mobility*, Glencoe, Illinois: The Free Press.
Siltanen, J. (1994) *Locating Gender. Occupational Segregation, Wages and Domestic Responsibility*, London: UCL Press.
Svalastoga, K. (1958) *Prestige, Class, and Mobility*, Copenhagen: Glydendal.
Treiman, D.J. (1994) *Social Stratification in Eastern Europe after 1989. Codebook*, Los Angeles: University of Los Angeles.
Tyree, A., M. Semyonow and R. Hodge (1979) "Gaps and Glissandos: Inequality, Economic Development and Social Mobility in 24 Countries," *American Sociological Review*, vol. 44, no. 3, pp. 410–427.
Wolf, W.C. and N.D. Fliegstein (1979) "Sex and Authority in the Workplace. The Causes of Sexual Inequality," *American Sociological Review*, vol. 44, no. 2, pp. 235–252.
Yamaguchi, K. (1987) "Models for Comparing Mobility Tables: Towards Parsimony and Substance," *American Sociological Review*, vol. 52, no. 4, pp. 482–94.
Zagórski, K. (1978) *Struktura i ruchliwo społeczna* (Social structure and mobility), Warszawa: PWN.

APPENDIX TO CHAPTER 5

Appendix Table A5.1 Odds-Ratios Lower Supervisors vs. Subordinates: 1983, 1988 and 1993

Year	Bulgaria	Czech Republic	Hungary	Poland	Russia
1983	1.3	1.3	1.7	1.5	1.1
1988	1.3	1.3	1.4	1.7	1.2
1993	1.3	1.5	1.8	1.5	1.2

Appendix Table A5.2 Distributions by EGP Socio-occupational Strata: Women (%)

Socio-occupational Categories	Bulgaria			Czech Republic			Hungary			Poland			Russia			Slovakia		
	1983	1988	1993	1983	1988	1993	1983	1988	1993	1983	1988	1993	1983	1988	1993	1983	1988	1993
Higher Professionals	8.0	8.1	8.6	6.6	7.2	6.7	7.3	7.1	7.0	7.6	8.0	6.5	21.1	21.3	21.2	10.4	10.8	10.6
Lower Professionals	38.1	38.9	40.8	49.2	50.4	47.8	41.5	44.2	47.0	42.6	44.0	45.1	41.9	42.6	42.5	29.8	30.6	31.6
Owners	0.8	2.4	5.5	0.4	0.8	7.6	2.5	47.0	7.8	1.5	1.9	6.7	0.4	1.1	2.3	0.4	0.5	3.8
Skilled Workers	11.0	10.7	10.7	12.2	12.4	11.0	25.3	24.2	21.9	18.2	18.4	15.8	16.0	14.7	13.5	29.3	29.0	26.8
Unskilled Workers	26.6	26.5	23.2	25.8	23.8	22.5	25.3	24.2	21.9	18.2	18.4	15.8	14.5	14.2	15.1	22.6	21.9	20.9
Farmers & Farm Laborers	15.5	13.5	11.3	5.8	5.4	4.3	6.4	5.1	3.5	18.1	16.1	16.2	6.1	6.1	5.3	7.5	7.2	6.4

Appendix Table A5.3 Distribution by EGP Socio-occupational Strata: Men (%)

Socio-occupational Categories	Bulgaria			Czech Republic			Hungary			Poland			Russia			Slovakia		
	1983	1988	1993	1983	1988	1993	1983	1988	1993	1983	1988	1993	1983	1988	1993	1983	1988	1993
Higher Professionals	8.6	8.0	7.7	13.4	14.2	11.4	10.5	9.8	8.8	11.7	10.1	14.2	21.4	20.9	19.9	11.7	10.1	14.2
Lower Professionals	14.1	13.0	12.7	17.0	17.1	16.8	12.1	12.3	13.9	12.5	11.9	11.8	11.4	12.6	12.1	15.3	14.7	14.8
Owners	1.1	3.7	9.4	0.5	1.2	14.3	2.6	5.3	12.0	3.7	6.1	13.8	0.7	1.9	5.6	0.4	1.1	9.6
Skilled Workers	28.9	29.1	27.2	34.2	34.1	28.5	39.0	37.9	35.5	32.4	33.0	29.6	34.8	34.4	33.2	40.6	41.2	38.0
Unskilled Workers	34.4	35.5	31.2	29.2	28.0	24.4	24.3	24.1	21.2	27.2	26.4	22.2	21.9	21.3	21.6	24.8	23.8	21.8
Farmers & Farm Laborers	12.1	12.6	11.3	5.6	5.4	4.6	15.4	14.8	15.1	8.6	8.3	7.6	9.7	8.8	7.6	6.0	6.1	5.1

CHAPTER 6

GENDER AND SUCCESS IN LIFE[1]

Analyses of the sources of feelings of personal success for men and women are in their infancy, with mainstream discussion generally focusing either on objective measures of socio-occupational position or on subjective differences in the value systems of the sexes. Taken in turn, these studies have two main conclusions: first, women are underpaid by about 30 per cent (Domański, 1992); second, women prefer 'soft', humanistic values (family, work on behalf of other people etc.), whereas men attribute greater significance to 'hard' values, such as material and professional success (Reszke, 1991; Moir and Jessel, 1993; Firkowska-Mankiewicz, 1997). However, work in these fields seldom controls for social background and level of intelligence. This is a serious omission insofar as these factors are known to shape human value systems and to affect future lives and careers via complex processes of socialization and cultural transmission that determine people's aspirations (Kohn, 1969; Kohn et al., 1986; Sułek, 1990). In addition, these factors also affect educational and professional opportunities (Blau and Duncan, 1967; Jencks et al., 1972; Kerckhoff, 1976, 1989; Słomczyński and Mach, 1996).

This chapter sets out to address whether the usual results with respect to earnings, professional activity and position, preferred value systems and patterns of success continue to hold when controls are applied for social background and level of intelligence, and whether personality traits can add to the explanation of gender differentiated outcomes. The particular issue addressed is what role—if any—did gender per se play in the development of the careers of a sample of intellectually gifted 30-year-olds? Did being born female or male have any significance for socialization within the family or education at school and university? Was gender a trump card or a handicap in the attainment of social, economic and professional position and in the subsequent subjective sense of success?

The study is based on the findings of follow-up studies of a special group of people with above-average intellectual competence when they were thirteen years old. This panel was studied initially in 1974–76, by the 'Warsaw Study of Intellectual Performance in Warsaw Children born in 1963' (Firkowska et al., 1978; Firkowska-Mankiewicz and Czarkowski, 1982; Wald and Firkowska-Mankiewicz, 1992; Firkowska-Mankiewicz, 1993). Twenty years later, in 1995, this group of 141 gifted teenagers was re-contacted and questioned about their current situation, educational and professional careers and sense of success in life (Firkowska-Mankiewicz, 1999). In order to control for the 'initial conditions' as far as possible and to eliminate any barriers to the future prospects of the subjects that might have arisen from differences in their social background, two equal-sized groups of men and women (N=24) were selected. Not only were these two groups extremely well balanced with respect to their IQs at the age of thirteen, they also had very similar social backgrounds, with both parents of all subjects having higher education and qualifying as members of the highest possible socio-occupational group, the 'intelligentsia'.[2] These rigorous criteria of group selection guaranteed that only genuine gender-based differences in life careers, uncontaminated by intellectual capacity and social background, would be detected in the analysis.

There are four substantive parts to the chapter. To begin, the first two sections examine the objective indicators and subjective determinants of the socio-economic and occupational status of men and women. These are followed by an examination of the psychological meaning of success in life. Finally, possible barriers to the careers of the subjects that might have been inherent in their family homes, education and job histories, family and social situations, health and personalities are investigated.

THE EFFECTS OF SOCIO-ECONOMIC AND OCCUPATIONAL STATUS

In order to provide an essential first building block for the analysis, this section contains a brief summary of the objective socio-economic indicators of the men and women under study, at the time of the time of the follow-up sweep.[3]

EDUCATION

The data presented in Table 6.1 speak for themselves. Nearly all the gifted women and 75 per cent of the men can boast at least of higher education. Although the proportion of Ph.D. holders is three times higher for the men, it is also true that three times more men than women did not get a full higher education. Likewise, while a significant proportion of males have only college or secondary vocational education, no females entered the labor market with such a 'low' level of education. In other words, the dispersion of education is much higher amongst the males than the females, with a tendency for the men to be relatively less well educated, albeit for reasons that have not yet been identified.

Table 6.1 *Educational Achievements by Gender*

Educational Achievement	Women (%) N=24	Men (%) N=24
Ph.D.	4	13
University Diploma	92	62
Incomplete University	4	13
Post-Secondary Vocational School	0	4
Secondary Technical School	0	8
p	0.17	

OCCUPATION

Unfortunately, the small number of women for whom there is information about the most recent job hampers a comparison of the current position of men and women in the social structure (Table 6.2). Thus, data for nine of the female cases are missing, driven by the fact that six were currently not working (one of them was still studying), four were on leave looking after small children and one was not working for other, unknown reasons. Nevertheless, and despite the lack of significant differences between the sexes, it is worth noting that the proportion of women in the group of professionals was lower than the proportion of men, despite the fact the women are more highly educated. On the other hand, four times as many women as men were medium-level administrative staff. These findings therefore confirm a pattern found in many other studies: women, though on average more highly educated than men, are located at lower positions in the occupational hierarchy

(Reszke, 1991; Domański, 1992). This raises the question of whether such a pattern will be replicated when more detailed dimensions of occupational stratification, such as job complexity, prestige, socio-economic status and promotion are considered?

Table 6.2 Socio-occupational Status by Gender[1]

Socio-occupational status	Women (%) N=15	Men (%) N=23
Managers & Senior Executives	0	0
Professionals	33	43
Technicians & Administrative Staff	40	9
Clerical Workers	7	13
Sales & Service Workers	0	9
Skilled Workers	0	0
Semi-skilled & Unskilled Workers	0	0
Farmers	0	4
Owners	20	22
Occupational Level Mean/Standard Deviation	2.6/1.5	3.0/0.90
p (Occupational Group)	Not Significant	
p (Occupational Level)	0.19	

[1] Occupational Level is coded as follows: 1) (top managers and senior executives), 2) (entrepreneurs), 3) (intelligensia & junior executives) and 4) (the rest).

Table 6.3 Complexity of Work, Prestige and Occupational Status by Gender

Indicators[1]	Women Mean	Women SD[2]	Men Mean	Men SD	*p*
Complexity of Work	61.8	14.2	63.4	16.1	Not Significant
Prestige	57.9	8.2	57.8	11.5	Not Significant
Status	49.4	13.7	51.8	17.8	Not Significant

[1] Scales adopted from Kohn and Schooler (1983).
[2] SD is the Standard Deviation.

In fact, the results presented in Table 6.3 suggest that the men and the women have very similar occupational positions in terms of job complexity, prestige and socio-economic status. None of the differences reported are significant and, as far as prestige is concerned, there is practically no difference at all. However, the considerably higher standard deviation of the male data suggests that the women's jobs are much more homogeneous in this respect. Overall, gifted women achieve a comparable position to similar men and, on this score, there is no evidence of discrimination against women.

MATERIAL AND HOUSING CONDITIONS

Material and housing conditions are factors that, together with education and occupational position, are the most important determinants of social status. The data presented in Table 6.4 show that, in principle, gifted men and women share similar conditions, although the own average earnings of the women are in fact slightly higher than those of the men. Even more striking, a very clear-cut difference emerges in the comparison of total family incomes, with those of the women in the sample being more than twice those of the men. This difference seems likely to be the result of the gifted women having partners who earn more than the partners of gifted men, a supposition supported by other features of the data. In particular, the partners of the women had significantly higher levels of education and occupational status than those of the men: 90 per cent of the their husbands had higher education and occupational positions that locate them either in the intelligentsia or in the class of private entrepreneurs. In contrast, the proportion of the partners of gifted men who belong to either of these categories does not exceed 65 per cent ($p<0.05$).[4]

Table 6.4 Material and Housing Conditions by Gender

Material & Housing Conditions	Women Mean	SD[1]	N	Men Mean	SD	N	*p*
Respondent's Monthly Income (Polish Złoty)	1611.9	1611.4	16	1378.1	1531.4	15	Not Significant
Family Monthly Income (Polish Złoty)	3339.5	2826.0	19	1496.3	1917.1	19	0.01
Material Possessions[2]	5.4	2.1	24	5.4	2.2	20	Not Significant
% of Respondents Owning a House/Apartment	58.3		20	58.3		20	Not Significant
Number of Rooms	3.4	1.1	23	3.5	1.7	20	Not Significant
Apartment Size (m^2) per capita	23.8	15.9	9	27.8	44.9	13	Not Significant

[1] SD is the Standard Deviation.

[2] The Material Possessions scale was constructed as the sum of ten items (coded 0/1) such as computers, cars, gardening plots, etc.

Unsurprisingly, the intellectually superior 30-year-olds surpass their peers from the general population as far as level of education, occupational position and material status are concerned. Data from a national sample document the well-known truth that intelligence increases an individual's chance of achieving a higher position on the stratification ladder significantly (Firkowska-Mankiewicz and Zaborowski, 1997).

SELF-ASSESSMENT OF SOCIO-ECONOMIC STATUS

The subjective assessments of the respondents' own positions were measured in terms of the degree of satisfaction they expressed with the level of education they had achieved, their own job and material and housing conditions and their assessment of their position on the hierarchies of socio-occupational and material status. Analysis of the data in Table 6.5 shows clearly that the self-assessments of the men and the women across this range of socio-economic indicators were very similar. The exceptions are education (the men were less satisfied than the women) and housing conditions (where it is the women who were less satisfied). As such, no evidence can be adduced from this source to suggest that women feel themselves to be the subjects of discrimination. In fact, if the objective and subjective indicators discussed so far are considered together—but especially those relating to educational attainments—the early conclusion, perhaps unexpected, must be that the situation of gifted women was actually slightly superior to that of equivalent men.

Table 6.5 Own Appraisal of Socio-economic/Occupational Position by Gender[1]

Percentage of Respondents Dissatisfied with:	Women	Men	*p*
Level of Education	4	21	0.19
Job	13	13	Not Significant
Material Situation	25	33	Not Significant
Housing Conditions	46	17	Not Significant
Position on Occupational Career Scale (Mean/SD[2])	(5.5/2.3)	(4.9/2.2)	Not Significant
Position on Property & Material Conditions Scale (Mean/SD)	(4.5/2.0)	(4.4/1.4)	Not Significant

[1] Both the occupational career and property & material conditions scales are measured on an 11 point scale ranging from 0 (very low) to 10 (very high).

[2] SD is the standard deviation.

THE MEANING OF SUCCESS IN LIFE

A major difficulty with the use of subjective indicators to assess well-being is that the responses may simply reflect different underlying value systems. This section, which examines the hierarchies of life values of talented men and women, is devoted to an exploration of this possibility.

VALUE SYSTEMS

In the event, the data presented in Table 6.6 indicate that the majority of the differences in the choice of the most important goals in life between the sexes are not significant. This result might be interpreted as a sign of a far-reaching convergence of orientations in the lives of women and men with high intellects and homogeneous social backgrounds. However, it must be noted that women gave higher priority to the attainment of a successful family life than did men. Another significant difference emerged in the case of self-realization, with women mentioning goals that fall under this rubric significantly more frequently than men and

Table 6.6 Life Goals by Gender

Life Goals[1]	Women (%) N=24	Men (%) N=24	p
Power over Other People	0	0	N/A
Leisure Time	4	17	Not Significant
Non-monotonous Life	25	21	Not Significant
Peaceful, Guaranteed Existence	13	4	Not Significant
High Income	4	25	0.10
Interesting Work	25	25	Not Significant
Awareness of Doing Something for Others	13	21	Not Significant
Clear Conscience	13	29	Not Significant
Successful Family Life	75	50	0.13
Human Respect	0	13	Not Significant
Great Love	0	0	N/A
Education, Knowledge	8	8	Not Significant
Occupation, Success, Promotion, Position	13	13	Not Significant
Friends	33	33	Not Significant
Independent Views	8	22	Not Significant
Personal Growth, Improvement, Self-Realization	50	13	0.01

[1] This list of life goals, excluding the last one, is taken from Bauman (1961).

ranking them second in their overall value systems, after a successful family life. Men, on the other hand, did not attribute much significance to self-realization and self-growth. The third significant difference centered upon income, with the attainment of a high income coming near the bottom of the value systems of females while being ranked relatively highly by the males in the sample.

Notwithstanding these significant differences, there were also notable similarities in the values most and least frequently identified by the sexes. The first five ranks in the women's value systems were occupied, in turn, by a successful family life, self-realization, devoted friends and *ex equo* an interesting job and an adventurous life. Men also gave priority to a successful family life and friends but, interestingly and unexpectedly, they mention a clean conscience, interesting work and a high income. In other words, men and women share values such as a successful family life, friends and an interesting job, whereas they differ with respect to several other values. Women identify self-realization and a life full of variety, adventures and risks as important (more 'imaginative' or maybe more 'egocentric' values), whereas men prefer more down-to-earth achievements, such as a clean conscience and a high income.

SUCCESS IN LIFE DEFINED

How do the visions of success in life of gifted women and men emerge against the backdrop of their value hierarchies? This question was explored by means of an open-ended question that asked respondents what 'success in life' meant for them and who they felt could be said to have achieved this. Responses to the question were grouped into several categories that defined success in terms of 'material success', 'professional work,' 'prestige', 'family life,''self-realization' (meaning achievement of self-defined goals), satisfaction with life and oneself, 'getting an education' and, finally, 'achievement of peace, stability and happiness'. It should be emphasized at this point that the current respondents differ radically from the average Pole of the same age with respect to their understanding of success. Above all, success for this elite group was most often defined in terms of self-realization (52 per cent) rather than material success (24 per cent). In contrast, their 'average' counterparts cite these categories in almost opposite proportions; 48 per cent identify success with material well being and only 27 per cent with self-realization (Firkowska-Mankiewicz, 1997).

While clearly different from the overall average, there was no difference between the success criteria espoused by the sexes in the current sample, with one telling exception. Intellectually gifted men, somewhat more often than similar females, associate success with material prosperity (35 and 17 per cent, respectively: $p=0.15$). This result is consistent with the data presented earlier regarding value hierarchies and is, to that extent, an expected finding. Meanwhile, although a certain degree of difference emerged in the proportions defining success in terms of self-realization (63 per cent of women and 48 per cent of men), it was not significant. Although this finding is surprising at first, it becomes more understandable when it is recognized that, in the hierarchy of life goals discussed earlier, self-realization meant, above all, personal development, self-improvement and the growth of ego and, in this context, it appealed to women more than to men. Here, on the other hand, self-realization as a vision of success in life means above all realization of one's own plans, ambitions and goals, and satisfaction with one's own achievements: and it is in this sense that self-realization was almost equally important for both sexes.

OVERALL ASSESSMENT OF LIFE

Three indicators of the respondents' psychological perceptions of their own success in life were compiled during the course of the study. The first was an index of the satisfaction that respondents expressed with the nine areas of their lives (level of education, educational specialization, marriage, children, health, professional work, material situation, housing conditions and achievement in life), computed as the sum of the scores (each on a scale of 1 to 6) that the subjects assigned to each of these. The second was formed from the assessments respondents gave of their own life, while the third recorded general opinions on the meaning of a successful life.

The data presented in Table 6.7 show clearly that the levels of satisfaction expressed by gifted men and women with different spheres of life is almost identical. Similar proportions (about one-half of the women and slightly fewer men) said that their life was wonderful, or at least successful, although slightly more women than men feel that they have done well in life. If to this are added the findings concerning successes and failures, women believed that they had achieved various kinds of success in life (significantly more than men): three-quarters of the women, but only one man in two, said they had achieved something (p=0.11). As far as failures are concerned, men and women responded almost identically: about 30 per cent of both admitted to them; although approximately 45 per cent said that they had never experienced any such events, while about one-quarter found it 'difficult to say.'

Table 6.7 Psychological Indicators of Success by Gender

Indicators	Women (%) N=24	Men (%) N=24	*p*
Satisfaction with Life[1] (Mean/SD[2])	(21/3.9)	(23.4/4.5)	Not Significant
General Assessment of Life:			
Quite Good	50.0	41.7	
Not too Good	37.5	37.5	Not Significant
Poor	12.5	20.8	
Opinion on Having a Successful Life:			
Definitely/Rather Yes	66.7	62.5	0.16
Definitely/Rather No	33.3	37.5	

[1] The satisfaction with life indicator is a composite measure with each of the factors being scored on a 6-point scale from 1 (very satisfied) to 6 (very dissatisfied).
[2] SD is the Standard Deviation.

All in all, the vast majority of intellectually gifted people with intelligentsia backgrounds have, according to their own appraisals, been successful in life, although women are perhaps slightly more aware of this than men. This is an interesting finding if it is noted that women's psychological well being is usually found to be inferior to that of men (Czapiński, 1992). The present results might be interpreted, on the one hand, in terms of personality traits (perhaps gifted women are more optimistic) and, on the other hand, in terms of value hierarchies. However, the first of these two hypotheses seems doubtful in view of the analysis presented below, which shows that gifted women and men do not differ significantly with respect to personality. The second hypothesis seems to be rather more plausible insofar as men care more for material success whereas women care more for family values and self-realization, as suggested earlier. Given this, it is possible to surmise that it was easier for the intellectually gifted women to realize their preferred values than it was for the men to achieve a satisfactory, and probably considerably elevated, material status. In other words, women and men differ in their definitions of success and this may be the reason why they differed (slightly) in their assessments of the degree to which they had been successful themselves.

SUCCESS IN LIFE: BARRIERS AND SPRINGS

In an attempt to better interpret the findings of the preceding section, respondents were asked to assess the influence on their success in life (positive or negative) of thirteen factors. As reported in Table 6.8, men and women differed significantly in their views on five of these. The factors on which they disagreed most were character, temperament and gender itself. As far as character is concerned, twice as many women as men said that this had been a negative influence on their life histories but, at the same time, slightly more women than men considered its effect to have been positive. In other words, women's ratings were the more polarized. A similar pattern was found for gender, with women more often than men indicating both positive and negative effects of their sex. On the other hand, while men perceived no negative consequence of their being male they also indicated positive effects of this factor much less often than women. The majority of men felt that gender had played no part in the course of their life histories.

Table 6.8 Life Histories by Gender

Factors	Women			Men			*p*
	0	+	–	0	+	–[1]	
Health	37	46	17	52	44	4	Not Significant
Aptitude	4	96	0	21	79	0	0.19
Gender	54	29	17	83	17	0	0.05
Character, Temperament	0	62	38	26	57	17	0.01
Parents' Socio-economic Status	25	71	4	33	67	0	Not Significant
Education	4	96	0	8	88	4	Not Significant
Occupational Qualifications	17	79	4	26	74	0	Not Significant
Love Mate	17	71	12	38	54	8	Not Significant
Colleagues, Friends	46	50	4	54	46	0	Not Significant
Religious Convictions	88	12	0	88	8	4	Not Significant
Political Convictions	83	13	4	92	4	4	Not Significant
Socio-political Transformation in Poland	9	86	5	30	55	15	0.08
Fate, Chance	30	65	4	54	46	0	0.18

[1] '0' = no effect, '+' = positive effect and '–' = negative effect.

The next factor viewed differently by women and men was the socio-political transformation in Poland. Almost all women (86 per cent) rated it positively whereas only 55 per cent of men were willing to say that the transformation was a good thing, although only 15 per cent were ready to admit that reform had negatively affected their biographies.

When asked to justify their opinions on this matter, certain of the men replied: "you never know what tomorrow will bring so you cannot plan or predict, you don't know what to do with your resources and skills". Others noted that "everywhere there is theft and dishonesty", or they complained of relative impoverishment, job loss, etc. In contrast, the women pointed, above all, to their greater opportunities for development and professional and material improvement. Typical statements proffered by the women included: "if I hadn't started up a firm of my own I would never have learned what potential I have", "[T]hanks to the transformation I can earn more for my work and my abilities"; "I have more opportunity to earn money, develop", etc.

In summary, only personal character and temperament emerged from this study as a serious barrier to the personal development and success in life of both sexes. Beyond this, the women identified gender and health as constraints on their progress, while the males felt that socio-political transformation was a negative influence on their lives. Respondents of both sexes felt that their own aptitude, education and professional qualifications had helped them to get on in life. At the same time, women—who are generally perceived as less reluctant to evaluate change positively—were much more enthusiastic than men about the effect of the Polish socio-political transformation on their lives. Furthermore, neither religious beliefs nor political convictions (although, admittedly, nothing specific was asked about either) were felt to have had any significant effect on respondents. This could be a sign of indifference on the part of gifted 30-year-old Poles, although it could equally be a sign of the independence of their careers and development from ideological opinions and of the overriding importance of high aptitude and qualifications in an emerging market economy.

FAMILY ENVIRONMENT

The intellectually gifted subjects in the initial sweep of this study came from the same social backgrounds and their parents—both mothers and fathers—had higher education, belonged to the intelligentsia and enjoyed good material conditions. In other words, the families of the subjects were very homogeneous in these respects. This, however, leaves open the question of whether the families of origin were also alike in terms of their socialization and culture; for example, in terms of childcare, value transmission and parental aspirations. In fact, no significant differences were found between the women and men in such things as the number of people caring for them as a child or whether their mothers undertook paid work (about one-half of the respondents' mothers had worked throughout their childhood). Neither were there any real differences in terms of household duties performed as a child, although girls more often than boys had regular chores. Also, the parents of the now-adult boys and girls declared similar conformist values for their offspring ("well groomed, knowing how to behave", "obedient, well-behaved", "should do well at school"). However, clear-cut differences did emerge in respect of self-direction, with the values "should have his/her own opinions, think independently", "should have a variety of interests", "responsibility" being assigned more frequently to boys than to girls ($p=0.08$). Similar differences were uncovered as far as aspirations involving the child's education were concerned: these were slightly higher for boys than for girls ($p=0.14$).

All in all, the twenty year-old data suggest that typical, culturally determined differences in parental values concerning the upbringing of children of the two sexes were discernible, despite the fact that the male and female teenagers were otherwise reared in identical, good for the time, socio-economic conditions. In comparison with the girls, the boys were expected to think more independently and to be more intellectually active and responsible. Parents also had higher educational aspirations for boys.

Analysis of the data from the 1995 study lent no support to the suggestion that intellectually gifted girls experienced more parental control than equally gifted males. Neither did it support the hypotheses that the girls enjoyed different opportunities to voice their personal opinions and decide for themselves, that their fathers had been more lenient or more strict towards them, or that their parents' had rewarded obedience and respect rather than partnership and mutual understanding. The only weak differences that could be discerned related to the maternal parenting style: mothers' of sons manifested a more partnership-oriented style than mothers' of daughters ($p=0.17$) and significantly more frequently evaluated their daughters on the basis of their shortcomings rather than their merits ($p=0.11$).

Despite these rather negligible, yet quite typical, differences, most subjects said that they had felt well or very well in their family home (58 per cent of women and 67 per cent of men) when looking back on their childhood. In other words, they did not feel that they had experienced any serious barriers to their intellectual development in their families of origin. Nonetheless, there were several culturally typical elements of the parental approach to the girls, including lower expectations with respect to independent thinking, intellectual activity, responsibility and level of education. Also, mother–daughter relationships were slightly more strained than other parent–child interactions. An earlier study of the socialization experiences and IQs of thirteen year-old girls and boys indicated that such a child-rearing climate might generally be expected to lower the level of intellectual competence in girls (Firkowska-Mankiewicz, 1996).

EDUCATIONAL CAREER

In exploring differences in educational careers it is notable, above all, that the girls had generally higher achievements in primary school. Whereas 42 per cent of the girls obtained the highest grades for all subjects in their final primary school certificates (p=0.01), the comparable figure for boys was only four per cent. However, this situation changed in secondary school where, although the girls were motivated to be top of the class in all subjects more often than the boys (p=0.10) and had more out-of-school activities than the boys, the final school certificates did not differ significantly across the sexes. Nevertheless, although all subjects passed their examination, all the girls graduated from their original school without delay whereas 12 per cent of the boys repeated a class and 21 per cent changed schools, mainly because of conflicts with teachers (p=0.01).

To conclude this discussion of secondary-school careers, it should be added that no significant differences between the personality traits of the girls and boys could be found. Both sexes were liked by their peers and could count on family support in difficult situations. Neither did they differ with respect to such characteristics as their approach to life, self-esteem and achievement motivation. All in all, gender had no significant effect on the final outcome of the educational careers of the gifted girls and boys in primary and secondary school, although those of the girls were generally more disciplined and conflict-free.

All the of girls, and all of the boys except one, wanted to go to college after secondary school, but the former had more difficulty deciding where to go (p=0.01). The main reasons for the problems confronting the girls were their greater variety of interests and personality factors, such as lack of self-confidence, test anxiety, etc. Yet once they had overcome their major and minor set-backs, all of the girls, with the exception of one who got a job, went to college: fewer boys followed suit, with two deciding to go to postgraduate vocational schools and two to take jobs.

In general, no significant differences were found between the women and men as far as their university careers were concerned, with one exception: the women were more serious about their studies than the men ($p=0.08$). Perhaps this is why 82 per cent of the women (but only 70 per cent of the men) finished the studies they had taken up without any problems and all but one, who is still studying, managed to get their degrees. Nonetheless, the graduates of both sexes obtained similar results: more than 90 per cent of the women and 80 per cent of the men graduated with very good or good grades. Somewhat more women than men had scholarships during their period at college (57 and 33 per cent, respectively).

Recalling the statistics presented in Table 6.1, it is clear that the women's educational careers were more successful than those of the men. Despite their equally favorable environmental backgrounds and intellectual capacities, several men lacked sufficient motivation to complete their studies. There were practically no such cases among the female respondents because, even though one woman has incomplete higher education, she is still studying and will probably graduate (to be fair one man is in an analogous situation).

OCCUPATIONAL CAREER

Analysis of the occupational careers of respondents begins with a presentation of their dreams and the realities of their first jobs. The discussion then proceeds to an examination of how many jobs, and in which sectors, the women and men have had and what factors facilitated or impeded their occupational achievements.

FIRST JOB: DREAMS

The majority of the data presented in Table 6.9 are not surprising. Both women and men had most frequently hoped that work would "give satisfaction and enjoyment; " "enable utilization of abilities, skills and interests; " "be meaningful, necessary, serve some definite cause", and "further enable development and improvement of qualifications". Women, much more frequently than men, wanted work that was "beneficial for others" (a finding confirmed by other studies). Men, on the other hand, much more frequently than women, dreamed of jobs that "offer great promotion and career opportunities" (see Firkowska-Mankiewicz, 1996; Moir and Jessel, 1993). However, several responses were also received that shattered popular stereotypes. For example, men more frequently dreamed of jobs "guaranteeing long holidays" (p=0.15), that were "easy and not very involving" (p=0.08) and "stable, sure and do not hold the threat of dismissal". Finally, men dreamed just as frequently as women of jobs that "give a certain amount of power and opportunities to manage people;" "help achieve fame" and "provide opportunities for competition and personal challenge".

Table 6.9 Desirable Job Characteristics by Gender

The Job Should:	Women (%)	Men (%)	*p*
Enable Utilization of Abilities, Skills & Interests	75	78	Not Significant
Offer Promotion & Career Opportunities	8	30	0.12
Be Beneficial to Others	46	8	0.001
Help Achieve Fame	8	10	Not Significant
Be Easy, Not Very Involving	0	19	0.08
Give Power, Opportunities to Manage People	4	5	Not Significant
Provide Considerable Financial Returns	42	57	Not Significant
Give Satisfaction/ Enjoyment	88	87	Not Significant
Be Stable, No Threat of Dismissal	17	29	Not Significant
Provide Opportunities for Competition, Personal Challenge	13	115	Not Significant
Provide Lots of Free Time/Long Holidays	29	55	Not Significant
Be Meaningful	67	55	Not Significant
Enable Further Development & Improvement of Qualifications	54	65	Not Significant
Be Tension Free, Peaceful	25	25	Not Significant

When asked to identify the job description that was most important for them, both women and men pointed to those that "give satisfaction and enjoyment" (35 and 25 per cent, respectively) and "enable utilization of abilities, skills and interests" (25 per cent of both sexes). Likewise, both women and men hoped for jobs that offered opportunities for self-realization (occupational fulfillment and utilization of all their potentials) and were equally scornful of job characteristics related to prestige (e.g., 'power,' 'fame,' 'competition'). Contrary to expectations, job characteristics associated with stability were indicated more frequently by men than by women.

FIRST JOB: AGE AT TAKE-UP AND TYPE

Both sexes earned their first money at about 15 years of age and both also began their first job at similar ages (women a year later than men, at the age of twenty, although the difference was not significant). Neither was there any significant difference in the nature of the first paid work undertaken; odd jobs for the majority of women (71 per cent) and men (58 per cent) alike.

NUMBER OF REGULAR JOBS

The data in Table 6.10 show clearly that, on average, the men have had a greater number of regular jobs than have the women; that is, they have been occupationally more mobile. Parallel, albeit less distinct, differences in occupational mobility also emerged with respect to the number of jobs held in the public and in the private sectors. It is noticeable though that the data indicate identical, although limited, experience of self-employment. Gifted men and women are equally (non-)dynamic as far as involvement in their own businesses is concerned.

Table 6.10 Number of Jobs Held by Gender

Number of Jobs	Women N=24		Men N=24		*p*
	Mean	SD[1]	Mean	SD	
Waged Work– Public Sector	0.9	0.8	1.3	0.8	0.16
Waged Work–Private Sector	0.8	1.0	1.3	1.4	0.20
Self-employed	0.3	0.6	0.3	0.6	Not Significant
Total	2.0	1.3	3.2	2.3	0.03

[1] SD is the Standard Deviation.

OCCUPATIONAL CAREERS: PAST, PRESENT AND FUTURE JOBS

A basic summary of the differences in the socio-economic status of the first and most recent jobs held by men and women is straightforward: they are not significant, as indicated in Table 6.11. All that can be found (data not shown in the table) is that the occupational status of the most recent job held by women was slightly higher than in the case of men (p=0.19). In particular, the former were situated nearer to the category of private entrepreneurs whereas men, on average, were more likely to be found amongst the ranks of the intelligentsia and junior managers. Curiously, women achieved marginally superior initial positions in terms of job complexity, prestige and socio-economic status, although the ordering is reversed for the most recent job, with men having slightly more complex positions and minimally higher socio-economic status. However, these differences are certainly not significant.

Table 6.11 Characteristics of First and Last Job by Gender

Job Characteristics		Women		Men		*p*
		Mean	SD	Mean	SD	
Job Complexity	First	66.6	16.1	63.9	17.8	Not Significant
	Last	61.8	14.2	63.4	16.1	Not Significant
Prestige	First	57.6	12.4	56.5	13.8	Not Significant
	Last	57.9	8.2	57.8	11.5	Not Significant
Socio-economic Status	First	52.4	14.2	52.0	17.8	Not Significant
	Last	49.4	13.7	51.8	17.8	Not Significant

Table 6.12 Subjective Ratings of Occupational and Material Hierarchies[1]

Rating of:	Women		Men		*p*
Position in Occupational Hierarchy					
10 Years Ago	0.8	1.2	1.4	1.3	0.15
Now	4.3	2.5	4.7	1.9	Not Significant
In 10 Years Time	8.0	2.2	7.3	2.1	Not Significant
Position in Material Hierarchy					
10 Years Ago	1.3	1.5	1.9	1.6	0.21
Now	4.5	2.0	4.4	1.4	Not Significant
In 10 Years Time	7.7	1.9	6.7	1.7	0.06

[1] As for Table 6.5.

Table 6.12 reveals the subjective standings of respondents in the occupational and material hierarchies through time: in particular, their perceptions of their status ten years ago, now and what they expect ten years hence. On average, the men rated their occupational career and material situation ten years ago slightly more favorably than did the women, while ratings for the present do not differ significantly. However, it is expected that the situation will have changed dramatically in favor of the women over the next ten years. Although the difference between the prospective ratings of occupational status by sex is not significant, the women's mean position in the occupational hierarchy is expected to be almost one rung higher (8.0) than the men's (7.3). This difference is even more pronounced (and significant) for the ratings of prospective material status: in this case, the women on average place themselves more than one rung higher in the hierarchy of material success than do the men. If the data in the columns of the table are analyzed, it can be seen that women tend to move more quickly in terms of both occupational and material ratings than men. The latter start out from higher assessments of their positions than women, but then seem to slow down and they expect to surrender the field to the women in the future.

No other significant differences in characteristics or situations relating to occupation could be found in the data. Women did not work longer hours than men (including additional work, both women and men worked 10–11 hour days on average). Neither was the work of either sex more or less related to formal education. Further, men and women equally frequently indicate people or situations (including foreign travel) that positively affected their professional careers: more than 50 per cent of both sexes mentioned such influences. Also, there is no difference in the frequency of complaints about people who, or events that, may have had a negative affect on careers: only about 10 per cent of both women and men recalled such events. The cause of the apparently greater dynamism of women's professional careers is therefore, on this evidence, hard to isolate.

FAMILY SITUATION AND SOCIAL RELATIONS

Nearly all the women (92 per cent) and 82 per cent of the men in the sample married at one time or another. One quarter of the women and 22 per cent of men were subsequently divorced, with three men and one woman later remarrying. Overall, the sample contains comparable proportions of married women and men (63 and 65 per cent, respectively), 17 per cent of the women were single; as opposed to 30 per cent of the men, and 21 per cent of women are divorced or separated; compared to four per cent of the men. In the general population, 69 per cent are married, 18 per cent are single, four per cent are divorced or separated and about 10 per cent are widowed. Therefore, the current sample has slightly lower proportions of married women and men and slightly higher proportions of single men and divorced women (see Czapiński, 1993). Nobody in this sample was widowed.

The majority of women (83 per cent) and slightly fewer men (67 per cent) were very happy with their marriages. The remainder claimed to be "quite happy", but the difference is not significant. Neither is there any substantial difference between ratings of the impact of their marriage partners on professional careers. While 33 per cent of women and 44 per cent of men said there was a positive impact, 56 per cent of women and 44 per cent of men said there was no impact and 11 per cent of both said there was a negative impact. More pronounced differences emerged, however, when the problem of partner's support in crisis situations (trouble, worries) was analyzed. Responses to this question revealed that more than half of the women (56 per cent) and one-third of the men said they always got support. Furthermore, 17 per cent of the women and 44 per cent of the men said they often got support, while 28 per cent of women and 22 per cent of men said they rarely received support. All in all, the women disagree more on this issue than do the men.

It might also be noted that slightly more women than men have children (74 and 58 per cent, respectively), which is interesting in view of the fact that the men much more frequently claimed that having a child/children did not interfere with their professional career at all, or that the effect was positive (62 per cent of men against 30 per cent of women). Women on the other hand identified the opposite effect of parenthood much more frequently than men (35 and 8 per cent, respectively: $p=0.12$).

Notwithstanding the high educational and professional status of both marital partners, the majority of respondents' families are quite traditional. Two types were dominant: in the first, only the husband worked (30 per cent of the women and 17 per cent of the men); in the second, the husband spent more time at work, while the woman not only worked but also took care of the house and children (44 per cent of the women and 56 per cent of the men had such families). Only 11 per cent of either sex had families based on true partnership, where the husband and wife devoted the same amount of time to their professional work and to the family.

This section concludes with a review of the answers given to the question of what pattern of family life would be most preferred, if life could begin anew. The distribution of responses is very typical. Nearly one-half of the women and almost 60 per cent of the men would like to work and have children, devoting just as much time to their families as to their careers. Significantly more women (38 per cent) than men (9 per cent) would like to be able to devote more time to their families, without resigning from work; that is, they favored an even more traditional, 'family-oriented' life-style. Only nine per cent of each group said they would like to give up work completely and have children instead. Slightly more men than women would prefer to spend more time in their work than devote it to their family (9 per cent and 5 per cent, respectively). Finally, 14 per cent of men (but not one woman) would rather not have any children at all ($p=0.12$).

Overall, the majority of respondents (surprisingly, more men than women) 'wishfully' declared preferences that inclined them towards the partnership model. Nevertheless, quite a number of women (four times more than men) perceived their role very traditionally; that is, although they worked, they were willing to take on the extra burden of housekeeping and child-care. The proportion of women who would like to devote themselves completely to their homes and children was much smaller than the proportion of women who actually did so (9 and 30 per cent, respectively). That said, a similar proportion of men would also like to have such a traditional 'feminine' role. More men, however, would prefer not to have any children, or at least to give precedence to their work rather than their family (23 per cent in all). There are therefore considerable discrepancies between reality and the ideal family model aspired to by respondents.

As far as wider social relations are concerned, the women pay more attention to the maintenance of close, warm family units, with 46 per cent of women (but only 25 per cent of men) admitting to such behavior. This does not mean that men do not care for such relations at all they are merely less earnest in their desire to maintain them ($p=0.15$). The majority of women (92 per cent) reported that, if necessary, they normally found support in their close or more distant family; slightly fewer men (75 per cent) reported that they could enjoy the same ($p=0.18$). But the men have more ramified social networks, maintaining permanent contacts with almost twice as many people as the women.[5]

A very small proportion of women (12 per cent) and slightly more men (29 per cent) were involved in non-professional and non-family activities (social, political, charity or religious), although the difference is not significant. Equally insignificant are the differences in responses to the question concerning interests, passions and hobbies, although 71 per cent of men and 54 per cent of women admitted that they did have a very distinct, concrete field of interest.

HEALTH AND PERSONALITY

The bio-psychological (health and personality) traits of the subjects were the final determinants of the life histories examined in the studies.[6] Respondents were asked four probing questions about their state of health: "[H]ow satisfied are you with your health?"; "[H]as your health in any way encumbered or limited your day-to-day functioning?"; "[H]as your state of health over the last 15 years in any way interfered with your career plans (e.g., forced you to change a chosen specialty, affected your level of education)?"; and "[H]as your state of health led to any general, non-professional changes in your life plans?". Only the last question yielded significant differences between the women and the men ($p=0.11$). Health complicated women's personal plans more often than men's (38 versus 13 per cent). In all of the remaining cases, a similar, albeit insignificant, trend emerged: women were less satisfied with their health than men; they more often said that their state of health makes life more difficult and they admitted slightly more often that health problems have interfered with their professional plans over the last 15 years.

Slightly more men (38 per cent) than women (29 per cent) rated their psychological well being as very good or good. However, many more women (42 per cent) than men (25 per cent) used the expression "it varies". Almost no respondents rated their psychological well being as "poor, bad or very bad" (one woman and two men). Yet again, therefore, this factor does not differentiate between the sexes in any significant way, a finding which contradicts the results of many studies that have found that women do not fare well on this score (see Czapiński, 1992). Perhaps intellectually gifted women of high social status (as in this study) cope better with poor psychological well being or distance themselves from it more easily than other members of the population?

Several dimensions of personality were analyzed, with respondents being asked questions relating to their optimism, self-esteem, locus of control, fear of success, Machiavellism and strategies for coping. Two measures of optimism were used, with respondents being asked to say whether life in general brings more bad things than good things and also to complete a version of Seligman's (1993) test of how people interpret failures. No significant differences emerged in response to the first question; the vast majority of females (85 per cent) and males (74 per cent) said that life in general brings more good things than bad things. Seligman's test could not differentiate between the responses by sex either: the mean for women being 6.0 and that for men 6.6, indicating that men interpret their failures slightly less optimistically. According to Seligman, all scores up to seven points are indicative of a higher than average level of hope and optimism.

Women's mean level of self-esteem (16.2) was slightly higher than men's (15.1), but the difference is not significant. This is an interesting result that suggests that the intellectually gifted women have a balanced self-esteem and a high sense of self-worth. Their self-esteem seems to be a logical consequence of their high occupational and material position and sense of success in life. As far as locus of control (LOC) is concerned, the mean scores for the men and women were –5.96 and –4.48, respectively. With p=0.20, this result may be interpreted as follows: the men in the sample had a slightly more internal LOC than the women. Both scores are, however, very high and oscillate around –4.65, the mean found in the 1995 national study of persons with higher education (Titkow, 1997). While the sexes in the present study did not differ in their levels of pugnacity—they were equally ready to take risks and accept challenges—men actually feared success slightly more than women (scores of 12.6 and 11.9, respectively). Although this difference is insignificant, its failure to accord with the popular stereotypes that bury women's desire for success under slogans such as the need to secure their happiness in their relations with people is very revealing. Gifted women are not afraid that their femininity or family life will be threatened or that they will be deprived of friends if they succeed either in their careers or in other facets of their life.

Differences on the Machiavellism scale were significant: women scored markedly lower (–0.05) than men (3.22). In other words, gifted men had a less idealistic vision of the world and human nature and tended, more often than similar women, to think that other people are either stupid or cunning. It is worth adding that this difference becomes slightly less distinct when men living abroad are excluded from the analysis. This suggests that living abroad has led to the development of a more negative image of human nature and the principles by which people live. The men and women differ clearly in the strategies they adopt to cope with economic hardship. In particular, women apply the 'hedgehog' strategy, while men more often employ the 'fox' strategy. Repeating this analysis excluding the respondents living abroad—a group using both of these strategies significantly less frequently than domestic residents (p=0.11 and p=0.16, respectively)—still left a small difference between the sexes in the use of the 'hedgehog' strategy, although they pursued the 'fox' strategy in equal proportions.

In summary, in this intellectually gifted sample, women seem to be in a poorer state of health than the men, although the sexes do not differ significantly with respect to several other psychological attributes: in particular, in their optimism, self-esteem, fear of success and application of the 'fox' strategy. At the same time, a number of weak, but rather characteristic, differences can be observed for the remaining psychological variables. Men have a slightly more internal locus of control but, on the other hand, they are less willing to adopt the 'hedgehog' strategy to cope with economic hardship and have a more cynical (or perhaps less distorted) vision of the world and human nature.

CONCLUSION

In general, the image of the sexes emerging from this analysis violates many stereotypes concerning women's position, potential, beliefs and personalities. The subjects of this study were equally gifted intellectually, yet the women were more highly educated and had at least equivalent, if not higher, occupational and material status. They also possessed a greater sense of success in life; more satisfaction with their own achievements; as high, if not higher, levels of self-esteem; little fear of success and high levels of optimism, pugnacity and enterprise. This is in spite of the fact that while their family socialization took place in equally favorable socio-economic conditions, their parents formulated lower expectations for them as far as independent thinking, intellectual activity and responsibility were concerned. They also had lower educational aspirations for their daughters than did the parents of sons. Furthermore, the mothers of girls were more critical of their daughters than the mothers of boys were of their sons. Fortunately, this cultural message did not manage to limit the educational aspirations and performance of the girls in the sample.

As a group, the girls ultimately achieved a higher educational level than the males while their intellectual competence, personality (particularly their weaker Machiavellism, stronger orientation towards self-growth, self-realization and work for the benefit of others) bore fruit in their professional life. They therefore achieved equal, if not higher, scores on objective and subjective measures of social position and had a stronger sense of success in life. Also, the women managed to achieve all this in spite of their significantly greater burden of household and family duties (only 11 per cent of the families covered by the study functioned on a partnership basis). Intellectually gifted women appear to agree to such a traditional distribution of roles, even though a large majority of them would prefer relationships that were otherwise. Nevertheless men also opt equally frequently for such a preferred style of relating to their families, while currently accepting a situation in which their wives either do paid work and devote time to the house and children or, often against their own preferences, withdraw from their professional careers altogether. It is in this 'voluntary' acceptance of traditional (not to say unfair, or at least non-preferred) distribution of professional and family roles that lingering effects of the cultural baggage collected in the family of origin may be detected (see Firkowska-Mankiewicz 1996). For all of their intellectual and personality qualities, and their professional and material achievements, intellectually gifted women are still under the pressure of powerful stereotypes.

NOTES

1 The author acknowledges the contribution made to the research project by Mirosław Czarkowski.

2 The mean IQ for the groups, as measured by the Wechsler Intelligence Scale for Children (Wechsler, 1974), exceeded 130. The groups were matched pairwise such that the difference in global IQ, verbal IQ and non-verbal IQ between the men and women in each pair could be no more than 3 points, the standard error of the data.

3 As the men and women analyzed were selected so rigorously with respect to their IQs and social backgrounds, it was felt justified to adopt a less stringent level of statistical significance (p=0.20) when pursuing relationships between variables that would otherwise never have reached the conventional threshold of significance (p=0.05).

4 The figures presented in Table 6.4 should be interpreted with caution due to the high proportion of missing data, particularly for women. It was also necessary to eliminate four men from the comparisons because they were living abroad. However it is known that the latter group possess material and housing conditions almost four times better than those of their peers in Poland (Firkowska-Mankiewicz, 1999).

5 The relevant statistics are Mean=28, Standard Deviation=27 and Mean=16, Standard Deviation=10, respectively; p=0.06.

6 Precise details of the psychological variables, together with an explanation of the scoring system, are provided in the Appendix Table A6.1 (p. 174).

REFERENCES

Bauman, Z. (1961) "Wzory sukcesu warszawskiej młodzieży" (Warsaw youth's patterns of success), *Studia Socjologiczne*, vol. 3, no. 3, pp. 103–138.

Blau, P. and Duncan, O.D. (1967) *The American Occupational Structure*, New York: Wiley.

Christie, R. and Geis, F.L. (1970) *Studies in Machiavellism*. New York–London: Academic Press.

Czapiński, J. (1992) *Psychologia Szczęścia* (The psychology of happiness), Warszawa: Akademos.

Czapiński, J. (1993) "Polski Generalny Sondaż Dobrostanu Psychicznego" (The Polish general survey of psychological well being), Warszawa: Polskie Towarzystwo Psychologiczne.

Czapiński, J. (1994) "Uziemienie polskiej duszy" (The grounding of the Polish soul), *Kultura i Społeczeństwo*, no. 3, pp. 17–37.

Domański, H. (1992) *Zadowolony niewolnik* (The happy slave), Warszawa: Wydawnictwo IFiS PAN.

Firkowska, A., A. Ostrowska, M. Sokołowska, Z. Stein, M. Susser, M. and I. Wald (1978) "Cognitive development and social policy," *Science*, vol. 200, pp. 1357–1362.

Firkowska-Mankiewicz, A. (1993) *Spór o inteligencję człowieka* (The debate about human intelligence), Warszawa: IFiS PAN.

Firkowska-Mankiewicz, A. (1996) "Gender and IQ—socialization and stratification determinants," *Polish Sociological Review*, vol. 1, no. 113, pp. 61–77.

Firkowska-Mankiewicz, A. (1997) "Successful life and what it means for contemporary Poles: The socio-demographic and psycho-social context," *Polish Sociological Review*, vol. 4, no. 120, pp. 269–286.

Firkowska-Mankiewicz, A. (1999) "Zdolnym być ... Kariery i sukces życiowy warszawskich trzydziestolatków w okresie transformacji ustrojowej" (To be gifted ... careers and success in life of Warsaw thirty year-olds in times of systemic transformation), Warszawa: Wydawnictwo IFiS PAN.

Firkowska-Mankiewicz, A. and M.P. Czarkowski (1982) "Social status and mental test performance in Warsaw children," *Personality and Individual Differences*, vol. 3, pp. 237–247.

Firkowska-Mankiewicz, A. and W. Zaborowski (1997) "Kariery życiowe uzdolnionych nastolatków warszawskich" (The careers of gifted Warsaw teenagers), *Kultura i Społeczeństwo*, vol. XL1, no. 4, pp. 155–165.

Jencks, C., M. Smith, M.J. Bane, D. Cohen, H. Gintis, B. Heyns and S. Michelson (eds.), (1972) *Inequality: A Reassessment of the Effect of Family and Schooling in America*, New York: Basic Books Inc.

Kerckhoff, A.C. (1976) "The status attainment process: Socialization or allocation?", *Social Forces*, vol. 55, pp. 368–381.

Kerckhoff, A.C. (1989) "On the social psychology of social mobility processes," *Social Forces*, vol. 68, pp. 17–25.

Kohn, M.L. (1969) *Class and Conformity. A Study in Values*, Homewood, Illinois: The Dorsey Press.

Kohn M.L. and C. Schooler (1983) *Work and Personality: An Inquiry Into the Impact of Social Stratification*, Norwood, New Jersey: Ablex Publishing Corporation.

Kohn, M.L., K.M Słomczyński and C. Schoenbach (1986) "Social stratification and the transmission of values in the family: A cross-national assessment," *Social Forum*, vol. 1, pp. 73–102.

Moir, A. and O. Jessel (1993) *Płeć mózgn* (Gender of the brain), Warszawa: PIW.

Potocka-Hoser, A. (1985) *Aktywiści organizacji społecznych i politycznych w zakładzie przemysłowym. Obraz własnej osoby i otoczenia społecznego* (Activists of social and political organizations in the industrial plant. Self-image and image of the social environment), Wrocław: Ossolineum.

Reszke, I. (1991) *Nierówności płci w teorisch* (Gender inequality in theory), Warszawa: Wydawnictwo IFiS PAN.

Rosenberg, M. (1985) "Self-concept and psychological well-being in adolescence," in: R. Leahy (ed.), *The Development of the Self*, New York: Academic Press.

Rotter, J.B., M. Seaman and S. Liverant (1962) "Internal versus external control of reinforcement: A major variable in behaviour theory," in: N.F. Washburn (ed.), *Decision, Values and Groups*, vol. 2, New York: Pergamon.

Seligman, M. (1993) *Optymizmu można się nauczyć* (Learned optimism), Media Rodzina of Poznań: Poznań.

Słomczyński, K.M. and B. Mach (1996) "The impact of psychological resources on status attainment: Poland 1978–1980 and 1992–1993," *Polish Sociological Review*, vol. 4, no. 116, pp. 337–352.

Słomczyński, K.M. and G. Kacprowicz (1979) *Skale zawodów* (The occupational scales), Warszawa: IFiS PAN.

Sułek, A. (1990) "Life aspiration of Polish youth: Intergenerational stability and generational changes. 'Sisyphus,'" *Sociological Studies*, vol. VI, pp. 189–205.

Titkow, A. (1993) *Stres życia społecznego* (The stress of social life), Warszawa: Państwowy Instytut Wydawniczy.

Titkow, A. (1997) "Poczucie kontroli nad zdarzeniami w latach 1984–1985" (The Locus of control of events in 1984–1995), in: H. Domański and A. Rychard (eds), *Elementy nowego ładu* (Elements of the new order), Warszawa: Wydawnictwo IFiS PAN.

Titkow, A. (1999) "Społeczna i kulturowa tożsamość kobiet" (The social and cultural identity of women), Mimeo., IFiS PAN.

Wald, I. and A. Firkowska-Mankiewicz (1992) "Implications of the Warsaw Study for social and educational planning," in: B. Tizard and W. Varma (eds), *Vulnerability and Resilience in Human Development*, London and Philadelphia: Jessica Kingsley Publishers.

Wechsler, D. (1974) *Manual for the Wechsler Intelligence Scale for Children*, Revised, New York: The Psychological Corporation.

APPENDIX TO CHAPTER 6

Appendix Table A6.1 Operationalization of the Psychological Variables

Optimism—This is defined from the responses to the following question that was used in Bauman's (1961) study:

"Generally speaking, does life bring ..."

1. more bad things than good things
2. rather more bad things than good things
3. rather more good things than bad things
4. many more good things than bad things.

Pessimism—This indicator is Seligman's (1993) test, it contains 48 items describing sad and happy, hypothetical, events. Each event is accompanied by two rival interpretations and the respondent is asked to choose the interpretation that he/she finds most appealing. For the purpose of the present study 16 items were selected that test the scope and stability of personal failures. The total score measures how often the respondent chose interpretations diagnostic of universal, and stable, failures. The scale ranges from 1 (an optimistic interpretative style) to 13 (a pessimistic interpretative style) [6.5, 2.2].[1]

Self-esteem—This variable was measured using the responses to 6 statements from the Rosenberg Self-Esteem Scale (Rosenberg, 1985). Each response is rated on a five-point scale (from 1—definitely disagree to 5—definitely agree) and is then re-coded so that high scores indicate a high self-esteem. Scores can range from 5 (low self-esteem) to 24 (high self-esteem) [16.7, 4.7].

Locus of control—This indicator, proposed by Titkow (1993), is partially derived from Rotter's Internal–External (I–E) Scale. The scale has 8 items and responses are rated on a five-point scale (from –2—definitely disagree to +2—definitely agree; 0—difficult to say). Scores can range from –12 (high internal locus of control) to +4 (low internal locus of control) [–4.67, 3.9].

Fear of success—This indicator was introduced by Titkow (1999) and used in a not yet published study of identity in Polish women. There are nine items:

1. I fear that if I am too successful in life people will stop liking me.
2. I am sure that successful people are often sad and lonely.
3. Sometimes I do not reveal my potential to others for fear that they may think that I am conceited.
4. In my opinion no woman can make a professional career for herself and have a successful family and personal life at the same time.
5. I believe that the price people often pay for their career and success is not worth the effort.
6. In my opinion a woman who is successful in her professional and public life loses her femininity.
7. It is sometimes worth doing something less well than one could so that nobody feels threatened by our achievements.

[1] In this Appendix the first figure in the square brackets refers to the mean, and the second to the standard deviation.

8. Most women are afraid to compete with men who hold similar positions.
9. I think that there are situations, not only at home or in the family, when women are better at what they do than men.

Responses are rated on a four-point scale (from 1—definitely disagree to 4—definitely agree) and are re-coded so that high scores indicate a high level of fear of success. Scores can range from 3 to 21 [12.5, 2.9].

Machiavellism—This variable is based on a scale (Mach IV) constructed by Christie and Geis (1970) and adapted by Potocka-Hoser (1985). The scale has 20 items rated on a five-point scale from –2 (definitely disagree) to +2 (definitely agree), re-coded so that negative values indicate low Machiavellism and positive values indicate high Machiavellism. Scores can range from –16 to +22. [2.0, 7.7]

Strategies of coping with economic hardship—Two scales, based on the work of Czapiński, 1994), were developed: the 'hedgehog strategy' and the 'fox strategy.' The following items were included in the scale:

1. I try to manage things so that as little is wasted as possible.
2. I shop at sales and hunt for 'bargains'.
3. I mend old things rather than buy new ones.
4. I cut down on current expenses.
5. I spend less money on my own pleasures.
6. I try to use less electricity, warm water and heating.
7. I take on extra work.
8. I have found or am looking for a better job.
9. I have begun to invest in production, trade or services.
10. I have begun to invest in shares, premium bonds or trust funds, to deal in shares or to transfer money from account to account.
11. I try to put my qualifications and skills to better use.
12. I develop new qualifications or skills with better earning opportunities in mind.

Responses were rated on a four-point scale from 1 (definitely agree) to 4 (definitely disagree) with responses to items 1–6 re-coded so that high scores indicated intensive utilization of the 'hedgehog' strategy and responses to items 7–12 indicated intensive utilization of the 'fox' strategy. Scores on the 'hedgehog' scale ranged from 0 (the respondent does not save and does not cut down on expenses) to 18 (the respondent saves very hard and cuts down on expenses) [8.8, 3.2]. Scores on the 'fox' scale ranged from 0 (the respondent does not seek new, active ways of earning money) to 15 (the respondent actively seeks new ways of earning money) [7.8, 3.3].

CHAPTER 7

STEREOTYPES: OPINIONS OF FEMALE ENTREPRENEURS IN POLAND

The position of women on the Polish labor market has attracted considerable academic attention since the beginning of the reform process, with Domański (*this volume*) echoing the usual finding that, notwithstanding systemic change, women are still failing to gain access to the most senior employment positions. This phenomenon is not unique to Poland or even to the bloc of ex-communist countries, and is a phenomenon that has attracted the universal epithet of the 'glass ceiling'. That is, women progress so far up hierarchies, but typically fail to attain the top positions within organizations. If indeed this is the case, one possible route over the barrier that might be available to women is that of starting their own businesses. Summary evidence from the early transition period suggests that some such process might actually have been taking place: as early as 1992, self-employed women accounted for some 21 per cent of all women in work (GUS, 1998).

However, there have been only a limited number of academic studies that have focused on female entrepreneurs in Poland. Research conducted by Lisowska (1997) revealed that women entrepreneurs were typically aged over 40, had a minimum of secondary education, grown-up children and a previous career. Although she found that both men and women cited the desire to earn a good income and to utilize their previous work experience as major motivators in the decision to become entrepreneurs, women were more likely than men to point to a wish to prove their own worth to their spouse as important. Lisowska (1996) attributes this finding to the persistence of the Polish stereotype, a creation that defines both the gender division of labor within the economy and the position of women in society in general. She also found strong echoes of the view, widely held in Poland, that "women are less predestined than men to manage and to participate creatively in the country's economic life because they have to fulfil their maternal function." (*ibid.*, p. 66). Jasiecki (1995) also points to the existence of cultural barriers that inhibit their progress on the labor market: female entrepreneurs are seemingly challenging deeply rooted, traditional mores. This chapter seeks to revisit these very issues.

The findings reported in this work are drawn from a survey, conducted in January 1997, of a random sample of eight hundred individuals aged between 18 and 70 who resided in towns of at least five thousand inhabitants that was designed to elicit information on the perceptions of females as entrepreneurs.[1] The results of the survey are reported in the following five sections, each addressing a particular aspect of women as business owners. In the following section, views regarding male and female stereotypes of business owners are analyzed. While the majority believed there to be no difference between the sexes, a significant minority thought otherwise. Further questions were put to the latter group in an attempt to discover the ways in which both they themselves, and society more widely, viewed female entrepreneurs to be different to seemingly equivalent males. The exercise revealed interesting contrasts between male and female respondents regarding gendered stereotypes of business owners.

Section 3 of the chapter reports the evaluations of the skills of male and female business owners, as these were perceived by the respondents to the survey. While the majority recognized no skill differential to exist between the sexes, a minority did perceive a difference, with the prevailing view being that women possessed superior skills. This discussion of skill portfolios is complemented, in Section 4, by an evaluation of the advantages and obstacles that women in business are believed to face in the eyes of the urban residents forming the basis of this study. The views of females contrast sharply with those of the males interviewed. In Section 5, the focus of the discussion switches to perceptions of the success of entrepreneurs, with the results indicating that, while many feel that women are equally likely to succeed as males, a large percentage believe that the path for females is harder.

The preceding considerations leave open the question of whether business ownership is considered to be a suitable career and Section 6 reports the responses received when interviewees were asked whether they believed such a choice to be suitable for their own offspring. The results, somewhat surprisingly, reveal that the majority of respondents would support both their sons and daughters in any entrepreneurial aspirations they may have. Those surveyed recognized that such a career choice offered the potential to earn high incomes, although the associated risks were not unrecognized. Finally, Section 7 summarizes and concludes the chapter.

STEREOTYPES OF MALE AND FEMALE BUSINESS OWNERS

While published data provide some information on the prevalence and gender division of business owners in Poland, they offer no insight into the public perception of women as entrepreneurs or of entrepreneurship in general. The first issue to be addressed by the survey was whether there exists, as is frequently supposed, a different vision of female and male business owners. In short, the strength of the traditional stereotype in the urban community was explored by the question: "[W]ould you describe a typical women entrepreneur in the same way as a man, or differently?". Two-thirds of the sample claimed that they would describe them in the same way, although one-quarter of respondents considered there to be a difference. Those falling into the latter group were

Table 7.1 Perceptions of Women Business Owners

Description Used by Respondents (N=208)	Total (%)	Male (%)	Female(%)
A Better Employer	24.5	25.5	23.7
Competent, Professional	21.1	23.4	19.3
Reliable, Conscientious, Responsible	14.4	13.8	14.9
Takes Care of Business, Active	11.5	13.8	9.6
Elegant, Well-Groomed, Well-Dressed	11.1	9.6	12.3
Decisive, Unyielding, Male in Character	8.7	8.5	8.8
Polite, Kind, Nice	7.7	7.4	7.9
Precise, More Scrupulous than Men	6.7	6.4	7.0
Energetic	6.7	8.5	5.3
Specific, Responsible, Calm	6.3	8.5	4.4
A Worse Employer than a Man	5.3	4.3	6.1
More Demanding than a Man	4.8	5.3	4.4
Cannot Envisage a Woman in this Role	2.9	4.3	1.8
Other Description	21.2	18.1	23.7
Other Answer	5.3	5.3	5.3
No Answer	1.9	2.1	1.8
Did Not Know	3.8	5.3	2.6

probed further in an attempt to ascertain why they perceived sex to be a relevant characteristic in differentiating between entrepreneurs, with the responses to this question being summarized in Table 7.1.

Most frequently, female entrepreneurs were actually considered by respondents to be better employers than males, and this view was more prevalent amongst men than women.[2] In a similar vein, more males than females considered women business owners to be competent and professional.[3] While the variation in the responses of men and women was not great, there is a suggestion in these findings that women are, at least in some ways, viewed as the better entrepreneurs. It would be incorrect, however, to assume that these results reflect an enduring Polish stereotype for, on being asked their views regarding the stereotypical/conventional image of women as entrepreneurs, the overall flavor of the survey responses was distinctly different.

Table 7.2 Stereotypes of Typical Female and Male Entrepreneurs

Description Used by Respondents (N=208)	Female (%)	Male (%)
Good Employer, Takes Care of Workers	24.5	14.6
Competent	21.2	11.9
Reliable, Conscientious, Honest	14.4	14.3
Takes Care of Business	11.5	6.9
Elegant, Well-Groomed	11.1	6.4
Decisive, Inflexible	18.7	6.4
Polite, Kind, Nice	7.7	8.4
Precise, Careful	6.7	..
Energetic	6.7	1.8
Specific, Reasonable, Calm	6.3	..
A Bad/Worse Employer	5.3	17.9
Demanding	4.8	..
Cannot See a Woman Playing this Role	2.9	..
Other Characteristics	21.2	12.1
Other Answers	5.3	2.3
Do Not Know	3.8	..

While female respondents perceived that the stereotype of businesswomen closely mirrored their own personal views, the same was not true in the case of males. Thus, despite the fact that over a quarter of the men questioned thought that women were better employers than males, fewer than 15 per cent considered this to be an element of the stereotype of female entrepreneurs. Likewise, while 23 per cent of men considered women business owners to be more competent and professional, fewer than one in eight thought that this was the stereotypical view (Table 7.2). These results suggest two things for female entrepreneurs in Poland today: they are highly regarded, at least among the urban community; but, more negatively, such sentiments contrast sharply with what people see as the prevailing stereotype. And this difference between the personal views expressed by respondents and those they perceived 'others' to hold was most marked amongst males. This might indicate a generational difference, insofar as women have historically been considered to be less adept at business ownership than men, while contemporary views are more open-minded. However, in a country in which gender stereotypes are so deeply rooted in the national culture, it might be unrealistic to assume that the change that this might imply will be effected rapidly. Nevertheless, the fact that certain of the negative characteristics which respondents felt were components of the stereotype of a male entrepreneur were not considered to be elements of the popular perception of female business owners is worthy of note.[4]

Table 7.3 Stereotypes of Female and Male Entrepreneurs[1]

View of Stereoptype	Females		Males	
	N	%	N	%
Negative	23	12.2	241	31.4
Ambivalent	14	7.4	90	11.7
Neutral	23	12.2	56	7.3
Positive	115	60.8	271	35.3
Stereotypes of Sub-Categories	8	4.2	88	11.2
Rejection of Stereotype	1	0.5	17	2.2
Unclear Answer	5	2.6	4	0.5
TOTAL	189	99.9	767	99.6

[1] The percentage sums do not add to 100 due to rounding.

In order to simplify the information obtained from the survey about gender stereotypes, the responses were aggregated into four categories; in turn created to represent whether the subject's assessment of the Polish stereotypical vision of women as business owners was negative, ambivalent or neutral. The results obtained from conducting this exercise are presented in Table 7.3.[5] There is a clear distinction between the sexes in their perceptions of the stereotype of a female entrepreneur. While over 60 per cent of women believe that this stereotype is positive, just over one-third of male respondents assumed this to be the case.

Nevertheless, more males elected for descriptions that are here considered to be positive than for any of the three other response aggregations. In a similar vein, while 31 per cent of male respondents thought that the stereotypical view of women business owners was negative, only 12 per cent of women were of the same opinion.

MANAGEMENT SKILLS OF MALE AND FEMALE BUSINESS OWNERS

In order to investigate further why respondents of both sexes seemingly viewed female entrepreneurs more favorably than males, interviewees were asked: "[D]o you think that women can manage a business better, the same or worse than a man?". Although the majority—61 per cent—believed there to be no difference in the managerial ability of the sexes, 16 per cent of respondents thought that women were the better managers and less than eight per cent held the opposite opinion.

Table 7.4 Why are Women Better Managers?

Response (N=208)	Total (%)	Male (%)	Females (%)
More Precise, Scrupulous	44.5	46.3	42.6
Better Communicators	19.5	20.9	18.0
Talented, Better Reasoning	18.8	16.4	21.3
More Dependable, Honest	17.2	19.4	14.8
Better Employers	16.4	13.4	19.7
More Persistent	14.8	13.4	16.4
Take Better Care of Business	14.1	13.4	14.8
More Operative, Smart	12.5	13.4	11.5
Better Qualified	4.7	3.0	6.6
Other Answers	8.6	10.4	6.6
Difficult to Say	0.8	..	1.6

Those perceiving there to be a difference in the management skills of men and women were asked to justify their beliefs. Table 7.4 reports the responses of those believing that women were the more able, with the modal reply for both sexes being that women managers were more precise and scrupulous, although this view was more widely held by males than females. The results also indicate that female entrepreneurs are viewed as better communicators, more talented, more honest and generally better employers. Few respondents cited qualifications as a source of this supposedly superior female entrepreneurial performance—less than seven per cent of the women surveyed, and only three per cent of the men stated this—despite the widespread conclusion that women are the better educated sex (Ingham and Ingham, 1997). Those respondents who considered female business owners to be worse than males most frequently (38 per cent of all interviewees) felt that women were more suited to non-market, domestic activities. However, 28 per cent believed that women were less decisive and courageous than men, while 23 per cent believed that women were too weak and would be unable to manage the stress.

HELP AND HINDRANCE FOR FEMALE ENTREPRENEURS

Throughout the world, women are less likely than males to be regarded as either members of, or potential recruits to, the entrepreneurial class, and the situation in Poland represents no exception. In view of this, those interviewed were asked to identify the factors that they considered most aided and most hindered women as business owners. A little over half of those surveyed cited domestic chores and family obligations as constraints, while one-fifth alluded to stereotyping and prejudice.[6] In comparison, a study conducted in 1995, which questioned businesswomen about the problems they faced, reported that 70 per cent of the female managers interviewed felt that their job gave them too little time for their private life, while two-thirds believed that they had too little time for leisure (Lisowska, 1997).[7] Domestic duties are clearly viewed as a hurdle to female entrepreneurial success, both by women business owners and the wider population.

Very rarely did interviewees express the view that women were psychologically weaker and thereby overwhelmed more easily by the demands of entrepreneurship. Less than four per cent of respondents thought that women lacked the requisite nerve, courage or willingness to bear risk, and only four and a half per cent believed that men would be reticent to have a woman as a business partner. Somewhat surprisingly, only two per cent of those questioned thought that employees would prefer not to have a women boss, a finding which contrasts sharply with the survey reported in Ingham and Karwińska (*this volume*).[8]

At the same time, unreported results indicate that those surveyed considered women business owners to possess a number of advantages that men did not have. Forty per cent cited attributes such as beauty, charm and elegance, while an additional 15 per cent pointed to superior communication skills, eloquence and straightforwardness. Other characteristics noted, albeit by a minority of respondents, were education, knowledge, hard work, precision, insight and kindness. However, and notwithstanding the inclusion of noble attributes in the foregoing list, the survey conveys clearly the message that it is physical characteristics that are believed most commonly to be the most likely to give female entrepreneurs advantages in the business world.[9]

That the responses portray a stereotype of women as business owners is confirmed by the fact that, when questioned about the characteristics successful business people were believed to possess, a completely different set of attributes emerged. Over 27 per cent of those surveyed pointed to professionalism, almost one-quarter to intellect and over 20 per cent to entrepreneurship and communication skills. Other important attributes highlighted included determination (18 per cent of respondents) and honesty and reliability (17 per cent). At the other end of the spectrum, only slightly more than three per cent thought that appearance was an important asset for business owners, while none admitted to a belief that domestic circumstances could be a constraining factor for entrepreneurs. It is therefore quite clear that male and female entrepreneurs are viewed differently in Poland: the career paths of women are hampered by domestic duties but aided by physical attractiveness, while males are helped by their professionalism and smartness and are untroubled by household affairs.

PERCEPTIONS OF THE SUCCESS OF WOMEN BUSINESS OWNERS

Ultimately, beliefs about the entrepreneurial capabilities of women reveal nothing about their ability to become successful businesswomen. The survey therefore also asked whether "it is easier for a woman or a man to become successful in business in Poland?". While more than one-half of the respondents (55 per cent) thought that there was no difference in the constraints facing the sexes in this regard, 34 per cent of those sampled considered that it would be harder for women. The latter figure contrasts sharply with the mere three per cent who believed that success would be achieved more easily by women. It is further noteworthy that the percentage of female respondents who believed women to face greater hurdles than men exceeded the corresponding percentage for males by a considerable margin; the figures being 39 per cent and 24 per cent, respectively. Furthermore, the more educated the respondent, the more likely they were to believe that women face greater obstacles in the business world. On the basis of this finding, it could be conjectured that those who are likely to be most familiar with the workings of business recognize more acutely the disadvantageous position in which women find themselves.

Table 7.5 Obstacles for Women Entrepreneurs

Response	Males		Females		Total	
	N	%	N	%	N	%
Stereotype/Prejudice/Tradition	45	42.1	56	33.3	101	36.7
Domestic Obligations	21	19.6	44	26.2	65	23.6
Discrimination against Women	19	17.8	37	22.0	56	20.4
Women are Worse Bosses	14	13.1	19	11.3	33	12.0
Women are not Forceful Enough	12	11.2	18	10.7	30	10.9
Disregard for Women	6	5.6	15	8.9	21	7.6
More Difficult for Women to Start a Business	3	2.8	6	3.6	9	3.3
Other Answers	8	7.5	17	10.1	25	9.1
Do Not Know/No Answer	2	1.8	1	0.6	3	1.1
TOTAL	130		213		343	

Those respondents who thought that the sexes were not equally likely to be successful were asked why they believed this to be the case, with the views of those who thought that it was harder for women to succeed being presented in Table 7.5. The most frequently cited reason was stereotyping/prejudice/tradition, although this was underpinned by marked differences between the responses of men and women. Thus, whereas only one-third of female respondents saw these factors as major difficulties, the corresponding figure for males was 42 per cent. Conversely, while less than one-fifth of male respondents felt that domestic responsibilities limited the achievements of female business owners, the corresponding figure for women exceeded 26 per cent. Also more females (22 per cent) than males (18 per cent) felt that the possible existence of discrimination constituted a constraint on the success of women entrepreneurs. A picture therefore emerges in which males believe that the stereotypical role of women hampers their achievements in the arena of business ownership, while females themselves feel less concerned about historical precedence and more concerned with outright discrimination and the pressures arising from household responsibilities.

If the female perception is indeed the correct one, there are grounds for optimism regarding the future of women as business owners. First, if the competitiveness of the Polish economy increases, as might be anticipated to ensue from the successful conclusion of the Mass Privatization Plan and increased trade liberalization, the distorting effects of discrimination should decline.[10] Second, the increasing availability of labor saving devices should decrease the amount of time households, and therefore *de facto* women, need to devote to domestic work. However, if the male view is correct, the belief that women should conform to the role set of the 'Polish Mother' may persist for many years to come. In addition, the number of respondents who thought that it was easier for women business owners to succeed was low and the prevailing view of this minority was that women's physical characteristics gave them their advantage, rather than any other objective asset.

IS A BUSINESS CAREER SUITABLE FOR A WOMAN?

A more accurate way of gauging public perceptions of females as entrepreneurs might be to shift the focus away from beliefs about those who are currently economically active towards the opportunities and threats that individuals perceive that such a career path might hold for future labor market entrants. To pursue this line of inquiry, those surveyed were asked how they would react to one of their own—suitably qualified—children starting up a business. The responses elicited by this question indicated a positive attitude towards entrepreneurship as a career; over 85 per cent of both the men and women surveyed would be in favor of their children opening their own business. Further probing highlighted a number of considerations underlying this strong level of support, as in Table 7.6. The most popular view was that entrepreneurship offers the potential to earn a high income; a belief held by over four in ten of both sexes. Other commonly cited benefits included the opportunity for independence, the chance for success and improvement, the opportunity to 'test' oneself, the potential for skill development and, of some note in an era which has witnessed the re-emergence of mass unemployment, the fact that starting a business of itself provides work.[11]

Table 7.6 The Suitability of a Career in Business for a Daughter/Son

Response	Daughter		Son	
	N	%	N	%
Definitely Yes	400	50.0	454	56.8
Probably Yes	284	35.5	243	30.4
Would Possibly Advise Against	44	5.5	45	5.6
Would Definitely Advise Against	16	2.0	12	1.5
Difficult to Say	52	6.5	45	5.6
No Answer	4	0.5	1	0.1

On the other hand, many small businesses came into being when the large state-owned enterprises (SOEs) divested themselves of peripheral activities. This out-sourcing has resulted in entrepreneurs now selling goods and services to their previous employers. However, these enterprises are highly vulnerable to the economic fortunes of their parent enterprises and, as restructuring is far from complete, this form of entrepreneurship carries risk (Scase, 1997). As shown in Table 7.7, such dangers represent the major reason why parents would reject business ownership as a career for their offspring. Nevertheless, there is some evidence of gendering in relation to attitudes towards risk, at least in terms of the career choices of offspring, with almost 47 per cent of respondents citing it as the reason why they felt that entrepreneurship was not suitable for their daughter, while the corresponding figure for male children was, at approximately 40 per cent, somewhat smaller.

Table 7.7 Reasons for the Approval of a Business Career for a Daughter/Son

Response	Daughter (%), (N=684)	Son (%), (N=697)
Chance for a Better Income	40.6	44.0
Independence	26.6	24.5
Chance of Success/Life Improvement	16.7	20.1
Possibility to Test Herself/Himself	17.7	10.5
Possibility for Skill Development	11.8	12.9
Work, Employment	10.8	10.5
Conditional Approval	10.1	6.2
She/He Will Decide for Herself/Himself	2.8	3.0
Family Tradition	8.0	..
A Man is More Responsible for Supporting the Family	1.5	1.0
Prestige	2.0	..
Other Answer	2.9	4.7
No Answer	0.5	1.1

Additional differences in attitudes towards daughters and sons were apparent in the other reasons cited for not supporting entrepreneurship as a career choice for children (Table 7.8). While almost 17 per cent of respondents felt that the inadequacy of legal regulations made business ownership unsuitable for a daughter, none of those surveyed considered this to be a reason to reject entrepreneurship for a son. Conversely, the tax problems associated with self-employment were cited more than two and one-half times more often in the case of a son than of a daughter. Also, while nearly twelve per cent of respondents expressed doubts whether their daughter could manage such work, no one expressed similar reservations about their son. However, more than twelve per cent doubted whether their son had the predisposition for entrepreneurship, although no one doubted that a daughter would be similarly troubled. Less than seven per cent of those questioned believed entrepreneurship to be unsuitable for a daughter because of the demands of their domestic duties but, unsurprisingly, no one considered this to be an important factor in the case of a son's choice of career.

Table 7.8 Reasons for the Rejection of a Business Career for a Daughter/Son

Response	Daughter (%) (N=60)	Son (%) (N=57)
Risk, Stress, Risk of Bankruptcy	46.7	40.4
Bad, Unstable Legal Regulations	16.7	..
High Taxes, Difficulties, Formalities	10.0	26.3
She/He Should go to Work First	6.7	7.0
Lack of Money, Expensive Credit	6.7	7.0
It is not Known if She/He will Manage	11.7	..
Lack of Suitable Disposition	..	12.3
Women Should Take Care of the Home	6.7	..
Other Answer	16.7	22.8
No Answer	3.3	3.5

SUMMARY AND CONCLUSIONS

The results of the research reported in this paper suggest that almost two-thirds of Polish city dwellers do not harbor what has been claimed to be the popular stereotype of women business owners; rather, they perceive there to be no difference between female and male entrepreneurs. Amongst the minority who did believe there to be differences between the sexes, the image of women business owners was actually more positive than negative: they were viewed as being better employers, more competent, more reliable, more decisive and more elegant than men. However, the traditional view of the role of women in Polish society has not disappeared completely and a small number of those surveyed expressed the opinion that women should stay at home and take care of the home and family.

The survey also unearthed some positive findings regarding the skills that women are thought to possess for business ownership. While 60 per cent of respondents believed that the sexes were equally well equipped in this regard, 16 per cent considered women's skills to be superior to those of men, while only eight per cent considered them to be inferior. However, in view of the following discussion, it seems likely that these beliefs are themselves predicated on stereotypical views of women rather than on any specific knowledge of the skills necessary for successful business management.

When questioned about the obstacles those businesswomen might face, over half of the respondents pointed to the constraints of home and family. This is in interesting contrast to the findings of Lisowska (1996, 1997) who, on asking women business owners about the problems they themselves faced, found many to feel that their business obligations meant that they did not have enough time for a family. Possibly this is a reflection of the country's history, with older generations having been thwarted in their entrepreneurial ambitions whereas the current generation of women business-owners have put their careers before children and marriage. On the other hand, the current survey's finding that the major advantages which female entrepreneurs enjoy are physical in character might be viewed as a not altogether encouraging reflection of the standard stereotype.

A large number of respondents expressed the view that female entrepreneurs would find it more difficult to succeed than would a comparable male. The justifications advanced for the possession of this view included prejudice, discrimination, stereotypes and family responsibilities. At the same time, a minority of those surveyed believed that women were not in fact suited to run a business. However, and more positively, owning a business was viewed by many respondents as a career for which their sons and daughters were equally suited. Nevertheless, this raises the question of whether this view is itself based upon a stereotype of the entrepreneur rather than on personal experience.

On the face of it, self-employment in Poland is extremely important and has accounted for between 22 and 25 per cent of all in work over the period May 1992 to August 1998 (GUS, 1998). Typically, however, the figure has been between five and six percentage points lower for women than for men (*ibid.*). Nevertheless, a superficial reading of the data could easily, but quite incorrectly, lead one to the conclusion that the extent of self-employment within the economy represents one of the miracles of the transformation. In truth, the country retained a sizeable private sector throughout the communist era as a result of the authorities' failure to collectivize the vast majority of the agricultural sector: and most of this was composed of extremely small family concerns. Thus, throughout the period covered by the Labor Force Survey (LFS), the proportion of rural workers reporting themselves to be self-employed has typically been three times greater than the equivalent proportion of urban workers (*ibid.*). While one cannot dismiss the 1.1 million urban dwellers who work for themselves, self-employment in Poland remains a distinctly rural phenomenon. Furthermore, outside agriculture, while some fifteen per cent of males were self-employed in August 1998, the corresponding figure for women was only 7.6 per cent (*ibid.*).

It is also important to recognize that the self-employed are not a homogeneous group but range from owners of large private companies, through professionals and trades persons to the proprietors of street stalls. Although by no means adequate to describe such variety, the LFS does distinguish between those who have employees from those who work on their own account. In August 1998, one-fifth of all self-employed had employees, although the figure was six per cent higher for males than for females (*ibid.*). However, outside agriculture, the equivalent percentages for males and females were 36.2 and 36.5, respectively. There is at least a good possibility therefore that, if the urban residents contacted in this study have personal experience of a self-employed worker of either sex, it will be of one who is at least overtly successful.

In summary, this survey revealed that the urban population, men as well as women, hold largely positive views of females as entrepreneurs. Notwithstanding the fact that it is precisely amongst this section of the population that one would expect traditional stereotypes to fade most quickly, this is an encouraging sign that urban labor markets might exhibit the genuine adaptability that will be necessary for the country to compete in the world economy of the new millenium. However, the findings must be tempered by the fact that, outside agriculture, there has yet to be an explosion of meaningful self-employment and that the views expressed in this study may reflect another stereotype; that of the western entrepreneur, as characterized by perhaps Bill Gates, Richard Branson or Anita Roddick. In truth, some entrepreneurs succeed, while others struggle to survive; and this holds for females just as it is does for males.

NOTES

1 The study was conducted by the Center for Social Survey Research at the Institute of Philosophy and Sociology of the Polish Academy of Sciences in Warsaw.

2 This description of female entrepreneurs encompasses the following: being better than men as employers; taking better care of employees; being less likely to fire workers; being more likely to help workers; being more understanding, tactful, protective, human, respectful, accessible and delicate, in addition to paying wages which are both higher and received on time.

3 The term 'competent' refers to attributes such as professional, qualified, better at conducting business and having a grasp of the market.

4 These included the following: operative, dishonest, upstart, rich, smart, workaholic, clever, arrogant, cheats the government, forceful, conceited, ignorant, and 'nouveau riche'.

5 In Table 7.3 positive expressions relate mainly to management skills and the fulfillment of the ownership role, whereas negative expressions relate primarily to the human resource issues that arise between owners and employees.

6 Included in the stereotyping and prejudice category were responses such as discrimination, tradition, the belief that women cannot cope with managing a business and male chauvinism.

7 Additional barriers reported by Lisowska (1996, 1997) included a lack of legal knowledge and frequent changes in legal requirements.

8 Although Ingham and Karwińska (2001) report results for Kraków, a parallel survey was also conducted in Warsaw, Budapest and Prague and, for those three cities, the belief was that employees did not like to have women as bosses. The results for all four locations are discussed in Grime et al. (1997).

9 This finding is somewhat worrying from a policy perspective insofar as beauty at least is, for most people, an unalterable personal characteristic to use the terminology of Spence (1974).

10 This follows because discrimination imposes a cost on firms and, in a competitive climate, where profit is eliminated, firms engaging in such practices will not survive.

11 The significance of the fact that starting a business provides young people with employment should not be understated, given the high levels of unemployment facing young people in Poland, including Warsaw (see Ingham and Ingham, 2000).

REFERENCES

Domański, H. (1999) "Social Mobility in Six East-European Nations," *this volume.*

Grime, E.K., V. Duke and M. Ingham (1997) Final Report of the European Commission project "The Social and Economic Consequences of Privatization in Central and Eastern Europe," European Commission.

GUS (1998) *Labour Force Survey in Poland, May 1998*, Warszawa: Główny Urząd Statystyczny.

Ingham, H. and M. Ingham (1997) "Unemployment, Gender and Education in Poland: A Legacy of History?" Discussion Paper EC7/97, The Management School, Lancaster University.

Ingham, H. and M. Ingham (2000) "Labour Market Reform and the Lost Generation: Youth Unemployment in Poland," *Geographia Polonica*, vol. 73, no. 1, pp. 5–23.

Ingham, H. and A. Karwińska (2001) "Women and Labor Market Reform in Kraków," *this volume.*

Jasiecki, K. (1995) "Przedsiębiiorcy 90" (Entrepreneurs 90), *Spoleczenstwo Otwarte*, no. 5, pp. 3–8.

Kotowska, I.E. (2001) "Demographic and Labor Market Developments in the 1990s," *this volume.*

Lisowska, E. (1996) "Barriers to a Wider Participation by Women in Private Sector Growth in Poland," *Women and Business*, nos. 1–2, pp. 64–67.

Lisowska, E. (1997) "Women Entrepreneurs in Poland, Lithuania and Ukraine—A Comparative Analysis." *Women and Business*, nos. 1–2, pp. 14–19.

Scase, R. (1997) "The Role of Small Businesses in the Economic Transformation of Eastern Europe: Real but Relatively Unimportant?" *International Small Business Journal*, vol. 16, no. 1, pp. 13–21.

Spence, M.A. (1974) *Market Signalling: Informational Transfer in Hiring and Related Screening Processes*, Cambridge, Mass.: Harvard University Press.

CHAPTER 8

WOMEN'S ORGANIZATIONS IN POLAND

The self-organization of a society, whether in the spheres of politics, economics or culture, or in the promotion of information exchange and the protection of group interests, underpins the notion of a civil society. Legal, freely organized activities oriented towards the satisfaction of the interests of people were not in the past normal phenomena in Polish society: prior to 1990, only three political parties existed; by 1991, this figure had risen to almost three hundred. At the same time, women started to undertake many activities in response to the challenges posed by the new economic, political and social order. A women's movement, organizing activities undertaken by women, either individually or collectively, which enabled them to express their opinions and to accomplish their goals, developed as a social force. Women no longer accept a given situation passively, but adopt an active stance towards the reality they want to change. The purpose of this chapter is to investigate the growth of women's organizations during the past decade using case material obtained from in-depth, case-study interviews.

Whatever the constraints on their operation, it is incorrect to argue that women's organizations were totally absent during the socialist era and the following section outlines the major characteristics of those that did exist. Section 3 then goes on to explore the rapid expansion of the women's movement during the 1990s; in particular, the growth in the number, as well as the diversity, of related organizations is discussed. Section 4 focuses attention on the constituencies of the various groups that have emerged. Not surprisingly, some of these are elitist in the stance they adopt towards their potential members, whereas others are more open. A rather different way of distinguishing between women's organizations is that based on territory of operation. Thus, just as large cities have tended to fare better in economic terms during the early years of transition, it is also in the major agglomerations that many of the organizations are most active. Nevertheless, bodies dedicated to the rural community do exist and Section 5 analyzes the areal differentiation that has emerged as the women's movement has developed. Having examined their constituencies and spatial spheres of influence, Section 6 provides an in-depth analysis of the activities of the various types of women's organization. A summary and concluding remarks to the chapter are contained in Section 7.

DYNAMICS

Until 1989, two major women's organizations existed in Poland; the Circle of Rural Housewives (CRH) and the League of Polish Women, both of which still operate today.[1] The first CRH was established in 1877, in a village near Skierniewice; its main objective being the provision of education in villages.[2] Nonetheless, it also played a very important role in the struggle for the preservation of the Polish national identity under the sequential periods of annexation by Russia, Germany and Austro–Hungary (Michalik, 1993, p. 347) and later became influential in the process of the professionalization of agriculture. The CRH entered the epoch of the (communist) Polish People's Republic as a longstanding organization, the major achievement of which was its widespread acceptance among village inhabitants, even though it was not legalized until 1957. As a body formed by a specific social category of women—female inhabitants of villages linked mainly, although not exclusively, to agriculture—it always retained a focus on raising the level of agricultural knowledge and on teaching its members how to run a household. The gathering and transmission of the traditions of folk culture were notable among its accomplishments. From the outset, the CRH relied primarily on its own initiative and funds. The specific nature of its activities, and its local community scale, thwarted attempts to include it within the family of other mass women's organizations, such as the League of Women.[3] In 1966, after a decision taken by the Central Committee of the Polish United Workers' Party, the CRH regained its status as a rural organization and began to co-operate with the Agricultural Circle, which was a farmers' movement, on matters concerning the division of labor within the peasant family.

The second organization, the League of Women, was founded in 1945 with the goal of promoting "educational and socio-educational work, the activation of women and their participation in the country's socio-political, economic and cultural life." (Encyklopedia Powszechna, 1984, p. 33). The statute of the League of Women states that it will seek 'to group the widest possible masses of women' and conduct 'ideological-educational work ... protecting the interests of women' (see Jaranowska, 1994).[4] Because the League was obliged to perform ideological functions, it found it difficult to win social support. Its statutes were changed several times and it became "an organization ... associating women from urban milieus." (Encyklopedia Powszechna, 1984, p. 733). As its membership straddled social classes, strata and social backgrounds it tended to identify more with local communities and interests than with some abstract 'female' aggregation. In 1983, the name of the organization was changed to the League of Polish Women in an attempt to divert women's attention away from the hardships of everyday life at the time towards more patriotic concerns.

The effects of the activities of these two groups were widespread and not confined simply to their members. Almost all rural women were eligible for membership of CRH, while most were not very active and were poorly represented in both CRH and in other political and social organizations (Tryfan, 1968). However, even though only some female villagers were involved in its work, almost all benefited from the functions it performed and almost all rural women must have come into contact with the activities of their local CRH.

Likewise, the League of Women, although hampered by not having explicitly defined goals of activity, also attempted to be useful in the community. Whilst its official representative role was to reassure the authorities of its ideological correctness, grassroots organizations were helping women with various aspects of their family and professional lives (Borkowska, 1973; Jaranowska, 1994; Kowalczyk, 1997).[5] Many women belonged formally to the League but never derived any benefits from membership, although numerous others sought, and received, its assistance, even though they had never been members.[6] Furthermore, non-members benefited occasionally from the cultural, recreational and educational events that the League organized, which typically were either free or required only a token payment. Conversely, many female inhabitants of cities never came into contact with the League's activities, even though they must have known of its existence.

Throughout the upheavals of 1989–1990, the CRH continued as an organization perceived to be engaged in economic and cultural activities. However, the League of Women was identified as a state organ that had adhered to communist ideological functions and it was widely believed that it had not been free from political pressure from the party in power. This was a crisis exacerbated by the fact that state financing of the League was suspended early in the current reform era. Nevertheless, some of its members became actively involved in controversial issues, including collaborating with other feminist organizations to oppose a restrictive draft of the anti-abortion Act.

Notwithstanding the activities of the CRH and the League, the need, and the capacity for creative social participation by women had lain dormant under communist rule and, as soon as the socio-political conditions in Poland permitted, independent women's social organizations began to emerge. The first of these were informal and had to wait several years for registration. In the spring of 1981, the Polish Feminist Association was established in Warsaw, although this group was not registered formally until 1989. Likewise, the Women's Self-Support Movement commenced operation in 1985 but was not registered until March 1994. The first Polish clubs of 'Amazons'—women after mastectomy—were set up in 1987 and, in 1989, the Independent Social Women's Movement began its activities and was registered formally in the following year. Also in 1990, the Polish Women's Council was revived; an organization originally founded in 1924. In addition, women MPs organized themselves in the Parliament, with their early activities laying the foundations of the Parliamentary Group of Women, which later came to comprise female representatives from both chambers of government. Other bodies established at the time included the Association for Natural Birth and Breast Feeding, the Women's Defence Movement and Pro Femina.[7] Overall, seven women's organizations commenced their activities in 1989 while, in the first half of the 1990s, an average of more than ten new ones were established each year.[8] Altogether, a total of 68 women's organizations operated in Poland during the period 1990–1995; that is, 66 new ones alongside the two of long-standing. The Federation of Women and Family Planning was also active, with seven of its total of nine associated groupings being exclusively for women.

In terms of size, six out of the 68 groups dominate: the Democratic Union of Women, the League of Polish Women, the Labour Union's Women's Section, the Federation of Polish Women's Clubs (Amazonki), the CRH and the Women's Section of Solidarity. Of these, both the Democratic Union of Women and the Labor Union's Women's Section have adopted structures similar to that of political parties. The Women's Section of Solidarity is a structural component of the main union, operating in every region where the parent has a presence. The CRH has preserved the organizational structure developed during its century long history. The Amazons' clubs tend to be associated with city hospitals, with which they co-operate in the fields of prophylactics and rehabilitation. Least transparent is the League, although it is evidently far less structured than it was during the socialist period. While it still maintains provincial, regional and urban boards, together with four local circles, it has lost its accommodation base and has also had to fight for financial resources.

A PICTURE OF THE POLISH WOMEN'S MOVEMENT

The heterogeneity of women's movements is well known and documented by inter alia French studies conducted in the 1970s and 1980s (Castelain-Meunier, 1986), although this diversity is neither exclusive to women's groups, nor is it a symptom of weakness or immaturity. It is also found, for example, in the ecological movement, both in Poland and elsewhere in the world (Gliński, 1996, pp. 228). The internal diversity of Polish women's organizations is due primarily to their operational characteristics (formal or informal, governmental or non-governmental), their natural constituency and their territorial distribution. Many began life as informal initiatives, whether individual or collective, but by 1995 only five had retained this informal status, the remainder having registered their activity and assumed the form of an association or foundation. Some were even established within existing formal structures; for example, as scientific-research units within Polish universities dealing with women's problems.

An alternative categorization of women's movements distinguishes between governmental and non-governmental bodies.[9] Not surprisingly, this typology emphasizes the civil character of the organizations established after 1989 and the independence of their power elite. The main governmental women's organization began life as the Office of Government's Plenipotentiary for Women's Affairs, a branch of the Council of Ministers' Office, which has since had a rich, albeit short, history. The first democratic Polish government (headed by Tadeusz Mazowiecki) set up the Plenipotentiary although, ironically, the first female

Prime Minister, Hanna Suchocka, abolished it. Reactivated during the coalition governments of the Democratic Left Alliance (the former communist party) and the Polish Peasants' Party, the scope of the organization was widened, as evidenced by its new title—the Office of Government's Plenipotentiary for Family and Women's Affairs. Its major function was to assist the government in tasks which included the initiation and co-ordination of activities promoting equal rights of women in all fields of life and shaping and implementing state policy in relation to the family, children and youth (DWOIP, 1995, p. 110).

In September 1997, when power transferred to the coalition of the Election Action 'Solidarity' and the right wing Freedom Union, the word 'women' was omitted from the Plenipotentiary's title. This could be taken to imply that women's problems have been identified as synonymous with women's role within the family. Alternatively, it could be a reflection of the fact that the government has decided no longer to deal with women's specific problems and is instead concentrating its attention on the general problems of the contemporary Polish family. In this context, it is worth remembering that the bill requiring the equal status of men and women was drafted on the initiative of the Parliamentary Group of Women under the Democratic Left Alliance–Polish Peasants' Party coalition. While this administration failed to pass the bill, equal opportunity legislation is currently once again under discussion in Parliament.

It is clear therefore that the existence of any governmental organization is dependent upon the will of the political grouping in power. Egalitarianism is a value identified with the political left wing, and this encompasses the problem of women's social status. Conversely, the right wing stresses family affairs and promises to pursue pro-family policies; in consequence, they give priority to the role of women in the private sphere of life, although not to the exclusion of their participation in the public sphere. This perception of the inseparability of the problems of women from those of the family strengthens the stereotype of the traditional division of activities between the sexes. It also serves to distract attention away from issues such as women's place in contemporary, democratic society and the role of men within the family. On the other hand, excluding women's participation in the public sphere from the orbit of the government's direct interest devalues the issue.

Other Polish governmental women's organizations include the Provincial Center of Crisis Intervention and the Żoliborz Women's Center in Warsaw.[10] The first offers psychological, social and legal counseling, individual and family psychotherapy for people in crisis situations, and provides education and training services. The second delivers professional courses and counseling services for women, primarily for those who are inhabitants of Warsaw's Żoliborz District, as well as running support groups for women with alcohol problems, parents of mentally handicapped children and women with weight problems.[11]

The remaining women's organizations in Poland are non-governmental, established through local initiatives and are not publicly funded. Their specific programs are influenced by many factors, including ideology and public opinion, which often enforce the hierarchy of priorities that should be dealt with by community organizations (Taylor, 1994, pp. 56–58). The tendency to emphasize independent status was evident at the world women's conference held in Beijing in 1995. At this event the non-governmental organizations claimed that they had at least equal rights to represent Polish women, while simultaneously expressing doubts as to whether the Office of Government Plenipotentiary for Family's and Women's Affairs would fulfill its mission in a reliable manner.[12] This conference also intensified the ideological divisions between the non-governmental organizations of the Polish women's movement. For example, certain groups, basing their programs on 'Christian values,' distanced themselves from the 'feminists' who, in their opinion, were neglecting the traditional social role that women played within the family.[13]

While public funds are provided for the governmental organizations—mainly from the budgets of the ministries, the Parliament and the National Bank of Poland—very few subventions for other women's groups come from this source. Also, the monetary aid given by local authorities is quite negligible.[14] Very often organizations that operate explicitly at the local level do not receive any financial support for their activities at all (DWOIP, 1995, pp. 40–42), even if they aim to tackle problems such as local unemployment. Many organizations are, at least partially, dependent on their own ability to generate income from sources such as cultural events and subscriptions. In addition, however, they have attracted a plethora of both domestic and foreign sponsors, with the United Nations Development Fund and the Stefan Batory Foundation being two noteworthy examples. Also, foreign women's organizations have helped their Polish counterparts although, most frequently, such assistance has taken the form of the provision of funding for a specific project. Finally, funds are provided by international religious associations for those groupings that have their roots in the same faith; for example, the Polish Union of

Catholic Women has received assistance from Catholic bodies in Germany, Switzerland and Canada, as well as from the International Union of Catholic Women's Organizations.

CONSTITUENTS OF WOMEN'S ORGANIZATIONS[15]

An alternative way to categorize women's organizations is by whether they accept men into their membership (mixed organizations) or are exclusively female (non-mixed). It is not only women who establish mixed organizations and neither are women the only activists within them. Moreover, they address a wide audience, not solely women. For example, the Federation for Women and Family Planning directs its activities towards both women and young people; Pro Femina, which champions the rights of women to abortion, counts men among both its founders and active members. The practice of restricting membership to women is primarily the custom of feminist organizations and is not, of course, unique to Poland: in certain cases their statutes even forbid men to accompany female members, as with the Maison des Femmes in Paris, for example.

Generally speaking, women's organizations are set up with females as the addressees of their activities. Most of them specify what characteristics a women should possess in order to be a member, what values they should share in order to be involved in their activities and, more specifically, to which particular audience they are directing their actions. In other words, being female is not a passport for entry into all women's groups. Taking into account the rather selective nature of the Polish women's organizations, it is possible to distinguish, first, groups for all women and, second, groups for particular social categories of women. Only a few organizations fall into the first classification and, generally speaking, they incorporate the word 'women' in their title. One obvious example is the Kowary Association of Women's Health Promotion, which implements a program covering women's physiology and biological functions. The more restrictive organizations typically differentiate potential members according to characteristics such as level of education, socio-occupational category, ideological-political orientation, membership of a given social milieu, or affliction with specific health problems.

Occupational position has evolved as an important eligibility criterion for membership, with unemployed women (and/or those threatened by the loss of a job) and businesswomen typically being targeted. The self-organization of women performing similar jobs indicates that they attach importance to their occupational activity, a sentiment that runs counter to a widely held Polish view. Thus it is typically accepted that women should concentrate primarily on issues such as their home, family, children and their husband's professional career (Domański, 1995).

With one exception, all of the organizations targeting a specific occupational group of women were established to counter female unemployment. The fact that some authors argue that women in Poland (like elsewhere) tend to lose permanent jobs easily, and have a lower probability than men of securing re-employment, mobilized other women. As early as the autumn of 1991, the International Women's Foundation was established as the first organization in Poland offering assistance to women losing jobs through group redundancies in liquidated firms. Other similar groups followed: the Center of Women's Activation and Employment, the Association of Active Women, the Żoliborz Women's Center, the Center for the Advancement of Women and the 'Aba' Unemployed Persons Agency. All of these have been actively involved in helping women to find jobs and to acquire new or supplementary qualifications. It is of some importance that they perceive the consequences of female unemployment not only in economic terms, but also from a psycho-social perspective and many women who have lost work have received their support.

At the other end of the spectrum there are organizations for educated women who already hold career positions. Such bodies aim to encourage increased levels of professionalism, for example, the Federation of Business and Professional Women Clubs, or to promote high ethical standards in professional life, for example, Centrum Praw Kobiet (the Center of Women's Rights) and Instytut Edukacji Obywatelskiej (the Institute of Citizenship Education). Members can win scholarships abroad to allow them to upgrade their qualifications, with one sponsor being the Polish branch of Zonta International.

Other bodies, such as the Parliamentary Group of Women and Soroptimists International, seek political influence and are frequently recognized as experts in their fields, both in Poland and abroad. One consequence of the formation of these exclusive women's organizations has been the creation of an elite, which has reinforced the strength of the contention that "occupational position and its attributes differentiate people to an increasingly greater extent in the 1990s." (Domański, 1998, p. 62). It is disturbing that this could lead to an even more pronounced shift of poorly educated and/or unemployed women to the margin of social life while female professionals continue to implement their own programs of advancement.

Ideology is another important factor differentiating social movements. In some cases, when formulating their program of activity, organizations define certain values that their members are required to espouse. In other cases the reverse is true and an 'ideological rationalization' is sought for activities already undertaken (Ślęczka, 1997, p. 20). Within the women's movement, organizations typically defend values that hold a high position in the hierarchy of society's values, such as egalitarianism, pluralism, tolerance, world peace, health and justice.

However, the same values can orient activities in a completely different direction. An interesting example is provided by those organizations that, while outwardly perceived as one stream of the women's movement, in reality adopt other theoretical underpinnings for their ideologies. These alternative foundations define the goal to be achieved and they adopt different strategies for its attainment. For example, in defending egalitarianism they can either fight discrimination against women by demanding a quota system, or they can provide women with education and training (Malinowska, 1997a). In this way similar programs of activity can be built on the basis of different ideologies (Ślęczka, 1997). Within the Polish women's movement there are no fundamental differences between the feminist organizations, although contrasts do exist between organizations of Christian Democratic, Social Democratic and feminist orientations.[16]

A representative goal for the female Social Democrats has been defined as "(the) protection of women's rights and interests as well as of their equal opportunities in all aspects of life; fighting social, professional, cultural and political discrimination against women; supporting women's professional aspirations; preparing women for public activities, and representing women's rights and interests towards state and local authorities as well as business associations." (DWOIP, 1995, p.15). It is stressed, of course, that this goal helps to 'support democracy.'

Female representatives of Christian Democratic persuasion similarly declared that their aim is to support women's desire to "perform functions in democratic institutions and in public life". Simultaneously, their task is to "shape public opinion in issues concerning the family" (*ibid.*, p. 128) from a position which recognizes that a woman's primary role is to be a mother and a wife. One of the female leaders of this group admits that the decision to found the organization was prompted by a desire to counteract the feminist movement, which was seen as attempting to impose on society a model of a woman 'liberated' from her traditional roles [2]. The support for women wishing to participate in the wielding of power is, on the other hand, justified by the necessity of increasing the participation of women with center-right and conservative orientations in public life. A particular aim being to increase their presence on elected ruling bodies, such as the boards of co-operatives the leadership of political parties, and within Parliament itself [2, 9].

In contrast, Polish feminists formulate their goals as "the dissemination of equality of rights principles and the struggle for the equal rights of women" [5] (*ibid.*, p. 58); "activities aimed at changing legal norms, practices of law enforcement and customs and culture, which discriminate against women" [2] (*ibid.*, p.120); and, "undertaking anti-discriminatory activities and supporting the development of women's culture." (The Women's Foundation eFKa) (*ibid.*, p. 132).

Interviews conducted with the leaders of selected Polish women's organizations indicate that ideological divisions in the women's movement are based on a set of opinions, as opposed to real knowledge, about the beliefs of other organizations. Frequently they renounce feminism and feminist organizations, a stance which may be attributed to the refusal of feminists to accept the traditional stereotype of women within Polish society [2]. Alternatively, it may be a reflection of dissatisfaction with the aggressive strategies adopted by feminists [7] and the revolutionary character of their programs [9]: "ideologies are the baggage of programs and policies of social movements and forces." Ślęczka (1997, p. 18). The same programs can have different 'baggage' while the same baggage can be seen in different programs. That is why, as the author remarks, the women's movement can, and does, attract people with different religious beliefs and various political views (*ibid.*, p. 18).

The women's movement is not however limited to activists and the founders of women's groups since it also includes those in the female population who derive benefits from the activities of the organizations. It quite often happens that, after meeting through the auspices of one organization, women form new coalitions. Sometimes they do not choose to set up a separate structure, preferring instead to become a component element of the original body. The Club of Businesswomen, which has operated since 1993 within the International Women's Foundation in Łódź, is one example of this latter practice.

The largest number (eight) of women's organizations covered by the survey are concerned with the provision of assistance for women who have found themselves in a 'difficult life situation'. The most comprehensive approach to this problem is that adopted by the Women's Self-Support Movement, which not only teaches what assistance means but also carries out therapeutic, educational and informational activities aimed at instructing women how to cope in the most diverse of life's situations. Likewise, the Association for Women and their Families offers assistance to a broad range of recipients: single mothers, women from families afflicted by alcoholism, female victims of violence, women and their families who find themselves in difficult life situations, and unemployed women. Other organizations focus their attention on a specific type of problem: the wives of alcoholics, for example, can seek assistance from the Self-Support Women's Aid Movement attached to the Abstinence Club. Several organizations were set up with the explicit purpose of providing support for single mothers, including the Parabola Foundation, the Help for Single Mothers Foundation and the St. Joseph Foundation Help for Single Mothers Foundation.

Of the 68 organizations that comprise the women's movement in Poland, eleven are elitist. To join these clubs it is necessary to fulfill definite criteria, and often it is necessary to have the support of at least one current member and the acceptance of others (e.g. Soroptimist International). These elite groups were established by women running their own businesses (the International Professional Women of Poland, the International Forum for Women); women-creators (the Creative Women's Club); women active in the public sphere of social life (the Parliamentary Group of Women, the International Forum for Women) or women holding important professional positions (Soroptimist International, Zonta International). Their members have in common a high level of education; however, they are primarily characterized by the same attitude towards life [7, 9, 11], sometimes referred to as 'individualistic orientation and self-reliance' (Domański and Dukaczewska, 1994).

The majority of these organizations were founded to help women from particular strata of society raise the level of their professionalism and heighten their independence and social position. In order to achieve this, they established both national and international networks of contacts among women entrepreneurs in different fields in the hope that they might exchange experiences, organize meetings with experts from different fields and discuss general problems connected with the promotion of entrepreneurship (the International Professional Women of Poland) (DWOIP, 1995, p. 30). Others deal with the promotion of members' creative output, strive to strengthen emotional ties between women, assist their creative work or attempt to integrate women actively involved in the different fields of art, science and culture (the Creative Women's Club) (*ibid.*, p. 32). They also promote women as owners of firms, conduct scientific analyses of new phenomena (such as the growing involvement of women in business activity) and propagate education helpful in starting and running a business (the International Forum for Women) (*ibid.*, p. 50).[17] The elite women's organizations play an important social role in propagating universal values and, through their example, they promote a new female image; one which is individualistic and professionally active (see Domański and Duckazewska, 1994). Such a role model for women is desirable in the present political—economic climate in Poland.

THE TERRITORIAL DISTRIBUTION OF WOMEN'S ORGANIZATIONS IN POLAND

Throughout the world, women's organizations operate mainly in large and medium-sized cities (Paquot, 1982, pp. 410–421). In Poland, the situation is similar: an overwhelming majority of women's organizations have their base in Warsaw—49 out of 68.[18] The other cities where more than two women's organizations operate are Kraków (7), Gdańsk (4) and Łódź (3), while Poznań, Katowice and Bydgoszcz each have two. In 1995, four new bodies were established in Warsaw and two were formed in both Toruń and Kraków. Groups with local sections usually locate in voivodship capitals: The Clubs of Women after Mastectomy ('Amazons'), for example, has branches in 16 voivodship capitals and the Democratic Union of Women has branches in 17 voivodship capitals, as well as in several medium-sized cities.[19]

In the case of those organizations associated with the feminist movement, one explanation for this spatial concentration is the fact that large cities ensure indispensable social support for their activities. Further, the new social movements, including the feminists, are generally the work of specific actors: usually the educated, the intelligentsia and professionals. Such a membership permits a faster orientation towards, and a more accurate assessment of, economic, political and technological transformation. The members are characterized by independent thought and, instead of readily accepting the place delimited for them and fulfilling their due role, they display creativeness and exhibit a need for active participation in the modeling of social relations (Touraine, 1992, p. 243). It is this so-called 'new collective actor' that is the "basic nucleus of new social movements" (Gortat, 1987, p. 52).

In contrast to the feminist movement, the wider women's movement comprises differentiated individuals who tend to be factionalized rather than identified with one single, common cause. The various interest groups are accommodated by the definition of goals that differ across organizations. On the other hand, some groupings, associated primarily with the feminist movement, attempt to define social conflict in terms of sex categories in such a way that it can concern the whole of society and hence become global in character (Malinowska, 1997b).

If the Polish women's movement appears insignificant in small towns and rural communities, it must be remembered that the focus adopted here has been exclusively on autonomous organizations. It is quite possible that in smaller localities the movement differs in character. For example, it could see its role as being that of involving women in the activities of other socio-political organizations as opposed to that of establishing a locally dedicated body. Involvement in trade unions, political parties and charitable organizations reflects a worldwide tradition of the women's movement (Molyneux, 1993, pp. 712–715). Nevertheless, and notwithstanding the theoretical rhetoric, issues related to the presence and the strategies of the Polish women's movement remain empirical questions.

ACTIVITIES OF POLISH WOMEN'S ORGANIZATIONS

Adopting categorizations that have been used in the study of other social movements, the intention here is to characterize the fields of activity of Polish women's organizations and the collective actions of the movement as a whole. In particular, attention is focused upon the ideological-political and the socio-economic arenas (Matuchniak-Krasuska, 1995; Pawlik, 1997).[20] In reality, the distinction between the two is chiefly analytical because there are also organizations which define their goals in very general terms and undertake actions in both of these fields simultaneously. For example, the feminist organizations operate in the ideological–political field but are frequently involved in intervention-type activity, with the Women's Rights Center being a case in point.

IDEOLOGICAL-POLITICAL FIELD

Involvement in the ideological–political field implies that activity is focused on the dissemination and realization of a professed ideology. This can occur in two ways; through modification of the law or by changing patterns of behavior and custom (Touraine, 1974). One example of an organization whose activities are aimed at the modification of the law is the feminist Women's Rights Center, which adopts as one of its defined tasks "acting to ensure an equal status of women and men through the change of legal norms (...) which discriminate against women" [3]. This organization became involved in the preparatory work on the draft of the new constitution, during the course of which it paid particular attention to citizens' rights and duties. According to one female activist, it was possible during this process to adopt two principles of behavior; either to strive to amend the existing rules concerning the rights of women or to focus on the creation of a new law without underlining differences between men and women [3]. Feminists from the Center are firmly in favor of the second solution: "in my opinion, neutral entries give better guarantees [of egalitarianism]. I was and remain opposed to the entries which can be found in the previous constitution that underline specifically the role and guarantees given to women due, for example, to maternity. I believe that the issues connected with parenthood should be approached neutrally without speaking only about maternity" [3].[21]

Neutral legal rules can also play an important role in breaking down stereotypes of social division according to sex. One example is the 'monitoring of legislation' (as one leader of an organization called it) in a way that ensures that legal prescriptions do not result in discriminatory practices. Thus, while the right to care for a sick child was nominally given to both parents, in practice it was only granted to the mother. This led to the conviction that by "discriminating in favor of/against one sex, we really restrict the rights of both sexes" [3].

The activities of the world feminist movement aim to 'integrate the rights of women within the main trend of human rights'; however, Polish feminists treat this concept as 'rather one for the future'. As the leader of the Polish Feminist Association stated: "today, at the end of the 20th century, the activists of human rights movements realize that, first, human rights were constructed for the man, with a thought about the man and, second, for the white man from a definite social stratum. This is why I believe that, until the equality of women's and men's status has been achieved, it is impossible to speak only about 'man' and his/her rights" [5]. Feminists also see the necessity of concluding "a new contract of the sexes" [5], the basis of which must be the legally guaranteed equality of females and males. The stance adopted by Polish feminists on this issue is very much in line with the general direction of activity pursued by their western European counterparts (Malinowska, 1997b).

Activists within the Christian Democratic organizations are also interested in the modification of the law. In their opinion, "a problem of fundamental importance in social life is the desire to base society on certain values, and we locate these values in Christianity" [2]. These values "have existed for two thousand years and they secure the social order, and we consider this to be the most important thing" [2]. The strategy of these bodies is to increase the share of women in the elected organs of power. As such, they are more interested in making law than in changing regulations and they do not object to a quota system as a means of facilitating increased female participation in order to achieve this aim [2].

The Social Democracy movement also pursues this strategy, with the most influential organization within this sphere being the Parliamentary Group of Women. Its members are also actively involved in the Democratic Union of Women and were, of course, members of the Section of Women in the Labour Party that, at the time, was the ruling party in the Polish parliament. For obvious reasons, these women had the best opportunity to influence Polish law. Outside this group there was a certain subset of the women's Social Democratic movement whose members had formerly been involved in the Solidarity movement. The main strategy pursued by this group was to increase the direct participation of women in the organs of power by means of the quota system, while undertaking simultaneously to train and prepare women for political roles [1, 7, 10, 11].

The examples cited above demonstrate that, irrespective of ideological differences, women's organizations seek to modify the existing law. However, each ideological orientation does this in the way it believes can guarantee that its values are implemented. In consequence, the strategies adopted vary and they depend inter alia on the political leverage possessed by the organization at any given time.

The second area of action in the ideological-political sphere consists of attempts to modify traditional patterns of behavior. Bearing in mind the internal diversity of the movement, it is not difficult to imagine the wide scope of influence it can exert in this direction. At the same time, it is also worth highlighting its attempts to change the model of woman's role in society. The most explicit and transparent actors in this field are those organizations that place the problems of women in the context of the global social system and in the relationships between the sexes; they include the feminist organizations fighting for an egalitarian model of sex roles. While it is easy to enact laws proclaiming gender equality, it is quite another thing to observe adherence to them, given that social relations are based on the domination of men and the policies that have underpinned this for "more or less six millenniums" (Funk, 1997, p. 5). Hence, it is not surprising that patriarchal relations are almost second nature (Pringle, 1997).

The main direction of change according to the feminist organizations should be towards the elimination of female stereotypes. Because they have developed in a patriarchal culture that discriminates between the sexes, they are "a dangerous instrument of restrictions upon women" [5]. Generally, the stereotypes are considered to restrict freedoms and "women's full subjectivity, personal freedom, freedom in basic rights and the possibility of realizing this freedom" [5] are the concepts which must replace them. The problems of a woman's situation, place and role in society do not have to be, and are not, perceived exclusively through the prism of domination or as a conflict of the sexes.

Activists from the Christian Democratic wing of the women's movement advocate "the freedom of choosing the path of life starting from school, selecting a husband, partner, occupational career", but not "an escape from something": abortion was given as an example of a misunderstood freedom [2]. Meanwhile, they do not refer to egalitarianism as a value in itself, but to the Christian concept of subjectivity. Female Social Democrats define the problem differently. They perceive the issue of the equality of women and men not as a global conflict of the sexes, but mainly as the result of discrimination against women; in pursuing egality they emphasize all expressions of inequality between the sexes. Women's problems are seen to be the result of their carriage of the main burden of transformation in Polish society [10], they are the category whose right of choice is restricted by economic weakness [8] and who are "commonly discriminated against", particularly in the labor market [6].

Other women's organizations strive to introduce new behavioral models into specific areas of life and, in so doing, they appeal less to general notions of 'freedom' or 'subjectivity' and more to values such as health and the generally conceived social good. It is in this area that the activity of women's clubs is of special importance. The elite women's organizations, comprising educated individuals in high social positions, are seen as credible when propagating values such as the "observance of moral norms in work, performing jobs and activities in other spheres of life, ... popularizing the spirit of social servitude and understanding among people which contributes to international consensus and friendship" (Soroptimist International, DWOIP, 1995, p. 78), and when "promoting high ethical standards in professional life" (Zonta International—Polish Region, *ibid.*, p. 108). According to the opinion of some members of these clubs, they already shape public opinion and, according to their particular aspirations, play the role of experts and do so not only in the domestic sphere, but also in an international context [7, 12].[22]

Activities aimed at changing the model of women's behavior can be divided roughly into two: those dependent upon direct contact with a broad cross-section of women and those that rely on indirect methods. Examples of the latter type of activity include supporting and conducting research, publications and, via the behavior of activists, providing a role model for other women. The opportunity to influence behavior directly can in practice come about as a result of personal contact with a given organization. Legal counseling, for example, is reinforced by advice compatible with the ideology of the organization providing it. The provision of training courses can also offer an opportunity for a group to present its ideology and it can also be helpful in promoting new attitudes towards life and its problems. Many women's organizations (e.g. the Center for the Advancement of Women and the International Foundation of Women) offer psychological training aimed at teaching assertiveness and the activation of the individual.

Certain organizations arrange functions at which views can be exchanged and popularized and many of them also organize conferences, seminars and meetings. For example, the Warsaw-based International Forum for Women, which has been operating for several years, is very active in this field. Amongst feminist groups, the Women's Foundation eFKa, based in Kraków, is another active participant and it organized the first feminist conference in Poland, held in March 1990 and entitled 'Maternity as a Choice and not Coercion.' It now hosts yearly conferences.

Organizations undertaking specialist activities pertinent to women can bring about change in cultural models as these refer to the place and role of gender in society. One such example is the provision of courses for women who are, or who wish to be, candidates in Parliamentary elections by the Toruń section of the Center for the Advancement of Women and Women Also. These bodies are recognized for both their work in teaching women new roles and for introducing new concepts relating to their role in society.

Numerous women's groups are involved in publishing activity, ranging from the distribution of their own programs to the publication of books and magazines. For example, the International Women's Foundation has produced two brochures and one book since 1996, including advisory hints for the unemployed. Likewise, the Center for the Advancement of Women has published successive directories about women's organizations and initiatives. The magazine *Pełnym Głosem* (In Loud Voice) is produced by the Women's Foundation eFKa and the Women's Rights Center specializes in publishing a compendium of knowledge entitled *Poznaj Twoje Prawa...* (Get to Know Your Rights), which deals specifically with labor market issues. One special form of popularization of the ideological—political tools available to the women's movement in Poland involves spectacular street actions such as demonstrations, events, entertainment, the distribution of leaflets, as well as organization and participation in shows, TV and radio programs and press interviews.

SOCIO-ECONOMIC FIELD

Activities in the socio-economic field focus upon a wide range of real life problems, with specific actions being targeted at issues recognized by a given organization to be urgent and important in certain social milieus, from the viewpoint of particular social categories of women. Generally speaking, socio-economic concerns are linked with local-level social relations. However, this local character tends to vary because of differences in social structures across regions, large cities, large city districts and medium-sized towns. There are very few organizations in small towns or rural communities, as demonstrated by the earlier territorial analysis. It is in the socio-economic field that collaboration between women's organizations is possible (Matuchniak-Krasuska, 1995), in contrast to the situation in the ideological-political arena, which is characterized by tensions between competing values. Nevertheless, in the 1990s, with the search for a new paradigm of the place and role of women and the existence of a peculiar social pressure towards individualism, the behavior of organizations can also be guided by implicitly defined, often divergent, motivations. Thus, the local scene is also potentially a good platform on which organizations can integrate their activities.

To illustrate the socio-economic activities of women's groups, attention will focus on examples that show how goals are translated into community actions. Apart from sporadic cases when organizations focus on specific needs and problems, most deal, at least in principle, with two issues: unemployment (primarily among women) and difficult situations within the family. The latter primarily relates to issues such as poverty, single motherhood and family life pathologies. Some organizations concentrate on just one of these issues; the Polish Women's Council, for example, provides assistance for women and their families who find themselves in difficult situations, while the Center of Women's Activation and Employment fights against unemployment and its effects. There are also those bodies that have focused their efforts upon a particular problem, such as the fight against unemployment, but when other problems have appeared, they have been ready to cope with them. Examples here include the Łódź branch of the League of Polish Women, which withdrew from organizing cultural-educational activity in favor of promoting charitable assistance [6]. Similarly, the Center for the Advancement of Women redirected its activities towards the promotion of female rights to return to the labor market, although it is still engaged in charitable activities, which remain very much in demand. Different forms of activity in the socio-economic field include counseling, consultations, psychiatric support, material assistance and the improvement of women's qualifications via the provision of various types of training courses. A common characteristic of such work is the desire to activate the individual in accordance with the principle of "helping means, first of all, not depriving the individual of autonomy, initiative and responsibility for their own actions" (Piwowarski, 1994, p. 12).

To develop the characterization of the direction and form of these activities, attention is focused on an in-depth study of The International Women's Foundation, an organization based in Łódź. This entity was founded in the autumn of 1991, on the initiative of a group of friends. Its membership comprised members of the academic staff of one of the universities, representing different scientific disciplines and practitioners from diverse fields and its formation was a reaction to the dramatic growth in women's unemployment, both in the city and its vicinity. The liquidation of many industrial plants that had previously dominated the industrial landscape and the bankruptcy of many companies caused a complete collapse of the local labor market. In consequence, the women affected had little chance of rapid re-employment and even those with higher education lost jobs. At this early stage, although not formally registered, it designed a course entitled 'How to Run One's Own Firm'. The syllabus included accounting, labor law, economic and commercial law, marketing, principles of compiling a business plan, social aspects of team work, psychological training and the reconstruction of a sense of one's own value. Between the autumn of 1991 and the end of 1997, 745 people completed the course, with 15 per cent of its graduates now running their own manufacturing (clothing, knitted goods and artistic products), trade (wholesale and retail) or service firms (artistic and printing services, building designs, accounting offices and fitness clubs). The Foundation also provided a second-stage training program entitled 'Marketing and Business Plans' and 101 persons had completed this course by the end of 1997.

The group's program of activity was determined by the local socio-economic situation. Hence the starting point was not to design an ideological platform, but the attainment of a specific goal. After a few months of operation, the organization was registered and, since March 1992, it has had official foundation status. Women dominate, both amongst the sponsors and on the management board, but men are also involved. It is a woman's organization insofar as its main objective is to promote female entrepreneurship and it was with women in mind that it was established. This example shows that organizations active in the socio-economic field are reacting to changes in the prevailing situation and that they adapt their activity to local needs.

After a few years of operation, men also began to benefit from the Foundation's activities. In addition, it extended its scope beyond the city boundaries to encompass neighboring medium-sized towns and even a nearby administrative provincial center that was experiencing similar labor market problems. One course (Modern Secretary) addressed another group vulnerable to the threat of unemployment: young women without any qualifications and those who wished to acquire new skills. The program included subjects such as office work organization and the operation of modern office equipment—including computing, principles of business correspondence, English language, etc.—and 218 people have graduated since 1993. Also in 1993, and again in response to signals emanating from the local labor market, a two-level computer-training program was introduced, with 220 persons now having been trained in this area.

In collaboration with the Edinburgh Chamber of Industry and Trade and the Foundation for Promotion of Entrepreneurship, the group organized a course entitled 'Managerial Training for Women', covering areas such as the identification of participants' strengths and weaknesses, effective communication methods, different management styles and the organization of working time. At present, the Foundation runs a two-stage course for individuals who have lost their jobs under the group redundancy program, encompassing, in part one, 'Return to Work' and, in part two, 'Professional Training', which covers topics such as small business, computers and crafts. It also provides regular counseling services in fields such as financial and tax issues, labor law, economic and commercial law, business plans and interpersonal training for small businesses. So far, 158 persons have benefited from these activities. It is worth adding that, for 18 months prior to December 1996, the Foundation had obtained credit from the 'Mikro' fund and had advanced some 300 loans to small firms.[23] The organization also embarked on charitable activities. For instance, in September 1996, it conducted an auction of garments and paintings, the income from which was designated for the assistance of the poor, children from orphanages, the co-funding of winter vacations for children from low-income families and New Year events for children.

Other women's groups also operate in the same city. The voivodship League of Polish Women fights local poverty and gathers and distributes second-hand clothes and provides summer vacations for children [6]. The activists of the League admit that its goal, defined in statutes such as "striving to ensure a full implementation of the principle of equal rights for women in political, social, economic, professional and cultural life, in accordance with the provisions of the UN convention concerning the liquidation of all forms of women's discrimination ... " (Kowalczyk 1997, p. 14) remains abstract, given that it is confronted with the real hardship faced by many unemployed women in the city. Furthermore, its modest funds do not allow it to develop other active forms of assistance with the consequence that "the goals which the organization wished to accomplish are obliterated" [6].

To summarize, certain characteristics of activity in the socio-economic field are prominent. First, organizations are sensitive to the real problems of the city, region and district. Second, they respond rapidly, thereby outpacing the systemic solutions of public administration. Third, they are flexible and adapt their programs and activity to the real needs and intellectual level of the social category that they wish to assist. Fourth, they frequently lack basic funds. However, those organizations created by individuals who possess education and/or skills that are valued in a market economy can survive even during the most difficult periods by exploiting their human resources. On the other hand, the relevant legal regulations allowing for co-funding of such activities by the local authority were absent until recently. It is also worth stressing that the active involvement of women's organizations in the socio-economic field is subjected constantly to a peculiar verification: their existence depends on whether they are needed and enjoy social recognition.

SUMMARY AND CONCLUSION

Notwithstanding the long history of women's organizations in Poland, the 1990s have witnessed rapid changes both in their number and in their diversity. Despite a common aim to enhance the position of women they differ markedly, both in their constituencies and in the means they employ to achieve their objectives. The ideological–political field is an area in which, at best, women's organizations operate alongside one another. Within this arena the internal divisions within the women's movement are obvious, whereas the potential possibilities for collaboration are not (Pawlik, 1997). This is not to say that such collaboration does not occur since, within a given ideology, there is scope for collaboration between women's organizations in Poland, Europe and beyond and, in this sense, Polish women already belong to a world network. Given that women's organizations in Europe have achieved a high degree of integration, despite their ideological differences, it is possible that this will also happen in Poland (Malinowska, 1997b). Enhanced collaboration would of course be desirable because at the present time the various factions of the women's movement are weakened both by their fragmentation and by their failure to co-operate.

Socio-economic activity, on the other hand, is considered to be the most fruitful platform for potential collaboration (Matuchniak-Krasuska, 1995). However, from a certain point of view, collaboration is a secondary issue. It is more important that women's organizations collectively constitute a significant force within the local nexus of groups actively undertaking work in some substantive area. Initiatives aimed at combating long-term female unemployment are arguably one of the best examples of the positive action on behalf of women that are being undertaken by these groups, an activity which is essential in Poland today.

NOTES

1 The CRH and the League, together with the elitist Creative Women's Club (established 1979) and the Episcopal Sub-Commission on Preaching to Women (established 1969), represented the full range of formal women's organizations in communist Poland. Unlike the League and the CRH, the latter two organizations operated outside the public domain.

2 Skierniewice lies 50 kilometers to the west of Warsaw.

3 The League of Women was established by the Socialist authorities.

4 This wording of the statute explains, in part, the desire of the authorities to include the CRH within the League of Women.

5 Being seen to be ideologically correct typically entailed participation at celebrations of national holidays. The organization of this participation was the responsibility of both the central and local boards.

6 The provision of legal advice is one example.

7 To this list should be added two research centers, established in the 1980s, dealing explicitly with women's issues. The Interdisciplinary Research Team on Women's Situation was founded in 1980 and this was followed, in 1989, by an interdisciplinary research team focusing on Women's Problems. The first group was attached to the Social Studies Institute of Warsaw University, while the second was based at the Adam Mickiewicz University in Poznań. Alongside purely women's organizations, the women's movement also includes domestic and foreign foundations that run programs addressed to women or those pursuing research projects concerning women.

8 The breakdown of the formation of these organizations is as follows: 1990–8; 1991–10; 1992–13; 1993–11; 1994–13; and 1995–13.

9 This division rests on the type of founder (government versus individuals) and upon the sources of the organization's funding (state budget versus other sources).

10 The first of these centers is attached to the Collegium Medicum of the Jagellonian University in Kraków.

11 Research centers in public universities dealing with women's problems can also be thought of as governmental organizations insofar as their work is state funded.

12 The main doubts of the non-governmental women's organizations derived from their earlier negative experiences with the office. In this particular instance, alongside the official government report entitled "Report for 4th UN World Conference on Women's Affairs Beijing 1995—Government Plenipotentiary for Family and Women," there appeared a rival report entitled "Women's Situation in Poland, Report of the Non-Governmental Organizations—Beijing 1995."

13 As a result of these ideological divisions both the pro-family and the rural party groupings prepared their own reports for the conference.

14 Two examples of local authority financial support for women's organizations are the Żoliborz District Council, which supports the Żoliborz Women's Center, and the City of Łódź Council, which supports the association 'Work and Home'.

15 Henceforth, the numbers in square parentheses refer to the list of women's organizations provided in Appendix Table A8.1.

16 The first group of organizations includes, among others, the Institute of Civic Education, the European Union of Women, the Young Women's Christian Association and the Polish Union of Catholic Women. The second includes, among others, the

Democratic Union of Women, the Women Also, the Women's Section of the Labor Union, the League of Polish Women and the Center for the Advancement of Women. Finally, the third group is composed of the Polish Feminist Association, the Women's Foundation eFKa, and the Women's Rights Center.

17 Among the elite women's organizations in Poland, the Independent Social Women's Movement deserves special attention due to the exceptional character of the social background of its members. It constitutes a close circle of women with a specific historical tradition: they are the former female instructors of the Military Training of Women for the Country's Defence, the girl guides of the 2nd Polish Republic, the female liaison officers of Szare Szeregi (Grey Ranks—a scouting organization which fought against Germany during World War II) and female soldiers of the Armia Krajowa (Home Army), along with their daughters (DWOIP, 1995, p. 54). The goal of this organization is "fighting against all forms of a woman's treatment as an object, all overt and covert forms of political and economic domination, striving to restore to women their due place in the political, professional and family life ...". (*ibid.*, p. 54).

18 Exceptions are the CRH and the Foundation for Development of Polish Agriculture that, unsurprisingly, are not located in major centers. The former has thousands of circles in villages and the latter seven local sections in smaller towns.

19 Until 1 January 1999, when their number was reduced to 16, Poland comprised 49 administrative regions, known as voivodships.

20 Fields are the areas where organizations focus their activity; it is in these that goals and slogans are formulated. In the ideological-political field, these goals are general, while in the socio-economic arena they tend to be operational.

21 The words in parentheses have been added by the current author.

22 For example, certain members of the Soroptimist organization have acted as consultants to the United Nations.

23 The 'Mikro' fund provides loans to firms that are considered by the banking sector to be too small to be trustworthy borrowers.

REFERENCES

Borkowska, E. (1973) *Funkcjonowanie organizacji kobiecych na wsi w śietle aktywnościspołeczno-zawodowej kobiet* (Women's organizations in the countryside against the background of occupational activity of women), unpublished M.A. thesis, Łódź: Zakład Metod i Technik Badań Społecznych, Instytut Socjologii, Uniwersytet Łódzki.

Castelain-Meunier, C. (1986) *Emancipation et mouvements culturels* (Emancipation and cultural movements), Center d'Analyse et d'Intervention Sociologiques, École des Hautes Études en Sciences Sociales.

Domański, H. (1995) "Równouprawnienie. Stereotyp tradycyjnego podziału ról" (Equal rights. The stereotype of the traditional division of roles), in: A.Titkow and H. Domański (eds), *Co to znaczy być kobietą w Polsce?* (What does it mean to be a woman in Poland?), Warszawa: IFiS PAN.

Domański, H. (1998) "Ruch na drabinie" (Movement on the ladder), *Polityka*, no. 10, pp. 60–62.

Domański, H. and A. Dukaczewska (1994) "Orientacje indywidualistyczne w Polsce" (Individualistic orientations in Poland), *Kultura i Społeczeństwo*, vol. XXXVIII, pp. 61–82.

(DWOIP) *Directory of Women's Organizations and Initiatives in Poland* (1995) Warszawa: Centrum Promocji Kobiet.

Encyklopedia Powszechna (General Encyclopedia) (1984) vol. II, Warszawa: PWN.

Funk, R. (1997) "Word from a German publisher," in: E. Fromm *Miłość, płeć, matriarchat* (Love, sex, matriarchy), Poznań: Rebis.

Gliński, P. (1996) *Polscy Zieloni* (Polish Greens), Warszawa: Wydawnictwo IFiS PAN.

Gortat, R. (1987) "O naturze nowych ruchów społecznych" (About the nature of new social movements), in: E. Lewicka-Banaszak, P. Marciniak and W. Modzelewski (eds.), *Studia nad Ruchami Społecznymi* (Studies on social movements), Warszawa: Uniwersytet Warszawski, Instytut Socjologii.

Gorczyńska, Z., S. Kruszyńska and I. Zakidalska (eds.) (1997) *Płeć–kobieta–feminizm* (Sex–woman–feminism), Gdańsk: Wydawnictwo Uniwersytetu Gdańskiego.

Jaranowska, I. (1994) *Liga Kobiet Polskich w procesie przemian*, (The League of Polish Women under change), unpublished M.A. thesis, Katedra Socjologii Wsi i Miasta, Instytut Socjologii, Uniwersytet Łódzki.

Kowalczyk, M. (1997) *Liga Kobiet Polskich jako organizacja obywatelska* (The League of Polish Women as a civil organization), unpublished M.A. thesis, Katedra Socjologii Wsi i Miasta, Instytut Socjologii Uniwersytet Łódzki.

Malinowska, E. (1997a) Europejski ruch feministyczny II fali (European feminist movement of the second wave), paper presented at the meeting "Sociology and the Polish society," Instytut Socjologii, Uniwersytet Łódzki.

Malinowska, E. (1997b) "Demokracja równołciowa jako nowy cel ruchu feministycznego w Europie" (Parity democracy as a new goal of feminist movement in Europe), in: Gorczyńska *et al.* (eds).

Matuchniak—Krasuska, A. (1995) "Ruch feministyczny i kobiecy w Polsce. Interwencja Socjologiczna 1994–95" (The feminist and women's movement in Poland. The sociological intervention 1994–95), *Folia Sociologica*, no. 27/98, Łódzkiego: Wydawnictwo Uniwersytetu.

Michalik, M.B. (ed.) (1993) *Kronika Kobiet* (Chronicle of women), Warszawa: Wydawnictwo 'Kronika.'

Molyneux, M. (1993) "Women's Movement," in: W. Outhwaite and T. Bottomore (eds.), *The Blackwell Dictionary of Twentieth-Century Social Thought*, Oxford: Blackwell Publishers.

Paquot, E. (ed.) (1982) *Terre des Femmes* (Women's land), Paris–Montreal: La Décou-vertee/Boréal Express.

Pawlik, W. (1997) "Ruchy kobiece i feministyczne w Polsce" (The feminist and women's movement in Poland), paper presented at the 10th Polish Sociological Congress, Working Group 32, Katowice.

Piwowarski, W. (1994) "Zasada pomocniczości a struktury pośrednie" (Rules of help and intermediary structures), in: *Stare i Nowe Struktury Społeczne w Polsce*, (Old and New Social Structures in Poland), vol. I, Lublin: UMCS.

Pringle, R. (1997) "Feminist Theory and the World of the Social," *Current Sociology*, vol. 45, no. 2, pp.75–89.

Ślęczka, K. (1997) "Feminizm czy feminizmy? Feminizm jako wiązka ideologii" (Feminism or feminisms? Feminism as a bunch of ideologies), in: Gorczyńska et al. (eds).

Sytuacja Kobiet w Polsce (The Situation of Women in Poland) (1995) Report of Non-governmental Organisations, Beijing, Warszawa.

Taylor, C. (1994) "Kiedy mówimy: społeczeństwo obywatelskie" (When we are saying civil society), in: K. Michalski (ed.), *Europa i społeczeństwo obywatelskie*, (Europe and civil society), Kraków: Społeczny Instytut Wydawniczy.

Touraine, A. (1992) *Critique de la modernité* (A critique of the modern), Paris: Fayard.

Tryfan, B. (1968) *Pozycja Społeczna Kobiety Wiejskiej* (The social position of rural women), Warszawa: Książka i Wiedza.

APPENDIX TO CHAPTER 8

Appendix Table A8.1 Women's Organizations

[1] Center for the Advancement of Women
[2] Institute of Civic Education and Women's Promotion
[3] Women's Rights Center
[4] Pro Femina
[5] The Polish Feminist Association
[6] The League of Polish Women
[7] Soroptimist International
[8] Union of Labor—Women's Section
[9] European Union of Women
[10] Democratic Union of Women
[11] Women Also
[12] Independent Social Women's Movement

CHAPTER 9

THE PARTICIPATION AND POWER OF WOMEN IN PUBLIC LIFE

Against the background of the majority of west European countries, one might consider the representation of women in Central and Eastern Europe during the communist era as substantial, if such is measured by their presence at various levels of the decision-making process. In Poland, as elsewhere in the CEE region, the percentage of women participating in the exercise of power was one of the propaganda elements highlighting the pursuit and achievement of gender egality. In the Polish Parliament (Sejm), women held up to 23 per cent of all deputies' positions.

Before 1989 the choice of candidates for the Sejm, and in consequence the deputies who eventually sat there, was meant to realize the principle that the body should represent the whole landscape of Polish society. That is, when considering the participation of women in the decision-making processes of the old eastern bloc, sight should not be lost of the role of quota systems, informal as this was in the case of Poland.[1] However, the female representatives were of lower than average educational and professional status, and so less politically experienced, a fact that condemned them to perform only a 'supplementary' role (Siemieńska, 1995). In short, the functions of political leadership were reserved for men (Regulska, 1994). Nevertheless, it must not be forgotten that those decisions essential for the functioning of the state were taken not in the parliament, but in the Political Bureau of the Central Committee of the Polish United Workers' Party (PUWP), from which women were generally absent.

Women's labor market participation in the communist countries of CEE was also impressive by western standards (Einhorn, 1993). As she points out, the growth in female labor market activity in the post-war period in those democratic economies which registered increases mainly took the form of part-time employment. This contrasts starkly with the position in the communist countries where most women worked full-time. In the case of Poland, 65 per cent of all working age women were economically active in 1988, a figure that amounted to 45.5 per cent of the total labor force (*ibid*., p. 266).

At least three factors underpinned the heavy representation of women on the labor market. The first two relate to the political principles of the ruling authorities and to the insatiable thirst for labor of the economic system over which they presided. The third related to the pressure emanating from the low level of wages, which necessitated that at least two incomes per household. Yet, in economics as in politics, representation was one thing, power quite another. Women failed to achieve the highest managerial positions, with Leven (1994, p. 30) reporting that, in the 1980s, they accounted for only 12 and 4.5 per cent of the vice-presidents and presidents of enterprises, respectively. Further, sight should not be lost of the fact that there existed a considerable overlap between the political and economic spheres under communism.

The rules underpinning women's participation in public life changed, apparently radically, with the collapse of the pre-existing system in 1989. While the past must frequently act as a point of reference, this chapter examines patterns of political power and economic domination in the years since that watershed.

Two areas of public activity are pivotal for women's position as set against that of men: their presence in political bodies—such as parliamentary membership and the occupancy of government positions—and their access to positions of economic power in firms and corporations. Other considerations that impinge on the hierarchy of power across the sexes are overshadowed by those that really matter: political power and economic domination. The two substantive sections that follow consider these issues in turn, while a concluding discussion closes the contribution.

WOMEN IN POLISH NATIONAL POLITICS: FACT AND PROSPECT

The decline in the parliamentary representation of women accelerated during the years of post-communist struggle in Poland. In this context it is necessary to examine again the displacement of women from parliament after the 'Round Table' agreements of 1989. As Fuszara (1994–

95) has shown, from the resumption of democratic political activity women had far less chance of being selected than men due to their low positioning on electoral lists. In fact, "the share of women in parliament fell drastically just as it, as an institution, acquired real power." (*ibid.*, p. 345).[2] This situation was mirrored throughout the post-communist countries and happened despite the existence of constitutional guarantees of gender equality.

A full description of the representation and power of women requires information not only on the parliamentary seats they hold, but also on their tenure of political office. For information on the latter, it is necessary to consult the Handbooks and Supplements of the Sejm and of the Senate. Up to 1996, there emerged a clear predominance of men over women in parliamentary institutions: of the 25 Standing Committees of the Sejm, only one had a woman presiding; and of their 68 vice-presidents, only four were women. In the Senate, only one committee had a woman president, the other 14 being led by men, and only two out of 27 vice-presidents were women. Furthermore, in one of the Sejm Committees (System of Economy and Industry) there were no women at all.

Even on those Sejm committees that deal traditionally with issues encompassing women's concerns (e.g. health and culture), they usually do not occupy more than one-quarter of the seats. This is surely significant; even if women do account for 34 per cent of the membership of the Committee on Education, Science and Technical Progress. The membership of Senate committees is even more 'masculinized': four do not possess a single woman member, while less than one-quarter of the members on two more are women (approximately 23 per cent on both the Committee for Science and National Education and the Committee for Local Self-Government and State Administration).

The low representation of women in the membership of particular committees simply reflects the numerical preponderance of men in parliament as a whole. However, the minute presence of women as presidents of committees, and also in the leadership of parliamentary political clubs, cannot be explained solely by 'objective' factors. In contrast to the situation prior to 1989, present-day women parliamentarians display a much higher level of educational attainment and greater political experience than do male deputies and senators. As one author comments "the path of women to parliament is longer and more complicated than the men's, ... the condition of their success—i.e., receiving the mandate to be a deputy—in comparison with men, requires them to have a greater range of political attributes" (Siemieńska, 1995, p. 33).

A still more important feature of women's parliamentary situation is their near absence from ministerial positions (Einhorn, 1993). In Poland in the 1990s, women have only held between six and seven per cent of all ministerial, vice-ministerial, and director-generalships (Fuszara, 1994–95). Details published in the 1990 Statements of the Government of Poland in relation to the application of the 1979 Convention on the Elimination of All Forms of Discrimination against Women indicated that women held only 13 per cent of senior posts within Ministries during the 1980s. The range extended from 0.5 per cent in the Ministry of Foreign Affairs to 35.4 per cent in the Ministry of Culture and the Arts. On the basis of information gathered by the author on fifteen offices of central administration for November/December 1996—presented in Table 9.1—the disproportionately low share of women in the current decade has continued to mirror the position at the end of the nineteen-eighties.[3]

Table 9.1 Men and Women in Senior Posts of Poland's Central Administrative Offices: 1996

Post	Men		Women		Total	
	N	%	N	%	N	%
Minister	15	100	0	0	15	100
Secretary & Under-Secretary of State	70	89.7	8	10.3	78	100
Director General	14	87.5	2	12.5	16	100
Ministerial Adviser	14	93.3	1	6.7	15	100
Director of Departments: Offices & Units	199	79.6	51	20.4	250	100
Deputy Director of Departments: Offices & Units	299	71.4	120	28.6	419	100

Comparing the proportions in particular columns of Table 9.1, it can reasonably be concluded that the numerical preponderance of men is significant in all senior positions. Further, while the domination of males is most evident at ministerial level, it is only slightly less so at lower levels of the hierarchy. On the basis of this evidence, a thesis might be formulated that the higher the position, the more difficult it is for a woman to acquire and the more evident the predominance of men.

Four offices had to be omitted from Table 9.1 for reasons of data incompatibility. However, of the 31 senior posts in the Ministry of Justice, men held 25 (80 per cent). In the Minister's Office itself there were only men, as was true of the Procurator-General's Office. In the Ministry of Foreign Affairs, there were 42 women in senior positions but 265 men. At the end of 1996 there were 19 women and 105 men in the central administration of that Ministry. In its foreign establishments, the senior positions (meaning ambassadors, consuls-general, charges d'affaires, directors of consulates and consular departments) were held by 160 men and 23 women, while there were only five women amongst its 69 ambassadors.

There is evidence of continued male dominance even in those Ministries in charge of issues regarded as 'for women.' Thus despite the fact that the school teaching profession is the most 'feminized' in Poland, only eleven women held senior positions in the Ministry of National Education, which is in charge of the school education of children and young persons. Of these, one was an Under-Secretary of State, one a Director of Department, while the remainder were Deputy-Directors of Departments. Men, on the other hand, held 29 senior posts.

Disappointing as these findings appear, they do not differ greatly from those noted for most countries of the world: the average percentage of women ministers in the USA and Europe was 5.4 per cent in 1994 (UN, 1995). At the same time, women held over 15 per cent of ministerial positions in only 16 countries, although appointments in six of those, they held over one-third of places. Nonetheless, a tendency for the share of women in the most senior state posts to grow has emerged in recent years (*ibid.*). Indeed, it should be noted that, following the elections of 1994, an 'equality of the sexes' occurred for the first time in Swedish government, with the percentage of women ministers reaching 52 per cent. This said, it is evident that women tend to play their most important role in the direction of those departments usually regarded as appropriate to their social role: that is, culture, health, education and social welfare.

Prediction of the future political role of women in the countries of CEE depends on whether the fall in women's representation in Poland's organs of power after 1989 can be called a watershed or simply a continuation of already apparent, earlier trends. Will women be able to take advantage of the new possibilities, as they have in other democratic systems, or will there be a failure to participate, thereby allowing men to hold the key positions? Einhorn (1993) takes the political activity of women during the socialist period as her starting point. She notes that, as argued above, the high representation of women in that epoch did not really reflect their influence in the decision-making process of the affairs of state. The women involved in politics were poorly educated and often came from low social strata, both of which limited their effective activity. Presently, the level of female representation in parliament is probably a better reflection of their real influence in political matters. Further, before 1989, the *de jure* equality of entitlement of the sexes in all spheres, including political activity, was more an element of official propaganda than practical intent. Thus, the presence of women in decision-making bodies, particularly at local level, was not an example of the exercise of their rights, but rather a measure of their obligations. Perhaps this previous pressure to undertake politics on 'the third shift' was the very reason why women rejected the political sphere at the precise moment when pressure from the state vanished.

The data presented so far only serve to raise the question of why there was a significant 'withdrawal' of women from political activity after 1989. The preponderance of men in the institutions of public life is so great that Heinen and Matuchniak-Krasuska (1992), for example, spoke of a 'male democracy' in Poland. Most intriguing of all is the political passivity of those women who, prior to 1989, were heavily involved in opposition circles. Several authors have sought an analogy to this outcome in the experience of South American countries, where former female oppositionists were pushed aside by men (Einhorn, 1993). There is not, however, much detail available on the women who were active in the Polish opposition movement; nor is it known how many of them moved into the new institutions of public life or how many abandoned political activity altogether. It is therefore impossible to say what the tasks of women active in the opposition movement in the eighties were, to what extent they confined themselves to the role of assistant or to what degree their involvement in decision-making proved fundamental.

Perhaps the fact that only two women were members of the 18 strong Inter-Factory Strike Committee in 1980—when women constituted about half of the membership of Solidarity—provides an important clue. Equally important may be the observation that, at the first national congress of Solidarity held a year later in Gdańsk, scarcely seven per cent of the delegates were women. Long (1994) has described the altogether curious example of women who, convinced that they—by reason of their sex—were unfit to hold leadership positions in underground Solidarity, resigned in favor of men. One heroine (Danuta Winiarska) relates how she held the direction of the 'Mazowsze' region while Solidarity remained outlawed. When, after several years, it became possible for her to reveal herself and to undertake open work, she was of the view that, as a woman, she would never attract support from her subordinates in the union. As such, she decided not to put her name forward for election and credited her contribution to someone else.

For women, there exist alternatives within the sphere of private life to public participation. The social vision of a woman's role presupposes the possibility of her limiting herself to activities in private life, and the climate at the end of the eighties contributed to the realization of this outcome. Viewed from this angle, the situation of men was in fact more difficult than that of women, given that the level of acceptance of male inactivity outside the home was, and is, low. Nevertheless, the time constraints imposed by the demands of guaranteeing a daily existence for the family functions as an additional factor that now serves to compromise women's activities outside the home. At the same time, it is quite conceivable that women have rejected politics as the domain of 'dirty business'. Conflicts between power elites, financial misdeeds and accusations about the political pasts of individuals might all have contributed to the unwillingness of women to engage in the arena of politics.

At the Ninth Extraordinary Congress of the Polish United Workers Party, as a result of the abolition of the 'quota' rule for women delegates, the percentage share of women declined by almost one-half in comparison with earlier Congresses. Similarly, in NSZZ 'Solidarność', both before the introduction of martial law and during the period of oppositional activity, women were relatively absent from leadership positions. This provides further evidence that the fall in the representation of women in leadership positions after 1989 should not be judged in terms of a return to a traditional system of roles, but as an expression of normal conditions in the real power structure (Siemieńska, 1995).[4]

Inspired by this fact, a Bill on Equality of Men and Women was drafted during the last parliament by the Parliamentary Women's Group. This proposed that neither sex should account for less than 40 per cent of the membership of representative bodies. Not only has the quota system been seen as an instrument for achieving equality of the sexes in public life, it has also been regarded as a natural consequence of the democratization of the political system (Bonder and Nari, 1995). Furthermore, political scientists of feminist orientation frequently stress the advantages that women bring to politics through their espousal of those values and purposes usually associated with the private sphere, including the experience of motherhood and the possession of virtues such as respect for others, respect for unorthodox opinions and an ethic of responsibility (Mansbridge, 1990). The difference in women's approach to politics brings society closer to the ideal of 'thinking democracy', a rather different conception to the Schumpeterian notion of politics as a market of competing interests.[5]

Quota systems in general, and the Polish draft bill, in particular, have never been without critics, even amongst feminists, some of whom view them as a device by which women become 'client citizens' taking advantage of assistance programs conferred on them, above all, by men (Hernes, 1984). Political scientists have also opposed them on grounds of 'justice', in that they take into account 'non-meritocratic' considerations (ascribed characteristics). They can further be seen to restrict the freedom of choice of electors by imposing upon them a predetermined list of candidates, derived on the basis of criteria of which they may not approve. Finally, there seems to be no guarantee that there will be a sufficient pool of women suitably qualified for the task, thus worsening the quality of work done in political bodies. Such arguments continue, for now, to hold sway in Poland and the Bill on Equality has yet to be passed into law.

While the significant representation of women, particularly in parliament, resulting from a quota system, if such is adopted, may be a change for the better, it may also have only propaganda value when the center of gravity of the power structure is shifting from the political to the economic system. Important economic decisions are now taken elsewhere, most particularly in the business sphere (Jones, 1988). As early as the 1960s, it was being argued that 'voting counts but money decides' (Rokkan, 1966). It is even claimed sometimes that the growth in the percentage share of women in parliament testifies to the fact that its significance is declining. This suggests that it is important to examine the position that they have acquired in the new economic establishment that has emerged in the years since 1989.

WOMEN AND THE ECONOMIC ELITE

The belief that it is necessary to differentiate representation based on electoral rights (a specified percentage) from representation based on financial assets has been gaining popularity in recent years (Epstein, 1981; Ferguson, 1988). Under this view, evidence of a significant growth in the share of women in the institutions of representative power exaggerates their real influence. Put another way, decisions involving direct financial consequences are taken outside parliament—amongst the management of the most influential economic actors. This approach implies the need to broaden the definition of politics in liberal democracies well beyond the confines of representative institutions.

Power, in this alternative view, is associated not only with parliament, local self-government or the leadership of political parties, but with the activities of economic elites. In this, one can detect a neo-marxist influence, emphasizing the connection of the political authorities with the ruling economic class. However, there are significant differences of emphasis within this general approach. Authors of extreme feminist disposition, particularly in the Scandinavian countries, are inclined to depreciate the value of parliament. Others of more open persuasion prefer to speak of a 'parallelism' in the exercise of power. Important as such differences may be, the ambition here is to examine how the adoption of this wider conception of power affects the apparent standing of women in Polish society. In so doing, use will be made of both a large-scale, official data-base, the Labor Force Survey (LFS), and a smaller specialized survey to address the important questions that arise from extending the boundaries of the 'political sphere'.

Under communism, there was considerable overlap between the economic and the political realms of activity. One crucial element of the transformation has been the severance of many of the direct links that existed previously. An important corollary of this has been the weakening of the standing of the public sector of the economy, even if its numerical size has not been reduced to the extent that many reformers have considered desirable. Arguably the degree of mobility between public and private sector economic elites in the more flexible western economies is now greater than at any time since World War II. Those focusing upon the emasculation of political institutions, however, are generally referring to the private sector as the new locus of power. This raises issues regarding the gender composition of the public and private sectors during the early years of transition.

In fact, over the period between 1990 and 1997, the share of women in the total employed labor force actually increased from 45.2 per cent to 46.6 per cent (GUS, 1998, p. 122). However, over the same period, the same source indicates that the share of women in public sector employment increased from 43.8 per cent to 51.0 per cent. That is, the public sector became increasingly feminized whereas the private sector, where women's share fell from 46.8 per cent to 44.0 per cent, did just the opposite. If the locus of power is indeed shifting from the public towards the private sector, this might represent one early sign that women are already disadvantaged.

In reality, simple representation within the private sector workforce is an insufficient guide to the evolving position of women within the economic power structure. To some, the emergent class of entrepreneurs represents a seed-bed of Poland's new middle class (Węcławowicz, 1996, p. 136). True or not, those who are self-employed with employees are certainly a minority group within the labor force and constituted less than four per cent of all those in work as of February 1998 (GUS, 1998a). Women, however, constitute only 32 per cent of these employers (*ibid.*).

Table 9.2 Selected Qualifications of Employees by Sector (%): 1998

	Public Sector	Private Sector
University		
Males	17.2	7.5
Females	23.6	5.7
Vocational Secondary & Post-Secondary		
Males	29.2	23.4
Females	40.3	30.2
Primary & Lower		
Males	10.3	21.9
Females	9.3	23.8

Source: GUS (1998a).

Both employment in the private sector and self-employment are really only suggestive of the relationship that women might have with the locus of true economic power and, as such, it is useful to examine the official statistics further. One important indicator of the nature of the emerging political economy of the country is provided by the educational attainments of those engaged in state and private undertakings. As shown in Table 9.2, a marked contrast has emerged between the composition of these spheres of the economy, with the former remaining the bastion of the intelligentsia. Most important though is the finding that male private sector workers are 30 per cent more likely than similarly located females to be university graduates.

While educational attainment is normally a useful indicator of the status of the positions that workers are likely to hold in market economies, this was certainly not the case in CEE under planning. To the extent that the handicaps of the past have yet to be overcome, this may find a reflection in Poland today. Furthermore, educational aggregates may still fail to capture the differing skill requirements of an emerging market economy in comparison with a tottering communist edifice. Table 9.3 therefore examines the evolving occupational composition of the employed population, disaggregated both by gender and by ownership sector.

Table 9.3 Percentage of Occupations Occupied by Women: 1998

	Public Sector	Private Sector
Legislators, Senior Officials, Managers	35.5	27.1
Professionals	66.1	47.5
Technicians, Associate Professionals	60.1	52.0
Clerks	77.4	62.7
Service Workers, Shop & Market Sales Workers	63.2	72.1
Skilled Agricultural & Fishery Workers	46.5	25.6
Craft & Related Trades Workers	12.9	23.9
Plant & Machine Operators & Assemblers	11.1	13.8
Elementary Occupations	63.7	41.5

Source: GUS (1998a).

The evidence indicates clearly that women are under-represented in the 'top' occupations of legislators, senior officials and managers. Their position in the private sector is much weaker than in the public sector, since they accounted for only 27 per cent of those in the prestige occupations in the former, compared to 35 per cent in the latter. To the extent that the locus of power is shifting towards the private sector in Poland's fledgling market economy, this does not augur well for women. A similar picture emerges for professional occupations, with women holding approximately two-thirds of the positions in the public sector but less than one-half in the private sector. This finding doubtlessly reflects the feminized nature of the teaching and health professions—which are still typically provided by the public sector—and also suggests that women are failing to gain positions of similar status in the private sector. Thus the evidence would seem to suggest that private sector professionals—lawyers, accountants, consultants, etc.—are predominantly male.

While useful for identifying the broad structure of Poland's new middle-class, national surveys such as the LFS are unable to identify precisely those in positions of real power in the new economic hierarchy. On the one hand, only certain private sector enterprises can be considered to be at the forefront of Poland's modernization drive and, on the other hand, not all of the senior management positions can rightly be regarded as belonging to the elite. Overcoming these reservations requires the identification of both the most dynamic private undertakings in the economy and the key players within them.

THE GENDER COMPOSITION OF HIGHER MANAGEMENT: A SURVEY

In 1997 a survey of the composition of the management and supervisory boards of two types of company was undertaken: (1) those registered on the Polish Stock Exchange; and (2) those included in National Investment Funds under the Mass Privatization Program (MPP). Two considerations underlay the focus on such firms. First, the former are new phenomena in the economy, constituting the leading players on the developing Polish capital market. Also, such companies belong to the group of enterprises currently posting the best financial returns in the country's corporate sector. Further, it is widely expected that the companies involved in the MPP will achieve similar results in the near future.

Second, the outcomes of the actions of managers of stock market companies are shouldered not by the managers themselves but by the individuals who have chosen to invest in them. In total, the number of investment accounts managed by stockbroking companies in 1995 exceeded 800,000 (Stock Exchange Annual Report 1995), while the number of shareholders is several times greater. However, the number of Poles with a potential interest in the functioning of companies involved in the Universal Privatization Program (those issued with Mass Share Certificates) is around 23 million (*Gazeta Wyborcza*, 23th November 1996).

Information on the management and composition of the supervisory boards of companies traded on the Stock Exchange was collected from their audited financial reports for 1995. However, in thirteen cases earlier data, from 1993 or 1994 reports or from the companies' share issue prospectuses, had to be utilized, either because of the impossibility of obtaining annual reports or the lack of information contained within them. To this database were added companies that registered on the Exchange in 1995 or 1996. In total, this provided a sample of 91 individual companies, 1,096 senior board-level positions which collectively laid claim to them.

As can be seen from the figures in Table 9.4, women were a clear minority, both in the management of Stock Exchange-listed companies and on their supervisory boards. If all individuals making up these bodies are taken as the base, the share of females on executive boards was

11.8 per cent and on the supervisory boards was 10.3 per cent. The predominance of men is very evident in particular management posts, with women representing only 4.4 and 8 per cent of the presidents of executive and supervisory boards, respectively. This evidence suggests that, the higher the managerial position, the more unlikely it is that a woman will hold it.

Table 9.4 Women's Share on Executive Boards of Floated Companies

Governing Bodies	Women		Men	
	N	%	N	%
Executive boards				
Presidents	4	4.4	91	95.6
Other members	42	16.6	253	83.4
Supervisory Boards				
Presidents	7	8.0	88	92.0
Other members	66	12.1	545	97.9

The situation is described more fully by the data displayed in Table 9.5, which groups the number of companies by the percentage of women holding management positions within them. It appears that on the executive boards of over 60 per cent of Stock Exchange-listed companies, and on almost half of the supervisory boards, there are only men. Women occupy no more one-quarter of the positions on executive or supervisory boards in over 80 per cent of companies. There are no cases where there are only women on executive or supervisory boards.

Data on the composition of the management boards of companies included in the MPP were collected from information available in the Registration Courts and direct from the companies themselves in 15 cases because of reporting difficulties. In total, this exercise yielded information for 228 companies, approximately 45 per cent of all companies covered by the Program at the time of the survey. Taking account of both the executive and supervisory boards of these organizations generated a sample of 2,471 individuals.

The picture is only marginally better for women in these companies covered by the National Investment Funds than it is in those listed on the Stock Exchange. Of the presidents of all management boards, the share of women, at 3.5 per cent, is minimal although, in the case of supervisory boards, the position is a little better, with every tenth president (10.8 per cent) being a woman. In terms of the membership of management boards, women accounted for 15.7 per cent of the global total and for one-fifth of those on supervisory boards. Still more significant is the finding that 50.7 per cent of all management boards, including 24 per cent of supervisory boards, contained no women at all. The degree of male dominance in the management personnel of the companies covered by the survey is indisputable.

Table 9.5 Women's Share in the Executive and Supervisory Boards of Floated Companies

Women's Share (%)	Number of Companies	% of Companies
	Executive Boards	
0	59	64.8
1–25	15	16.5
26–50	14	15.4
51–75	2	2.2
76–99	1	1.1
100	0	0
Total	91	100
	Supervisory Boards	
0	40	45.5
1–25	36	40.9
26–50	9	10.2
51–75	2	2.3
76–99	1	1.1
100	0	0
Total	88	100

CONCLUDING DISCUSSION

Under communism, the economic sphere overlapped to a considerable extent with the political sphere and, at least in Polish conditions, formal co-option seems to be an appropriate way to describe the public activities of women during that era. Although there were no formal barriers to women holding positions of real power, in practice the key posts were held by men and the presence of women in the parliament and local authorities did not contribute much to political life: they fulfilled a token role only. In the new circumstances, this chapter has shown that women have so far failed to ascend the commanding heights of either of the newly separated political and economic domains. Only when they do so will there be 'equal power' for the sexes.

However, the fact that male dominance is so pronounced in the economic and political elites, does not enable us to state to what degree this is connected with the gendered division of social roles, discriminatory practices or other forms of segregation connected with sex. It does, nevertheless, allow us to state that the regularities determining the lower position of women in sectors that directly exercise power in western countries are apparent within the Polish context also. Collectivist orientations appear to be relatively strong in our society and these operate against the acceptance of women as equally endowed participants in public life. This underpins the separation of a male sphere (the public) from a female sphere (the private). The ideology of the equality of the sexes propagated during the socialist era depended mainly on women's mass occupational activation and was never a sufficiently strong stimulus to overcome this division nor to introduce deep changes in the system of social roles connected with gender.

The possibility of reintroducing co-option as a means of granting greater access to positions of power is often discussed by analysts researching the political activities of women in the Anglo–Saxon countries and perhaps it should not be discounted in the Polish situation. However, it would appear that the need for official co-option has been superseded. The increasing educational and political attainments of women participating in public institutions leads one to believe that their influence will come to reflect their quantitative presence in a way that was never true in the past. Nevertheless, the decline of the share of women in parliament, their modest presence in local government, central administration and the directorates of enterprises leads one to doubt whether their position will improve significantly in the near future.

NOTES

1 This tactic is particularly well known in the Scandinavian countries and the 40% rule adopted there has recently been proposed for the Council of Europe (COE, 1997).

2 The decline in women's representation can equally be observed at local government level. Before the 1990 local elections, women held 22 per cent of positions in councils of different levels (Fuszara 1994–95). In 1990, only 15 per cent of the candidates standing in local elections (17 per cent four years later), and 11 per cent of those

elected (13 per cent in 1994), were women. Furthermore, women constituted a minority of political leaders. The failure encountered by women in local government elections is all the more surprising in the light of findings that they are more inclined to involve themselves in activity with a local, rather than a central, focus. The more informal local spheres of activity are an alternative for women to the centralized, and formalized, arenas preferred by male political activists (Ferguson, 1988).

3 These 15 offices comprised 13 Ministries plus the Central Planning Office and the Office of the Council of Ministers.

4 This said, it is at the local level that women may exhibit a tendency to greater involvement over the coming years (Einhorn, 1993). Such activity is easier to integrate with family life, running a household and the obligations attendant on bringing up a family, is less formalized and is concerned with issues which have a direct impact on daily life. The same arguments hold true for the non-governmental organizations that are often considered to be a constituent element of civic activity and which have shown marked growth in Poland since 1989 (Wygnański, 1996). The great bulk of these organizations are concerned with matters connected to culture and the arts, physical culture and sport, health protection, defence of children's rights and social welfare. These are activities somewhat subversive of the public/private dichotomy and it is precisely in these areas that one can observe the opportunity for women's extra-familial activity on a mass scale in western countries. In Poland, a similar tendency can be noticed, with Kozińska-Bałdyga (1996) estimating that they account for 80 per cent of all members of such organizations.

5 Scandinavia represents the best example of a group of countries in which the quota system has been applied at various levels. There, it is often stressed, however, that women do not get co-opted on the basis of only one socio-demographic criterion, but enter party leadership by a process of natural selection based on qualifications and aptitude for leadership (Skjeie, 1995).

REFERENCES

Bonder, G. and M. Nari (1995) "The 30 Percent Quota Law. A Turning Point for Women's Political Participation in Argentina,"in: A.Brill (ed.), *A Rising Public Voice. Women in Politics Worldwide*, New York: Feminist Press at the University of New York.

COE (Council of Europe) (1997) "A Women's Place is also in the Parliament," *http://www.coe.fr/europa40/e/9702/awomens.htm*, Strasbourg: COE.

Einhorn, B. (1993) *Cinderella Goes to Market. Citizenship, Gender and Women's Movements in East Central Europe*, London: Verso.

Epstein, C.F. (1981) "Women and elites: a cross national perspective,", in C.F. Epstein and R.L. Caser (eds) *Access to Power*, London: Allen und Unwin.

Ferguson, K.E. (1988) "Subject-centredness in Feminist Discourse,"in: K.B. Jones and A.G. Jonasdottir (eds.).

Fuszara, M. (1994–5) "Równe prawa, równe szanse? Z zagadnień równości praw kobiet i mężczyzn" (Equal rights, equal opportunities? Issues concerning the equality of male and female rights), *Roczniki Nauk Społecznych* (Social Science Yearbook), vol. XXII–XXIII, Book 1.

GUS (1998) *Rocznik Statystyczny 1998* (Statistical yearbook), Warszawa: Główny Urząd Statystyczny.

GUS (1998a) *Aktywność Ekonomiczna Ludności Polski w 1998 Roku: Luty* (Labour Force Survey in Poland: February 1998), Warszawa: Główny Urząd Statystyczny.

Heinen, J. and A. Matuchniak-Krasuska (1992) "Polska demokracja jest rodzaju męskiego" (Polish democracy is male), in: *Aborcja w Polsce. Kwadratura koła* (Abortion in Poland. The unsolvable problem), Towarzystwo Religioznawcze.

Hernes, H.M. (1984) "Women and the Welfare State: The Transition from Private to Public dependence," in: H. Holter (ed.), *Patriarchy in a Welfare Society*, Oslo: Universitetsforlaget.

Jones, K.B. (1988) "Toward the Revision of Politics," in: K.B. Jones and A.G. Jonasdottir (eds).

Jones, K.B. and A.G. Jonasdottir (eds) (1988) *Developing Theory and Research with a Feminist Face*, London/Newbury Park/New Delhi: Sage Publications.

Kozińska-Bałdyga, A. (1996) "Women, Democracy and Civil Society," A paper presented at the conference: *A World in Transition. Feminist Perspectives on International Relations. An Interdisciplinary Conference*, University of Lund: 14–16 June.

Leven, B. (1994) "The Status of Women and Poland's Transition to a Market Economy," in: N. Ashlanbeigui, S. Pressman and G. Summerfield (eds), *Women in the Age of Transformation*, London: Routledge.

Long, K.S. (1994) *We All Fought for Freedom: Women in Poland's Solidarity Movement*, Boulder, Colorado: Westview Press.

Mansbridge, J. (1990) "Kobiety, rządzenie i dobro powszechne" (Women, ruling and the common good), *Ameryka*, Autumn.

Regulska, J. (1994) "Transition to Local Democracy: Do Polish Women Have a Choice?", in: M. Ruschemeyer (ed.) *Women in Politics of Post-communist Eastern Europe*, New York: Sharpe.

Rokkan, S. (1966) "Norway: Numerical Democracy and Corporate Puralism,"in: R.A. Dahl (ed.), *Political Oppositions in Western Democracies*, New Haven, Connecticut: Yale University Press.

Siemieńska, R. (1995) "Dostęp do władzy i podejmowania decyzji na wszystkich szczeblach" (Access to the authorities and the decision process on all levels), in: *Raport na IV światową konfrencj Narodów Zjednoczonych w sprawach kobiet* (Report prepared for the IV world conference on women), Bejing.

Skjeie, H (1995) "From Movement to Government. Women's Political Integration in Norway," in: A. Brill (ed.), A Rising Public Voice. *Women in Politics Worldwide*, New York: The Feminist Press at the University of New York.

UN (United Nations) (1995) *The World's Women 1995: Trends and Statistics*, New York: United Nations.

Węcławowicz, G. (1996) *Contemporary Poland: Space and Society*, London: UCL Press.

Wygnański, J.J. (1996) "Podstawowe statystyki dotyczące działań organizacji pozarządowch w Polsce"(Basic statistics referring to non-govermental organisations in Poland), in: B. Synak and M. Ruzica (eds), *Sektor pozarządowy w zmieniającym się społeczeństwie* (Non-governmental sectors in a changing society), Gdańsk: Gdańsk–Indianapolis.

CHAPTER 10

GENDER AND EARNINGS: A REGIONAL APPROACH

Although the distribution of earnings was narrower than that observed in market economies, inequality was not eradicated during the communist era and the gender earnings differential in Poland was typically of the order witnessed in the west (Einhorn, 1993).[1] The situation in that period was complicated, however, by the pervasive use of non-pecuniary payments to reward workers and the presence of a welfare system that has been viewed as delivering 'mainly women's benefits' (Fuszara, 1993, p. 47). It is impossible to say whether these considerations would have altered popular impressions regarding earnings differentials, and the data sets available to researchers at the time were certainly not of sufficient quality to expect that reasoned analysis of the possibility could have been undertaken. In any event, the primary interest in this contribution is with the present.

As the labor market has become driven progressively more by market principles, the overarching reach of the state has receded and the quality and accessibility of data have improved, meaningful examination of earnings differentials has become a realistic possibility. Reform notwithstanding, it is perhaps unsurprising that in Poland, as elsewhere in the world, women continue to earn less than men. This simple stylized fact is nevertheless insufficient to demonstrate that it is gender per se that is the underlying cause of the difference. Before being able to arrive at this conclusion, it would be necessary to control for the fact that, amongst other things, men and women are concentrated in different industries and occupations, have differing educational backgrounds and do not work for the same number of hours per week.

The goal of what follows is to examine the extent to which a model based upon certain empirical regularities, but one supported by theoretical argument, can help to explain the significant differences in the female-to-male differential in median earnings to be observed across Polish space, using cross-sectional data for 1997.[2] It is therefore to be regarded as but one input to a much needed, but far from complete, program of research directed towards answering the question of whether discrimination adversely affects women's earnings on that country's labor market. The choice of the region (voivodship) as the unit of analysis requires little justification, given that they are well known to exhibit marked variation on virtually every economic and social indicator (Węcławowicz, 1996). Communism proved insufficient to eradicate the spatial legacy of the Partitions and, at least in its formative stages, the current modernization of Poland's economy did little to change the inherited situation (*ibid.*).

At the same time, the adoption of a regional focus has a wider justification, insofar as much of the literature exploring female labor market disadvantage within the country has cultural underpinnings and culture is assuredly not constant across the territories of the country. While various, simple dichotomies—rural/urban, east/west etc.—are often adopted to capture this differentiation, it would be premature to assume that any such simple device is sufficient for the analysis of the geographical disparities in the earnings gap during the current decade, hence the finer disaggregation utilized in this treatment.

The following section provides the necessary descriptive background for the analysis to follow by highlighting certain key features of the earnings distribution and placing them in the context of the significant differences in economic structure that prevail across Polish regions. It is established that although disaggregation of the data does not bring into question the finding that women earn less than men, the differential is by no means a geographic constant. As such, Section 3 develops a model to attempt to explain the observed spatial differences in the earnings gap and this is estimated empirically in Section 4. The specification of this model is then subjected to statistical test in Section 5 and, on the basis of the results of this analysis, corrected earnings differentials for each of the country's voivodships are derived. The final section of the chapter contains a summary of the principal findings and a concluding discussion.

A PORTRAIT OF SPATIAL AND GENDER EARNINGS DIFFERENTIATION

The prospect that the overall dispersion of earnings would widen with the onset of liberalization was widely welcomed; resources, particularly labor, had to flow into those activities that would help to modernize the country's economy and promote growth. Much less certain, notwithstanding some of the arguments to be found in the literature, was the impact that reform would have on the relative earnings of women. Utilizing official survey data for 1997, this section first reviews some of the salient characteristics of the distribution of median gross earnings of full-time workers in enterprises with more than five employees. This then serves as a context within which to explore regional differences in both economic structure and the earnings gap in more detail.

Even though large changes have been observed in the national hierarchy of earnings (Rutkowski, 1996), Map 10.1 indicates that significant regional differences continue to exist.[3] Furthermore, these bear a striking resemblance to the distribution of income observed throughout the communist era (Węcławowicz, *op cit*; Zienkowski, 1997). In the past, the pattern could be ascribed to the dual character of the Polish labor market, in which there was a primary sector comprised of strategic heavy industry and a secondary sector whose activities were devoted largely to the satisfaction of consumption demands (Rutkowski, 1994). Workers in the former were rewarded more generously than those employed in the latter, lower priority undertakings. As the role of the planner disappeared, it would be natural to expect that the wage structure would be re-aligned and for labor to flow into those activities demanded in the free market.

In fact, at least at the level of broad industry groups, the changes in the earnings distribution to 1997 were perhaps not as great as might have been expected, particularly when account is taken of sector of ownership. Thus, while Table 10.1 indicates that manufacturing earnings had regressed towards the national median, the advantages enjoyed by the mining and power sectors remained intact, especially in the sections of those industries that remained in public control. As the following quote from one of its chief architects attests, this could be regarded as one symptom of the failure of the Polish restructuring program to achieve a number of its early goals: "every economic system has a specific hierarchy of pay and prestige, and the hierarchy typical of a non-market, state-dominated economy is very different to that typical of a

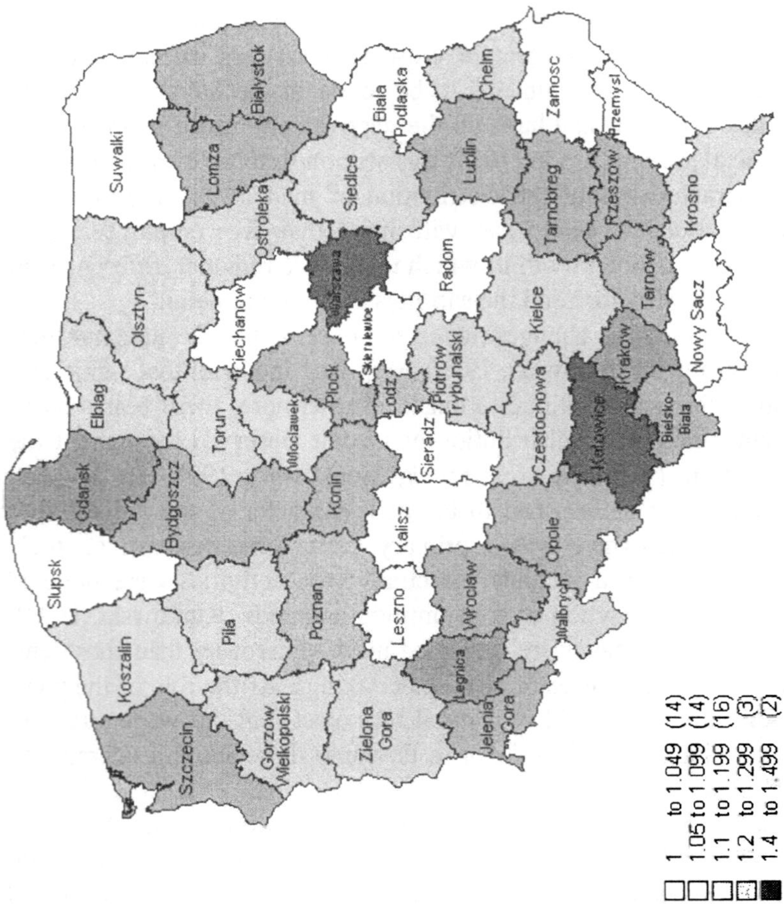

Map 10.1 Region to Lowest Median Earnings: 1997
[*Source*: Calculated from GUS (1998)].

competitive market economy. ... Some groups move up and others go down. The latter include, for example, workers in heavy industry and mining, sectors which were once the backbone of wasteful centrally planned economies." (Balcerowicz, 1994, pp. 45–46). At the same time, while the earnings premium observed for the financial sector is typical of all market economies, and was one of only two industries in which private sector pay exceeded that in public undertakings in 1997, it was also evident in Poland in the period before the current reforms began (GUS, 1997, p. 243).

Table 10.1 Earnings: Industry by Sector to National Grand Median: 1997

Industry	Public	Private
Agriculture, Hunting & Forestry	1.12	0.68
Fishing	0.76	0.59
Industry:	1.32	0.93
Mining and Quarrying	2.04	1.23
Manufacturing	1.10	0.92
Electricity, Gas and Water	1.42	1.09
Construction	1.05	0.98
Trade and Repair	1.08	0.84
Hotels and Restaurants	0.97	0.59
Transport and Communication	1.08	1.05
Finance	1.28	1.37
Real Estate	1.11	1.00
Public Administration	1.17	1.36
Education	0.97	0.95
Health and Social Work	0.84	0.73
Community Services	0.97	0.82
SECTOR	1.05	0.92

Source: Computed from GUS (1998a, p. 84–92)

A major feat of the communist authorities in the years following the Second World War was to increase dramatically the level of industrialization of the economy. However, the achievement of this goal was in some conflict with the stated objective of leveling out spatial inequalities in living standards and it has been argued that the drive to industrialize actually did little to reduce the areal discrepancies in development inherited from the past (Węcławowicz, *op. cit.*, p. 38).[4] In fact, in spite of over forty years of planning, the importance of industrial employment across the regions of Poland exhibited the same general pattern in 1988 that it had in 1946 (*ibid.*, p. 36–37) and Map 10.2 suggests that eight years of transformation did little to alter the overall complexion of

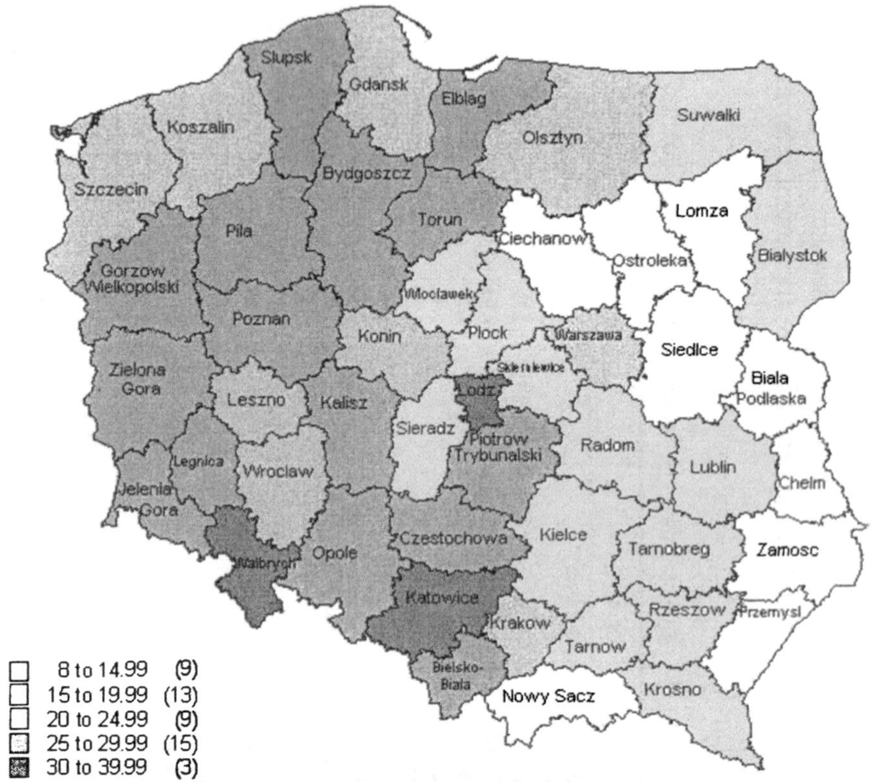

Map 10.2 **Percentage of Employment in Industry: 1997**
[*Source*: Calculated from GUS (1998)].

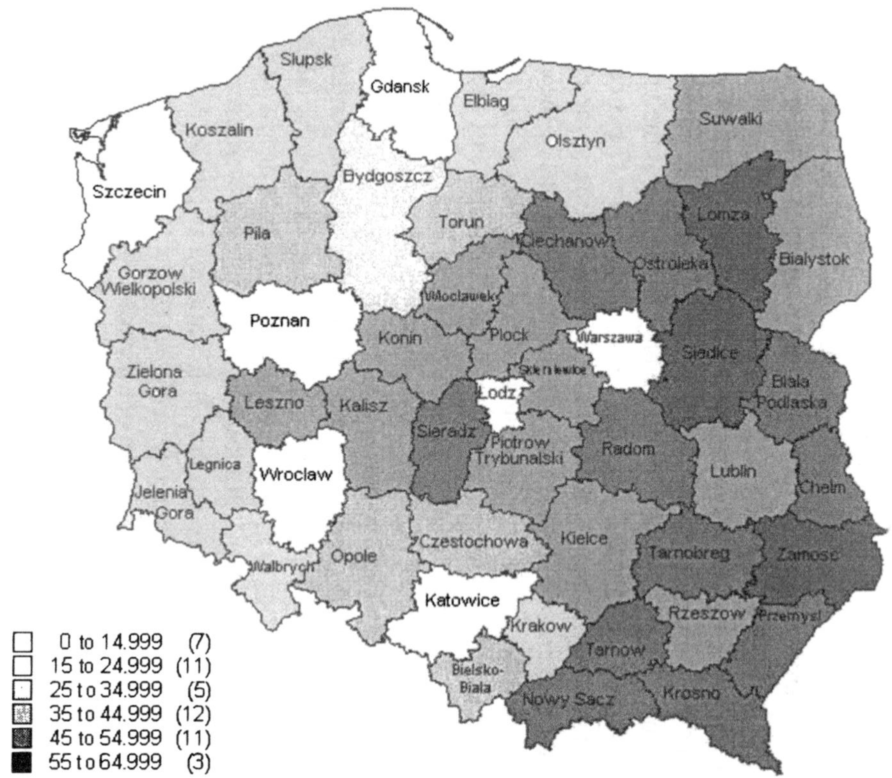

Map 10.3 Percentage of Employment in Agriculture: 1997
[*Source*: Calculated from GUS (1998)].

the country. In particular, the importance of industry continued to exhibit a distinctly west–east gradient, with the highest concentrations being found in the south–west and in the central voivodship of Łódź.[5] Against a national figure of 23.6 per cent, industry accounted for 38.9 per cent of Katowice's workers; indeed, that region alone was responsible for almost one-sixth of all such jobs in the economy. On the other hand, none of the voivodships on the eastern border of the country had more than twenty per cent of their workforces engaged in these activities.

An even more vivid demonstration of the prevailing spatial imbalance in the structure of economic activity is provided by the distribution of the importance of agriculture in the employment totals of the voivodships, as shown schematically in Map 10.3. While some 27 per cent of Poland's total employment was to be found in agriculture at the end of 1997, the range prevailing in the 49 administrative regions of the country ran from less than six (in Łódź and Warsaw) to almost sixty-three per cent (in Zamość). Once again, there exists a distinct east–west divide, with all western border regions having less than one-quarter of their workers in agriculture, while no voivodship on the eastern border had fewer than thirty-eight per cent.

On the face of it, the foregoing does not suggest that the gender differential will vary regionally; indeed, if the finding that, in the late socialist period, "industry wages tend to be relatively high or low regardless of skills or occupation" (Rutkowski, 1994, p. 155) were generalizable to the sexes in the present era, little variation might be expected. However, Ingham and Ingham (*this volume*) report that the differential continues to exhibit a wide dispersion across industries which, when taken in conjunction with the preceding discussion of the unbalanced character of Polish regional economic structures, clearly opens up the possibility of spatial imbalance in the earnings gap. Also, Rutkowski (1996) found that women gain relatively more than men from being employed in the private sector of the economy and, as shown in Map 10.4, there is a distinct regional pattern to its importance in employment totals. Thus, whereas 31.8 per cent of national employment was to be found in the public sector in 1997 (GUS, 1998b, p. 12), its spatial distribution is similar to that of industry and, at the very least, reveals a much stronger presence of the state in the west of the country. This is somewhat paradoxical given the twin assumptions that it is the private sector and the more westerly territories that will drive the country's integration with the west (Johnson and Loveman, 1995; TFRDP, 1996).

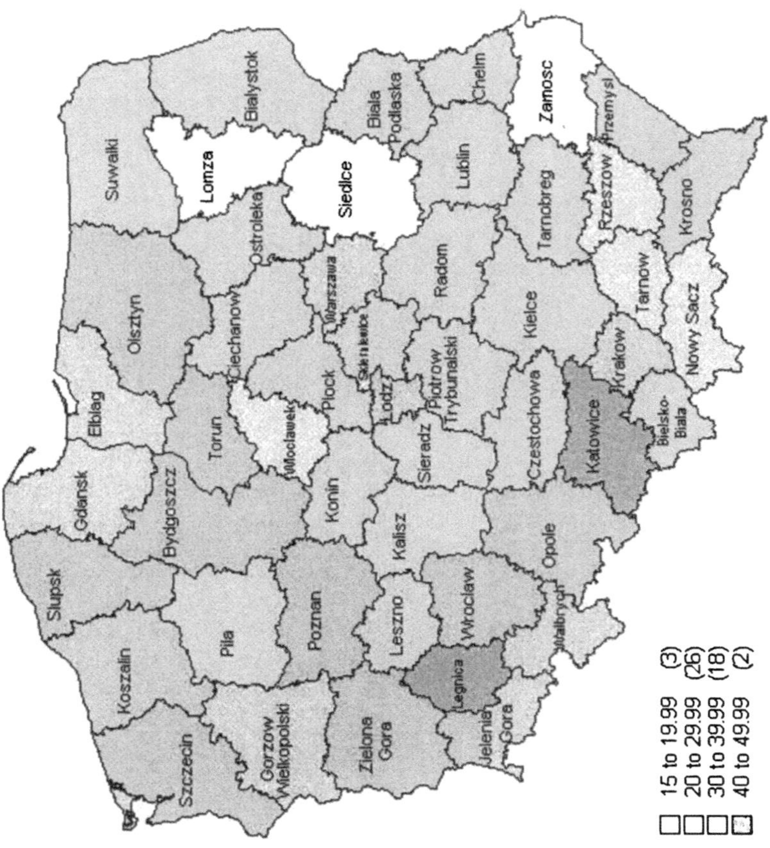

Map 10.4 **Percentage of Employment in the Public Sector: 1997**
[*Source:* Calculated from GUS (1998b)].

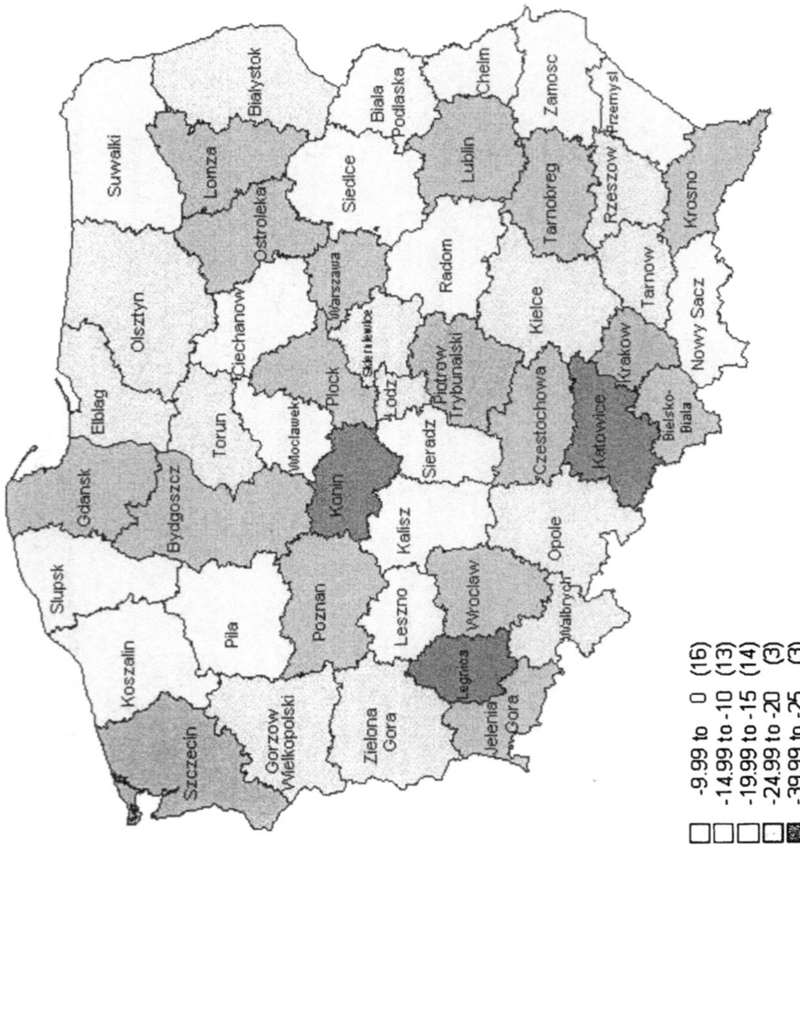

Map 10.5 **Female-to-Male Median Earnings Differentials (%): 1997**
[*Source:* Calculated from GUS (1998)].

In any event, the percentage shortfall of female from male median earnings in 1997 ranged from just over three per cent in Ciechanow to almost 39 per cent in Katowice, figures which should be placed in the context of a national difference of slightly less than one-fifth (GUS, 1998a, pp. 85–86). Map 10.5 indicates that there is a general tendency, albeit not one that is without exception, for the differential to be larger in the west of the country; a pattern which suggests that the variation in the earnings gap has its roots more in national industrial and sectoral influences than in specific regional factors.[6] The following section is devoted to a formal, statistical examination of these and related hypotheses.

Before proceeding to the analysis, however, it is important to emphasize one important point; namely that the focus in this paper is upon regional differences in the earnings differential between the sexes. While a worthy subject of study, the absolute earnings of women in Katowice, for example, where they fare particularly badly on the chosen measure, exceed those of men in Zamość, where women obtain virtual parity. Although this might appear to be trivial, and a more sophisticated analysis might in any case falsify it by introducing cost-of-living considerations, it nevertheless injects a necessary caveat into the interpretation of all studies such as this.

MODELING SPATIAL VARIATION IN GENDER EARNINGS INEQUALITY

The relevant literature on earnings, earnings differentials and discrimination in market economies is both voluminous and diverse. As such, no attempt is made here to review it with any rigor and the reader is referred to the papers in Ashenfelter and Layard (1986) for good, all be they a little dated, introductions to the area. These reveal that aggregate earnings analyses are inevitably restricted in the range of theoretical hypotheses they can test adequately and that the current exercise must be considered to be one seeking empirical regularities rather than as one designed to differentiate between specific competing theories. In the economies in transition, the data sets necessary to undertake these latter more sophisticated analyses are only just beginning to emerge.[7] The ensuing discussion first establishes the general arguments to be included in the present model and then specifies precisely how the relevant influences are to be measured.

INDUSTRIAL MIX

The preceding section provided strong empirical grounds for the inclusion of some control for industrial structure in a model purporting to explain variations in the earnings gap in Poland, an argument that can also be supported by a good deal of evidence from other countries (Rubery, 1992). Nevertheless, it is of some comfort to note that the empirical inducement to take account of industrial structure is also supported by theoretical argument. Thus, if industries differ in the degree of monopoly power they possess, they may differ in the extent to which they are able to discriminate against women (Becker, 1971, p. 46). In addition, the extent to which an industry possesses monopsony power within a given region will influence its opportunity to engage in rational, profit maximizing wage discrimination across groups of workers with differing supply elasticities.[8] However, the assumption under which this monopsony model will generate unfavorable wage payments to women—namely that their supply is less elastic than that of males—is empirically somewhat dubious (Killingsworth, 1983).[9]

PRIVATE–PUBLIC SECTOR MIX

Fears have often been expressed that women will face discrimination from the new private sector employers expected to emerge in the Polish economy as a result of reform (e.g. Zajicek and Calasanti, 1995, p. 184). While the argument is open to objection, insofar as private firms are driven by the profit motive, when taken at face value it suggests that the more significant the presence of the public sector within a labor market, the lower should be the associated gender differential. On the other hand, the numerous restrictions on female employment in the Labor Code apply largely to industries that continue to be located mainly in the public domain (EIU, 1999; Fong and Paull, 1993, p. 235). This legislatively driven reduction in the demand for female labor suggests that the importance of the public sector within different voivodships might actually serve to widen the earnings gap.

HOURS OF WORK

When analyzing female and male earnings it is important that like be compared with like. Unfortunately, this is not the case with the published data, in which the earnings figures are for the total month covered by the survey and hence pay no regard to the number of hours worked. As it is known that the latter vary by sex (Ingham and Ingham, *this volume*), this is an important shortcoming of the data to be analyzed. As no suitable hours of work information, disaggregated by sex and voivodship, is available, there is a need in this case to resort to measurement by proxy. In particular, the *ILO Yearbook of Labor Statistics* indicates that the weekly hours of work of females are below 90 per cent of those of males in both agriculture and education in Poland.

FIRM SIZE

There are a number of plausible theoretical explanations—efficiency wage considerations, training policies, compensating differentials—why large firms are often observed to pay more than small ones (Oi, 1990). It could also be argued that earnings differences between men and women will be lower in large firms simply because they are more likely to adhere to equal pay legislation (Ferber and Spaeth, 1984) or because they have structured labor force allocation procedures that are more gender-blind than those operated by smaller employers. On the other hand, large firms usually have stronger monopoly positions that potentially they will be able to exploit in discriminating against any particular group of workers.

RELATIVE LABOR SUPPLY

If female and male workers were perfect substitutes for one another, their relative supplies would have no bearing on the wage differential. Once allowance is made for the possibilities that discrimination exists (Becker, 1971) or that men and women form non-competing groups—there is crowding—(Bergmann, 1986), then labor supply becomes an important consideration. It likewise assumes significance if the sexes are for some reason not perfect substitutes in production. Under any of these scenarios, it would be expected that the earnings of women relative to those of men would be negatively influenced by their relative supply.

LABOR MOBILITY/MARKET OPENNESS

In freely functioning labor markets the flow of workers from low to high wage regions might be expected to exert some degree of equalizing pressure across space. Even in developed economies, however, there are reasons—movement/commuting costs, uncertainty, inertia, etc.—to expect that this effect might not be particularly strong. In Poland, with its notoriously malfunctioning housing market (Mayo and Stein, 1995), there are grounds for believing that the effect will be weaker still.[10] Nevertheless, it is changes on the margin that influence wage rates and the issue of whether net migration flows tend to equalize relative earnings across voivodships is worthy of exploration.

REGIONAL DIVERSIFICATION

Numerous taxonomies of the likely ability of Polish regions to meet the challenge of integration into the world economy have been proposed during the course of the last decade, although it is probably fair to say that the Scarpetta and Huber (1995) classification has received the most attention. They developed a six-fold grouping of the voivodships, derived from cluster analysis on 1992 data, which identified seventeen regions as diversified and therefore possessing the potential to meet the challenges of transformation largely unaided. If their ranking has substance—and this has not been proven—it might be imagined that the more developed local areas they isolated would have lower gender earnings differentials. At the very least, their economies are not dominated by single industries and hence, it might be assumed, characterized by competitive environments, thereby allowing workers a choice of employer. As such, it is to be expected that ceteris paribus such areas will exhibit less discrimination than others.

OMITTED VARIABLES

A number of variables to be found in many studies of earnings have necessarily had to be omitted from the model because of the non-availability of relevant data, although two of these deserve particular mention. The first is some measure of the educational attainments of the sexes within particular regions, which is central to the standard human capital approach to earnings determination (Becker, 1975). This is troublesome but, while annual graduation data for different educational levels are published, there is no contemporary measure of the total stocks of those with particular qualifications and this is what would be desirable here. Undoubtedly, this will be proxied in some way by the industrial variables included in the model, but there is no way of knowing just what biases its omission introduces.

Second, the construct is deficient insofar as unions retain any power to influence earnings and their distribution across individuals. It has been argued for some time that unions might discriminate against women (e.g. Booth, 1986) and, if they do, then given that unionization varies across industries in Poland, as it does elsewhere in the world, their uneven spatial presence may cause the extent of female disadvantage to vary regionally.[11] In the same vein, Ingham and Ingham (1998) argue that such vestiges of union power, or at least membership, as remain within the Polish economy are to be found in the public sector. The proxies are included in the model, but a measure of spatial patterns of unionization would clearly be preferable.[12]

VARIABLE DEFINITIONS, MNEMONICS AND SOURCES

EARNINGS

Median gross earnings by sex and voivodship.
Computed from GUS (1998, pp. 126–143).[13]

INDUSTRIAL MIX

Manufacturing: the percentage of voivodship employment in manufacturing in 1997.
Mining: the percentage of voivodship employment in mining in 1997.
Utilities: the percentage of voivodship employment in gas, electricity and water supply in 1997.
All computed from GUS (1998, pp. 100–101) and GUS (1998b, pp. 12–23).

SECTOR MIX

Public: the percentage of voivodship employment in the public sector in 1997.
Computed from GUS (1998b, pp. 12–23).

FEMALE-TO-MALE HOURS OF WORK

HoursEd: the percentage of voivodship employment in education in 1997.
HoursAg: the percentage of voivodship employment in agriculture in 1997.
Calculated from GUS (1998b, pp. 12–23).

FEMALE RELATIVE LABOR SUPPLY

Frls: females as a percentage of total voivodship labor supply (employed plus unemployed) at December 1997.
Fru: females as a percentage of the voivodship unemployment stock at December 1997.

Employment data from GUS (1998b, pp. 12–23), unemployment data from GUS (1997c, pp. 20–22).

EMPLOYMENT IN LARGE FIRMS

501+: the percentage of voivodship employment in firms with more than 500 employees in 1997.

Calculated from GUS (1998b, pp. 27–35).

LABOR MOBILITY

Mig: net internal migration as a percentage of total voivodship population in 1997.

Calculated from GUS (1998d, pp. 325–332).

REGIONAL DIVERSIFICATION

Diverse: a dummy variable taking the value 1 for the 17 voivodships Scarpetta and Huber (1995) classified as diversified and 0 otherwise.

Before proceeding to estimate the explanatory power of this model, it is necessary to specify more precisely how the dependent variable is to be calibrated. Taking the simple difference itself would be open to the objection that the model was merely explaining earnings levels across regions. For example, if it were the case that men earned ten per cent more than women throughout the country, then the bigger absolute differences would occur in those voivodships with the highest overall levels of earnings. Given this, it is more appropriate to examine some measure of relative earnings. In the simplest case this would be w^f/w^m, where w stands for earnings and the superscripts f and m refer to females and males, respectively. Following the work of Mincer (1974), it is usual for this ratio to be transformed as $lnw^f - lnw^m$ and for the model to be estimated in semi-log form. It should be noted, however, that the theoretical rationale for the logarithmic transformation present in human capital driven models applied to micro-data is absent in the present case. Given this, a second variant of the estimating equation will focus upon the percentage difference in earnings, $[(w^f - w^m) / w^m] \times 100$. The behavior of the gender differential, measured in both of the foregoing ways, is then to be modeled as a function of the influences discussed above.

ESTIMATION

Preliminary investigation of the data revealed three constraints on the specification of the model. The first was that the sum of the percentages of employees in manufacturing, mining and the utilities (that is, industry) was highly collinear with the percentage of the workforce engaged in the public sector (r = 0.77). The model was therefore estimated using the two sets of regressors as alternatives. Second, the percentage of employees in agriculture had to be omitted because of its strong correlation with the importance of both industry (r = –0.84) and of the public sector (r = –0.86). Third, employment in large firms is still dominated by public sector undertakings and the percentage of employment accounted for by all enterprises with over 500 workers is highly collinear with the percentage of total employment in the public sector (r = 0.81). In the light of this consideration, the variable *501+* was redefined to measure the percentage of total employment located in private firms with over 500 workers.

Table 10.2 presents the results of estimating, by means of OLS, four versions of the semi-log variant of the model.[14] While all coefficients of determination are reasonable for a cross-section analysis, they indicate that separate identification of the importance in the regional labor market of manufacturing, mining and the utilities represents a superior specification to that which incorporates simply the strength of the public sector. The reason is clear: to the extent that significance can be attached to the coefficients, mining and the utilities have adverse impacts on the relative earnings of women, while an increase in the role of manufacturing improves them. Within the preferred specifications, there is also some evidence, from column 1, that increases in the importance of large firms and the degree of openness of a region serve to lower the relative earnings of women but that increases in their share of the labor force are associated with improvements in their earnings position.

Table 10.2 $Lnw^f – Lnw^m$: All Workers[1]

Manufacturing	0.0038	0.0033		
	(1.948)	(1.652)		
Mining	–0.0174	–0.0199		
	(4.335)	(5.129)		
Utilities	–0.0239	–0.0253		
	(1.748)	(1.749)		
Public			–0.0069	–0.0089
			(2.976)	(4.448)
HoursEd	–0.0041	–0.0028	0.0216	0.0299
	(0.412)	(0.274)	(1.490)	(2.100)
Frls	0.0130		0.0816	
	(2.147)		(2.568)	
Fru		–0.0033		–0.0060
		(1.357)		(2.193)
501+	–0.0102	–0.0078	–0.0059	–0.0019
	(2.477)	(1.740)	(1.237)	(0.372)
Mig	–0.0002	–0.0001	–0.0001	0.0001
	(2.259)	(1.035)	(1.047)	(0.566)
Diverse	0.0271	0.0102	0.0415	0.0184
	(1.147)	(0.457)	(1.426)	(0.670)
Constant	–0.7360	0.0885	–0.9455	0.3099
	(2.397)	(0.631)	(2.515)	(1.995)
Adjusted r^2	0.682	0.661	0.484	0.464
N	49	49	49	49

[1] Absolute values of t-statistics are given in parentheses.

Although the model accounts for a good deal of the variation in the data when the earnings of all workers are taken together, it is of interest to disaggregate the workforce into its manual and non-manual components. Preliminary analysis of this division of the primary source, in conjunction with additional data from GUS (1998a, pp. 84–92), indicates that while there is a high degree of correlation (r = 0.79) between the relative earnings of females in blue and white-collar occupations across voivodships, there is less evidence of a relation between them by industry within the two ownership sectors. This suggests that different forces might be at work in determining the manual and non-manual earnings gaps observed across regions and justifies an analysis of the two sets of data separately.[15]

Table 10.3 presents the results obtained when the model is applied to the earnings of manual workers. Once again, the identification of separate industries provides a superior fit to the data than does the inclusion of the simple measure of the importance of the public sector. Focusing therefore upon the findings in the first two columns of the Table, women fare badly in those areas with high concentrations of employment in mining and more equivocally where large private employers are important in a region's labor market. The first of these findings is in line with expectations, insofar as women are legally excluded from the highest paid jobs in the industry, although the second may seem a little surprising in view of the arguments expressed above. On the other hand, female earnings approach more closely those of males as the share of women in the local labor force increases and as the manufacturing sector grows in importance. However, the findings in the second column indicate that the earnings position of females deteriorates as they become more prominent amongst the stock of regional unemployed. The suggestion is therefore that it is their employment share which drives the results regarding their labor force presence in the first column of the Table; that is, women earn more where there is a high demand for their labor.

Table 10.3 $Lnw^f – Lnw^m$: Manual Workers[1]

Manufacturing	0.0058	0.0052		
	(2.687)	(2.285)		
Mining	–0.0167	–0.0202		
	(3.712)	(4.526)		
Utilities	–0.0135	–0.0170		
	(0.877)	(1.027)		
Public			–0.0046	–0.0077
			(1.766)	(3.376)
HoursEd	0.0019	0.0044	0.0240	0.0368
	(0.169)	(0.371)	(1.484)	(2.272)
Frls	0.0213		0.0284	
	(3.124)		(3.502)	
Fru		–0.0063		–0.0091
		(2.246)		(2.947)
501+	–0.0099	–0.0055	–0.0037	0.0023
	(2.132)	(1.061)	(0.692)	(0.395)
Mig	–0.0002	–0.0000	–0.0001	0.0001
	(2.235)	(0.374)	(1.182)	(1.009)
Diverse	0.0291	0.0028	0.0461	0.0108
	(1.097)	(0.111)	(1.415)	(0.348)
Constant	–1.3766	0.0146	–1.6611	0.2544
	(3.996)	(0.091)	(3.950)	(1.442)
Adjusted r^2	0.640	0.602	0.420	0.379
N	49	49	49	49

1 As for Table 10.2.

The choice of labor supply indicator influences the apparent impact of migration on the earnings gap. Using total labor supply allows migration to achieve statistical significance at the five per cent level, while use of the unemployment measure renders the variable completely insignificant. It would appear therefore that areas with relatively high female unemployment levels are associated with relatively high out-migration. Although there is a clear need for further investigation, mobility appears to be selective and does not serve to reduce the overall excess supply of women manual workers. Finally, neither the education proxy for hours of work nor the dummy variable purporting to capture diversified regions approach statistical significance in the preferred specifications of the model.

Table 10.4 Lnw^f–Lnw^m: Non-Manual Workers[1]

Manufacturing	–0.0012	–0.0018		
	(0.892)	(1.210)		
Mining	–0.0083	–0.0110		
	(2.916)	(3.817)		
Utilities	–0.0260	–0.0283		
	(2.668)	(2.628)		
Public			–0.0056	–0.0075
			(4.005)	(6.018)
HoursEd	0.0106	0.0124	0.0247	0.0324
	(1.489)	(1.600)	(2.792)	(3.644)
Frls	0.0159		0.0172	
	(3.694)		(3.878)	
Fru		–0.0045		–0.0056
		(2.464)		(3.273)
501+	–0.0083	–0.0051	–0.0090	–0.0053
	(2.805)	(1.510)	(3.104)	(1.643)
Mig	–0.0001	0.0000	–0.0001	0.0001
	(1.546)	(0.546)	(0.879)	(1.551)
Diverse	0.0282	0.0081	0.0336	0.0123
	(1.676)	(0.490)	(0.1889)	(0.719)
Constant	–1.0180	0.0134	–1.0572	0.1029
	(4.661)	(0.128)	(4.606)	(1.063)
Adjusted r^2	0.730	0.685	0.677	0.651
N	49	49	49	49

[1] As for Table 10.2.

The results of estimating the model for non-manual workers are provided in Table 10.4, with the ordering of the specifications in terms of goodness of fit mirroring that obtained for manual workers, although the differences are less marked in this case. White-collar females evidently earn less where mining and the utilities are more important, a finding that is consistent with high pay in those activities continuing to be reserved for elite groups of manual workers. Although they remain fairly unimportant in most areas of Poland, the findings for the impact of large private sector employers on non-manual earnings differentials are again contrary to what was expected initially. Women tend to earn less, compared to men, as the proportion of the local employment stock accounted for by such enterprises increases. By way of ex-post rationalization, this finding may reflect either the privatization of non-restructured state enterprises or it might, to resurrect an already challenged but still troubling argument, be connected with large private employers being more willing to offer flexible working arrangements, with lower hours, to their female staff. The labor supply measures indicate that a greater total presence of women in the market is associated with higher earnings, while they receive lower rewards the greater is their weight among the unemployed. In contrast to the findings for manual workers, the results provide no suggestion that the rate of migration might influence the pay differential: a result that could be a reflection of the historically low rates of internal migration witnessed in Poland during the first decade of reform (Kotowska, *this volume*).[16] Finally, the diversification dummy variable once again possesses no explanatory power at all.

As indicated earlier, the model was also estimated in standard linear form using the percentage earnings gap as the dependent variable. In all cases, the results obtained were inferior to those generated by the semi-log specification, although they were not in any other way at variance with the preferred equation. Therefore, rather than considering these alternative findings in detail, attention turns to further statistical tests of the model discussed above.

MODEL RESTRICTIONS AND RESIDUAL ANALYSIS

The model reported in the first columns of Tables 10.2–10.4 represents the best in each case, in terms of overall goodness of fit. However, none of these estimated equations provide any evidence that either employment in education (the hours proxy) or Scarpetta and Huber's index of diversification play a role in the determination of relative earnings. This section therefore aims to explore whether it is acceptable, in a statistical sense, to impose the restriction implied by omitting these variables.

Having done this, the best fitting specifications are then used to highlight the difference between the prevailing spatial pattern of female earnings disadvantage and that implied by the preferred model.

Table 10.5 Lnw^f–Lnw^m[1]

	Total	Manual	Non-Manual
Manufacturing	0.0033	0.0056	–0.0012
	(1.797)	(2.670)	(0.827)
Mining	–0.0195	–0.0196	–0.0121
	(5.601)	(5.009)	(4.494)
Utilities	–0.0229	–0.0107	–0.0210
	(1.713)	(0.710)	(2.025)
Frls	0.0098	0.0167	0.0101
	(1.879)	(2.850)	(2.496)
501+	–0.0100	–0.0095	–0.0077
	(2.441)	(2.054)	(2.411)
Mig	–0.0001	–0.0001	–0.0000
	(2.021)	(1.810)	(0.116)
Constant	0.0585	–1.1356	–0.6751
	(2.266)	(3.899)	(3.366)
Adjusted r^2	0.687	0.642	0.683
N	49	49	49
F[3,40]	0.666	0.889	4.632

[1] As for Table 10.2.

The F-statistic presented at the foot of each of the equations reported in Table 10.5 refers to the test statistic for the joint linear restriction implied by the omission of the variables *Diverse* and *HoursEd* from the original specification. Given a critical value of F[2,40] at the 5 per cent level of 3.23, these restrictions are not rejected by the data for the regressions on all workers considered together and on manual workers alone, although they are rejected in the case of non-manual employees.[17] In summary, the evidence therefore suggests that women earn less the greater is the presence of mining and quarrying and of large private enterprises, irrespective of their professional standing. On the other hand, higher earnings for all women are associated with more feminized workforces. Female manual workers benefit in labor markets with larger manufacturing sectors, while white-collar women are disadvantaged where the utilities are important. In addition, there is somewhat weaker evidence that women in blue-collar trades earn less in more open regions.

Accepting these results as the basis for further investigation, Maps 10.6 and 10.7 plot the prediction errors for the percentage gender earn-

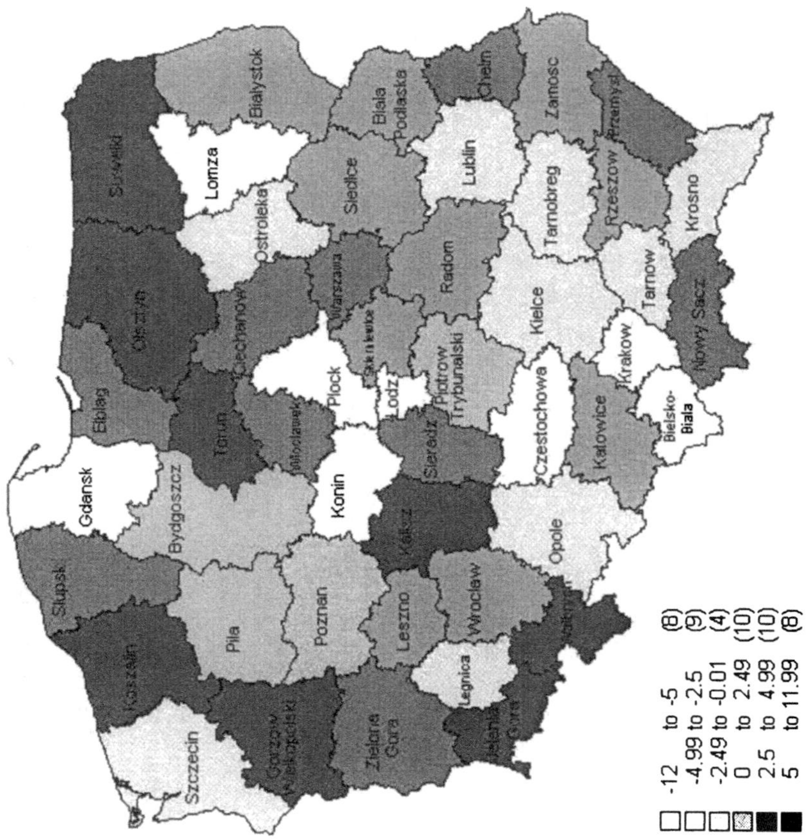

Map 10.6 **Residual Female-to-Male Earnings Differentials: Manual Workers**

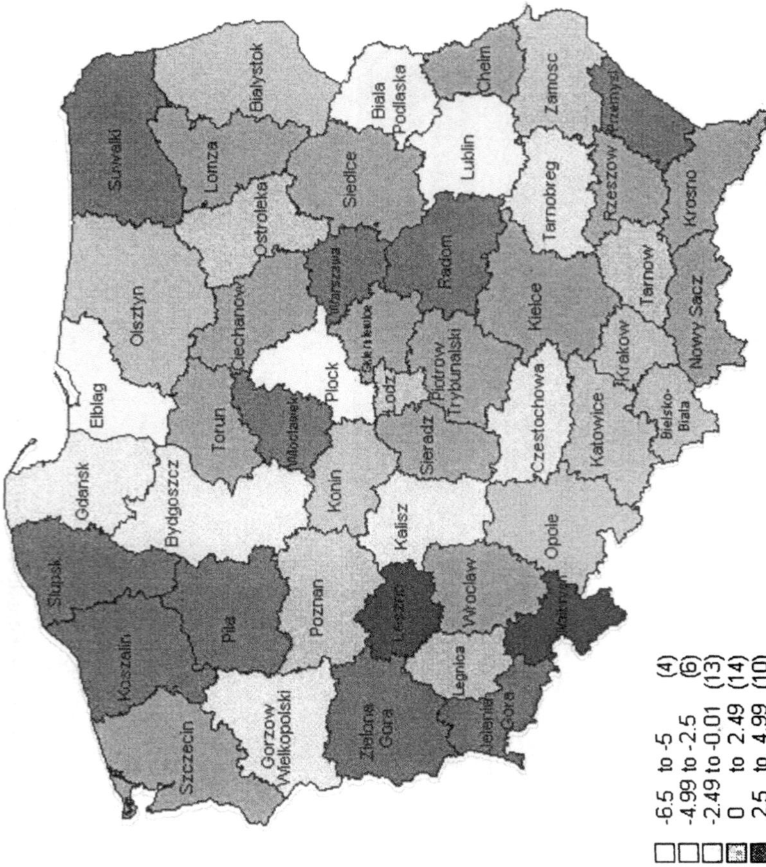

Map 10.7 Residual Female-to-Male Earnings Differentials: Non-Manual Workers

ings gap implied by the preferred equations for blue- and white-collar workers, respectively.[18] Positive values in these maps indicate that women earn relatively more than is implied by the model, while negative values imply the opposite. No clear spatial pattern emerges in the case of manual workers, save that women fare relatively well in two clusters of voidvodships, one along the western border and one in the north–east of the country. Each of these regions has a relatively slack labor market and the overall correlation of the prediction errors with the unemployment rates prevailing in December 1997 (r = 0.37) is in fact significant at the ten per cent level. Given the discussion in much of the literature, it is further noteworthy that women's earnings are also under-predicted in Katowice. The areas in which over-prediction is greatest appear more random and range from the heavily agricultural (Łomża) to the heavily industrialized (Łódź), the latter of which is centered on the female-intensive textile industry.

As befits the somewhat better performance of the model in their case, the prediction errors of the equation for white-collar workers are smaller than for manual workers. Although clearly not without exception, there is a tendency for under-prediction on the western border and for over-prediction on the eastern fringes of the country. While neither of the same magnitude (r = 0.23) nor as significant as in the case of blue-collar workers, there is some suggestion of a positive relationship between the prediction errors and the overall health of local labor markets for non-manuals. Although it is not possible to undertake a detailed consideration of this finding here, it could point towards a composition effect whereby high paying male jobs are lost first in the process of labor market restructuring and the expansion of new, higher productivity jobs is slow. Such a possibility is at least consistent with the findings of Ingham and Ingham (*this volume*) that males experienced a bigger burden of employment loss in the first years of transformation.

CONCLUSION

This chapter has provided further confirmation of the usual finding that women continue to earn less than men in the Polish economy and, by way of extension to most other studies, that the differential exists in each region of the country. Furthermore, the picture of countrywide disadvantage remains unaltered when the workforce is disaggregated into its blue- and white-collar strata. The size of the prevailing gaps are not, however, constant, although it has been shown that most of the spatial variation can seemingly be explained by a relatively simple empirical model containing a limited number of structural and labor supply variables. The findings obtained from conducting that exercise convey rather a mixed message for the future trajectory of the relative earnings of the sexes, albeit one that must be treated with caution because of an inability to incorporate direct measures of hours of work, labor quality or unionization into the model.

That women, regardless of skill, appear to be more handicapped where the importance of mining is greater is surely a legacy of history, and one that competitive pressures must eliminate in the near future. The same applies to the disadvantage experienced by female non-manual workers from large concentrations of public utility undertakings. It might also be regarded as encouraging that the earnings gap has been shown to be flexible: women earn relatively more where the demand for their labor is high. As several contributions to this volume have noted, women have enjoyed more favorable employment changes than men over recent years and the prospects are that this will continue into the future. On the other hand, the finding that large private enterprises appear to be associated with relatively lower female earnings constitutes a cautionary omen: much of Poland's future growth momentum will almost certainly be brought about by large scale foreign investment.

NOTES

1 Throughout this paper, this percentage difference will be referred to interchangeably as the gender differential, relative earnings or, following Lewis (1963), the earnings gap.
2 The choice of the median as the object of analysis was to a large extent dictated by the presentation of the original data in grouped form. With the highest earnings category being unbound at its upper end, calculation of average earnings is problematic.
3 The differentials in Map 10.1 are calculated in relation to the voivodship with the lowest median earnings (Ciechanów) and are defined as proportionate differences.
4 This is a contested point: certain authors argue to the contrary that the communists actually managed to reduce previous spatial inequalities, at least over certain periods of time (e.g. Wróbel, 1980).
5 Industry includes manufacturing, mining and quarrying, and gas, electricity and water.
6 The differentials in Map 10.5 are defined as percentage differences between female and male median earnings.
7 Reilly (1999) represents an interesting early study, although the reliability of the Russian data set upon which it is based must be questioned.

8 Discrimination proper, in the Becker (1971) sense of the term, is financially irrational insofar as it is costly to the employer, although compensating utility is derived from the practice.
9 It must, however, be noted that the voivodships do not constitute travel-to-work areas.
10 Hughes and McCormack (1986) found that the housing market was a major factor underlying limited internal migration in the UK.
11 On the other hand, it is quite possible to argue that unions have egalitarian goals.
12 Strictly speaking, a measure of union power rather than unionization would be desirable.
13 National median earnings from the data source were 945.56 złoty; 1052.86 złoty for males and 856.67 złoty for females.
14 As structured, the model has potential problems of simultaneity. However, preliminary investigation revealed the results to be robust when two-stage least squares was applied to the estimating equations, hence the findings reported in the text.
15 Nationally, the median earnings figures, in złoty, were as follows:

	Manual	Non-Manual
Males	958.89	1369.64
Females	674.27	975.16

Source: computed from GUS (1998, pp. 132–133 and 138–139).

16 In the usual case, one would expect non-manual workers to have more numerous external opportunities than manual workers, for the additional rewards from mobility to be higher for the former and for them to be more likely to be able to finance the cost of moving.
17 See Greene (1993, chapter 7) for further discussion of testing restrictions.
18 The differentials in Maps 10.6 and 10.7 are defined as the percentage difference between the actual and predicted values of w^f/w^m.

REFERENCES

Ashenfelter, O. and R. Layard (1986) *Handbook of Labor Economics*, vols. 1 and II, Amsterdam: North-Holland.

Balcerowicz, L. (1994) "Common Fallacies in the Debate on the Transition to a Market Economy", *Economic Policy*, no 19, Supplement, pp. 18–50.

Becker, G. (1971) *The Economics of Discrimination*, 2nd edition, Chicago: University of Chicago Press.

Becker, G. (1975) *Human Capital*, New York: National Bureau of Economic Research.

Bergmann, B. (1986) *The Economic Emergence of Women*, New York: Basic Books.

Booth, A. (1986) "Estimating the Probability of Trade Union Membership: A Study of Men and Women in Britain," *Economica*, vol. 53, no. 1, pp. 41–61.

Einhorn, B. (1993) "The Impact of the transition from Centrally Planned Economies on Women's Employment in East Central Europe," International Labor Office Briefings on Development and Gender (BRIDGE), Report No. 18, November, Geneva.

EIU (Economist Intelligence Unit) (1999) *Country Report Poland: 1st Quarter 1999*, London.

Ferber, M. and J. Spaeth (1984) "Work Characteristics and the Male–Female Earnings Gap," *American Economic Review Papers and Proceedings*, vol. 74, no. 2, pp. 260–264.

Fong, M. and G. Paull (1993) "Women's Economic Status in the Restructuring of Eastern Europe," in V. Moghadam (ed.), *Democratic Reform and the Position of Women in Transitional Economies*, Oxford: Clarendon Press.

Fuszara, M. (1993) "Women's Legal Rights in Poland and the Process of Transformation," *Beyond Law*, vol. 3, no. 8, pp. 35–47.

Greene, W. (1993) *Econometric Analysis*, 2nd edition, Englewood Cliffs, NJ: Prentice-Hall.

GUS (1997) *Rocznik Statystyczny Pracy 1997* (Statistical yearbook of labor 1997), Warszawa: Główny Urząd Statystyczny.

GUS (1998) *Rocznik Statystyczny Województw 1998* (Voivodship statistical yearbook 1998), Warszawa: Główny Urząd Statystyczny.

GUS (1998a) *Zatrudnienie w Gospodarce Narodowej Według Wysokościm Wynagrodzenia za Wrzesień 1997* (Earnings distribution in the national economy as of September 1997, Warszawa: Główny Urząd Statystyczny.

GUS (1998b) *Pracujący w Gospodarce Narodowej w 1997* (Employment in national economy in 1997), Warszawa: Główny Urząd Statystyczny.

GUS (1998c) *Bezrobocie Rejestrowane w Polsce I–IV Kwartał 1997* (Registered unemployment in Poland I–IV quarter 1997), Warszawa: Główny Urząd Statystyczny.

GUS (1998d) *Rocznik Demograficzny 1998* (Statistical yearbook of demography 1998), Warszawa: Główny Urząd Statystyczny.

Hughes, G. and B. McCormack (1986) "Migration Intentions in the UK: Which Households Want to Migrate and Which Succeed?", *Economic Journal*, vol. 95, Supplement, pp. 113–123.

Ingham, H. and M. Ingham (1998) "Who Joins the Liberated Unions of Poland Now That Choice is Free," *Research Bulletin*, Research Centre for Economic and Statistical Studies, Central Statistical Office, Warsaw, vol. 7, no 2, pp. 5–21.

Ingham, M. and Ingham, H. (2001) "Gender and Labor Market Change: What do the Official Statistics Show?", *this volume.*

Johnson, S. and G. Loveman (1995) *Starting Over in Eastern Europe*, Boston, Mass: Harvard Business School Press.

Killingsworth, M. (1983) *Labor Supply*, Cambridge: Cambridge University Press.

Kotowska, I.E. (2001) " Demographic and Labor Market Developments in the 1990s," *this volume.*

Lewis, H. (1963) *Unions and Relative Wages in the United States*, Chicago: University of Chicago Press.

Mayo, S. and J. Stein (1995) "Housing and Labor Market Distortions in Poland: Linkages and Policy Implications," *Journal of Housing Economics*, vol. 4, no. 2, pp. 153–182.

Mincer, J. (1974) *Schooling, Experience and Earnings*, New York: National Bureau of Economic Research.

Oi, W. (1990) "Employment Relations in Dual Labor Markets ('It's Nice Work If You Get It')," *Journal of Labor Economics*, vol. 8, no. 1, pp. S124–S149.

Reilly, B. (1999) "The Gender Pay Gap in Russia During the Transition, 1992–96," *Economics of Transition*, vol. 7, no. 1, pp. 245–264.

Rubery, J. (1992) *The Economics of Equal Value*, EOC Research Discussion Series No. 3, Equal Opportunities Commission: Manchester.

Rutkowski, J. (1994) "Wage Determination in Late Socialism: The Case of Poland," *The Economics of Planning*, vol. 27, no. 3, pp. 135–164.

Rutkowski, J. (1996) "High Skills Pay Off: The Changing Wage Structure During Economic Transition in Poland," *Economics of Transition*, vol. 4, no. 1, pp. 89–111.

Scarpetta, S. and P. Huber (1995) "Regional Economic Structures and Unemployment in Central and Eastern Europe: An Attempt to Identify Common Patterns," in OECD (ed.), *The Regional Dimension of Unemployment in Transition Countries*, Paris: OECD.

TFRDP (Task Force for Regional Development in Poland) (1996) *Regional Development in Poland: 1990–1995*, Warsaw.

Węcławowicz, G. (1996) *Contemporary Poland: Space and Society*, London: UCL Press Limited.

Wróbel, A. (1980) "Industrialization as a Factor of Regional Development in Poland," *Geographia Polonica*, no. 43, pp. 187–197.

Zajicek, A. and T. Calasanti (1995) "The Impact of Socioeconomic Restructuring on Polish Women," in B. Łobodzińska (ed.), *Family, Women, and employment in Central–Eastern Europe*, Greenwood Press: Westport, Connecticut.

Zienkowski, L. (1997) "Why do Regional Gross Products Differ?", *Research Bulletin*, Research Centre for Economic and Statistical Studies, Central Statistical Office, Warsaw, vol. 6, no. 4, pp. 7–31.

CHAPTER 11

AGRICULTURAL CHANGE AND THE LABOR MARKET STATUS OF WOMEN

The significance of women within Polish agriculture was highlighted by Tryfan (1996, p. 93) when she found that "about 60 per cent of agricultural produce results from women's work". Of course, female contributions to agriculture of this magnitude are neither confined to Poland nor to the last decade: in both Europe and the rest of the world, women have for many decades been a valuable source of labor on farms, and they have typically combined such farm activities with domestic duties. In the case of Poland, however, the situation is particularly interesting because the various political epochs through which the country has passed have each had differing implications for rural women. The current chapter explores what these have been via an examination of both the historical development of the position of women in rural Poland and the challenges and opportunities facing them today.

Section 2 contains an overview of the various theoretical approaches that have been adopted to explain the position of women in rural communities. In Section 3, the unique nature of agricultural work is described, with particular attention being paid to the fuzzy distinction between market and non-market work within traditional peasant farming. This is followed, in Section 4, by a discussion of the development of Polish agriculture since World War II and, in particular, an analysis of the impact of the existence of a two-track economy—rapid industrialization combined with an enduring small-scale, private family farming sector—on women's labor market opportunities.

Women's position in agriculture in the years following the events of 1989 constitutes the subject matter of Section 5. The collapse of industry that characterized the transition period led to a severe contraction in off-farm labor market opportunities and farm owners have been among the first to be dismissed by contracting state enterprises. An important consequence has been a net inflow of labor back into family farming, with many rural women thereby being forced to surrender the managerial roles they played previously. This has served to increase the degree of over-employment within Polish agriculture. Section 6 concludes the chapter by noting that, although the prospects for rural women appear to be poor in the short-term, their superior level of education could be of benefit to them in the medium to long-term.

THEORETICAL PERSPECTIVES

A number of contrasting theoretical approaches to the analysis of the position of women in agriculture have been adopted in the literature. According to two sociologists who examined women's issues in the context of rural Norway, three major perspectives can be identified in this debate. First, the 'equal rights' paradigm views differences between men and women as the result of discrimination; proponents of this school of thought support policies that aim to provide women with the same rights and opportunities as men (Brandth and Haugen, 1997, p. 327). The second approach, which might be termed the 'women's perspective', regards men and women as fundamentally different. Therefore, instead of trying somehow to make them equal, this strand of feminism identified itself with measures to increase the prominence of the activities that are specific to women and to ensure that these are recognized and valued (Brandth and Haugen, *ibid.*, p. 327). Finally, the 'gender perspective' recognizes that women are not of themselves homogeneous and that within the female population there will be those who are suited to a wide range of tasks.

Which of these approaches is the most useful when analyzing issues concerning rural women? Following convention and accepting that agriculture is traditionally a male-dominated activity, it would probably be correct to focus on the 'equal rights' perspective, thereby stressing the dominated position of women. This would appear to be the viewpoint of one analyst who, in her analysis of Irish farmers' wives, argued: "[F]arming is a peculiar case in that the vocational–educational link is reversed; people know that farming will be their occupation before training is undertaken. Men more usually inherit farms, and therefore they are more likely to participate in agricultural education and training. However, the extent to which educational structures can and do reinforce this link, and thus contribute to the low participation rate of women is frequently neglected." (Shortall, 1996, p. 269). This explains how the educational system might reinforce the traditional dominance of males in agricultural property ownership since it implies that, as women typically will not become farm owners, they are less likely to undertake the education necessary to fulfill the role.

When applied to the case of rural women, the 'women's perspective' stresses the differences between the sexes, both in their farming and their social lives. Proponents of this approach regard women as equal in status to men, even if they do not possess the same rights. Appealing as this theory may appear, it contrasts sharply with the opinions of women in agriculture who consider themselves to be on an equal footing with their husbands when it comes to managing the family farm. A study conducted in Lower Saxony, Germany, illustrates this point: "like men ... they plan, organize, carry out banking transactions. And all women agree: 'the farm couldn't be run without us.'" (Modelmog, 1998, p. 112). In fact, the only identifiable difference between men and women lies in the type of occupation that they would choose if they had to leave their farms. While men would prefer to enter technical occupations, women would be more inclined to undertake typical urban work, for example, office employment or to continue with their education. This demonstrates quite clearly that, contrary to the 'equal rights' approach, while women are different to men they see themselves as equal partners.

It could be argued that both the 'equal rights' and 'women's perspective' strands of the theoretical literature focus on the comparison of women and men in various areas of social life. The phenomena and processes analyzed by the adherents to these views have been employed both in the context of male dominance and in studies of co-operation between men and women. In this respect, the 'equal rights' theorists stress conflict whereas those professing the 'women's perspective' focus on co-operation, at best, or on the independence of the activities of the sexes, at least. Such unresolved differences of emphasis increase the attraction of the 'gender' approach, which is more clearly consistent with the fact that women within farming households perform a wide range of different duties, both on and off the farm. Indeed, the approach is particularly relevant for the study of rural women because "women's roles in agricultural production show enormous variation across time and space" (Flora, 1988, p. 265) and it is adopted in the remainder of this chapter.

THE PRISON OF THE INTERNAL MARKET: WOMEN IN TRADITIONAL AGRICULTURE

In order to provide an appropriate contextual background, it is important to consider the role played by women in traditional peasant agriculture, a starting point that can be justified on at least two grounds. The first, which could be termed ideological, relates to the impact of modernization, both on agriculture, in particular, and on the rural areas, in general. It is the contention of this chapter that the radical changes experienced by the Polish economy in the 1990s have altered the situation of those living in rural areas significantly and that these changes have transformed the position of women in these communities. The second reason is historic insofar as it focuses on the uniqueness of Polish agriculture within the former Soviet bloc.

Poland's agriculture, in common with that of other central and east European countries, was concentrated in traditional peasant farms at the close of World War II. This meant that, on assuming power, the communists were faced immediately with the problem of how they should treat the sector. Contrary to the experience of all other communist countries, except Yugoslavia, Polish agriculture retained its largely peasant character throughout the socialist period, despite frantic efforts to impose collectivization in the late 1940s and the early 1950s. According to one prominent economic historian, the majority of Polish farms still remained 'peasant post-traditional' at the end of the communist period (the late 1980s), with the farms typically being small and self-sufficient, although most had market connections (Kochanowicz, 1992). Thus, notwithstanding a limited degree of modernization, they preserved the traditional organizational structure within which tasks and responsibilities were delimited by both sex and age. Therefore, in order to examine the current situation of rural women in Poland, it is first necessary to examine their role within this type of milieu. However, in doing so it must be borne in mind that the form of peasant agriculture described above was not unique to Poland, since other types of pre-modern farming based on family labor shared common organizational characteristics: "In peasant agricultural systems ... and in frontier agriculture in the United States, custom and necessity determined agriculture to be a family affair." (Flora, 1998, p. 267).

Co-operation and conflict exist simultaneously within the traditional family farm. Family members are obligated to participate in production and, in return, receive the right of access to the produce of the enterprise. Historically, this right was regulated by custom, although latterly this has been replaced by legal regulation. The structural division of labor is the fundamental organizational characteristic of the family farm, with age and sex being its central dimensions in most peasant societies. Flora, commenting on peasant agriculture in Africa, noted that men assume responsibility for clearing the fields and killing lions while women engage in tasks such as seed selection, planting and the post-harvest processing of food (*ibid.*). In the case of Poland, Kocik (1976) also stressed the existence of 'his' and 'her' types of activity: while men are responsible for working in the fields, women take care of the livestock (cows, pigs and poultry) and undertake non-market chores, such as gardening and housework. In a similar vein, Chałasiński (1964) points out that the underlying feature of the lives of rural women is the on-going conflict between their quasi-market work on the farm and their domestic duties.

Tryfan (1968) describes the peculiar nature of the family farm in terms of it being an organization which functions as a self-contained labor force. A very similar situation was evident in certain regions of the United States, both before and after World War II. Based upon oral history interviews conducted in the Appalachian region of Kentucky, the author of one study points out that:

> The descriptions of farm work ... indicated a fairly consistent gender division of labour on these farms. Specifically, women and girls were responsible for work done in the house and the yard area—cooking, cleaning, sewing and textile work, child care, laundry, food preservation, vegetable gardens, poultry care, and dairy work. Men and boys, on the other hand, plowed the land, maintained and repaired machinery, and constructed buildings and fences. Men usually controlled cash crops production and, in some cases, oversaw the marketing of women's poultry and dairy products. They also maintained a virtual monopoly over the operation of large farm machinery which, on these under-capitalized farms, usually included draft animals, plows and, after about 1940, a tractor. (Scott, 1996, p. 214)

During peak times, such as the harvest, however, all family members work together, a phenomenon that is as visible on African and Latin American traditional farms as it is in Polish peasant families (see Tryfan, 1968; Kocik, 1976).

On the basis of research such as that discussed above, it might be concluded that there is a strong internal labor market in traditional farming that creates only limited opportunities for women, with their choices restricted to either work on the farm or chores within the family.

Nevertheless, the contribution made by women is as important as that of men. Modernization, by creating an external labor market, provides opportunities for rural inhabitants outside farming and undermines the status quo. The following section explores how change during the communist era affected women in Polish agriculture.

ENTERING THE EXTERNAL MARKET: WOMEN IN MODERNIZING AGRICULTURE

Following a Soviet-type policy of economic development, the Polish authorities introduced a program of rapid industrialization in 1949, beginning with the so-called 'Six Years Plan.' The focus of this blueprint was the development of heavy industry in order to move the country from an agriculture-based economy to an industrialized one. This industrialization drive had some important peculiar characteristics, with domestic sociologists pointing to the 'socialist' (Szczepański, 1973) and 'imposed' (Morawski, 1980) nature of the process. The 'socialist' characteristic stresses both political and ideological elements, such as the significance of heavy industry, the creation of a new working class, the bright future for a quickly changing country leaving behind its backward rural past, etc. The 'imposed' characteristic focuses on the leading role of the power elite in the process, as well as the lack of democratic mechanisms to permit either the emerging working class, or other groups involved in the social change, the opportunity to express their interests. Both Szczepański (*op. cit.*) and Morawski (*op. cit.*) also stress the significance of peasant farming as a primary source of the capital accumulation required for an industrializing economy.

One impact of these policies was to bring about change in a system in which the peasantry could be temporary laborers who relied on their plots of land for subsistence produce in times of economic hardship (Flora, 1988). Thus, the prevailing development model of the time, and the economic policies implemented to bring it about, meant that the fall-back position for the masses was eliminated in many countries. For women, these processes changed their opportunities on the internal market and opened up new ones on the external market. Industrialization provided the rural population with the opportunity to work outside agriculture without simultaneously necessitating migration to an urban center. Of course, this change also impacted upon the gender division of labor on the farms.

Certain phenomena associated with the Polish industrialization process—perhaps the most peculiar of all—are illustrated in Table 11.1. The agricultural labor force fell by less than 20 per cent over the period 1970 to 1984, although gender differences in this limited decline are marked. Thus, female employment in the sector declined continuously and, by 1984, was some 30 per cent lower than it had been in 1970. Conversely, male employment, while falling by nearby seven per cent between 1970 and 1978, actually grew by almost five per cent between 1978 and 1984. The result was that women accounted for over 55 per cent of the agricultural labor force in 1970, but their share had fallen to less than 47 per cent by 1984.

Table 11.1 The Agricultural Labor Force: 1970–1988

	1970		1978		1984	
	'000	%	'000	%	'000	%
Men	2852.0	44.4	2661.4	50.2	2788.1	53.4
Women	3568.9	55.6	2638.2	49.8	2495.9	46.6
Total	6420.9	100	5299.6	100	5224.0	100

Source: Wojciechowska-Ratajczak (1989, p. 132).

Table 11.2 People Working on Private Farms

Year	Total	Farming as a Primary Source of Income				
		Total '000	Those Aged 18–59			
			Men '000		Women '000	
1950	6800	6430	2356	41.4%	3331	58.6%
1960	6604	6018	2110	41.9%	2929	58.1%
1970	6883	5285	1527	38.7%	2417	61.3%
1978	5392	3919	1260	42.0%	1741	58.0%
1986	5653	3501	1304	48.3%	1397	51.7%

Source: Frenkel (1990, p. 54), elaborated by author.

A similar picture is painted in Table 11.2, which concentrates on those individuals for whom farming was the primary source of income. The data presented in the second column indicate that whereas 95 per cent of those in private Polish agriculture relied on farming as their primary source of income in 1950, this figure had fallen to 62 per cent by

1986. Confining attention to those of working age (18–59) reveals that there was once again a significant gender imbalance underpinning the decline. Over the period to 1986, the number of males dependent primarily upon agriculture fell by less than 45 per cent, while the corresponding reduction for females was 58 per cent. In consequence, the female share of those reliant on farming fell from almost 59 per cent to less than 52 per cent over the same period.

Enforced industrialization also gave a new impetus to the older industries of Poland, some of which had developed during the inter-war period, although others were established as early as the nineteenth century. A prime example is the textile industry in the Łódż region, an area that came to be regarded as a land of promise for rural women. Not only could they remain in their villages and commute to work, they could thereby enjoy improved conditions and hours of work as well. In addition, they received benefits in kind, such as free health care, dental services, regular health checks, generous maternity leave, subsidized factory shops for both the products of their own enterprise and other goods and foodstuffs, as well as bonuses for high productivity (Pine, 1995).[1]

The opportunities created by industrialization also caused mass migration from the rural areas, which resulted in changes in the agricultural labor market. As Lewis (1973) observes: "During the fifties, as young people were drawn into non-agricultural occupations, the agricultural work-force aged considerably. 58 per cent were aged thirty-five years or over; ten years later this had risen to 67 per cent, the greatest rise being recorded for the over-sixties. Fewer women than men were being drawn off the farms and in the ten-year period the number of women in charge of peasant farms nearly doubled." (Lewis, 1973, p. 47). However, this early picture changed considerably when the developing economy began to demand not only manual labor but also more highly educated people able to fill positions throughout industry, within the growing administration field, as well as within education and the service sector. According to Szemberg (1985, p. 89), in the late 1970s and the early 1980s, there was again a significant gender dimension to the flows into and out of agriculture, although this time women accounted for 53 per cent of the outflow stream, but constituted only 30 per cent of the total labor inflow.

The processes described above caused important changes in the demographic structure of the rural population. Based on data for 1981, it was noted that: "[T]he level of feminization shows an increasing decline in the number of women compared to men in the age cohort between 18 and 39. ... The most dangerous factor is the lack of women between 18 and 29. It is, however, significant that this demographic 'deformation' has been highest in the East–Central and North–East regions of Poland, where living conditions in the rural areas are the worst. In central Poland the situation is also worsening as a result of labour market developments in two of the largest cities in Poland, Warsaw and Łódź." (*ibid.*, p. 75).

This process underscored changes in the underlying characteristics of both the urban labor market and in the nature of farming during the period of modernization. The industrialization of the 1980s offered more opportunities for women than did its predecessor in the 1950s. An additional cause of the outflow of women from the industry in the later period was the changing nature of peasant farming: modernization had changed the nature of fieldwork, with tractors, and later combines, reducing the labor requirement in areas traditionally regarded as male, but housework, child-care and the traditional female roles on the farm remained untouched by such changes. The outflow of young women from villages in later years can therefore be seen as rooted in a desire to escape from the hard reality of farm and rural life. Moreover, the changes to traditional value systems that were associated originally with the stereotype of the 'urban promised land' further exacerbated the exodus. These trends led to a shortage of women in rural areas, particularly among the younger generations, as is shown in Table 11.3.

Table 11.3 Women as a Percentage of Men in Age Cohorts of the Farm Population in 1978 and 1981

Age Cohort	1978	1981
Below 17	93	95
18–29	91	90
30–39	101	94
40–49	105	105
50–59	115	114
60 and above	127	127
Total	103	102

Source: Szemberg (1985, p. 75).

The economic changes that accompanied industrialization also resulted in growing multiple job holding among the farming population, the obverse of which was a growth in the importance of part-time farming within the overall structure of agriculture. The latter is not, of course, a new phenomenon and dates back to at least the nineteenth century in parts of Western Europe and North America. In the post-World War II period, part-time farming was seen as a transitional phase for people entering or leaving agriculture, although today it is recognized as a persistent and prevalent feature of the economic landscape, albeit one that exhibits many national, regional and even local variations. For example, Blekesaune et al. (1993) show that in Germany it is traditionally the case that men work off the farm, leaving women to do the majority of the agricultural work; in Norway, on the other hand, both men and women juggle off-farm and farm work and most modern farm households are dual-career families, although women also undertake domestic duties.

In the case of Poland, Pine (1995) suggests that the failure of the communist government to collectivize agriculture, coupled with the favorable treatment afforded to the state farms and material production, forced many private farmers into industry. While most were linked to industry through either household ties or the 'kin' economy, others were classic worker-peasants straddling the sectors of waged work and subsistence farming. The same author also describes some specific patterns of plural activity within the rural communities of the southern highland region (Podhale) of Poland. In this locality, although migrant wage labor was the most lucrative source of income, villagers also worked outside farming. While women knitted, sewed and were involved in spinning activities for the market, in addition to their farm tasks, local men were also engaged in off-farm activities, including carving wooden boxes and other trinkets, and fashioning large baskets that were used in the area for everything from collecting potatoes in the fields to storing grain in the barn. Both men and women worked with leather, making tooled slippers and belts, as well as a variety of products, from cushions to coats, out of local sheepskin. Men worked as builders and laborers, while women dominated local and long distance trade, selling local crafts and produce at regional markets both within and outside Poland (*ibid.*, p. 52).

The Łódż area provides a further example of the specificity of local labor markets. In addition to the established opportunities for women in the textile industry, local traditions resulted in a very different picture of women's work from that prevailing in Podhale. Women in this region, with the exception of widows, were far less likely than men to run farms: even those women who effectively worked full-time on the farm did not consider themselves to be farmers. The majority of them, including those who were married to farmers, worked in the textile trade and believed that there had always been work in this industry and that this would continue to be the case (*ibid.*, p. 53).[2]

Industrialization thus affected females in rural labor markets in two ways. New job opportunities were created, particularly during the later phase of the industrialization process, which offered them the prospect of off-farm employment and gave them the opportunity to leave their traditional peasant households to begin new lives in the cities. However, industrialization also provided new job opportunities for men that forced women to assume responsibility for some 'male' work on the farms. This was especially true in the case of the so-called 'peasant-worker' farms, on which men typically divided their time between farm and off-farm jobs. In the late 1970s, nearly 40 per cent of Polish farms were of this type (Tryfan, 1984, p. 87). Ironically, it was on these undertakings that women assumed a greater proportion of the traditional male tasks while not enjoying a corresponding reduction in their traditional duties, such as housework and child-care. Although industrialization undoubtedly brought about changes within Poland's rural communities, it was not the only factor at work; the related process of urbanization also radically transformed social life in the country (Reissman, 1970).

The impact of urbanization may be viewed as two-dimensional. On the one hand, it generated demographic changes in Polish society as an increasing percentage of the population became city-dwellers (Rybicki, 1982). On the other hand, it also brought about cultural changes as people abandoned their traditional patterns of behavior, customs and values in favor of more modern ones. In an indirect way it also had a tremendous impact on farm and rural labor markets because it altered both individual aspirations and patterns of behavior, particularly among young women who eschewed rural life in favor of a career in a city. Allied to the process of urbanization is the concept of the 'urbanized village', a term that refers to the interaction of the traditional communities with urban centers and, over a quarter of a century ago, it was noted that: "[O]n the basis of economic dependence the relative isolation and self-sufficiency of the village population would seem to be a thing of the past." (Lewis, 1973, p. 52).

Thus urbanization had important impacts upon peasant culture: it changed almost everything from patterns of behavior to demands and aspirations, particularly among younger generations. It also brought about a division between 'time for work' and 'time for leisure', a distinction that would have been alien in traditional farming households

(Olszewska, 1969). Furthermore, attitudes towards the farm changed; no longer was it viewed as an object of ultimate value, but came to be regarded as a business (Jagiełło-Łysiowa, 1967). It also changed the concept of the internal labor market among farming families. Children, for example, were no longer considered to be part of the workforce (Tryfan, 1996). Likewise, women were treated as autonomous individuals and were allowed to decide whom they wanted to marry (Tryfan, 1968) and, as a result, farms lost their previous importance on the matrimonial market. At the same time, the strict division of labor into 'his' and 'her' types of work became less significant for the younger generation (Kocik, 1976).

BETWEEN INTERNAL AND EXTERNAL MARKETS: RURAL WOMEN DURING THE POST-COMMUNIST TRANSITION

Notwithstanding the major changes noted above, the present situation of rural women mirrors that which pertained during the communist period in certain respects and, as then, certain common processes shape social life. During the socialist era, industrialization and urbanization, together with state attempts to collectivize private agriculture, were of importance. Post-1990, the move to a market economy and the adoption of a liberal–democratic political regime have had a significant impact on rural communities. However, this impact has not been uniform across the country and the diverse nature of Polish localities has resulted in mixed economic, social, political and cultural outcomes. For example: "I would argue that part of this problem stems from the fact that even within each individual country, different regions had diverse histories and local economies, which have provided the context for a variety of reactions both to the socialist period, and the current period of 'transition.'" (Pine, 1995, p. 49).

In order to consider women's strategies on the contemporary labor market, it is instructive to begin by considering their attitudes to the market economy. From Table 11.4 it is clear that the most significant threat perceived by rural women in 1995 was the feeling of general uncertainty. It might be argued that this finding reflects a fear of unemployment, which has undoubtedly been the most dramatic manifestation of labor market change during transition. However, it is should be noted that only 12 per cent of respondents to the survey cited the fear of losing their off-farm job as their major worry. This finding is somewhat surprising given that, during the early years of reform, off-farm opportunities all but collapsed and large labor surpluses emerged in the rural areas. Furthermore, many large industrial enterprises shed labor, thereby further exacerbating the increase in unemployment. According to Frenkel (1997), 440,000 peasants lost their alternative employment, including 175,000 women, either through the collapse of plants or via employment reduction programs. Prior to 1990, non-agricultural employment was able to absorb all of the excess labor from the rural areas; however, the structural changes forced on the Polish economy under the Balcerowicz Plan eliminated this capacity. As such, it is no longer easy for rural men to migrate to urban areas to take off-farm jobs and this has radically altered the situation of rural women.

Table 11.4 Rural Women and the Threat of the Market Economy

Threats	Opinions	
	First Choice (%)	Total (%)
General Uncertainty	57.1	28.0
Fear of Losing Off-farm Job	12.2	12.6
Decline of Income	10.3	16.2
Lack of Welfare Benefits	8.2	12.6
Lack of Opportunities for Children's Education	6.1	21.6
Decline of Health Services	6.1	6.3
Lack of State Help in Organizing Vacations for Children	..	2.7
Lack of State Assistance for Disabled Persons and Handicapped Children	..	..

The data presented in this table are taken from a national survey on rural women conducted in 1995. For further details see Tryfan (1996).

The emergence of open unemployment at the start of the 1990s affected rural women particularly badly. In fact, one author has suggested that they, along with disabled persons previously employed by state or co-operative enterprises, are the two groups who suffered most from rising joblessness. As she notes: "the chances for rural women to get a new job are significantly less ... . Men who worked previously off-farm as typical 'peasant workers' returned to their farms which were run by women in past years. We may identify about 600 thousand such farms in Poland." (Tryfan, *op. cit.*, p. 47). This finding is consistent with the survey evidence reported in Table 11.5 showing that only 12 per cent of respondents felt that the major benefit of a market economy was the increase in entrepreneurial opportunities available for women. However, what the table also reveals is that rural women perceive the improvement in shopping facilities to be the major benefit of transformation.

Table 11.5 Rural Women and the Opportunities of the Market Economy

Opportunities	Opinions	
	First Choice (%)	Total (%)
Easy Shopping	51.0	31.5
More Time for Family Life	14.3	14.8
More Opportunities for Entrepreneurial Women	12.2	24.1
Women Are Able to Seek for New Sources of Income	10.2	6.5
Opportunities to Learn new Skills	8.2	18.5
Women Feel Free to Make Decisions on Their Own	4.1	4.6

As for Table 11.4.
Source: Tryfan (1996, p. 101).

Nevertheless, evidence from the Polish Labor Force Survey (LFS) indicates that although the unemployment rate in rural areas reached ten per cent as early as 1992 (GUS, 1998), which of itself is high, this was some five percentage points lower than that in urban areas.[3] But as unemployment has fallen from its peak, this differential has narrowed; in May 1998, while the rural unemployment rate areas was 9.4 per cent, the rate in urban areas was 10.7 per cent (*ibid.*). Notwithstanding any urban–rural divide, women in the latter localities have been consistently more prone to unemployment than men. In May 1992, the unemployment rate among rural women was 10.2 per cent, with the comparable male rate being one percentage point lower and, in 1998, the female rate remained over ten per cent while that for males had fallen to eight per cent (*ibid.*).

Predictably, these figures mask important differences within the rural population. According to Andrychowicz (1995), for farming households the unemployment rate was as low as 3.8 per cent in 1992, while in non-farming rural households it had reached 24 per cent. Similarly, Frenkel (1995) notes that by 1993 whereas the unemployment rate within private farming households had reached only 6.2 per cent, the corresponding figure for non-farming households exceeded 25 per cent. By 1996, although the unemployment rates for both groups of households had fallen, the figure for farmers had declined only modestly (by 0.1 per cent), whereas the rate for non-farming families had dropped by more than five percentage points, to 19.7 per cent (Frenkel, 1997). Among farming households, while the male unemployment rate stood at five and a half per cent in 1995, the female rate was seven per cent. Thus, although the data do support the existence of a female–male unemployment differential, it is clear that the major difference in the experiences of individuals within rural communities derives from whether or not they are members of a farming household.

It is, of course, inappropriate to proceed with the discussion without reference to the phenomenon of hidden unemployment in rural areas. While this is prevalent amongst the farming community, it can be argued that it was a general phenomenon during the communist era. Thus the Polish economy, in line with those of most socialist countries, exhibited a tendency towards over-employment, in essence because the prevailing ideology portrayed unemployment as an illness of capitalism that would not exist under the prevailing, alternative system. According to one source: "recent data show that there are about 2.4 million 'useless' people in peasant farms in the whole country." (Rosner, 1955, p. 108) and, of this total, approximately one-third live on small farms.[4] What is observed in Poland today is so-called 'agrarian over-population', a characteristic typically associated with developing economies.[5]

It is of some importance to note that the rate of 'uselessness' differs considerably between men and women. While it reaches almost 30 per cent among men in the age cohort 18 to 59, the corresponding figure for women is only 16 per cent (*ibid.*, p. 108). The difference arises because of the traditional gender delineation of agricultural work: women are useful on small farms because they undertake tasks which cannot be mechanized, in part because of the small-scale nature of the operation, but also because of low incomes. Such duties typically include the care of animals and children and the running of the household. This situation would appear to be yet another trigger for the elimination of the traditional gender division of labor within farming families.

Notwithstanding the fact that hidden unemployment remains widespread within Polish farming, some movement of rural inhabitants has occurred in the course of the current decade. Thus, whereas only 27 per cent of male rural inhabitants were economically inactive in May 1992, this figure had reached almost 34 per cent by May 1998 (GUS, 1998).

This apparent tendency to withdraw from the labor market has been even more pronounced amongst females: whereas fewer than 44 per cent of women in the rural regions were economically inactive in May 1992, the figure had risen to over 50 per cent by May 1998. These changes in economic activity status have been driven by the introduction, in 1990, of the Farmers Social Security Fund (KRUS), which provides assistance to over two million households, of whom 1.4 million are farming families (Christensen and Lacroix, 1997). KRUS provides two types of social security: retirement and disability pensions, and accident, sickness and maternity insurance. Any farmer who claims a retirement pension from this fund must give up all his/her land in excess of one hectare. While this scheme has reduced the problem of over-employment within farming to some degree, it is recognized that the scheme imposes a heavy burden on government resources and ultimately, by raising the dependency ratio, on those working in the legitimate economy (*ibid.*).

Although economic reform has resulted in both open and hidden unemployment, in the rural communities it has also brought employment opportunities. Pine (1995), for example, notes that, in the course of the transformation, certain new divisions of labor within the household have emerged. In some families it is now the young women with children who assume responsibility for the domestic and farming tasks, leaving the older women with grown children to become long-distance traders. In other households, younger women and couples with children are taking advantage of the relaxation of border regulations and traveling abroad to work as cleaners, nannies, farm laborers or builders while their parents care for the offspring.

In short, women are not simply useful on the farm, they are also obtaining work on the external rural labor market and this is serving to blur the gender division of labor. As a case in point, Wieteska (1995, p. 225) points out that 53 per cent of the employees of the Centers for Agricultural Advice (ODR—Ośrodki Doradztwa Rolniczego) are women. However, in contrast to the situation in the agricultural service industry, where the education of both sexes is broadly comparable, the same is not true of those engaged in farming proper. For example, only 13 per cent of male farm operatives graduated from secondary school and 1.4 per cent from colleges and universities, but the figures for females were 24 and 3.1 per cent, respectively (Gorlach, 1995). The necessary reform of Poland's agricultural sector need not, in principle, be disproportionately harmful to its female workforce, although ensuring that this is the case in practice will require vigilance on the part of the policy makers.

CONCLUSION

In summary, it is instructive to focus upon two issues that are likely to shape the position of women on the rural labor market in the foreseeable future. First, the opportunities for men to obtain positions in heavy industry are declining rapidly, with little if any likelihood of the trend being reversed. There is therefore little prospect that women who had previously been running farms will be able to resume their past role. In addition, the flow of men into rural labor markets has increased the competition for off-farm employment. In this respect, reform has limited women's opportunities on both the internal and external labor markets. This is not, of course, unique to Poland; the same process has, for example, been observed in Hungary: "[T]he post-communist welfare state, facing men's high unemployment rate and its own budgetary hardships, seems to have difficulties both to prioritize women's labor force participation and to continue the support of women's unpaid reproductive service in the households." (Asztalos-Morell, 1999, p. 20).

Second, the general problem of rising unemployment during the period of post-communist transformation is particularly severe for those individuals with the lowest educational levels. As women, and particularly those who run farms, are better educated than men in the same position, they should in theory find more openings on the evolving external labor market. The fear, however, is that the persistence of traditional rural cultural mores, under which women are expected to perform virtually all domestic duties, will continue to limit their opportunity to take advantage of the emerging opportunities.

NOTES

1 Pine (1995) does however note that conditions of work, as well as health and safety standards, remained poor by western standards.

2 The current situation of women in Łódź is discussed in Malinowska (*this volume*).

3 The first LFS was conducted in Poland in May 1992. The survey is a more accurate source of unemployment data for rural areas than the registration data because individuals who own a farm, or whose spouse owns a farm, are not eligible to register.

4 Small farms are here defined as being below 2 hectares.

5 For a more detailed analysis see Gorlach (1990).

REFERENCES

Andrychowicz, B. (1995) "Aktywność zawodowa ludności wsi w różnych typach gospodarstw domowych" (Occupational activity among members of various rural households), in: Klank (ed.).

Asztalos-Morell, I. (1999) "Rural women and the gender division of labor in the post-communist transition," in: Starosta et al. (eds).

Blekesaune, A., W.G Haney and M.S. Haugen (1993) "On the question of the feminization of production on part-time farms: evidence from Norway," *Rural Sociology*, vol. 58, no. 1, pp. 111–129.

Brandth, B. and M. S. Haugen (1997) "Rural women, feminism and the politics of Identity," *Sociologia Ruralis*, vol. 37, no. 3, pp. 325–344.

Chałasiński, J. (1964) *Młode pokolenie wsi Polski Ludowej* (The young rural generation in people's Poland), Warszawa: LSW.

Christensen, G. and R. Lacroix (1997) *Competitiveness and Employment: A Framework For Rural Development in Poland*, Washington, D.C.: World Bank.

Flora, C. (1988) "Public policy and women in agricultural production: a comparative and historical analysis," in: W.G. Haney and J. B. Knowles (eds), *Women and Farming. Changing Roles, Changing Structures*, Boulder and London: Westview Press.

Frenkel, I. (1990) "Dynamika, struktura i wykorzystanie zasobów siły roboczej w rolnictwie polskim" (The labor force in Polish agriculture: its structure, dynamics and use), *Wieś i Rolnictwo*, vol. 66, no. 1, pp. 50–77.

Frenkel, I. (1995) "Zmiany bezrobocia i zatrudnienia na wsi w latach 1992–1994" (Changes in rural unemployment in the 1992–1994 period), in: Klank (ed.).

Frenkel, I. (1997) *Ludność, zatrudnienie i bezrobocie na wsi w latach 1988–1995* (Population and unemployment in rural areas between 1988–1995), Warszawa: IRWiR PAN.

Gorlach, K. (1990) "Socjologia polska wobec kwestii chłopskiej" (The peasant question in Polish sociology), Kraków: Universitas.

Gorlach, K. (1995) *Chłopi, rolnicy, przedsiębiorcy: "kłopotliwa klasa" w Polsce postkomunistycznej* (Peasants, farmers, entrepreneurs: the 'awkward class' in post-communist Poland), Kraków: Jagiellonian University Press.

GUS (1998) *Labour Force Survey in Poland: May 1998*, Warszawa: Główny Urząd Statystyczny.

Jagiełło-Łysiowa, E. (1967) "Od chłopa do rolnika" (From peasant to farmer), in: *Młode pokolenie wsi Polski Ludowej, t. 2* (The young rural generation in people's Poland, vol. 2), Warszawa: LSW.

Klank, L. (ed.) (1995) *Wieś i rolnictwo w okresie transformacji systemowej* (The countryside and agriculture in the process of systemic transformation), Warszawa: IR-WiR PAN.

Kochanowicz, J. (1992) *Spór o teorię gospodarki chłopskiej. Gospodarstwo chłopskiew teorii ekonomii i w historii gospodarczej* (Discussion on the theory of the peasant economy. Peasant farms in economic theory and economic history), Warszawa: Warsaw University Press.

Kocik, L. (1976) *Przeobrażenia funkcji współczesnej rodziny wiejskiej* (Changes of functions in contemporary rural families), Kraków: Ossolineum.

Lewis, P. (1973) "The peasantry," in: D. Lane and G. Kolankiewicz (eds), *Social Groups in Polish Society*, London: MacMillan.

Malinowska, E. (2001) "Women's Organization's in Poland," *this volume*.

Modelmog, I. (1998) "'Nature' as a promise of happiness: farmers' wives in the areas of Ammerland, Germany," *Sociologia Ruralis*, vol. 38, no. 1, pp. 109–122.

Morawski, W. (1980) "Society and the strategy of imposed industrialization: the Polish case," *The Polish Sociological Bulletin*, vol. 42, no. 4, pp. 69–82.

Olszewska, B. (1969) *Wieś uprzemysłowiona. Studium społeczności lokalnej w powiecie opolskim* (An industrialized village: studies of local community in Opole county), Wrocław: Ossolineum.

Pine, F. (1995) "Kinship, work and the state in post-socialist rural Poland," *Cambridge Anthropology*, vol. 18, no. 2, pp. 47–58.

Reissman, L. (1970) *The Urban Process. Cities in Industrial Societies*, New York: The Free Press.

Rosner, A. (1995) "Bezrobocie ukryte w rolnictwie rodzinnym" (Latent unemployment in family farming), in: Klank (ed.).

Rybicki, P. (1982) *Społeczeństwo miejskie* (Urban society), Warszawa: PWN.

Scott, S.L. (1996) "Drudges, helpers and team players: oral historical accounts of farm work in Appalachian Kentucky," *Rural Sociology*, vol. 61, no 2, pp. 209–226.

Shortall, S. (1996) "Training to be farmers or wives? Agricultural training for women in Northern Ireland," *Sociologia Ruralis*, vol. 36, no. 3, p. 269–285.

Starosta, P, I. Kovach and K. Gorlach (eds) (1999) *Rural Areas under Communism and Beyond: Polish–Hungarian Perspectives*, Łódź: Łódź University Press.

Szczepański, J. (1973) *Zmiany społeczeństwa polskiego w procesie uprzemysłowienia* (Changes in Polish society under the process of industrialization), Warszawa: PWN.

Szemberg, A. (1985) "Ludność i praca w indywidualnym rolnictwie" (People and work in family farming), *Wieś i Rolnictwo*, vol. 46, no. 1, pp. 73–94.

Tryfan, B. (1968) *Pozycja społeczna kobiety wiejskiej* (Social position of rural women), Warszawa: Ksiąka i Wiedza

Tryfan, B. (1984) "Kobieta siła robocza w rolnictwie a dylematy emancypacji" (Women's labor force in farming and dilemmas of emancipation), *Wieś i Rolnictwo*, vol. 45, no. 4, pp. 75–96.

Tryfan, B. (1994) "Wiejscy inwalidzi i kobiety wobec przedsiębiorczości" (Rural disabled persons and women facing entrepreneurship), in: K. Duczkowska-Małysz, and M. Kłodziński (eds), *Rozwój przedsiębiorczości na terenach wiejskich* (Development of entrepreneurialism in rural areas), Warszawa: SGGW Publishers, pp. 47–48.

Tryfan, B. (1996) *Ochrona socjalna rodziny wiejskiej* (Rural families under welfare programs), Warszawa: IRWiR PAN.

Wieteska, E. (1995) "Rola doradztwa w procesie przemian społeczno-ekonomicznych na wsi i w rolnictwie" (The role of the advisory system under the process of socio-economic changes in countryside and agriculture), in: Klank (ed.).

Wojciechowska-Ratajczak, B. (1989) "Ewolucja poziomu i struktury ludności pracującej w rolnictwie polskim w latach 1970–1986" (Changes among the population employed in Polish farming in the years 1970–1984), *Wieś i Rolnictwo*, vol. 65, no. 4, pp. 125–148.

CHAPTER 12

WOMEN AND LABOR MARKET REFORM IN KRAKÓW

The Balcerowicz Plan envisaged the radical restructuring of industry in Poland and recognized that the move to a market economy would necessitate the eventual elimination of the over-manning in large state-owned enterprises (SOEs) that had been a pervasive feature of the Communist period.[1] At the same time, the growth of the private sector was seen to offer the prospect of employment opportunities that had been absent under socialism. Such dynamics are seemingly not, however, unique to central and eastern Europe: Hannon and Freeman (1989), for example, argue that the pervasive industrial momentum in the United States is for new firms to emerge, grow and displace large firms that have declined due to their inability to adapt to changing circumstances.[2] Nevertheless, much of the human capital embodied in large industrial enterprises typically depreciates when workers are forced to seek employment in emerging sectors; although individuals with skills suited to the new industries are likely to be able to capture high financial rewards.

The beneficiaries of restructuring in Poland were seen as likely to be young and highly educated city-dwellers, although numerous authors identified women as one group liable to suffer hardship through their being most likely to be fired first and hired last (Kuratowska, 1991). Early evidence seeming to support this contention emerged as women, while consistently less than half of the workforce, constituted in excess of half of the registered unemployed (Malinowska, 1995). It is notable, however, that the expectations of academics contrasted sharply with the initial impressions of the public: for example, when asked what kinds of people they believed to constitute the majority of the unemployed in 1992, only 6.6 per cent of respondents to one sample survey mentioned women, whereas, 35.5 per cent cited graduates (Reszke, 1995, p. 111).

At the time, official data indicated that women constituted 52.6 per cent of the registered unemployed, while only 5.3 per cent were graduates (*ibid.*). Nonetheless, it would be surprising if firms were overtly discriminating against women, given that they were more lowly paid than males under the former regime (Fong and Paull, 1993; Kramer, 1995) and remained so after 1989.[3] In addition, females tended to have higher educational attainments than males (Białecki and Heyns, 1993), although the distorted remuneration system that operated under communism did not reward this.[4] Better educated women were concentrated in professions that are typically both high status and highly paid in the west, such as accountancy (Leven, 1993), but which were seen as ancillary functions in the eastern bloc.

Public opinion has changed since the early study by Reszke; for example, a survey of women conducted in 1996 revealed that 67 per cent of those polled believed that females had fewer opportunities than males to find work, while 55 per cent felt that women were more likely than men to lose their jobs (CBOS, 1996).[5] Nonetheless, while over half of respondents felt that women had fewer opportunities than men on the labor market because of their domestic duties, only one-quarter saw employer discrimination to be the root of the problem. However, interpretation of such national surveys is confounded by the spatial dimension of transition (Gorzelak, 1996; Kukliński et al., 1997; TFRDP, 1996). For example, it would be expected that the labor market experiences of women in major urban centers, where western companies have established a presence and where buoyant domestic private sectors are emerging, would differ from those of women in rural areas where, outwardly at least, transition has had little impact. This chapter constitutes a case study and focuses on the position of women in the urban labor market of Kraków, albeit a study conducted against the backdrop of national developments.

Located in the Małopolska region in the south of the country, the Kraków voivodship is an area of contrasts.[6] On many counts it can be considered to be privileged: it is the historic capital and center of academia; it possesses a highly educated workforce, and it is located close to the tourist resorts in the Tatra Mountains.[7] However, the 'gift' of the Huta Sendzimira (HTS) steelworks by the Communist authorities ensured that, for all of the post-Second World War period, the region lacked a diversified economic base and suffered the highest pollution levels in Poland.[8] In reality HTS was located in Kraków as a punishment for the bourgeois character of the local population. During the 1980s,

HTS was the largest steelworks in the country, although, somewhat ironically, it had the highest paid workforce (Kennedy, 1991). Despite this, living conditions in Kraków deteriorated compared to those in other cities. In particular, the policy of intensive industrialization was accompanied by a growth of the local population between 1950 and 1984 of more than 450,000 (Sowa, 1988).

In the 1990s, when the health of labor markets has most frequently been measured by their unemployment rates, Kraków appears to have fared well. While the national registered unemployment rate peaked at 16.4 per cent in 1994, the corresponding figure for Kraków rose only to 10.2 per cent (GUS, 1995).[9] However, this may reflect the difficulty of restructuring HTS as much as any particular vitality in the local economy (Hardy and Rainnie, 1996, p. 94). For example, while the statistics suggest that there has been significant rationalization at the plant—at its peak HTS employed 40,000 workers, a figure that had fallen to 17,500 by 1995 (*ibid.*, pp. 196–97)—the raw data are misleading. Primarily because of strong union resistance, there have been no compulsory redundancies and manpower reductions have been achieved via voluntary severance schemes and 'spin-offs.'[10] The importance of the latter might be gauged from the fact that HTS is a shareholder in 20 new companies, with holdings ranging from 50 per cent to less than one per cent. In consequence, 250,000 of Kraków's employees still work for either HTS or its associated companies.

The actual outcome at HTS contrasts sharply with the plan proposed in 1992 by a team of Canadian consultants. They suggested that, in the short term, HTS should be merged with the neighboring Katowice steelworks and, in the long run, the plant should cease production. Unsurprisingly, the plan generated severe opposition and was not implemented. Instead, HTS became a State Treasury Company in 1992, with future technical innovation and spin-offs to be financed through government-guaranteed loans and it continues to consume state subsidies. Although wages that are low in an international context ensure that its output remains competitive, its access to western markets is limited and its problems are exacerbated by the continuation of economic instability in the former rouble market.[11]

Under the adopted transition strategy, Poland's immediate future is held to lie with the growth of the private sector, stimulated, at least in part, by foreign capital. However, Kraków has so far attracted less foreign direct investment (FDI) than had been hoped initially, although the same is equally true for the rest of the country. A ranking produced by the Task Force for Regional Development in Poland (TFRDP) (1996) placed Kraków seventh in terms of accumulated FDI, behind major centers such as Warsaw and Poznań.[12] Nonetheless, there have been some notable joint ventures established in the city; the local tobacco plant ZPT has had a long established relationship with the US manufacturer Philip Morris and this has been strengthened in the 1990s, while Heineken has secured a substantial stake in the Okocim brewery. Overall, recent data reveal that there are currently 70,990 private businesses in Kraków, compared to 1,156 state enterprises (Kraków, 1998). However, the income generated by the private sector in 1996—6,003,193 thousand złotys—only marginally exceeded the figure of 5,753,493 thousand złotys for the public sector. The resulting picture is therefore of an industrial landscape still dominated by large state firms, but dwarfed in numerical terms by small private firms. Some authors (e.g. Johnson and Loveman, 1995) point to the failure of early transition governments to adhere to the stringent anti-inflationary policies outlined in the Balcerowicz Plan as the restraining factor on private sector development.[13] If this is true, then it is necessary to recognize that the problems in Kraków have not been unique, but Poland's desire for full European Union (EU) membership early in the new century should provide an impetus for increasing the speed of restructuring.

The outcome of the restructuring that has taken place in Kraków is unlikely to have been gender-neutral and it is frequently assumed to have harmed women more than men. Whereas industrial employment has been protected more than had been anticipated at the start of the 1990s, the peripheral activities of the SOEs (for example child-care and catering) have either been divested or closed. Where the latter has occurred, it has been female jobs that have been lost. Nevertheless, small-scale privatization has been relatively successful and, in addition to individuals leasing city center shops and restaurants from the voivodship (Hardy and Rainnie, 1996), Kraków has attracted retailers such as the Italian company Benetton and the US food giant McDonalds. Western experience suggests that the jobs created within these enterprises will be largely for females. Furthermore, the growth of private sector business activities has generated well-paid employment in fields such as accountancy and law, professions that were historically dominated by women in Poland.

This chapter utilizes both survey and official data in order to obtain further insights into how women have fared in Kraków in the last decade. In the following section, evidence is presented on how women and men view the changes that have taken place in the economy since 1989. In Section 3, these views are contrasted with official data showing how the sexes have fared in the ongoing process of job creation and job destruction. While women appear to be more pessimistic about the effects of the market than men, the objective evidence contradicts at least some of their impressions: for example, they lost fewer jobs during the early 1990s and enjoyed greater employment growth in the more recent upturn. Following this, Section 4 investigates the gender profile of unemployment through time and reveals that not only has the female unemployment rate been consistently above that for males, but also that the differential is now increasing. The apparent contradiction between these jobless figures and the earlier data indicating that women have experienced superior employment growth constitutes a natural focus of attention in this section. Section 5 explores the views that firms hold of women as employees and, in the event, these seem to underscore the favorable interpretation of recent female labor market history. Employers express no bias against women workers and offer no evidence that they are more likely to fire them before men. A summary and conclusion to the chapter is provided in Section 6.

PERCEPTIONS OF THE IMPACTS OF CHANGE

Pessimistic forecasts regarding the impact of reform on the labor market position of women are echoed by the findings of certain past research projects undertaken in Kraków. For example, it was found that at both ZPT and the confectionery manufacturer Wawel, women felt that they were being forced to work full-time out of economic necessity, while simultaneously being in fear of losing their jobs (*ibid.*, p. 235). Additional evidence on the perceived impacts of reform in the city was provided by a survey conducted on a sample of 1,000 households in 1996.[14] This section explores the views of the employed respondents to that study on market control, restructuring and economic conditions. The responses in the tables that follow are disaggregated according to sex and ownership sector of employment.

Table 12.1 presents the views of respondents on market versus state control, showing that less than half of females, irrespective of employment sector, believe that Poland should be a market economy. Although this rises to more than half of males working in the public domain, the major supporters of the market are men employed in the private sector, of whom over 70 per cent voice their support. At the same time, while more than 50 per cent of women working in the private sector—in public enterprises—believe that industry should be state-controlled, the ordering is reversed for males. These findings provoke two conjectures: first, women are dissatisfied with working conditions in the private sector; second, men working in SOEs fear that if their firms are privatized, it is their jobs that are most at risk.

Table 12.1 Views on State vs. Market Control

	Private Sector (%)		Public Sector (%)	
	Females	Males	Females	Males
Poland Should Operate a Market Economy	48.1	71.4	48.5	54.6
Industry Should Be State- controlled	52.0	42.9	48.5	52.1
Shops Should Be Privately Owned	83.2	98.0	90.6	95.8
Housing Should Be Privately Owned	37.7	63.7	37.0	51.3
Health Provision Should Be Divided Equally Between the Private and Public Sectors	42.9	39.0	35.5	32.8
Education Should Be State-provided	50.7	43.5	52.9	54.6
N	77	154	138	119

Source: Household Survey, Kraków, 1996.

The survey revealed widespread support amongst both sexes for privately owned shops, a reflection presumably of the increased availability and choice of goods in Kraków in recent years. On the other hand, women do not hold the same positive views about private ownership of the housing stock, irrespective of their employer. Males in the private sector are the strongest supporters of private housing. In the case of health, the most common view is that there should be shared provision between the public and the private sectors. Finally, over half of the respondents of both sexes working in public enterprises believe that education should be state-provided, although men working in the private sector reveal somewhat less enthusiasm for the public provision of schooling. Overall, women appear to be more cautious towards private ownership than men, but the difference in views is far more pronounced for private sector employees than it is for those working in the public domain, with males employed in private enterprises being the major supporters of private ownership.

Table 12.2 Views on Privatization

	Private Sector (%)		Public Sector (%)	
	Females	Males	Females	Males
Privatization Too Fast	19.5	14.3	15.2	14.4
Privatization Too Slow	45.5	62.4	44.5	60.1
Satisfied with Large- scale Privatization	3.9	6.6	7.2	9.2
Not Satisfied with Large- scale Privatization	37.7	49.4	40.6	50.2
Satisfied with Small-scale Privatization	61.0	46.1	53.6	58.0
Dissatisfied with Housing Privatization	15.6	29.2	19.6	23.5
N	77	154	138	119

Source: Household Survey, Kraków, 1996.

The impression of greater enthusiasm for reform amongst males is reinforced by the data presented in Table 12.2, which reports attitudes towards the pace of privatization achieved in Poland to date. Over 60 per cent of men in both sectors of the economy believe that privatization is proceeding too slowly, with the corresponding figures for females being less than 50 per cent. Only a minority of respondents feels that privatization has been too fast, but more women than men hold this view, irrespective of employment location. Widespread dissatisfaction was reported by both sexes with the process and progress of large-scale privatization, with men being some ten percentage points more likely to be discontent than women.

There is more support for the small-scale privatization program, with more than 60 per cent of women working in the private sector expressing their satisfaction, although the corresponding figure for men is 15 per cent lower. Gender differences are smaller amongst public sector employees, nevertheless a greater percentage of males than females responded positively. Finally, respondents' views on housing privatization exhibit greater disparity across the sexes than across sectors and, in general, men are more dissatisfied than women. This appears to reflect the fact, noted above, that men are more in favor of the private ownership of housing than are women. In any event, it must be noted that, to date, housing reform has proceeded slowly.

To conclude this discussion of the attitude survey, Table 12.3 describes the views of respondents on the economic conditions experienced during the first years of the post-communist era. Once again the difference between the sexes is more marked than that across employment locations. While the modal response from men in both sectors was that the economic position of the country has improved, women hold just the opposite opinion. More uniformity is apparent in the responses regarding the economic situation of the family, with over half of public sector workers of both sexes believing that the position has worsened and only 18 per cent of men and 11 per cent of women perceiving any improvement. A more positive attitude was found amongst those in private enterprises, where one-quarter of females and only slightly fewer males are of the opinion that the economic conditions of the family have got better in recent times.

Table 12.3 Views on the Economic Condition of the Economy and the Family

	Private Sector (%)		Public Sector (%)	
	Females	Males	Females	Males
The Economic Position of the Country Is Better	27.3	41.6	29.7	42.0
The Economic Condition of the Country Is Worse	44.2	33.1	49.3	38.7
The Economic Position of the Family Is Better	24.7	22.7	10.9	17.6
The Economic Position of the Family is Worse	37.7	29.9	55.1	56.3
The Government Should Provide Jobs for Those Who Want to Work	81.9	78.5	83.3	71.4
N	77	154	138	119

Source: Household Survey, Kraków, 1996.

Finally, the survey revealed that views about the 'right to work' were similar across both sex and sector. When asked whether the government should provide jobs for those who want to work, over three-quarters of the respondents responded in the affirmative. In general, women in the public sector hold this view most strongly, although it is noticeable that a higher percentage of males in private firms believe that the state should provide work when necessary than do their contemporaries in the public sector.

The survey evidence presented in this section provides useful background information about how workers in Kraków view the impact of the process of transition. Overall, women voice less support for the market, feel less enthusiastic about accelerating the large-scale privatization process and believe that the changes to date have been detrimental at both the macro and individual levels. It therefore seems reasonable to conclude that women view the reforms that have taken place in the 1990s in a less favorable light than do men. The two following sections confront these findings with official data that describes the impact of reform on the relative labor market positions of the sexes in the area.

EMPLOYMENT

Various authors have suggested that women have borne a disproportionate share of the burden of employment change, insofar as they have been more likely to be made redundant than males with three arguments commonly being advanced in order to justify this belief. First, there exists outright discrimination that manifests itself in the preferences of managers who choose to dismiss women first. However, the increased emphasis on financial performance must cast doubt on the likelihood of such actions on the grounds of gender alone. This is particularly so as women in Poland possess relatively high educational endowments while, at the same time, being comparatively poorly paid (Białecki and Heyns, 1993).[15] Also, the occupational 'crowding' of women into careers such as accountancy and law that occurred under Communism equipped them with human capital far better suited to a modern market economy than the vocational, but often obsolete, skills acquired by many males.

A second, and more convincing, argument used to support the hypothesized vulnerability of women to job loss, relates to the evolution of the SOE sector during the transition period. Notwithstanding the success of the small-scale privatization program, the privatization of large public enterprises has been slow, particularly in comparison with the progress made in the Czech Republic and Hungary (Estrin, 1994).[16] In consequence, a large part of Poland's industrial production has remained concentrated in the state sector. However, many of these enterprises are experiencing, at best, financial difficulties, while others are technically insolvent. Indeed, it was only in 1997, after the passage of the 1996 Mass Privatization Act, that the transfer of many of these state assets into private ownership could begin to take place (Lubiński, 1998, p. 67), with the voucher scheme for privatizing the large SOEs only finally being introduced into Parliament on 18th July.[17] Given these delays, many jobs in the public enterprise sector have been preserved for longer than might have been expected initially. However, in the face of severe financial pressure, the survival strategy adopted by such undertakings has often been to reduce the importance of the peripheral activities associated with the typical socialist undertaking, or even to eliminate them entirely. As these auxiliary functions were normally in female-intensive operations such as child-care, basic education, catering etc., the threat this strategy posed to women is evident (Gregory et al., 1998).

Third, it must be recognized that women may have been more eager to accept redundancy, insofar as this presented them with the 'choice' of resuming the full-time domestic role that was denied to them under communism (Einhorn, 1993). At the same time, it is widely accepted that the notion of the family in Poland is still far more traditional than is the norm in most advanced economies (e.g. Siemieńska, 1997). In contrast to the situation during the communist epoch when women were expected to work full-time, on ideological grounds, their primary role nowadays is considered to be within the home.

Table 12.4 Employment Change, 1988–1993 and 1993–1998[1]

	1988–1993			
	Poland		Kraków	
	Male	Female	Male	Female
Absolute	–1,967,320	–1,366,925	–43,832	–40,299
Percentage	–30.6%	–25.2%	–20.4%	–21.1%
	1993–1998			
	Poland		Kraków	
	Male	Female	Male	Female
Absolute	+465,713	+694,188	+20,8353	+33,953
Percentage	+5.9%	+10.0%	+7.9%	+14.6%

[1] 1988–1993 excludes certain private sector jobs, most notably in agriculture.
Source: GUS (1994, 1994a, 1999).

In the event, the fundamental premise that women would be more prone to job loss than males is not substantiated by the official data presented in Table 12.4, which examines employment change over the two sub-periods 1988–1993 and 1993–1998.[18] During the course of the former, approximately 3.33 million jobs disappeared from the Polish economy, the majority of which were previously held by males. In the particular case of Kraków, both sexes suffered lower percentage reductions in employment than were experienced nationally. However, the burden was shared more equally in the region and women actually lost marginally more jobs than men, compared to five per cent fewer in the aggregate economy. Over the later period, employment had begun to grow again and women were the major beneficiaries in both Kraków and the country as a whole, gaining approximately twice as many jobs as men. In addition, women in Kraków enjoyed a rate of employment growth almost fifty per cent higher than the national average.[19]

Table 12.5 presents the distribution of employment across the four main branches of the economy and shows that material production continues to be an important source of work for men.[20] Women, on the other hand, are most heavily concentrated in the two service branches, but particularly those in the public sector. Nevertheless sight should not be lost of the significance of agriculture as an employer. Thus, even though Kraków is less dependent upon this sector than the national average—with some 27 per cent of all workers being engaged in agriculture in 1998 (GUS, 1999)—farms employ 22 per cent of the female (18 per cent of the male) workforce in the voivodship. This is one of the most critical features differentiating both the Polish and Kraków labor markets from those of their western neighbors in the EU that the country aspires to join.[21]

Table 12.5 Employment Distribution, 1998[1]

		I (%)	II (%)	III (%)	IV (%)
Poland	Males	26.50	38.47	17.53	17.51
	Females	28.29	18.28	32.07	21.36
Kraków	Males	18.03	40.17	19.87	21.93
	Females	22.28	16.98	34.77	25.97

[1] The data are based on the Europejska Klasykikacja Dzialalnosci (EKD, known as NACE in western Europe) classification and are aggregated as follows: Sector I=Agriculture, Forestry and Fishing; Sector II=Manufacturing, Electricity, Gas and Water, Construction and Mining and Quarrying; Sector III=Transport, Finance, Public Administration, Education, Health and Other Services, and Sector IV=Trade, Hotels and Real Estate.

Source: GUS (1999)

The distribution of employment across the branches of industry can be examined more formally by the use of an industrial concentration index. Denoting the share of total employment accounted for by the ith industry as S_i, the index employed her takes the general form:

$$n_\alpha(S) = \left[\sum_{i=1}^{N} S_i^{\alpha}\right]^{1/1-\alpha}$$

where: $\alpha > 0$ and $\alpha \neq 1$. In the particular case where $\alpha = 2$, the index becomes the inverse of the Hirschman–Herfindahl index and this is the measure reported in Table 12.6.[22] This index has natural bounds: in the hypothetical case where one industry accounts for all employment, the index would take the value 1; if employment were distributed equally across all sectors, then the value of the index would be equal to the number of industries in the classification utilized. In short, the lower is the value of the index, the higher the level of employment concentration. The measure indicates that the degree of employment concentration is lower in Kraków than it is in the economy as a whole for both sexes. Also, female employment concentration in Kraków was below that of males in every year, although male employment was becoming more diversified between 1996 and 1998 while the female workforce was becoming more concentrated, a finding that is not mirrored at the national level. However, Kraków ranks only ninth in the regional hierarchy of female employment diversification, behind cities such as Katowice, Warsaw, Szczecin and Gdańsk (Ingham, 1998).

Table 12.6 Employment Concentration, 1994–1998[1]

	1994	1996	1998
POLAND			
Females	6.40	6.29	6.53
Males	6.34	6.18	6.35
KRAKÓW			
Females	7.47	7.52	7.50
Males	7.03	6.90	7.09

[1] The data are based on the EKD (NACE) classification which contains 15 industries; thus $1 \leq n_\alpha \leq 15$. Data prior to 1993 were published according to the KGN (Klasyfikacja Gospodarki Narodowej) scheme, which contained 19 industries, hence the indices would not be comparable to those of later years.

Source: GUS (1994, 1996, 1999).

Table 12.7 presents data on the private/public sector employment distribution. In Kraków, as nationally, proportionately more males than females are located in the private sector, although the fact that more than seventy per cent of Poland's employment is now in private enterprises conceals the further fact that approximately 27 per cent of all workers are engaged on private farms (GUS, 1999). Excluding private sector agriculture widens the private sector employment differential between the sexes considerably, with less than half of all women workers then to be found in the non-state sector at both the national and the local level. This reflects the concentration of women in the core public sector services, such as education and health care.[23] Additional evidence on the position of females in the private sector comes from an examination of labor market flows, which show that while women accounted for over forty per cent of all gross new hiring in Kraków between 1994 and 1996, their share of gross private sector new hiring was only thirty per cent (US, 1997).

Table 12.7 Private Sector Employment as a Percentage of Total Employment, 31st December 1998

		PRIVATE (Total) (%)	PRIVATE (Excluding Agriculture) (%)
POLAND	Total	70.7	43.9
	Males	74.5	48.8
	Females	66.5	38.5
KRAKÓW	Total	68.0	48.2
	Males	72.5	54.8
	Females	63.3	41.3

Source: GUS (1999).

In summary, the official employment data suggest that women in Kraków have fared relatively well during the first seven years following the launch of the Balcerowicz Plan. They lost fewer jobs than men in the initial shake-out, enjoyed greater job generation in the years 1993–1998, and ended the period with a more diversified employment distribution. However, the pattern of female employment in Kraków still does not yet mirror that of a western economy. As Zienkowski (1997, p. 25) notes, although the contribution of the service sector in Poland is seemingly high, this is the result of the importance of 'traditional' functions, such as health care and education. The services that are most important in highly developed economies are those such as financial services, consultancy, tourism and recreation, all of which are immature in Poland. Indeed, less than one-quarter of females are employed in such activities, even in Kraków. Finally, even though the area has a relatively low reliance on agriculture, its importance as an employer, particularly for women, further serves to highlight the gulf between even an 'advanced' Polish region and the countries of Western Europe.

UNEMPLOYMENT

Having experienced fewer job losses in the early years of the reform and greater employment growth post-1993, it is tempting to conclude that women should therefore have experienced lower unemployment rates than males. However, the stock of the unemployed is determined not only by the inflows to the pool—including job losers, new entrants and re-entrants—but also by the outflows to employment, economic inactivity or disability.[24] From a comparison of Figures 12.1 and 12.2, it is apparent that female unemployment rates in Kraków have consistently been below those in the country as a whole since 1993.[25] For example, nationally women's unemployment was almost 18 per cent in 1993 and

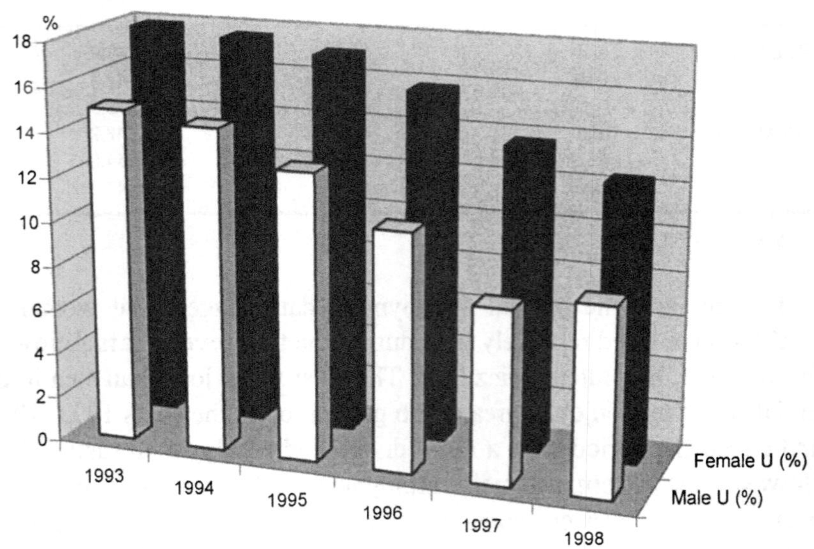

Figure 12.1 **Unemployment Rate by Gender, Poland, 1993–1998 (*Source*: *Employment in National Economy*, GUS, various years, *Registered Unemployment in Poland*, GUS, various years).**

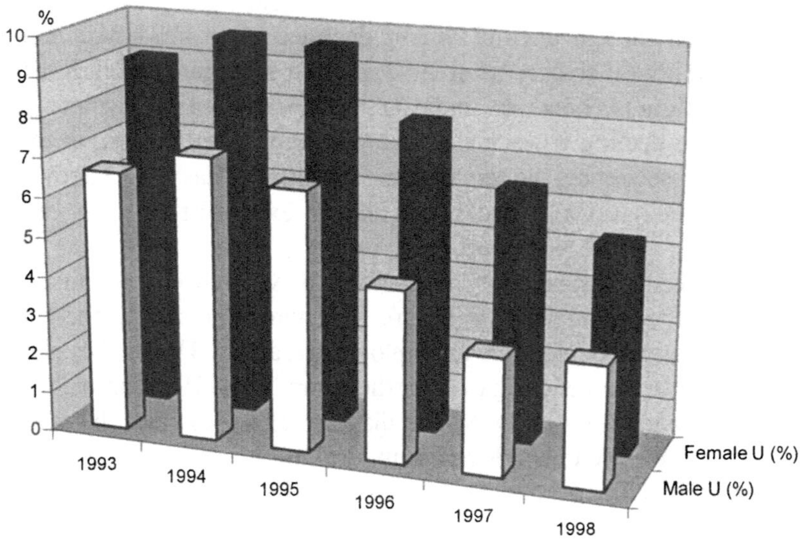

Figure 12.2 Unemployment Rate by Gender, Kraków, 1993–1998 (*Source*: *Employment in National Economy*, GUS, various years, *Registered Unemployment in Poland*, GUS, various years).

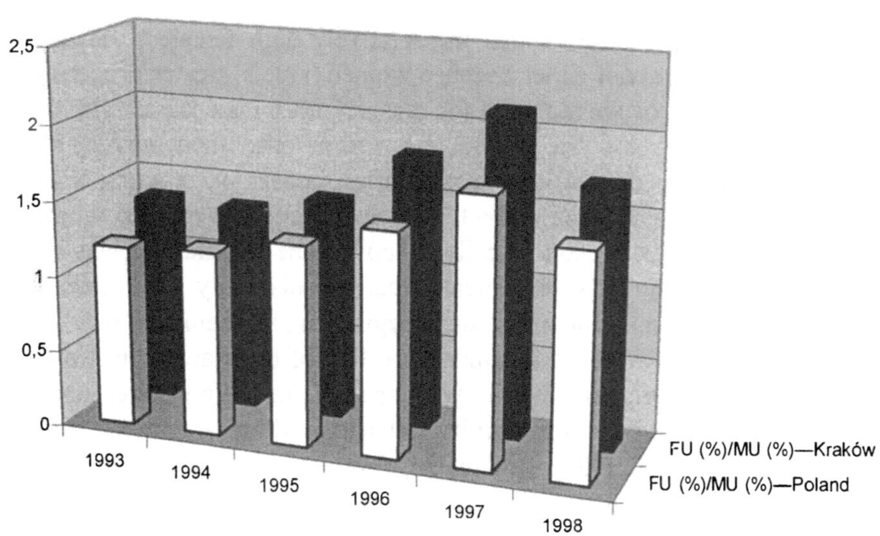

Figure 12.3 Female-to Male-Unemployment Relativities, 1993–1998 (*Source*: *Employment in National Economy*, GUS, various years, *Registered Unemployment in Poland*, GUS, various years).

1994, while the figure in Kraków remained below ten per cent. Nevertheless, even though unemployment declined after 1994, the female/male differential increased until 1997, both in aggregate and in Kraków. The 1998 figures, however, indicate that female unemployment rates continued to decline when male unemployment rates had begun to rise again. In consequence, the female/male differential has now narrowed to four per cent nationally and to slightly in excess of two per cent in Kraków.

Further confirmation that the position of women has begun to improve recently can be found in Figure 12.3, which presents a short time-series of relative female/male unemployment rates.[26] This makes explicit the increase in the gender gap over the years 1994–1997, as well as its subsequent narrowing in 1998. The diagram also illustrates the fact that even though female unemployment in Kraków is relatively low, it is not as favorable as that of men. It remains necessary to therefore attempt to explain the conflict between the employment and unemployment data for the region.

Nationally, it has been noted that higher unemployment rates for females are not the result of their higher incidence of job loss, but of their low outflow from the unemployment pool (Ingham et al., 1998). Women in Kraków are also more likely than men to be unemployed, notwithstanding the fact that the employment data would tend to suggest the reverse. The implication is that the relatively high female unemployment rates come about either because women have a greater propensity to join the stock of unemployed for reasons other than job loss or that men leave—or avoid—the register for reasons other than moving into employment. The first of these possibilities focuses on re-entrants and new entrants to the labor market, namely school leavers and women who were previously economically inactive. The second suggests that men are accepting early retirement, receiving disability allowances or working in the black economy and not registering as unemployed.

There is some evidence to support the first of these arguments in the case of the economy as a whole, with one-fifth of the registered unemployed in 1997 having never been in work and, of these, almost two-thirds were women (GUS, 1998). In Kraków, data for 1996 reveal that 13 per cent of unemployed females had never been employed, while the corresponding figure for males was two percentage points lower (Kraków, 1998). It is also noteworthy that women occupied only 22 per cent of temporary positions in the Kraków labor market over the years 1994–1996 (US, 1997). Although such jobs are typically short-term and state subsidized, they do reduce unemployment and this impact is clearly greater for men. The data therefore present a rather mixed picture. Despite the fact that women have lost fewer jobs and enjoyed higher job generation since 1993, there is a wide gender gap in the unemployment statistics. One possible explanation is that women recognize that the labor market is 'female friendly' after all and are more willing than men to queue to take advantage of the current economic upturn. A recent survey of employers in the locality might throw some light on this issue.

PERCEPTIONS OF WOMEN AS EMPLOYEES

A survey of one hundred Kraków employers that enquired about labor market and industrial relations practices was undertaken in 1997.[27] An early question established that during any planned reduction in manpower only seven per cent of firms felt that their policy was to place women 'at the head of the queue' and, even in this minority of cases, such apparent gender discrimination applied only to white-collar workers. Further evidence regarding the attitudes of the firms in this sample towards female employees is provided in Table 12.8.

Table 12.8 **Firms' Views of Women as Employees, Kraków, 1997**[1,2]

Views on Women Employees	Yes (%)	No (%)
Women Are Less Reliable	6	91
Women Are More Reliable	37	47
Customers Prefer Men	23	41
Women Have Higher Levels of Formal Education	22	56
Women Have Greater Work-Relevant Skills	31	48
Training Is Wasted on Women	22	56
Males Do Not Like Women as Colleagues	9	79
Employees Do Not Like to Have Women as Bosses	4	34
Women Do Not Like to Have Women as Bosses	41	35

[1] N=100.
[2] Because of non-respondents the 'yes' and the 'no' answers do not sum to 100.
Source: Firm Survey, Kraków, 1997.

More than one-third of those questioned perceived women to be more reliable employees than men, against only 15 per cent who considered them to be less so. However, over 70 per cent of the firms did not believe that women possess higher levels of formal education, even though it is generally recognized that this is the case.[28] Also, thirty per cent of responding firms felt that training was wasted on women, a finding mirrored by the results of the associated household study, which revealed that women were less likely to receive training than men, whether it be provided by an employer, the state or any other organization.

Arguably the most interesting findings from the firm survey relate to employers' impressions of how women are viewed as colleagues by their co-workers. The returns suggest that men are more than happy to work alongside women, with only ten per cent of respondents replying otherwise. It is nevertheless clear that employers perceive women as not favored by their co-workers as superiors, with almost sixty per cent of the responding organizations stating that workers do not like to have women as bosses. Somewhat provocatively, 54 per cent of the sample thought that this sentiment also applied to their female employees.

The evidence from this survey of employers reinforces the picture painted by the official statistics: enterprises do not hold adverse views of women as employees and there is virtually no evidence to suggest that women are likely to be the first to be fired.[29] Nevertheless, stereotyping persists, insofar as employers do not believe that women are acceptable in managerial roles, even to other women. Notwithstanding this caveat, it must be noted that these findings are more positive than the results provided by certain national surveys. For example, a recent study reported that women consider themselves to be more likely to lose their jobs, less likely to be able to find work, have a career and gain promotion to a managerial post, and to have less chance of successfully running their own company (CBOS, 1996).

SUMMARY AND CONCLUDING REMARKS

The evidence presented above provides a somewhat mixed picture of the position of women on the Kraków labor market. They lost fewer jobs than men during the early years of the reform era and have enjoyed greater job growth in later years. In addition, they are also more likely to work in the expanding service sector, while males are still heavily dependent on industry for employment. However, women have faced consistently higher unemployment rates than men, although the rates for both sexes have remained amongst the lowest in Poland. On balance, the results from the firm survey suggest that the greatest emphasis should be placed on the positive indicators of the impacts of change to date.

For the future, the priority for Kraków must be to reduce its reliance on HTS, but this must be achieved in a way that does not destabilize the entire local economy. In the past, HTS has attracted the interest of foreign companies: in particular the Austrian firm Voest–Alpine Stahl and the Dutch Hoogovens consortium (Jelonkiewicz, 1999). However, both companies withdrew from negotiations, blaming the national government for its lack of a clear privatization strategy for the steel industry. In 1999, the government adopted a new approach whereby the Sendzimir plant would focus on more expensive outputs, while Huta Katowice would produce low value-added products (*ibid.*). It was hoped that it would then be possible to find a single investor to buy both plants. Unfortunately, there was marked change in tactics in May 2000 when Huta Katowice was split into three parts and the government appeared to have been successful in its quest for foreign investors. The Italian company Danielli signed an agreement to build a new plant and the hope is that the company will purchase the flat-metal division. In addition, an agreement with the British–Dutch Corus group was sought that would have seen the company purchasing the long-metal products division and possibly the steel division (Koza, 2000).[30] These developments at the Katowice plant do not augur well for the survival of HTS and neither does the fact that Poland cannot delay the implementation of its agreement with the EU to reduce its import tariff on steel from nine per cent to three per cent for much longer. More ominous still, should Poland accede to the EU, it would have to abolish the import tariff altogether. In its present form, HTS would be unlikely to be able to survive even the milder of these increases in competitive pressure (Nicholls, 1998) and its long-term future undoubtedly depends on its ability to attract foreign capital. Such external assistance has proved the salvation Huta Lucchini Warszawa, for example, which is 51 per cent owned by an Italian company that is investing 161.6 million ECU in the plant in order to make it one of Europe's most modern steel mills (Ratajczyk, 1997).

In any event, women look set to benefit—at least relative to men—as Kraków's labor market evolves further. First, more restructuring at HTS will cause the loss of more male than female jobs, and employment at the plant is scheduled to fall by 10,000 early in this new century. Unlike past pronouncements, this threat looks likely to materialize because, as Redman and Keithley (1998) note, piecemeal amendments to the Labor Code have reduced job security considerably. For example, there has been a significant dilution of union involvement in the redundancy process. This should allow the planned manpower reductions at HTS to be achieved by resort to compulsion, if necessary.

Developments in other sectors look likely to generate significant female job growth. The French Casino company has opened a Géant hypermarket and demand is high for space in the Kraków Business Center, as well as for sites elsewhere in the town center, with rents three times higher than in out of center locations (European, 1998b). These companies will generate jobs in the retail sector and in occupations allied to office work; that is, in typical female employment. However, on a more cautious note, such jobs frequently require low skills and consequently offer low pay. It is also noticeable that Kraków earned $160 million from 3.7 million visitors in 1997 (European, 1998b), although it cannot be assumed necessarily that growth in the tourism industry will be to the disproportionate benefit of women. Superior opportunities for women are likely to arise from the planned developments in health, education and finance in the region (Karwińska, 1998) which will generate high skill jobs that will be well paid.

Historically, Kraków's southern location and its poorly developed transportation links have hampered its development. The latter of these will be improved by the construction of the Gdynia–Vienna motorway that will provide the city with much needed, high quality road connections to western markets. However, Poland's aspiration to EU membership, perhaps as early as 2003, may alter radically pre-existing patterns of wealthy and poor regions. Thus, whereas Silesia has long ranked amongst Poland's most prosperous areas, "the new core area of the Polish space is the Polish part of the grand European development axis of the twenty-first century—the axis Paris–Berlin–Poznań–Warsaw–Minsk–Moscow" (Kukliński et al., 1997, pp. 47–48).

In response to the challenges it faces, Kraków city council has drawn up an ambitious local plan to encourage development and establish laws relating to land use; its aim is that Kraków should develop as a center of science, culture and tourism (Kraków, 1998). In order to promote economic development seven 'strategic' spatial areas have been identified and one of these—East Kraków—includes HTS. Within these zones, local government provides property tax exemptions and special incentives to commerce, industry and to hotel and tourist businesses. In addition, three Special Economic Zones (including one encompassing HTS) were established in 1997. They are defined as areas for business, research centers and institutions dealing in the transmission of advanced modern technology and are projected to exist until the end of 2009.[31]

Whilst such initiatives are necessary, their emphasis is on the macro development of the region, with little or no focus on more micro issues. On a small scale, the Labor Office in Kraków did instigate a special program to help women who had been unemployed for more than a year in 1996 that involved both training courses and assistance in finding work, although there were only 216 participants in total (Krajowy Urząd Pracy, 1997).

There is, therefore, no evidence to suggest that resolving the problem of female unemployment is high on the policy agenda in Kraków. It is possible that this inaction reflects a stereotyped view of joblessness for men and women, as discussed in Reszke (1995), who found that unemployed males are viewed as socially undesirable, insofar as they are believed to resort to activities such as burglary and to develop diseases such as alcoholism. In contrast, the vision of unemployed females is far more positive: as they are perceived as spending their time productively engaged in household activities. Alternatively, the apparent indifference to female unemployment could be due to the belief, expressed by Siemieńska (1997), that if there are not enough jobs to go round, men have the right to take those that are available.

Unemployment for either sex, particularly when it persists over time, has severe economic and social consequences, both for the individual and for the local economy (Sen, 1997). In an area such as Kraków, which is still experiencing radical labor market change, it is necessary to equip the unemployed with the skills required in the growth branches of industry. However, both in Kraków and the country as a whole, the evidence suggests that the high levels of female unemployment that have arisen are, at least in part, a consequence of previously economically inactive women entering, or re-entering, the labor market. Given the limited funds available for active labor market measures, it is imperative that monies are targeted on those unemployed women who genuinely want to work, with the mounting evidence suggesting that such a policy will meet with considerable success.

NOTES

1 Góra and Rutowski (1989) estimate the degree of labor hoarding to have been as high as 50 per cent.

2 From the mid 1980s to 1994, the private sector share of non-agricultural employment in Poland rose from less than 10 per cent to more than 40 per cent (Johnson and Loveman, 1995, p. 2).

3 This line of argument does not preclude the possibility that firms discriminated against women because of their right to take leave to care for sick children, etc.

4 The system of pay that operated was a result of the different priorities that existed under Communism.

5 This was a nationally representative survey based on a sample of 1,101 adult women.

6 Poland's regional structure comprised 49 administrative areas, known as voivodships, prior to 1 January 1999, when their number was reduced to 16.

7 In 1995, 12.2 per cent of Kraków's workforce had graduated from high school, or better, compared to a national figure of 6.8 per cent (Francik, 1998).

8 The plant was previously known as the Lenin Steelworks.

9 The unemployment rate peaked in Kraków in September 1992.

10 Spin-offs are divestments of peripheral activities including child-care, education and restaurant facilities that have left HTS concentrating on core steel production.

11 Within the EU, steel is regulated by the ECSC (European Coal and Steel Community) and is regarded as a 'sensitive' good. As such, the trade concessions afforded to Poland by the EU under the Europe Agreements do not apply (Lavigne, 1995, pp. 214–215).

12 On a national base of 100, Kraków's FDI per head was estimated to be 117.3 compared to a figure of 610.5 for Warsaw—these figures reflect the reality that the majority of foreign investment entering Poland is attracted to the capital (TFRDP, 1996).

13 Whereas Balcerowicz aimed to peg annual inflation to rates below 10 per cent, the actual outcomes were above 50 per cent. This had a dampening effect on both output and employment in the private sector, as individuals were unwilling to use debt to finance business ventures. By 1998, inflation in Poland stood at 12.2 per cent (European, 1998).

14 Details of this survey are given in Grime et al. (1997).

15 The wage structure under Communism gave high rewards to those employed in traditional male occupations in heavy industry and mining. This provided a disincentive for men to pursue university education.

16 However, a simple headcount of SOEs might generate a biased impression. As noted by Balcerowicz (1994), many of the SOEs have undergone radical restructuring in the 1990s, including significant divestments. This is indeed true of the Sendzimira steelworks, although it is important to note that the parent company remains a shareholder in the spin-off enterprises.

17 In addition, accession to the EU requires that incomers operate 'market' economies. As one of the early contenders for membership, Poland will wish to demonstrate its commitment by increasing the speed of reform within the state sector.

18 The choice of the two sub-periods is determined by the data. For the years to the end of 1993, certain private sector jobs, most notably in agriculture, were not included in the official employment statistics. The data is available on both bases only for 1993. When all private sector activities are enumerated, total employment increases by approximately 6 million, or by over 40 per cent of total employment.

19 It should not be concluded that the observed growth in female employment is due to an increase in part-time jobs, as has been common in the west. In Kraków, over 90 per cent of employed women worked full-time in 1996 (US, 1997).

20 Material production is here defined as Manufacturing, the Utilities, Construction and Mining. This definition should not be confused with 'net material product', the communist equivalent of national income, which refers to all activities generating a 'visible' output (Lavigne, 1995, p. 45).

21 In 1993, Greece had the highest proportion of its workforce—21.3 per cent—engaged in agriculture in the EU. The EU5 (Belgium, Germany, France, the Netherlands and the UK) benchmark figure was 3.6 per cent (EC, 1996).

22 The measure reported here is based on employment shares and is described in detail in Hannah and Kay (1977) and is the one used by Kauttman and Domański (1997).

23 Whatever the rhetoric, education and health provision still remain largely state responsibilities in the west.

24 The inflow to unemployment of those who were previously economically inactive has been particularly important in Poland since many local labor offices actually encouraged women to register as unemployed, thereby increasing their unemployment rate and rendering them eligible for special assistance from central government. Also, disability allowances are a very importance source of income in the country, particularly for those individuals domiciled on family farms who are not eligible for unemployment benefit. Of course, transferring individuals from the unemployment to the disability register reduces the unemployment rate.

25 1993 has been used as the start date for the analysis of unemployment because the non-availability of comprehensive earlier employment data renders the construction of meaningful unemployment rates impossible.

26 These relativities are calculated simply as the female unemployment rate divided by the male unemployment rate. A figure of unity would indicate that there was no gender differential, while a figure of two would signify that the female unemployment rate was twice as high as the corresponding rate for males.

27 The firm surveys were face-to-face interviews with the individual responsible for the Personnel/Industrial Relations function within the company. The majority of respondents were, in consequence, male. Details of the survey can be found in Grime et al. (1997).

28 The responses from firms may quite conceivably be a hangover from the communist over-valuation of the blue-collar skills for which most men trained.

29 This contrasts with the assumption that women are viewed unfavorably as employees because they frequently require time off from work for domestic duties, such as caring for sick children (Kramer, 1995).

30 The negotiations with Corus collapsed in 2000.

31 It should be noted that the future of the Special Economic Zones is uncertain, given Poland's aspiration to join the EU (Meth-Cohn, 1999).

REFERENCES

Balcerowicz, L. (1994) "Transition to the Market Economy: Poland, 1989–93 in comparative perspective," *Economic Policy*, vol.19, April, supplement, pp. 72–97.

Białecki, I. and B. Heyns (1993) "Educational Attainment, the Status of Women and the Private School Movement in Poland." in: Moghadam (ed.).

CBOS (Centrum Badania Opinii Społecznej) (1996) "Women on Sex Equality," *Polish Public Opinion*, December.

EC (European Commission) (1996) *First Report on Economic and Social Cohesion*, Luxembourg: Office for the Official Publications of the European Communities.

Einhorn, B. (1993) *Cinderella Goes to Market: Citizenship, Gender Women's Movements in East Central Europe*, London: Verso.

Estrin, S. (1994) "Economic Transition and Privatization: The Issues," in: S. Estrin (ed.), *Privatization in Central and Eastern Europe*, Harlow: Longman.

European (1988) 3rd–9th August, p. 54.

European (1988a) 13th–19th July, p. 59.

European (1998b) 30th March–5th April, p. 38.

Fong, M. and G. Paull (1993) "Women's Status in the Restructuring of Eastern Europe," in: Moghadam (ed.).

Francik, A. (1998) "Charakteryka Krakowskiego Rynki Pracy Według Wykształcenia" (Education and the labor markets of Kraków), *Rynek Pracy*, vol. 73, no. 1, pp. 43–55.

Góra, M. and M. Rutowski (1989) "The Demand for Labor and Disguised Unemployment in Poland in the 1980s," *Communist Economics*, vol. 2, no. 1, pp. 323–335.

Gorzelak, G. (1996) *The Regional Dimension of Transformation in Central Europe*, London: Jessica Kingsley Publishers.

Gregory, A., M. Ingham and H. Ingham (1998) "Women's Employment in Transition, 1992–4: the Case of Poland," *Gender, Work and Organization*, vol. 3, no. 5, pp. 133–147.

Grime, E.K., V. Duke and M. Ingham (1997) "The Social and Economic Consequences of Privatization in Central and Eastern Europe," Report to the European Commission.

GUS (1994) *Zatrudnienie w Gospodarce Narodowej w 1993* (Employment in the national economy 1993), Warszawa: Główny Urząd Statystyczny.

GUS (1995) *Bezrobocie Rejestrowane w Polsce I–IV Kwartał 1994* (Registered unemployment in Poland I–IV quarter 1994), Warszawa: Główny Urząd Statystyczny.

GUS (1995a) *Zatrudnienie w Gospodarce Narodowej w 1994* (Employment in the national economy 1994), Warszawa: Główny Urząd Statystyczny.

GUS (1997) *Pracujący w Gospodarce Narodowej w 1996* (Employees in the national economy 1996), Warszawa: Główny Urząd Statystyczny.

GUS (1998) *Bezrobocie Rejestrowane w Polsce I–IV Kwartał 1997* (Registered unemployment in Poland I–IV quarter 1997), Warszawa: Główny Urząd Statystyczny.

GUS (1999) *Pracujący w Gospodarce Narodowej w 1998* (Employees in the national economy 1998), Warszawa: Główny Urząd Statystyczny.

Hannah, L. and J.A. Kay (1977) *Concentration in Modern Industry*, London: Macmillan.

Hannon, M.T. and J. Freeman (1989) *Organizational Ecology*, Cambridge, Mass.: Harvard University Press.

Hardy, J. and A. Rainnie (1996) *Restructuring Capitalism: Desperately Seeking Capitalism*, London: Mansell Publishing Limited.

Ingham, H. (1998) "Employment Change in Poland during Transition," unpublished mimeo.

Ingham, M., H. Ingham, A. Karwińska and G. Węcławowicz (1998) "Women in the Polish Labor Market: Is Transition a Threat?", in: M.J. Bull and M. Ingham (eds), *Reform of the Socialist System in Central and Eastern Europe*, Houndmills: Macmillan.

Jelonkiewicz, W. (1999) "Full Metal Packet," ***Warsaw Voice***, no. 12, 12th March.

Johnson, S. and G.W. Loveman (1995) ***Starting Over in Eastern Europe***, Boston, Mass.: Harvard University Press.

Karwińska, A. (1998) "Problemy Rozwoju Krakowa do Roku 2000. Dziedzictwo Przeszłości. Obawy I Nadzieje na Przyszłosc" (Development problems in Kraków by 2000: heritage, fears and hopes for the future), in: R. Borowiecki (ed.), ***Problemy Inwestowania i Rynku Nieruchomości*** (Problems of investment and the real estate market), Kraków: Akademia Ekonomicznsa w Krakowie.

Kauttman, P. and R. Domański (1997) "Industrial Concentration Under Shock Therapy: Poland in Early Transition Years," WP76, ESRC Center for Business Research, University of Cambridge.

Kennedy, M. (1991) ***Professionals, Power and Solidarity***, Cambridge: Cambridge University Press.

Koza, P. (2000) "Any Old Iron," ***Business Central Europe***, May, p. 3.

Krajowy Urząd Pracy (1997) ***Bezrobocie Kobiet w Pierwszym Póroczu*** (The unemployment of women in the first half of the year), Warsaw: Krajowy Urząd Pracy.

Kraków (1998) Kraków Home Page—business, ***www.um.krakow.pl/bp/business.***

Kramer, M. (1995) "Polish Workers and the Post-Communist Transition, 1989–1993", ***Communist and Post-Communist Studies***, vol. 28, no. 1, pp. 71–114.

Kukliński, A., A. Mync and R. Sul (1997) ***Polish Space at the Turn of the 20th and 21st Century***, Warsaw: Polish Agency for Regional Development.

Kuratowska, Z. (1991) "Present Situation of Women: Poland," in: UN Center for Social Development and Humanitarian Affairs, ***The Impact of Economic and Political Reform on the Status of Women in Eastern Europe***, Proceedings of a UN Regional Seminar, Vienna 8–12 April.

Lavigne, M. (1995) ***The Economics of Transition***, Basingstoke and London: Macmillan.

Leven, B. (1993) "Unemployment Among Polish Women," ***Comparative Economic Studies***, vol. 35, no. 4, pp. 135–145.

Lubiński, M. (ed.) (1998) ***Poland: International Economic Report***, Warsaw: World Economy Research Institute, Warsaw School of Economics.

Malinowska, E.(1995) "Socio-Political Changes in Poland and the Problem of Sex Discrimination," ***Women's Studies International Forum***, vol. 18, no. 1, pp. 35–43.

Meth-Cohn, D. (1999) "Danger Zones," ***Business Central Europe***, July/August, pp. 31–32.

Moghadam, V.M. (ed.) (1993) ***Democratic Reform and the Position of Women in Transitional Economies***, Oxford: Clarendon Press.

Nicholls, A. (1998) "Sticking to Steel," ***Business Central Europe***, February, pp. 28–30.

Ratajczyk, A. (1997) "Forging a Brighter Future," ***Warsaw Voice***, no. 12, 23rd March.

Redman, T. and D. Keithley (1998) "Downsizing Goes East: Employment Restructuring in Post-Socialist Poland," ***The International Journal of Human Resource Management***, vol. 9, no. 2, p. 274–295.

Reszke, I. (1995) "Stereotypes of Unemployed Men and Women," in: ***Women: The Past and the New Roles***, Center for Europe, Warsaw University Information and Documentation Unit on the Council of Europe, Bulletin no. 1, pp. 110–122.

Sen, A. (1997) "Inequality, Unemployment and Contemporary Europe," Development Economics Research Programme (DERP), No. 7, Suntory and Toyota International Centers For Economics and Related Disciplines (STICERD), London School of Economics and Political Science.

Siemieńska, R.(1997) "Wartości i postawy Warunkujące Obecność Kobiet na Rynku Pracy" (Values and attitudes affecting women's labor market activity), in: R. Siemieńska (ed.), *Wokół Problemów Zawodowego Równouprawnienia Kobiet i Mężczyzn* (On the problems of occupational equality between men and women), Warsaw: Wydawnictwo Naukowe SCHOLAR.

Sowa, K.Z. (1988) "Kraków—Trwanie i Zmiana" (Kraków—duration and change), in: B. Jałowiecki, E. Kaltenberg and E. Kwiatkowska (eds), *Procesy Urbanizacji i Przekształcenia Miast w Polsce* (Processes of urbanization and transformation of cities in Poland), Wrocław: Ossolineum.

TFRDP (Task Force for Regional Development in Poland) (1996) *Regional Development in Poland 1990–1995*, Warsaw: TFRDP.

US (Urząd Statystyczny) (1997) "Rynek Pracy w Województwie Krakowskim w Latach 1994–1996" (The labor market in Kraków voivodship between 1994–1996), Kraków: US.

Zienkowski, L. (1997) "Why do Regional Gross Products Differ?", *Research Bulletin*, Research Centre for Economic and Statistical Studies, Central Statistical Office, Warsaw, vol. 6, no. 4., pp. 7–32.

INDEX

For Product Safety Concerns and Information please contact our EU representative GPSR@taylorandfrancis.com Taylor & Francis Verlag GmbH, Kaufingerstraße 24, 80331 München, Germany

Batch number: 10725853

Printed by Printforce, the Netherlands